# Catullan Provocations

CLASSICS AND CONTEMPORARY THOUGHT

*General Editor: Tom Habinek*

I. *Catullan Provocations: Lyric Poetry and the Drama of Position,*
by William Fitzgerald
II. *Reading Sappho: Contemporary Approaches,*
edited by Ellen Greene
III. *Re-Reading Sappho: Reception and Transmission,*
edited by Ellen Greene
IV. *Tragedy and Enlightenment: Athenian Political Thought and the Dilemmas of Modernity,* by Christopher Rocco
V. *Warriors into Traders: The Power of the Market in Early Greece,*
by David W. Tandy

# Catullan Provocations

Lyric Poetry and the Drama of Position

William Fitzgerald

UNIVERSITY OF CALIFORNIA PRESS
*Berkeley / Los Angeles / London*

University of California Press
Berkeley and Los Angeles, California

University of California Press
London, England

First Paperback Printing 1999

© 1995 by
The Regents of the University of California

Library of Congress Cataloging-in-Publication Data

Fitzgerald, William, 1952–     Catullan provocations : lyric poetry and the drama of position / William Fitzgerald.
    p.   cm.—(Classics and contemporary thought : 2)
    Includes bibliographical references and index.
    ISBN 0-520-22156-7 (pbk. : alk. paper)
    1. Catullus, Gaius Valerius—Criticism and interpretation.   2. Verse satire, Latin—History and criticism.   3. Love poetry, Latin—History and criticism.   4. Epigrams, Latin—History and criticism.   5. Rome—In literature.   I. Title.   II. Series.
  PA6276.F52   1995
  871'.01—dc20                                          94-40303

Printed in the United States of America

08   07   06   05   04   03   02   01   00   99
9   8   7   6   5   4   3   2   1

The paper used in this publication is both acid-free and totally chlorine-free (TCF). It meets the minimum requirements of ANSI/NISO Z39.48-1992 (R 1997) *(Permanence of Paper).* ∞

*To Edward and Deirdre*

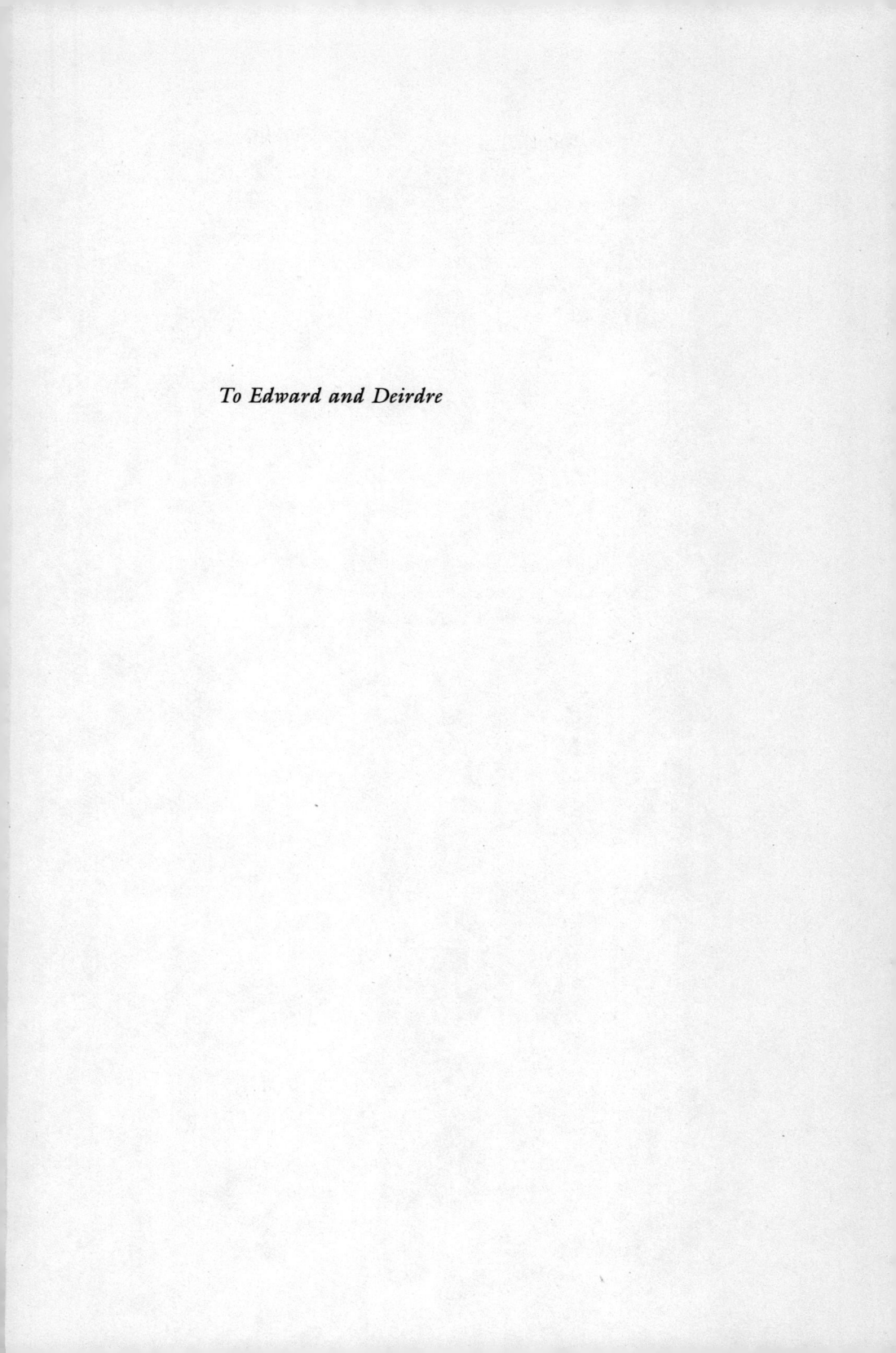

# Contents

ACKNOWLEDGMENTS ... ix

INTRODUCTION ... 1

1.
The Collection and Its Author ... 19

2.
Catullus and the Reader: The Erotics of Poetry ... 34

3.
Obscenity Figures ... 59

4.
Urbanity: The Poetry of Exclusion ... 87

5.
The Wronged Lover and the Poet's Isolation ... 114

6.
Gazing at the Golden Age:
Belatedness and Mastery in Poem 64 ... 140

7.
The Ruse of the Victim: Poems 10 and 11 ... 169

8.
The Death of a Brother: Displacement and Expression    185

9.
Between Men: Catullan Literature    212

CONCLUSION    236

NOTES    241

BIBLIOGRAPHY    289

GENERAL INDEX    303

INDEX OF CATULLAN POEMS CITED    310

# Acknowledgments

Without the encouragement, criticism, and advice of Tom Habinek, this book would probably not have come to publication, and I am very grateful to him for seeing the potential and diagnosing the problems of an earlier version with his customary generosity and acuity. The three anonymous readers for the press all had important criticisms and observations to make, and I have benefited greatly from their careful readings. My colleagues in the Classics program at UC San Diego read versions of several chapters and made valuable comments; Page duBois, in particular, has provided inspiration and encouragement at all stages of my work on Catullus. Micaela Janan, Michael Putnam, Amy Richlin, Dan Selden, and Marilyn Skinner—great Catullans all—have stimulated my thinking about this author either in conversation, through their work, or both.

At the University of California Press, Mary Lamprech supportively shepherded this book through the many stages from submission to publication, and Scott Norton edited the manuscript with incredible thoroughness and care. My thanks to them both. If errors remain, they are my own fault.

Chapter 2 appeared in an earlier version as "Catullus and the Reader: The Erotics of Poetry" in *Arethusa* 25 (1992) and is reprinted here by kind permission.

# Introduction

This book has three layers of argument. At the level of broadest application, it explores the drama of position and relation in lyric poetry through a reading of Catullus; I hope that this reading exemplifies an approach that can be applied to other authors, genres, and even media, for all aesthetic transactions involve some kind of positional drama. As a study of Roman literature and culture, it situates Catullus' poetry within the dynamics of a particular cultural context and identifies the concerns, anxieties, norms, and contradictions that enabled Catullus' particular orientation to lyric poetry. Finally, as a reinterpretation of a canonical author, it examines the investments that modern writers (scholarly and creative) have had in the canonicity of this author. How have these writers felt themselves authorized by Catullus? How have they imagined their relationship to him? What has been at stake in Catullus' canonicity? My own purpose is to argue for a Catullus who authorizes different enterprises, and in many cases this approach means responding to provocations that the modern construction of the author Catullus has been intended to control.

Let me begin with the first of this book's concerns, what I call *aesthetic positionality*. The consumer stands in a relation to a work of art that we call aesthetic, a relation that positions the consumer insofar as it determines the sense in which the work and its world are available, the conditions to which the consumer must agree in order to let the work exert its power, the satisfactions that are blocked or enabled, and so on. In every medium or genre, this aesthetic relation is inflected differently, and in any given work of art it may be engaged dramatically so as to become an important part of the work's content.

Poetry, among the other things it does, positions us in relation to the language we use every day: when we read poetry, we delegate speech to another, which means that the poetry positions the poet and the reader, or audience, differentially in relation to language. As an example of how the drama of this positionality might function in a particular poem, let us take William Carlos Williams's "This is Just to Say":

> I have eaten
> the plums
> that were in
> the icebox
>
> and which
> you were probably
> saving
> for breakfast
>
> Forgive me
> they were delicious
> so sweet
> and so cold.[1]

Like "This is Just to Say," most of Catullus' poems are addressed to someone and purport to have specific occasions or purposes (invitations, accusations, warnings, and the like). As this poetry is conventionally understood, the reader witnesses a portion of a drama going on between the poet and another person who, being neither the writer nor the reader of this poem, exists on a lower level of reality than poet or reader. Because *we* weren't saving the plums that Williams ate, and which we now enjoy with enhanced orality, the addressee's loss is our gain: she must accept the loss of her anticipated pleasure for his sake and for ours. But, insofar as she too is a reader, the position of Williams's addressee overlaps with our own: like us, she is asked to acknowledge that she has enjoyed the plums more in his mouth than she would have in her own. Her forgiveness depends on the delicious and unexpected enjoyment of the familiar (words like "cold" and "sweet") to which she is given renewed access through the detour of his note. Williams's poem is celebrated for being nothing more than a domestic note of the kind many of his readers will have written, its language plain and direct and its purpose quotidian. It is an objet trouvé claimed by the poet in much the same way as he claimed the plums that he found in the icebox. As a poet, he finds the words we have used and will use again, and he speaks them in such a way that we are forced to acknowledge they are rightfully his. The drama of this poem resides in the theft to which we, like the poem's addressee, find ourselves the willing victims.

"This is Just to Say" exploits the structure of the relation between everyday users of language, now also readers, and the poet who has preempted our intentions on that language. But why would we allow him to do such a thing? As readers or audience, we have implicitly licensed the poet to take any kind of advantage he can of a position of complete power in relation to language, to show us what can be done.

Williams's poem suggests that there is some relation between poetry and the note left for someone who will come on the scene when the poet is gone. Once the poet is dead, this relation becomes more poignant; in the following poem by Keats, the poignancy lent by death is quite aggressively anticipated, and the poet casts himself as something of a vampire in relation to the reader:

> This living hand, now warm and capable
> Of earnest grasping, would, if it were cold
> And in the icy silence of the tomb,
> So haunt thy days and chill thy dreaming nights
> That thou wouldst wish thine own heart dry of blood
> So in my veins red life might stream again,
> And thou be conscience-calmed. See here it is—
> I hold it towards you.[2]

The fact that we are reading this poem after Keats is dead, and that our own lives are suspended as we infuse the beating of time and the materiality of voice into these written words to realize the poem once more, means that the prophecy has been fulfilled. Jonathan Culler says of this poem that we fulfill the prophecy by forgetting our own empirical lives and by trying to embrace a fictional time in which the hand "is really present and perpetually held towards us through the poem." The drama of this moment is that "the poem predicts this mystification, dares us to resist it, and shows that its power is irresistible."[3] I would add that this "mystification" is simply an extreme and provocative version of the reader's position in reading any poem, the resurrection of whose voice depends on the reader's suspension of empirical time as he or she realizes its meter. The poem's extraordinary ending, in which the most immediate gestural challenge coincides with the closure that *contains* the poem, poses the problem of what the aesthetic object wants of us, and it does so through the paradoxical character of closure, which is both a form of epiphany (of the completed object) and of severance or release from the world of the work.

These two modern poems suggest that, whatever else it does, poetry distributes differential relations to language to poet and reader. In any artistic genre, the consumption of the work involves a drama of position involving at least the producer and the consumer. Frequently, as I show in the case of Catullus, the content of the work serves to elaborate that drama, which usually remains unconscious for the reader; nevertheless, the interest of the viewer, reader, or listener in the content of the work may stem from his or her investment in a particular structure of positionality characteristic of the medium or genre.

## Overhearing Poetry

Cast in the form of a note, Williams's "This is Just to Say" encourages us to see a continuity between poetry and our everyday linguistic transactions. John Stuart Mill's influential statement that poetry is not heard but overheard might seem to offer the same encouragement, but in fact it has been received and elaborated in such a way that the emphasis has been put on the *illusion* rather than the *relation* of overhearing.[4] Recently, in a very interesting study of poet and audience in Latin poetry, Kenneth Quinn credits Catullus with the invention of a poetry that seems to be overheard; Quinn situates this invention in the transition from an audience of listeners to an audience of readers for whom the poem creates the illusion of being overheard:

It is the difference between hearing a planned performance and overhearing a private conversation, even if the poem has been written with the thought in mind that it will be overheard, so that the feeling we have with such poems when we hear them or read them is that we have come along afterwards, that we are intruders, that the text of the poem has, as it were, fallen into our hands by accident is largely an illusion. A new way of writing poetry has come into existence whose success depends on the skill with which the writer can create that illusion.[5]

But overhearing is not only an illusion, it is also a relation. It disposes us, as intruders, to say apologetic things like "I couldn't help overhearing what you said . . . ," and it tends to affect the speech of the speaker, who is aware of the possibility of being overheard. The overheard speaker is both vulnerable to the possibility of giving something away and endowed with the power to tantalize the listener; Catullus, as we shall see, makes a great deal of this ambiguous relation to the reader. But these dimensions of the metaphor are scarcely ever explored by those who use it, any more than, for instance, the metaphor of poetry as confession leads to discussions of the reader's power to give or withhold absolution, or of the reader's standing in for a God who hears and understands all.[6] The continuity between poetry and other transactions or relations centered on speech is actually *suppressed* by the way these metaphors are (or rather, are not) elaborated.

But the idea that poetry is overheard or confessional is no longer as influential as it was. In the last two or three decades, and particularly through the work of Paul de Man, we have learned to read the lyric as an exploration of epistemological problems and aporias. This kind of reading is interested in the illusions in which we are persuaded to believe (e.g., that somebody is speaking, that nature can be addressed, etc.) and in how the figurality and textuality of poetry support or undermine these illusions. Because the focus has been on romantic or modernist lyric, the rhetorical structures of the lyric have been related to post-Kantian philosophical issues of knowledge and perception; commentary has played out a drama of mystification and demystification, either in tandem or in argument with the poet.[7] Chapter 8 is the nearest I come to these kinds of issues. Mostly, though, I am concerned less with the tendency of the lyric to solicit the reader with certain illusions (or to challenge those illusions) than with the lyric's exploration of the position of the speaker in relation to other (real or potential) speakers and, more broadly, with the relations and dramas of power that the poet's exploration of his position engage. A large part of my project in this book is to read the positional structures of the lyric through Roman concerns and relations; I argue that an alternative set of issues about the lyric can be elaborated from Catullus' poetry and its Roman cultural context, in which questions of performance, positionality, and power are more central than are those of subjectivity, authenticity, presence, voice, and anthropomorphism.

## The Roman Context

If Catullus provides a particularly rich opportunity to study these aspects of the lyric, it is because of the nature of Roman culture and society, and also because of Catullus' own moment in Roman literary history. This Roman context is the concern of the second layer of my argument. Quinn 1982 locates Catullus' poetry at a transition between spoken performance and written text, and, as he points out, this transition was slow. The ambiguous status of the Catullan poem enhances its elusive quality, the fact that it seems both casually occasional and yet fixed in its polished rightness of expression.[8] Art concealing art? Perhaps this is rather a function of the ambiguous status of its receivers, who have different kinds of access to the poem depending on whether they situate themselves as audience or as readership. The poem may be performed, or else read as a text; either way, the consumption of the poem is incomplete.[9] Because the written poem is the record of a performance we have missed, and the spoken poem can never realize the possibilities of the written text, the poem is always either more immediate or more enduring than what we experience.[10] The interpretive attempt to reconstitute the poem is always excessive with respect to the implied original performance; ultimately, we are made to feel that "you had to be there."

Catullus' collection reflects the existence of a group of like-minded poets (Licinius Calvus, Caius Cinna, and others) who profess literary principles derived from the Alexandrian poets, primarily the cultivation of perfection in small forms and a display of learning. These poets, who engage in polemics against the poetry of which they disapprove, are usually identified with the "neoterics" referred to disparagingly by Cicero (*Att.* 7.2.1).[11] The lively literary scene of Catullus' time was embedded within the Roman social context of the patron (*patronus*) and his circle of clients and friends (*clientes, amici*). At this time, the circle would have included professional critics, such as the poet-scholar Valerius Cato, who were beginning to involve themselves with contemporary poetry. These critics would have had the power to recognize the poets who performed at the gatherings of the *patronus* as worthy of study and commentary by the side of the canonical poets of the past. But the performance of poetry would still have been tied to that central occasion of ancient social life, the dinner, and the circle of the *patronus* would have included, as Quinn puts it, "people who can be invited to dinner . . . because they are witty talkers and, in a society infatuated with wit, can earn their place at table. These last are the *parasiti* and *scurrae* of whom we hear so much; many of the friends of Catullus are clearly of this social status" (136).[12] The poem, then, looks toward two different contexts united in the same situation, and it solicits two different kinds of attention. Like the transition between the spoken and the written, this ambiguous context problematizes the relation between poet and audience or readership. In some respects, the poet is like the dinner guest whose wit holds our attention, whose gossip piques our curiosity, and to whom we listen because or when he outshines us.

Because we are situated at the end of a long tradition of the criticism of written texts and of the perpetuation of a classical canon in which Catullus has played a major role, questions about the consumption of poetry have been increasingly buried by the business of interpretation. Even the modern critical movement that has addressed itself specifically to the issue of reception has been concerned with literary reception on the part of a community of *interpreters*. In the concluding essay to her anthology of reader-response criticism, Jane Tompkins (1980, 225) makes the point that, even where it describes the strategies by which the text stymies the process of interpretation, modern reader-response criticism has confirmed interpretation as the preeminent mode of the reader's response. But the position of the reader or audience of a poem is not adequately described as that of interpreter, nor can the poet disappear into the text's clues and resistances. We have to understand, for instance, how the poet plays the role of *scurra* (wit, raconteur, "man about town") in relation to those who have "invited" him just as much as how he makes his bid to be recognized by the critic as a worthy object of commentary and a candidate for canonization.

My conception for this book was formed while reading and thinking about Paul Veyne's brilliant and provocative *Roman Erotic Elegy* (1988), a book that combines a new understanding of the Roman elegiac poets with a polemic against the modern investments in sincerity and intensity that have prevented us from asking about the relation between poet and audience.[13] Veyne has been accused, with some justification, of flogging a dead horse, because at the time of writing—the French edition was published in 1983—few classicists still thought of Roman elegy as autobiographical and sincere.[14] Nevertheless, the residual assumption that it is self-evident that (and how) audiences will be interested in the intense erotic experience of a poetic persona has prevented us from asking what kind of taste is being addressed by this poetry. Veyne reads Roman elegy as "a pseudoautobiographical form of poetry in which the poet is in league with his readers at the expense of his own Ego" (44). It is the nature of the league that interests him, a league that he situates in relation to the peculiar, almost unreal world of Roman "irregular" society and to the complicated role it plays within upper-class Roman society as a whole. Veyne's description of the dialectic of author and reader, the shifting relations of power between them, and the contract that governs this game, is worth quoting in full:

> There is a whole dialectic of author and reader here, real society merely serving as a pretext for a semiotic game. Decreed to be superior to Ego by his morality the implied reader is next discretely knocked down (Ego comes from high society) and humiliated (Ego frequents alluring women) and then raised up again well above Ego, that naive creature. But who organized this game in which the implied reader gets to see the coarse side of life before his final triumph? It was the other Ego, the one who is his own editor. Is the reader made a fool of? No, for he knows all this. Visiting the carnival of books, he had gone into the palace of mirrors precisely to experience these highs and lows and to laugh (94–95).

Roman society, deeply concerned with hierarchy and with the maintenance of the decorum that befits one's position, but at the same time permeated by anomalies and complexities of status, was the obvious place for this form of entertainment to flourish.[15] For poet and reader, the effort of maintaining a clear sense of one's position in the complex, labile, and sometimes contradictory hierarchy of Roman rank and prestige could be suspended, and the whole question of hierarchy could become the premiss of an amusing game.[16]

Veyne's characterization of what he calls the semiotic game of Roman elegy has the great virtue of correcting the one-sided perspective that fails to recognize the cooperation of the audience in this enterprise. All too often, the elegiac poets, and Catullus himself, are represented as counter cultural heroes resisting straitlaced Roman orthodoxy: the *gravitas*, the stern morality, and the militarism of the political elite. But from the middle of the second century B.C.E., the frivolous distractions commonly associated with Greek culture had been part of the life of the Roman elite, separated spatially and temporally from the world of *negotium* (business) by the creation of a private life often centered on the Campanian villa.[17] The elite simply got used to living in two different worlds, of *negotium* and *otium* (leisure) respectively, and adopted a dual standard of ethics. The situation was always a bit precarious because political enemies would regularly attack, in speeches before the Roman people, the pleasures a rival member of the elite enjoyed in private. The pleasurable aspect of that precariousness was explored by the poets who professed (or confessed) to have substituted the values of *otium* for those of *negotium*. The elegiac poets (Propertius, Tibullus, Ovid) belonged to the rank of knights (equites), a rank from which one might choose to launch oneself on a political career leading to the Senate or, avoiding the struggles of *ambitio*, to devote oneself to *otium*, for which "leisure" would be a misleading translation because it could include business pursuits as well as various kinds of studies or artistic activities.[18] The elegists, obviously, had chosen the latter course, and one might say that in their poetry they performed the ambiguities of their equestrian status, which put at issue the relative claims of *ambitio* (potentially glorious but burdensome) and *otium*. Veyne's semiotic game, in which the reader feels alternately superior to and envious of the persona of the poet-lover, explores the ambivalence of the choice to embrace equestrian status.

As for Catullus, though he came from provincial Verona, he was a member of a family wealthy and important enough to be on social terms with Julius Caesar, and at Rome Catullus' connections brought him into intimate contact with members of the highest aristocracy.[19] It is unlikely that Catullus earned money from his poetry or that he needed to; he was a professional poet only in the sense that poetry was what he professed. And yet, as a Cisalpine (or Transpadane) Gaul at Rome, he made his way into high society through his literary talents. At the age of twenty seven (57–56 B.C.E.), he accompanied Gaius Memmius to Bithynia as one of the entourage (cohors) of the governor (cc. 10, 28). The aristocratic Memmius was a man of considerable literary culture, to whom Lucretius had addressed his *De rerum natura*, and besides Catullus he brought with him the poet Cinna, another Transpadane. Catullus spoke to his audience not as an outsider, nor as a paid entertainer, but as one whose performance of his membership in high society compensated for a social handicap. Many of the provincials who made their way into Roman high society became champions and performers of the urbane wit (urbanitas) on which elite Roman society prided itself by contrast to the "rusticity" of life outside the capital.[20] Catullus and his fellow Transpadanes might have felt pride at the cultural achievements and growing importance of their place of origin and at the same time the need to detach themselves from the boorish rusticity that was still attributed to them by the Roman elite. This cultural schizophrenia duplicated the situation of all Roman intellectuals with respect to the older culture of Greece, of which imperial Rome was now both the proud owner and the humble debtor.

Both as a Roman and as a Transpadane, then, Catullus' cultural position was ambiguous, and, as we shall see, this ambiguity intensified the focus on positional drama in his poetry.

## Roman Talk

Poetry, and particularly Catullus' poetry, is talk, and the Romans had a passion for it: sonorous speeches, obscene insults, moralistic tirades, witty barbs, urbane dinner conversation, profuse encomia, sly innuendos, solemn contracts, and copious lists. The canonical status of Roman literature has profoundly influenced the way the West has talked. Cicero (in both his speeches and his letters), Catullus, Tacitus, Horace, and Juvenal have all authored linguistic attitudes that centuries of education based on translating and composing Latin have fixed in our repertoires, although their names are beginning to be forgotten. Even in such unlikely places as modern journalistic accounts of trends and gossip in the big city we can recognize the epistolary attitude of Catullus' friend Caelius reporting to Cicero on the life of the city, with the same self-congratulatory ellipticism creating a community of those who are "tuned in."[21] All of these forms of speech create specific kinds of relation and of community.

Catullus' poetry, like Williams's "This is Just to Say," parades its relation to everyday acts of speech or writing: invitations, insults, dinner-table witticisms, gossip, obscene graffiti, and the like. More often than not, this aspect of his poetry is taken to display Catullus' ability to make a silk purse out of a sow's ear, proving, for instance, that even a crude insult can be raised to the status of art if enough care is taken with it. But each of these acts of speech or writing creates a particular kind of relationship that throws its own light on the society that a poem creates, at the same time as the particular poem in turn reveals something about the way these acts of everyday speech function.

Catullus' name is particularly associated with urbanity and obscenity, two very different forms of speech that both play an important role in creating the sense of a lively society around the poems and in the gaps between them. In fact, urbanity and obscenity are not as opposed as they might seem, for both forms of speech, in their Roman form, concern the relations within a particular community of speakers. Roman obscenity is preponderantly concerned with the impure mouth, for the word of the

Roman is sacred and the place from which it issues must be kept pure by members of the community of speakers; the obscene act to which Catullus most frequently refers is oral rape (irrumatio), and the most shameful perversion in Roman society is fellatio or cunnilingus. Like Greek obscenity, the Roman variety is also concerned with relations of power, with the penetrator and the penetrated, but its primary focus on the mouth makes it a site for exploring relations between speech and silence, between pure and impure speakers, and, as I argue, between the body of the poem and the bodies of poet and reader.

Catullus' urbanity—the various forms of elegant behavior, attitude, and speech that distinguish insiders of his circle from outsiders—is intended to be something that can only be exemplified, not defined; as a new kind of social performance that is continually improvising its own rules and limits while creating its excluded opposite, urbanity is more like a game than a quality. This game, which is a kind of "turf war," can be seen as poetic provided we are prepared to understand poetry itself as an event that takes place within an imagined community of speakers: perhaps the poet will reconstitute his audience as worthy members of his circle, returning to us our own speech with its potentialities now better appreciated; but perhaps he will thumb his nose, reminding us that there will always be something missing in our everyday speech, something we can't put our finger on, which separates the way he speaks from the way we do. Many of Catullus' poems invite us to think of poetry in terms of this kind of drama.

I am concerned throughout this study with the light that some distinctively Roman forms of speech and rhetoric can throw on the poetic relation and vice versa. All of these kinds of speech are trying to do something; they have their distinctive strategies for positioning the speaker and for engaging others in a certain relation to that speaker. My readings show how Catullus uses this dimension of various kinds of Roman speech to explore aspects of the poetic relation; at the same time, I hope they show how poetry reflects and magnifies the positional drama latent in all kinds of linguistic intercourse.

## The Author Catullus

The third layer of my argument concerns Catullus the author, both the author that has been constructed by modern scholarship to inhabit and rationalize the collection and the author who has authorized modern writers to produce "Catullan" literature. It is concerned with the focal position of the author in the collection and with the position from which others are authorized to speak by this canonical author. An author, Foucault has argued, is constructed, not born, for an author is the product of critical and scholarly operations, the fulfiller of educational and ideological purposes, and the occupant of a differentiated role and position within the total field of a particular canon.[22] A distinct set of investments governs the construction of any author and determines how that author in turn authorizes others, not necessarily critics, to speak in his name or from his position. Throughout the book, I ask how the author Catullus has been constructed in modern times and what roles he has been contructed to play; in other words, what has been at stake in our author Catullus?

The following words of a Catullan scholar commenting on an apparent paradox in the posture of Catullus the lover might be a good place to start:

There is no point in asking how Catullus can speak of Lesbia's *culpa* [fault] when he himself entered the relationship while she was still another man's wife, since his poetry, obviously, presents the relationship from his, not Lesbia's, much less Metellus' [Lesbia's husband's], point of view.[23]

We could learn much about how the criticism of lyric poetry is conventionally understood by reflecting on the force of the word "obviously" in this statement. If Catullus had not been issued a poetic license, he would look pretty shabby, but in fact he has more often than not been treated as a kind of saint. It appears that as critics we ("obviously") have a duty to speak from the position of the poet we are explicating, and this explication may involve amplifying the rhetoric of the poet in order to fix that position. Here is the same critic explicating Catullus c.11, a bitter farewell to his faithless mistress:

Like some huge, obscene monster, Lesbia wraps her thighs about the middle of countless lovers simultaneously and through this gripping embrace, again and again, breaks the groins of them all. By her insatiable sexual rapacity she crushes their manhood and thus renders them limp, useless, and impotent.[24]

The passage is notable, first of all, for the misogynistic relish with which it echoes Catullus' more modest, though still violent words.[25] But, ironically, the critic who sets out to speak from the position of Catullus with respect to Lesbia ends up taking the position of Lesbia with respect to Catullus' poetry. Fixing on Catullus' words, repeating and amplifying them in an excess of expository zeal, he ends up by wringing them dry and leaving them "limp, useless, and impotent." This rapacity bears not a little resemblance to that of Lesbia, who is accused of reducing the act of love to meaninglessness through her excessive lust.

What this passage shows, along with many like it in Catullan scholarship, is that an author is a position from which others are authorized to speak.[26] My final chapter examines Catullan literature, poems and novels inspired by Catullus and informed by Catullan scholarship. Some of that literature explicitly resurrects the Catullan voice to deal with amatory traumas of the writer or his persona, and it will be no surprise to anyone that much of this literature adopts the misogynistic tone of the passage quoted above. Several poems I cite in that chapter are addressed to Catullus himself in tones that recall Catullus' own tender graveside address to his dead brother (c.101); Catullus' readership as reflected in this literature is a brotherhood formed through the triangular relation between the Catullan figure, the woman, and another man. For these writers, "Catullus" means a certain emotional structure in which the unfaithful or unworthy woman plays an instrumental role in facilitating an understanding between men. I argue in other parts of the book that the Catullan scholar typically situates him- or herself in the position of a substitute for Lesbia, a substitute who understands the poet in ways that Lesbia was incapable of understanding him. My version of the position of the Catullan reader will, I hope, upset this tendency of that reader to feature in a drama of betrayal and its often misogynistic agenda.

Fortunately, the criticism of Catullus has been taking some new directions in recent years; the work of Skinner (especially 1979a, 1982, and 1989), Richlin (1983), Selden (1992), and Janan (1993) has suggested different, and various, ways of reading Catullus without relying on the sentimental narratives of the past.

## Provocation and Recuperation

Catullus is a provocative poet.[27] He tells us himself that poetry should incite a sexual itch,[28] but his poetry can also be stunningly trivial, breathtakingly obscene, or breast-tappingly self-righteous. Sometimes we are inclined to turn away or pretend we didn't hear, but for the most part we have been concerned to show that there is more here than meets the ear. My intention is both to recover the more radical implications of the provocation of Catullus' poetry and to describe the strategies by which this provocation has been neutralized or, more significantly, used as a pointer to higher things. The process of provocation and response that governs the creation of lyric value in the mainstream tradition of Catullan scholarship is not always acknowledged. In his exculpation of Catullus the adulterous hypocrite, the critic quoted above tries to make something invisible; he appeals with his "obviously" to an aesthetic rule about what is "out of play," or bracketed, when we agree to read a text as lyric poetry. The point is discreetly tucked away in a footnote because it must not become an issue. But the elaboration of the poet's point of view by the critic doesn't just *overlook* issues of justice and one-sidedness, for the points of view that are excluded (Lesbia's, Metellus') represent values that must be trumped by the successful poet, who makes it worth our while to take his side. The unsuccessful poet fails to persuade us to ignore other points of view and is usually called self-indulgent. It is therefore a requirement of the appreciation of poetry (as traditionally conceived) that we overcome a resistance to its one-sidedness in the name of values constituted as poetic by that very act of overcoming. This procedure is occluded by the "obviously" that pretends we have not made the first move in the interpretive game because there is no move to make. In fact, the paradox that the adulterer Catullus complains of his mistress's infidelity ensures that, in order to take his side, we must assume (and elaborate) a higher or more intense experience of love on his part that takes precedence over the experiences of others.[29] This, at any rate, has been the usual approach of Catullan criticism, which understands Catullan provocation as an invitation to find higher reasons to take the poet's side.

Another potentially provocative aspect of lyric poetry is its slightness. Catullus referred to his poems as "trifles" (nugae, c.1, 4) and often he challenges us not to agree. We have responded by making various kinds of virtue of this slightness. Here is an example from a novel of the thirties:

"There is a good deal of English laughter going on, and a certain number of people reading Catullus."
"Why is Catullus so important?" asked Algernon.
"Because no one could possibly pretend that he was a Fascist or a Communist or belonged to the Right or belonged to the Left, or indeed was anything but just a damned good poet, worth reading for the fun of the sound."[30]

Slightness becomes a virtue here because it leaves no room for the compromised and compromising interests of the public world, a position that accords with the widespread image of Catullus as a man who stood aloof from the corruption of politics in the late Republic, maintaining a purity of purpose in the small, private arena that he could control.[31] A more portentous version of the ethics of slightness is implied by a quotation from Auden that serves as the epigraph to a chapter called "The Poetry of Social Comment" in Quinn 1972:

> Even a limerick
> Ought to be something a man of
> honour, awaiting death from cancer or a firing squad,
> could read without contempt.[32]

Death from cancer is a clumsy business, unlike death before a firing squad, but the implication of Auden's lines is that there is an analogy between the redemption of the limerick by artistic responsibility and the redemption of a messy, meaningless death by the man of honor, perhaps even that the one guarantees the possibility of the other. That the ritualized precision of the firing squad can be read into the progress of cancer is "guaranteed" by the way that Auden's loose versification is tightened up from the word "honour" to achieve the wonderful concentration that is supposed to descend on those faced with the prospect of death. When he quotes these lines, Quinn implies that Catullus, with his careful use of colloquial language and often unprepossessing subject matter, is engaged in a similar redemption of the everyday.

These characterizations of the Catullan ethic of slightness have their own ideological force.[33] A Catullus who cannot be claimed by any particular political community, and yet mysteriously proves himself worth reading for the sake of something apparently so private and irreducible as a joy in "the sound alone," is a Catullus who guarantees the community of the most basic human experience beneath the divisions of social and political interests and struggles. Auden's man of honor, retired into the private temporality of reading in the face of his oppression by the inevitabilities of a time he cannot control, guarantees the commensurability of all experience. In the face of the various, though potentially commensurable, death sentences under which we may stand, Auden seems to say, waiting is all, and the quality of waiting is the field of the aesthetic.

My own version of Catullus the author will, I hope, raise some questions about why we read lyric poetry, bringing out what is unconscious about both the modern reception of Catullus and about the lyric genre as a form of entertainment. If the modern reception of Catullus has tended to celebrate a brotherhood between poet and readership, through both its sentimental narratives and its ethics of slightness, my own reading stresses our consumption, as readers, of positional dramas that are more dynamic. The provocation of Catullus has served for the most part to prompt a stabilizing reaction from those who would prove they are "in the know" by confirming certain values against the philistines whose misunderstanding Catullus courts. But I hope to show how Catullus' poetry might provoke us to question the nature of the reader's relation to poetry and of the drama that the licensing of a poetic position enables.

❖ ❖ ❖

A brief synopsis of the chapters follows to orient the reader. In the first chapter, I examine the construction of the author Catullus as a position within the Catullan collection, a position by means of which the promiscuous variety of the poems is rearranged into a sentimental narrative that controls some of its more provocative aspects. In this chapter, I also describe the position of the Catullan scholar within this sentimental narrative.

Chapters 2–5 all relate to the positional drama activated by various kinds of Roman talk. In Chapter 2, I examine the erotico-aesthetic language that Catullus uses about his own poetry and the provocative relation of this language to Roman social and sexual norms. I then describe the provocative game that Catullus plays with the positionality of reader and poet, and in particular his use of erotic models to explore the ambiguity of power relations in the transaction between them. Chapter 3 is closely related to my discussion of the erotics of poetry; it describes how obscenity *figures* in Catullus' poetry, that is, both how it figures as a form of diction with its own distinctive ways of engaging the reader and how it functions figuratively to explore power relations within the society of speakers created by a poem. Again, Catullus uses the dynamics of distinctly Roman forms of obscenity to frame the transaction of the poem. In Chapter 4, I consider the increasing importance of the concept of urbanity in Catullus' time and the strategies employed by those who lay claim to *urbanitas* to position themselves in relation to the excluded. As an indefinable quality that becomes visible only in relation to those who lack it, *urbanitas* in Catullus' poetry is often displayed in the context of a struggle for power. The performance of *urbanitas* involves an act of appropriation or theft of language that dramatizes the privileged position of the poet. Chapter 5 focuses on a group of Catullus' Lesbia poems, written in elegiac meter, which consist largely of accusations against Lesbia for betraying her lover; these accusations are accompanied by protestations of the poet's fruitless fidelity to an unreciprocated love from which he is unable to tear himself away. The language of these poems is pervaded by the rhetoric of aristocratic obligation, which is wrenched from its usual social context to speak of a radically unconventional relationship, whose distinctive features are emphasized by this misuse. In this chapter, I read the situations of the lover as dramatizations of the situations of the poet. The poems in which Catullus parades his inability to break off an unreciprocated love, I argue, dramatize the performing poet's isolation and immobility before his audience: the special status of the isolated performer who must sustain the illusion of his persona before an audience is reflected by that of the lover trapped in an unreciprocated love. The poems in which Catullus expresses doubts about the sincerity of Lesbia's amorous protestations dramatize the separation of poetic speech from what is spoken outside the poem.

Chapters 6–8 are concerned with various ways in which the poet negotiates an apparent weakness in order to locate strategically the power of his position. In each case, the distinctive capacities of poetic speech are realized in relation to a problem that has some characteristically Roman cast to it. In Chapter 6, on Catullus' "little epic" (c.64), I describe how Catullus both raises and solves the problem of the latecomer's relation to a lost but longed-for Golden Age. The poem consists mainly in the story of Theseus and Ariadne as represented on the coverlet of the nuptial bed of Peleus and Thetis, whose wedding is ostensibly the subject of the poem. But if this poem, which not only calls on an age that has passed but also describes another work of art, parades its own secondariness, it also proceeds to turn that position into one of power and mastery. Most important, an elaborate play between the gaze of the characters represented in the poem and the gaze to which they are subjected dramatizes the power of the latecomer to re-present what he has missed. I argue that the issue of secondary power is peculiarly relevant to Roman culture, which stands in a secondary but dominant position in relation to the Greeks, from whose literature and art the stories and figures of this poem have been both (humbly) borrowed and (imperiously) appropriated.

The following chapter focuses on two poems (cc.10, 11) in which the poet represents his persona as victimized by a woman; both poems consist of an elaborate scenario involving a three-way relationship between Catullus (or his persona), a woman, and other men, and they find the speaker using the woman to negotiate his relation to other men and vice versa. The attempt of the *persona* to master his situation fails in each case, but this only serves to locate the position of the *poet* that transcends the problematic situation in which his persona is caught. Set in a metropolitan Rome that presides confidently and arrogantly over an empire, these poems both feature a speaker who attempts unsuccessfully to manipulate this position of power; it is the persona's failure at this gambit that sets off the transcendent position of the poet.

Chapter 8 deals with the poems related to the death of Catullus' brother (cc.101, 65–68), which is represented as causing a crisis in poetic activity. Though on the one hand his brother's death makes it impossible for Catullus to communicate with his brother, on the other hand his bereavement also renders it impossible for him to write of anything else but his grief, in spite of other claims on him from friends. The negotiation of two different and conflicting kinds of *officia* (duties), threatening mutually to displace each other, and the displacement of communication caused by his brother's death, provoke Catullus to explore the nature of poetic speech, and particularly its potential for multiple origins and stratified texture. Woven into this problem of expressive displacement is the problem of cultural displacement for this Roman poet from Cisalpine Gaul who professes literary affiliations with the poets of Greek Alexandria. The death of Catullus' brother raises the question of where the poet speaks from, and it raises this question both from a cultural and from a generic perspective.

Catullus' poem on his brother's death (c.101) is one of his most famous and has spawned many imitations and adaptations. Readers and imitators of Catullus have often situated the pathos of this tender farewell in relation to the bitterness of Catullus' rejection of the faithless Lesbia (c.11). In the final chapter, I discuss Catullan literature and the use by late-nineteenth- and twentieth-century writers of Catullus' voice, figure, or story to construct brotherhoods between men that are mediated by women; much of this Catullan literature is explicitly or implicitly misogynistic, and this chapter describes the strategies of Catullan misogyny as reflected in his imitators.

CHAPTER I

# The Collection and Its Author

The construction of Catullus the author is first of all the process by which scholarship has dealt with the puzzling book of poems that has come down to us under the name Catullus: this book, in all its promiscuous variety, has acquired an author by being rearranged as something more like a novel, a sentimental narrative with a hero who goes through a process of development. Catullus the author has served to resolve the provocation of the book's miscellany and of its varied levels of intensity by anchoring it to a single psyche with its own center and periphery. At the same time, the author Catullus has also been situated in a particular relationship to the Catullan scholar, a relationship that establishes the sense in which the author *needs* the scholar; this relationship is also underpinned by a sentimental narrative. In this chapter, I concentrate on these two aspects of the scholarly construction of the author Catullus, but I would like to begin with a brief consideration of Catullus' position in the Roman pantheon.

## Catullus the Roman Author

Catullus is not just an author, he is a Roman author, and as such his name also designates a place on a map. As students of Latin literature, we learn our way around this map by putting the various authors in the Roman canon in relation to each other, placing Catullus, for instance, in relation to Horace, Vergil, Martial, Ovid, and Cicero.

We find Catullus in Vergil's more poignant moments, and at the same time he inhabits our sense of the "Roman" as a resistance to the imperial world-historical vision;[1] Martial (we learn to say) got him wrong in a way that reminds us of how crude the Romans could be.[2] Ovid shows what happens when Catullan sophistication is unleavened by deep feeling.[3] Horace is a much saner lyricist, but we miss the passion and immediacy.[4] Cicero is trying too hard to be urbane, whereas for Catullus urbanity is a natural element. For many, Catullus is the supplement necessary to make the Romans tolerable, to prove their wholeness:

When we have taken the trouble to notice Cicero's ponderous public humour, have allowed Horace's skittishness to amuse us, and have savored Martial's wittier epigrams, doubt remains whether one could laugh in Latin or make love in it, until we come upon the verse of Catullus.[5]

Catullus, it seems, rescues the Romans by showing us in their perfect balance tendencies that become dubious in others.[6] As we shall see, in some respects this is what he has told us himself.

A complete description of Catullus' modern position within the Roman canon would also have to consider certain recurrent types in this canon. Most important is that Catullus, with his "odi et amo" (I love and hate), is the emblem of the Roman poet divided against himself. This self-division is not simply a recurring psychological pattern, it is a manifestation of something contradictory about Roman culture, which is always in some way at odds with itself. Critical discourse about several Roman poets has elaborated this idea. Catullus, as the rebellious aesthete who professes the light touch but summons up the weightiest of Roman ethical language to express the disappointment of his hopes for a lasting relationship with Lesbia, represents a type that is exemplified in modern critical discourse by Lucretius and Vergil as well.[7] In Lucretius we find traces of the anti-Lucretius, the irrational passion that disturbs the message of Epicurean calm. In Vergil we hear two voices: the voice that glorifies Roman imperialism and the voice that pities the victims of its relentless march.[8] Seneca, the poet of both Stoic calm and Roman spectacular sensationalism, and Juvenal, the ranting preacher who positively relishes the abundance of contemporary perversion, might be two further representatives of this figure. In all of these cases, the self-division of the poet proves the impossibility of the poet's most radical stance, and it is perhaps with some relief that the critic sights the return of the repressed. In this respect, the conventional representations of Catullus and Vergil are complementary, the one being ultimately unable to repress beneath his dandyism a commitment to profoundly Roman moral standards, and the other unable to disguise his sympathy for the victims and opponents of Rome's glorious imperial mission. Having internalized this reciprocity of outlook, we can, Janus-like, have our Rome both ways. Every canonical author performs a role within the economy of a particular canon that the student absorbs, consciously or not, in the process of being initiated into a particular tradition. The position of Catullus in the Roman pantheon points to the ambivalence of modern attitudes toward the Romans.[9]

## Understanding Catullus

If the author is first of all a position within a pantheon whose layout accommodates certain agendas, the author also categorizes a position or perhaps a role to be adopted by the reader/critic. How has the Catullan scholar positioned him- or herself in relation to Catullus? For the most part, this position can be understood in terms of a narrative of love and betrayal that has been elaborated from the collection: Catullus' betrayal by a woman who failed to understand the nature of his love, and by a society that gave him no context in which to pursue this love, is compensated by the understanding of the modern scholar.

The founding act of modern scholarship on Catullus is the identification of the woman behind the name Lesbia, the beloved who features in a number of poems, scattered throughout the collection, that together imply a love affair rich in vicissitude and emotional drama. Catullus' Lesbia was identified by the founder of modern criticism of Catullus, Ludwig Schwabe, with the infamous Clodia, scion of one of the most distinguished Roman families, sister of the rabble-rousing tribune Clodius and wife of the consul of 60 B.C.E., Metellus.[10] We know of Clodia almost exclusively from hostile male sources, mainly Cicero, the antagonist of her brother Clodius. With this identification, the scholarly project of reconstructing a chronology of Catullus' poetry is inaugurated, and with it the critical project of elaborating the archetypal story of a love affair, told, of course, from the point of view of the disappointed and betrayed Catullus. The identification of Lesbia with Clodia Metelli has become the orthodoxy at least partly due to the overwhelming power of Cicero's vitriolic portrayal of Clodia in the *Pro Caelio*. In that speech, Cicero claims that the charges against his client, Clodia's erstwhile lover

Caelius, have been trumped up by Clodia as revenge for his rejection of her, and he spends a great deal of the speech defaming Clodia with a scurrilous, heavy-handed wit.

In a very real sense, Cicero has been made into the first reader and critic of Catullus.[11] The recognition of the Lesbia of Catullus in the Clodia of Cicero's *Pro Caelio* comes with the adoption of a certain rhetoric about Lesbia. It also provides an analogy for the position of the critic with respect to Catullus in Cicero's advocacy of Caelius, the spurned lover of Clodia. Just as Cicero cleverly detached his client Caelius from the moral opprobrium he heaped on Caelius' mistress Clodia, so the Catullan critic has spoken with stern morality about one member of an adulterous liaison (Lesbia) and deep understanding about the other (Catullus).[12] The critic's job, like the advocate's, would seem to be to make the best possible case for his client's point of view.

The critic who is advocate of Catullus and antagonist of Lesbia is also, potentially, a substitute for Lesbia. In "The Scholars," Yeats milks the irony of bald scholars toiling over their Catullus:

> Bald heads forgetful of their sins,
> Old, learned, respectable bald heads
> Edit and annotate the lines
> That young men, tossing on their beds
> Rhymed out in love's despair
> To flatter beauty's ignorant ear.[13]

As any of the respectable bald heads could have told Yeats, Catullus' Lesbia was anything but ignorant, hence the pseudonym that associates her with Sappho.[14] But Yeats, like so many poets, has found in Catullus a soulmate, and in doing so he has destroyed his own irony, for if beauty's ear is ignorant then it is entirely appropriate that bald heads should edit and annotate the lines that their intended audience failed to appreciate. Although no modern scholar would cast Lesbia as a philistine, it is a commonplace of Catullan criticism that Lesbia was unable to comprehend Catullus' conception of love, a conception that it is the critic's task to explicate. So the understanding that the critic extends to Catullus compensates for Lesbia's failure, which in turn situates the critic's labor.

A recent study of Catullus, Eve Adler's *Catullan Self-Revelation*, explicitly adopts this model of the relation between poet and reader that underlies so much work on Catullus.[15] According to Adler, the poems are a systematic self-revelation whose aim is "the perfection of others' ability to know him rightly, and thus the disavowal of false friends and the education of true ones. In this way it could come about that the reader of Catullus' poems becomes his pupil and even, possibly, his friend" (41). In Lesbia Catullus "has created for himself in her, by the relationship he assumes with her, the one woman who is loved both as man and woman. This is the unique woman to whom his love poems are poems of self-revelation, as are his poems to friends, and whose betrayal of him, like his friends' betrayals, can be understood as . . . her failure to know him as he knows himself" (163). Lesbia's betrayal of Catullus here stands for all betrayals that must be rectified by the critic, who understands Catullus better; paving the way for the work of the critic, Lesbia's betrayal situates the reader in a triangular relation between poet, lover, and reader.

Adler understands the relation between poet and reader or critic as personal, but others would have us understand Catullus better than those who betrayed him by virtue of our historical perspective. "Catullus" in this case is the name of a relation to the past, a voice that we recognize calling to us from its Roman prison, a yearning to which we can give a name better than he could. What Catullus feels for Lesbia, according to the most common understanding, is something for which there is no language in Latin, a feeling that will have to await Christianity, Romanticism, and modern conceptions of marriage to find an adequate linguistic and institutional expression.[16] Catullus, according to one of his most recent interpreters, is the frustrated prophet of "whole love," a position first espoused by Copley in 1949.[17] Commenting on poem 85 ("I hate and I love"), Copley diagnoses the torment of Catullus:

> At the risk of oversimplifying and importing into an ancient author concepts strictly modern, one might say that it is not so much his heart as his conscience that is putting him on the rack. . . . Well might his contemporaries ask "quare id facis?" ["Why do you do this?" i.e., hate and love] for they could have had no conception of his feelings. For that matter, Catullus himself does not know why he suffers so—witness the despairing nescio ["I don't know"] which he offers in reply. . . . The modern, backed by his tradition of romantic love, can understand Catullus better than could the poet himself, for it is now commonly accepted . . . that desire is right only when it is accompanied by love. . . . To be conscious of doing wrong, but not to know why the wrong is wrong—this is indeed excruciari [to be tortured].[18]

Victim of his own historical moment, this Catullus allows us both to experience the past as the birth-pangs of the present and to rescue his suffering soul from its own confusion and from the incomprehension of his beloved. In Catullus we are supposed to witness the Roman wanting to become modern, and in this respect reception of Catullus is similar to that of Vergil as the "naturally Christian soul." The historical novels that locate an alienated and, to his fellows, enigmatic Catullus in the exciting but decadent world of the last decades of the Republic use the figure of Catullus to project into the ancient world a sensibility that is potentially modern. It is the modern reader who claims to possess the key to this contradictory and complex character, hence the title of the most recent of the Catullan novels, Benita Kay Jaro's *The Key*.[19] My point here is that the theme of betrayal and incomprehension in Catullus' poetry has been elaborated by criticism so as to position the reader/critic as someone who can supply what the text and its author need and at the same time to give an affective content to the labor of intepretation.

## The Collection: Locating the Center of Gravity

Probably the most disturbing feature of Catullus' poetry is the promiscuity of the collection, a promiscuity that scholars have been much exercised to control by giving the collection a center of gravity. What has been at stake in the interpretation of the collection as a whole is the maintaining of the proper relation between surface and depth in a collection that is so mingled. How are we to understand the nature of the book that we know as "Catullus"?

Catullus' latest translator responds to Yeats's "The Scholars" by pointing out that without the shuffling of bald men there would be no text of Catullus to read.[20] True as this is for all ancient authors, it is particularly true for Catullus, who remained virtually unknown for six centuries from the last datable ancient reference to his work in Isidore of Seville (d. ca. 636) to the rediscovery of the text of Catullus around 1300.[21] In spite of Catullus' evident importance and fame in antiquity— for he is cited, imitated, and praised quite frequently—the survival of his work was a precarious affair. The manuscript that eventually turned up in Catullus' hometown of Verona was said to have been discovered "under a bushel."[22] Though the original manuscript (known as V or *Veronensis*) disappeared, it was not before copies had been made, giving us our three fourteenth-century manuscripts (O, G, and R), the ancestors of all modern editions. The corruption of V—one modern estimate puts this at over a thousand mistakes—[23] was admitted by the despairing scribe of G, who hoped that one would come after him who could correct this mess. The first to answer his call and the ancestor of Yeats's geriatrics was the eighteen-year-old Angelo Poliziano, whose annotations of the first edition of Catullus, as he tells us, cost him so much labor and kept him up so many nights that he believed that he had achieved more than any other scholar of his time.[24] Catullus enters the modern world, then, not as the passionate lover but as the bafflingly corrupt text that excites the ambition of the teenaged Poliziano.

If the Renaissance editors of Catullus, inheriting a manuscript in which blocks of poems had been conflated, faced the problem of establishing the proper boundaries between individual poems,[25] Catullus' modern scholars have been more concerned with relating the poems to each other in order to mitigate the baffling miscellany of the collection and its inscrutable order.[26] The collection is one of the most bewilderingly varied to have reached us from antiquity. It includes love poems, invective, obscenity, epithalamia, literary manifestos, social satire, anecdotes, political squibs, mythological epic—and more. Perhaps even more confusing than this proliferation of genre is the range of seriousness in the collection: some poems aggressively parade their flippancy, whereas others make an almost embarrassing spectacle of sincerity, and a third group is pokerfaced and could be taken either straight or as jokes. Restoring the author to life, or rather giving the text an author, becomes a matter of relating the poems to each other through some narrative.

But the subjectivity that subtends the narratives through which Catullus has been resurrected by modern criticism is different in kind from the subjectivity that an ancient Roman might have brought to such a miscellaneous collection. Pliny's descriptions of collections of poetry descended from Catullus, including his own, make it clear that ancient Roman audiences positively relished the chaotic variety with which the author displayed the range and changeability of his off-duty moods and attitudes. These descriptions feature asyndetic lists of activities, emotional states, and stylistic qualities that value capaciousness and inclusiveness over stability.[27] The late Republic sees the increasing cultivation of private life as an alternative, even an escape, from the rigors of the public image and its demands of *constantia* (steadiness, constancy).[28] By Pliny's time, the display of this private life, which became the locus of the same kind of competition that governed the political life of the upper classes, was common. But, according to Cicero, even Catullus' contemporary Piso had Philodemus celebrate his various, and often disreputable, private activities in "the most risqué [or 'exquisite'] verse."[29] Cicero himself provides us with another model for Catullus' collection, or for the kind of taste that would have delighted in its chaotic variety, when he writes to his friend Atticus, who keeps him apprised of what is going on in Rome while he is out of town:

Ut scribis, ita video non minus incerta in re publica quam in epistula tua, sed ista ipsa me varietas sermonum opinionumque delectat; Romae enim videor esse cum tuas litteras lego et, ut fit in tantis rebus, modo hoc modo illud audire (*ad Att.* 2.15).

As you write, so I see it: the uncertainty of the State is no less than that in your letter. But that very variety of speech and opinions delights me, for I seem to be in Rome when I read your letter and, as is the case in matters of such moment, to hear now this, now that.

However, the Catullan *libellus* (little book) does show some signs of order, as for instance in its tripartite division. The book begins with sixty short, personal poems in a variety of meters featuring the language and manner of urbanity (urbanitas), a section that is usually referred to as the "polymetrics"; it has at its center seven longer poems, for the most part lacking in personal references, and it ends with forty-eight short poems of love and hate in the elegiac meter, often awkward in style and full of the vocabulary of traditional Roman morality. In all three divisions, there are poems about a love affair with Lesbia, which is clearly represented as having a narrative dimension, although the poems do not appear in any narrative order.[30] Other characters, sometimes historical ones under their own names, appear and reappear, often reflecting strong, but not always consistent, feelings on Catullus' part.

How are we to constitute an author for this book that we call "Catullus"? Modern scholarship on the author begins with the work of Ludwig Schwabe, whose *Quaestiones Catullianae* (1862) constructed a fairly detailed biography of Catullus using the poems themselves and material from Cicero (particularly the *Pro Caelio*) about Clodia and Caelius Rufus. Schwabe produced from the collection a story of love, betrayal, and jealousy, and the influence of his work has been enormous.[31] The scholarship that has followed Schwabe's project has aimed to recover the novel latent in the jumbled collection that has come down to us. There is a neat analogy in this project to the work of textual criticism, traditionally understood as reconstructing an original text that has been "corrupted." On this analogy, the original text is the correct order of the poems as they were composed by the historical Catullus, and to reconstitute this original text is simultaneously to interpret the poems by translating them into the quintessential modern literary form, the novel.

The project of criticism, then, is to produce a plausible narrative out of the poems in the collection and an explication of individual poems in terms of such a narrative. Catullus, constructed by this work as the author of the restored text, becomes the author of an autobiographical novel.[32]

As they stand, the poems about Lesbia are a chaotic mix of the superficial, the passionate, the vitriolic, the heartfelt, the irreverent, and the moralistic. To acquire an author, they must be made to yield a story that turns this variety into coherence, a story in which the lover Catullus maintains a stable core while progressively realizing the truth about a changeable and fickle Lesbia from whom he finally succeeds in separating himself.[33] The story that Catullus authors, and that has been rescued by commentary from the promiscuous variety of the collection, is, in its most common modern form, a story of passion that turns, on the man's part, into something deeper; the progressive knowledge of his own deeper feelings and of the woman's unworthiness leads to Catullus' final break with his Lesbia.[34] So the elaboration of the story that is central to the collection is also the construction of an author whose journey from surface to depth and whose struggle to separate from a woman of threatening promiscuity could be parables of the interpreter's relation to the disturbing variety of the collection.

## The Novel of Catullus

Though few would now claim that the Lesbia poems reflect the history of a real love affair, the poems are almost always read as composing a story, even if fictional. Dominating the opening of the collection is what is usually referred to as a "Lesbia cycle," a sequence of poems that presents the basic narrative of a love affair. These love poems (cc.2, 3, 5, 7, 8, and 11) have been scanned for signs of change in Catullus' (fictional) relationship with Lesbia, which is said to undergo a progression from light to serious and from optimistic to bitter.[35] Full-blown versions of the novel of Catullus' love see a similar progression through the whole book, with Catullus discovering deeper feelings in himself at the same time as he realizes Lesbia's unworthiness, and not uncommonly he ends up turning to God.[36] That this story has been so endlessly elaborated in Catullan scholarship is due to the need to find some way of stratifying the collection and, above all, of siting the playful, trivial poems so that they become part of a story of transcendence. Even versions of the structure of Catullus' book that do not revolve around a Lesbia narrative use amatory metaphors to describe a turn from the light and playful to the weighty and serious. Hallett 1988, for instance, argues that Catullus distinguishes the playful, polymetric poetry (cc.1–60) from the more serious longer poems and elegiacs through sexual metaphors for his poetry that distinguish "pleasurable, playful, sexual activity" from "dutiful, reproductive sex and . . . shared commitment to long-term perpetuation generally" (399). Her motto for this shifting of gears in Catullus' collection is a passage from one of the wedding poems: "Play as it pleases you, and in a little while produce children" (ludite ut lubet, et brevi / liberos date, c.61, 204–5).[37] This motto neatly suggests that there is a development from the playful to the serious within Catullus' career.

The most thoroughgoing recent attempt to see Catullus whole, to plot the psychic history beneath the collection, is to be found in W. R. Johnson's *The Idea of Lyric*.[38] It is worth dwelling on Johnson's interpretation because it is a satisfying and sophisticated narrative construction of the author Catullus that takes this kind of enterprise as far as it can go, revealing in its engaging eloquence the investments that have guided much modern criticism of this poet. For Johnson, the tripartite division of the collection tells a story: the three kinds of poetry represent different moments in a subjectivity that is gradually overcome by its darkest and deepest instincts. It is a story profoundly congenial to modern sensibilities, for within the Catullan oeuvre Johnson finds a finished and accomplished collection (*The Sparrow*, i.e., the polymetrics) arranged by the author himself, and then two different kinds of poetry, written in the last years of Catullus' life and published posthumously, in which tendencies only implicit in *The Sparrow* break out and overwhelm the artistic optimism of the earlier collection. Here is Johnson's own synopsis:

> To put it briefly, Catullus sees himself, at the core of himself, as the victim of the world and the victim of himself. This overwhelming sense of alienation and of hopeless vulnerability, which is almost hidden in *The Sparrow*, enhances its hilarity and energies in retrospect: so when we turn to the narratives and elegiacs, the zest and swagger of *The Sparrow* foil and heighten the powerful feelings of impotence and isolation that find their full unfolding in these poems, which I believe to have been written just before the poet died (115).

Johnson sees the collection in two different ways. First, as a narrative that moves from a controlled artistic triumph to the uncollected works in which the "hilarity and energies" of *The Sparrow* begin to unravel, culminating in the problematic poem 68 (both narrative and elegiac) where "an elaborate, profoundly felt artistic discourse . . . imagines the ruin of artistic discourse" (162). But this narrative of Catullus' psychic history and death is compensated by a lyric simultaneity in which the two portions of what is now Catullus' oeuvre, collected and uncollected, themselves form a new artistic whole, each providing a foil for the other.

Johnson is full of admiration for *The Sparrow* as the product of a young man's "delight in the world and in himself" (116), in which the richness and jumble of the world Catullus so passionately experiences is only enhanced by the severe artistic control of the poetry. And yet Catullus, the provocative champion of an elegant and un-Roman frivolity, "came to see that perhaps he had got out of his depth, that perhaps he was wasting—had wasted?—his life" (117). What breaks out in the uncollected poems has been repressed by the vibrant and rebellious young poet who shed his provincial values to make a splash in the exciting world of sophisticated Roman society. Let down by Lesbia, Catullus "realizes that *pietas* and 'the bond inviolate' (*fides*), the values of his childhood, are and always were his real values" (120). Similarly, Catullus' commitment to art had always exceeded the forms in which it had been expressed, which, like Lesbia, were an unworthy field for the deployment of Catullus' deepest urges. In both the amatory and the aesthetic spheres, then, Catullus was bound to experience disillusionment. Nemesis, whose human form is Lesbia, punishes Catullus for having denied his own deepest self, and the love story becomes an allegory for Catullus' relation to his art, "for art demands of the artist what love demands of the lover—total, complete devotion" (113).

Johnson's version of the "novel" of Catullus allows him to understand the frivolity or preciosity of so much of Catullus' work as a pose, beneath which lies "a sense of identity and of life as passionate as the art that informs it is rigorous" (112). Readers of the novel of Catullus, then, are invited to look past the pose at what it conceals, to find hints of what is waiting to break out. Here, as elsewhere in Catullan scholarship, the story of a progression from surface to depth in the artistic and moral spheres revolves around Lesbia's betrayal of her lover and Catullus' rejection of her as unworthy of his love.

## Stratification: Surface and Depth

In his influential essay "What Is an Author?" Foucault (1979) reverses the conventional understanding of the relation between author and work. Though "we are accustomed ... to saying that the author is the genial creator of a work in which he deposits, with infinite wealth and generosity, an inexhaustible world of significations," Foucault argues that "the author is ... the ideological figure by which one marks the manner in which we fear the proliferation of meaning" (159). In what sense do we fear the proliferation of meaning? One way of answering this question is to consider how Catullan criticism unweaves the text of the collection to produce a stratified model of the ensemble in which layers are isolated from each other to prevent contamination. The production of an author for the text that has come down with Catullus' name involves the search for the *essential* Catullus: Johnson's *pius* Catullus, Havelock's lyric Catullus, or Kroll's impetuous child of nature, for instance.[39] Poems that fully engage the poet's distinctive capacities are to be isolated from those that do not, and of course we need the latter in order to find the former. Another form of stratification, Quinn's theory of levels of intent, is intended to provide a model that preserves the unity of Catullus' work as an object of criticism against the earlier contentions (of Havelock and Kroll, for instance) that Catullus wrote successful poems and unsuccessful ones.[40] Catullus is there in all of his poems, according to Quinn, but in different degrees (32). Applying the category of intensity to organize the stratification of the text determines how connections are to be made within the collection. Let us consider an example of this principle at work.

On the face of it, it would seem natural to compare the kiss poems addressed to the boy Juventius (cc.48, 99) to the kiss poems addressed to Lesbia (cc.5, 7), and so Quinn does:

Poems 5 and 7 show the same form [as cc.48 and 99] at a level of intent that was, I think, quite unprecedented in Roman poetry. We are dealing no longer with ideas Catullus found it fun to toy with: we are dealing with things that were carried to their proper, logical conclusion—the possession of Lesbia as his mistress. To fail to distinguish between Poems 5 and 7 and Poems 48 and 99 is carrying open-mindedness too far. We might as soon fail to distinguish Catullus and Ovid.[41]

The affair with Lesbia must not be contaminated by association with the homosexual relation, which evidently could not be carried to its "proper, logical conclusion," and the comparison of the two groups of poems serves to isolate the playfulness of 5 and 7 from the toying of 48 and 99, to distinguish the surface of something deep (full possession) from mere surface. Looked at from a Foucaultian point of view, the author Catullus with his levels of intent serves as a way of preventing the communication between these two groups of poems in the collection, and I would argue that constructing an author for this collection has been more than anything else a matter of managing the relation between surface and depth, which in this case coincides with the distinction between homosexual and heterosexual desire.

The isolation of a deeply felt heterosexual love from homosexual toying is one of the most important areas in which the mapping of surface and depth in this collection has been carried out. In this connection, the much-cited article of Colin Macleod, "Parody and Personalities in Catullus" (1973), is particularly interesting. The purported burden of this article is to argue "that these poems are fictions, and that sometimes they embody a form of humour whose appreciation partly depends on recognizing the gap between fiction and reality" (302). Now it so happens that the poems treated in this article (cc. 50, 55, 58b, 24, 15, 21, 23, 16, 11, 89) are all, with one very important exception (c.11), to a greater or lesser extent homosexual, though nothing in the title or in the beginning or the end of the article suggests that this is its focus. The one exception to the homosexual thematic is poem 11, Catullus' bitter farewell to Lesbia, which stands out also because it is the only poem in this group that Macleod does not treat as parody or, in fact, as a fiction; those who have detected "tasteless hyperbole" in the beginning of the poem have failed to sound the poem's level of intent.[42]

The real agenda of Macleod's article is not to draw attention to the fictional nature of Catullus' poems but to separate the serious and heartfelt relation with Lesbia (so that any infusion of irony into c.11 is dismissed as "cheap") from the parodic eroticism of the homosexual poems. Here the author Catullus serves to prevent that staple of classical scholarship, the parallel, from producing a dangerous promiscuity; Macleod takes his parallels in some cases to prove the presence of literary parody but in others to indicate heartfelt sincerity.[43] I argue in the next chapter that the eroticism of the poems Macleod is dealing with cannot be separated from that of Lesbia poems such as poems 2, 5, and 7. Though Macleod's article contains much that is interesting and useful in spite of its methodological confusion,[44] his claim to philological objectivity—"to use the identification of poetic forms and conventions to approach the poem's significance"—masks an agenda about the stratification of Catullus' oeuvre that the philology is serving. What appears to be a rather loose series of observations on miscellaneous poems of Catullus is in fact a masterpiece of economy, for the expulsion of "cheap" irony from the deeply felt poem 11 is accomplished at the same time as the homoeroticism in Catullus' poems is banished into the category of literary parody.

It has been an important component of the notion of the classic author that, while reflecting his times, he has also managed to rise above them. This has been particularly important in the case of Catullus, who seems to relish fashionable life at Rome while he rails against the corruption and betrayal with which it is rife. For some, the figure of Catullus protesting his fidelity and commitment to a Lesbia who repeatedly betrays him demonstrates the survival of personal integrity in a disintegrating society.[45] So parallels that would assimilate the Lesbia poems to others, breaking down the hierarchy of intensity, may also threaten the privileged status of the author in relation to his times.[46]

## The Pure Catullus

Ironically, the poet whom Quintilian valued for the "sharpness" (acerbitas, 10.1.96) of his iambics became known to the Victorians as the "tenderest of Roman poets."[47] The potential contamination of tenderness with violence and obscenity in a collection that jumbles them together has been a major concern of modern scholarship, which has responded by producing an author whose inmost core remains unspoiled by the world in which he participates with such gusto. In 1885, Baehrens presented to us a Catullus who was "good, upright, lovable and good-natured" (40); those who object to his morals are told that they should remember that we are dealing with a poet of Roman times, not of our own, and that Catullus' environment was one where "the dissolute morals and unbridled license infected many of his fellows with the utmost corruption, where nobody could avoid accustoming his eyes and mind to all manner of filth, even if he did not himself sink into it" (41). Catullus, provoked by men he despised, "himself unsullied and pure, pursued bitter hatreds bitterly, little caring what pus and venom he exuded in expressing his contempt" (41).[48] Wiseman 1985, who provides fascinating documentation of this model of the conflict between innocence and corruption in the Catullus myth, has enough sympathy with it to try to put it on a sounder basis. Arguing, in a chapter called "The Beauty of Innocence," that Catullus' poetry betrays a fascination, even an identification, with virginity, Wiseman attributes this moral innocence to Catullus' Transpadane background, commenting that "it was a dangerously vulnerable set of attitudes to take into the corrupt and cynical world of Roman high society" (122). Echoing Baehrens, Wiseman goes on to say that Catullus learned to "hit back when he chose, and hold his own with those who held his moral standards in contempt" (123).[49] In the various versions of the innocent Catullus, *in* his time but not *of* it, the function of the author is to provide a psychological model for the way that the obscenity inhabits the collection without contaminating it.[50]

In the rest of this book, I do not try to reconstruct a life or a psyche from the Catullan collection; in fact, frequently, by reading together poems that are usually treated in separate categories, I undermine the narratives and stratifications that have been supported by traditional constructions of Catullus the author. Often I engage contiguous poems in a dialogue with each other even, and perhaps especially, when they would seem to involve different "levels of intent"; in other cases, I take groups of poems that are traditionally linked together but deal with them in relation to different issues. There is now a copious literature on whether Catullus himself ordered the collection as we know have it, whether it was published as a single book, and, if not, what is referred to by the expression "little book" in the first line of poem 1.[51] I do not believe that a definitive answer can be given to these questions, so I will not claim that my groupings and the relations they establish were intended by Catullus himself. Rather, I hope to give a new look to a familiar collection by reading it while keeping in mind the kinds of issues outlined in my introduction.

CHAPTER 2

# Catullus and the Reader
## The Erotics of Poetry

Catullus tells us in one of his most famous poems that the success of his poetry can be measured by whether it sexually excites hairy old men (c.16, 7–11). Scholars have not been quick to hail this as the key to Catullan poetics, though they have made a great deal of the same poem's supposed distinction between the poet's verse, which may be indecent, and the poet's life, which need not.[1] So Catullus' most provocative statement has been buried beneath a reassurance of his personal purity. But in what sense might sexual provocation be a factor in Catullan poetics, and how might this affect our understanding of the position of poet or audience in relation to the poet?[2]

In this chapter, I describe the context of Catullus' statement, focusing on a group of poems (cc.1, 2, 15, 16) that, directly or indirectly, casts the relation between poet and reader in sexual terms. I begin by considering some of the aesthetic terms that Catullus uses of his poetry and their provocative relation to Roman cultural norms, and then I describe how this provocation functions in the constitution of the aesthetic object. Catullus' dedication poem situates the book's recipient (and consumer) in a particular relation to the book that defines its aesthetic status; the gesture with which he offers his book, I argue, is a form of teasing that is duplicated in some of his love poetry, poetry that concerns the relation between poet and reader as much as that between poet and beloved. In the rest of the chapter, I describe how Catullus explores, unsettles, and manipulates the power relations between poet and reader, the shifting of vulnerability and control. I argue that Catullus is exploring an aesthetic relation that unsettles the rigid framework of Roman conceptions of power and position as they are metaphorized by sex and gender.

We begin at the beginning, the dedication of the book to Cornelius Nepos (c.1) and the first of the two poems about the pet sparrow of Catullus' mistress (c.2). Although these are juxtaposed in the book as we now have it, they are usually treated in two different contexts, the first being read as a literary manifesto and the second as the beginning of a "Lesbia cycle" in which Catullus unfolds the drama of his turbulent love affair. But both poems offer something to their audience, whether it is the book itself, in which Catullus' "trifles" (nugas, 1.4) are collected, or a titillating glimpse of the erotic world of the poet and his mistress, and it is this relation between poet and audience that provides the framework in which I compare them.

### Catullan Aesthetic Language: Pets, Toys, and Toying

What immediately strikes the reader about the much imitated poems on the death of the mistress's pet sparrow (cc.2, 3) is their *insistent* triviality, and I emphasize the word because this triviality is intended to provoke;[3] combined with a delicate eroticism, this insistent triviality culminates in the final lines of poem 3, where Catullus berates the dead sparrow, whose dirge he has sung, for spoiling his mistress's eyes with weeping:

> o factum male! o miselle passer!
> tua nunc opera meae puellae
> flendo turgiduli rubent ocelli. (3.16–18)[4]

> What a pity! Wretched sparrow!
> Because of you my girlfriend's eyes
> Are red and swollen from weeping.

The bathos, with its knowing eroticism, winks at the audience, addressed specifically in the second line of this poem as the "men of elegance" (hominum venustiorum) who are invited to join in the dirge for the dead sparrow. *Venustus*, the adjective with which the audience of this poem is summoned, is a particularly important word for Catullus because it spans what we would call the erotic and the aesthetic spheres.[5] The bird that the *venusti* of poem 3 are called on to mourn is described as the *deliciae* of Catullus' mistress (3.4, compare 2.1), a word that is also of crucial importance to Catullan aesthetics. *Deliciae* is not unlike our word "pet" in its range of associations. "Pet" can be a noun or a verb: the verb conveys a way of indulging a being referred to by the noun, an indulging that is at the same time self-indulgence. *Deliciae* also refers both to a pleasurable form of activity (lovemaking, most notably) and to a person or thing that serves our pleasure or is indulged by us for our own pleasure (compare the word "toy"). In both languages, the words also signify a form of behavior that results from excessive self-indulgence; the now obsolete English expressions "to pet" or "to take the pet," meaning "to sulk" or "to take offense," seem to derive from the primary sense just as the Latin word *deliciae* can mean "airs" or "caprices." The negative associations of the word in Latin are extensive: most significantly, they include the implication of effeminacy that to the Roman mind goes with any form of nonpurposive or nonessential activity.[6] *Deliciae*, then, is a complex word, denoting at the same time an object or being, a status (favorite, darling), and a form of behavior; to call something or somebody your *deliciae* is to point in two opposite directions, to the object and to oneself, and it is also to mark one's behavior, quite self-consciously, as questionable.

*Deliciae* is the word for Lesbia's pet, for the games she plays with it, and for the game Catullus is himself playing in these poems, for *deliciae* and the closely related adjective *delicatus*[7] are words with which Catullus sometimes represents his own poetic activity.[8] As "delicious" and "delicate," these words have entered our own aesthetic vocabulary, but though they are still associated with the trivial (the culinary and the ornamental arts respectively), they have been severed from the language of behavior and attitude in which their Latin counterparts are embedded. It is significant that the word Catullus uses to refer to his poetry in the first poem of the book, *nugae* (trifles, triflings), seems to have meant, among other things, "mime"; in other words, it too may refer to performance as well as product.[9]

When Catullus describes the game in which he and his friend Calvus improvise responses to each other's compositions, he portrays them as *delicati* engaged in an erotically tinged performance (c.50):

Hesterno, Licini, die otiosi
multum lusimus in meis tabellis,
ut convenerat esse delicatos:
scribens versiculos uterque nostrum
ludebat numero modo hoc modo illoc,
reddens mutua per iocum atque vinum.
atque illinc abii tuo lepore

incensus, Licini, facetiisque,
ut nec me miserum cibus iuvaret . . . (50.1-9)

Yesterday, Licinius, a day of leisure,
we fooled around a lot in my tablets,
since we'd agreed to be a little precious:
writing little verses each of us
played around in this meter and that,
giving and taking while we joked and drank.
I went away from there inflamed
by your suave, sophisticated humor;
even dinner couldn't interest me . . .

The mutual provocation of the two poets may remind us of Lesbia teasing the sparrow with her finger (c.2.3-4); certainly, the variation of meters reminds us of the kissing in the famous poem (c.5) in which Catullus and Lesbia play with different rhythms and numbers ("Give me a thousand kisses, then a hundred," etc). Poem 50's erotic language aligns the games of the two poets with the thousands of kisses that Aurelius and Furius read about in poem 5 and find "a bit soft and not quite straight" (molliculi ac parum pudici, c.16.8)—in other words, characteristic of the *delicatus*. Swapping verses back and forth in an analog of foreplay leaves Catullus in a state of frustrated excitement (50.7-13); like the endless kissing of poems 5 and 7, the *deliciae* of Catullus and Calvus are a deliberate indulgence in the inessential and a refusal to get to the point, which in Rome is taken as a sign of effeminacy.[10] Catullus claims and performs the position to which this kind of language would assign him, but in doing so he puts at question some of the assumptions that underlie it. Because poetry concerns relations, and not just objects, it is in terms of the behavioral and relational associations of an ambivalent word like *deliciae* that Catullus explores the drama of poetic positionality.

The first two poems of Catullus' little book present us with two delightful objects, almost toys: the "smart new little book" (lepidum novum libellum, 1.1) itself, with its smooth surfaces, and the sparrow that is the *deliciae* of its mistress. Not only are these both eroticized objects, as we shall see, but they are also components of a game that the poet is playing with his audience. Just as there is something ambiguous about the book that Catullus offers its dedicatee in poem 1 (physical object or poetic work?), so there is an ambiguity about the sparrow, which may be an innocent pet or the vehicle of a sexual metaphor. In these poems, Catullus plays with surface and depth to eroticize our relation to the objects, which are both offered and withdrawn, and which both hide and reveal: the poetic trifles (nugae) might, after all, *be* something (1.3-4), and Lesbia's play with the sparrow might be part of the narrative of a love affair. So the two poems take their character from the gesture with which these objects are offered to us.

But the one who offers is both powerful and vulnerable, and my second pair of poems (cc.15, 16) are spoken from the potentially vulnerable position of the poet whose words are entrusted to readers who may take them as they will. Of these poems, one is explicitly about the relation between poet and readers (c.16), and the other appears to be an episode from the erotic life of Catullus (c.15). In the former, Furius and Aurelius are attacked for concluding, from all those kisses they have read about in his poetry, that Catullus is effeminate, and it is here that he retorts that his poetry only has the requisite charm (*sal* and *lepor*, 16.7) if it can excite hairy men. In poem 15 Catullus simultaneously commends to Aurelius a beloved boy and warns him to keep his hands off. The violent phallic threats with which poem 15 ends, and which frame poem 16, reflect the Roman obsession with relations of dominance and subordination, an obsession that is amply attested by Catullus' poetry.[11] In both cases, Catullus has made himself vulnerable by virtue of what he has entrusted to Furius and Aurelius; the combination of entrusting and withholding in poem 15 recapitulates the giving and withholding that characterizes poem 1, but in a much more aggressive context. By raising the question of the relation between poet and reader from the standpoint of the poet's vulnerability, his lack of control over the transaction, these poems provide the counterpart to poems 1 and 2, which speak from a position of confidence. That the vulnerability of the poet is expressed in relation to a phallic threat from other men has to do with the provocative performance that Catullus stages, and with the culture's determination of the particular form of pleasure that he purveys as effeminate. For Catullus, the aesthetic is a function of the positionality of agents in a transaction and, more particularly, in the case of these poems, of a *play* with positionality that upsets what has been described as the Roman puritanism of virility.[12]

## Teasing: The Aesthetic Relation

The first poem in Catullus' book is not simply an act of dedication, for what Catullus does in this poem is to put the book into circulation, to give it to its readership, and the nature of the object is to some extent constituted by the form of this gesture.[13] The dedicatee, Cornelius Nepos, stands at a nodal point between the production of Catullus' *nugae* and their reception by posterity: because he approved them, or saw something in them, they have now been published and committed to the care of time.[14] Once his trifles have been given value by a reader, they cease to belong to the poet, but publication also removes them from any other individual's appropriation:

> Cui dono lepidum novum libellum
> arida modo pumice expolitum?
> Corneli, tibi; namque tu solebas
> meas esse aliquid putare nugas
> iam tum, cum ausus es unus Italorum
> omne aevum tribus explicare cartis
> doctis, Iuppiter, et laboriosis.
> quare habe tibi quidquid hoc libelli
> qualecumque; quod, ⟨o⟩ patrona virgo,
> plus uno maneat perenne saeclo. (c.1)

> To whom do I give this chic new little book
> freshly smoothed by the dry pumice?
> Cornelius, to you; for it was you
> who used to think my trifles *were* something
> when you yourself had dared, alone
> of the Italians, to expound all history
> in three most learned and laborious volumes.
> So have this little book for what
> it's worth, and, O my virgin patron,
> may it remain fresh for more than one generation.

The modest detachment of "have this little book for what it's worth" acknowledges that Nepos, by seeing something in Catullus' bits and pieces, is responsible for their publication; but it also recognizes the fact that what this book *is* depends on how its future readership receives it. So the object that Catullus is giving to Nepos is both a delightful physical object and a polished work of art that is not confined to any one of its instantiations, and this duality is what complicates the gesture of giving, because the book as work of art cannot actually be given. Paradoxically, then, the approval of Nepos, which earned him this book, is what removes the "trifles" to another time.

Catullus is publishing his trifles; every reader of Catullus knows that "now you have it, now you don't" feeling produced by a combination of casual spontaneity and high finish;[15] at the end of poem 1, the book is given to Nepos with a gesture that dramatizes this relation between poet and reader. The phrase "habe tibi" (have it, 8) is, as Fordyce (1961 ad loc) points out, "a regular phrase of Roman law in reference to the disposal of property." Both in the legal and colloquial senses (the latter implies, as Fordyce puts it, "a certain indifference"), there is often a contrast between what is given and what is retained. But in this case it is the same thing that is both given and retained ("have this little book . . . may it remain"; habe tibi . . . quod maneat, 8–10), and there is a real connection between the lightness of Catullus' relation to his *nugae* and their continued freshness as aesthetic objects.[16] The poet himself keeps nothing, for the book goes on the one hand to anyone who now finds something in these trifles, and on the other to a posterity that continues to find them fresh. Nepos, though he gets this attractive little book because he made something of Catullus' *nugae*, can't really have it because the virgin sees to it that the book will remain fresh for future generations.

This virgin is the poet's Muse, addressed here as patron (patrona virgo, 9) instead of Nepos. As a virgin the Muse plays her part in the erotic figuration introduced when the newly completed book appears "freshly smoothed by the dry pumice" (2). Pumice has two uses in the literary sphere: to smooth the ends of the scroll in the final stages of the book's preparation, and to erase and correct the work prior to publication. The first use draws attention to the book's attractions and availability, as Horace shows us when he berates his book of epistles for its eagerness to prostitute itself to the public:[17]

> Vertumnum Ianumque, liber, spectare videris,
> scilicet ut prostes Sosiorum pumice mundus
> odisti clavis et grata sigilla pudico. (*Ep.* 1.20.1–3)
> You seem, book, to look towards Janus and Vertumnus
>                       [booksellers' area],
> Wanting to offer yourself smooth from the pumice of the Sosii
>                       [booksellers],
> You shun keys and seals, which are welcome to the chaste.

Horace's "smooth from the pumice" plays on the fact that pumice was used as a depilatory, and Catullus' phrase also associates the book's appealing exterior with sexual attractiveness and availability. But this aspect of the book, its immediate appeal and consumability, so to speak, is conveyed by the same words that also express the labor of composition and literary perfectionism implied by liberal use of the eraser, features of the book that ensure its continued life beyond this generation.

For the most part, modern commentators have concentrated on showing how the poem functions as an Alexandrian or neoteric literary manifesto: the lightness and modesty with which Catullus offers his book is all part of a display of allegiance to Alexandrian principles.[18] This approach usually generates a contrast between surface and depth that says as much about modern scholarship as it does about the poem: this apparently light and unprepossessing poem conceals references to Alexandrian watchwords and aesthetic attitudes, and once these have been identified by the scholar, the poem reveals itself as a serious work of high art.[19] The work of the scholar, then, protects us from the poem's trivial surface. Although the interpretation of this poem as a coded and concealed masterpiece posing a riddle for the learned reader is compatible with much of what we know of the Alexandrians, the poem has another dimension that is more distinctively Roman, and that is its social gesture. The associations of words like *pumex* and *expolitum* (smoothed, polished) in Latin are not only Alexandrian: smoothness and polish in a literary context tend to be given dubious sexual connotations by Roman writers who play on the coincidence of the language of the toilette with that of literary polish; so Catullus' book has a teasing sexuality that is provocatively effeminate.[20]

What I am arguing here is that Catullus is playing with the particularly complex relation between poet and reader when he both gives and withholds the book in a kind of teasing.[21] The poetics implied by this poem is neither one of surface and depth (Catullus professes an urbane indifference to the trivialities he offers Nepos, but finally reveals his sense of their true worth) nor paradox (it takes the harsh application of dry pumice to make something that never dries up: perenne, 10). In fact, it is Nepos' own work that exemplifies the deceptive or paradoxical results of "artistry": he has managed to unfold (explicare, 6) the whole of time in a mere three volumes.[22] By contrast, Catullus focuses the temporal paradox concerning his own book on the act of giving: Nepos is welcome to the book (this attractive, smooth little volume), which becomes his as Catullus utters the formula "habe tibi"; but, as the poet prays for the same book that the Muse may preserve it fresh throughout posterity, he withdraws it from its dedicatee (maneat).[23] The same pumice that gives the book its sexy air of availability also gives its content the kind of polished definitiveness that takes it out of the field of consumption and consigns it to the care of posterity and the *virgin* Muse. Standing in for any reader who sees something in these trifles, Nepos is the figure through whom we experience the studied carelessness of these poems as a relation both to the poet and to posterity. Catullus' contradictory act of giving offers us the bifurcated sensation of participating in two different time-scales: we acquiesce in our frustrated possession of these trifles in order to participate in the eternal freshness of the work. What exactly it is that gives these trifles substance (esse aliquid, 3) we forbear to explore in order to leave them fresh for posterity. Here an aesthetic drama of loss and compensation takes on an imperial character, for this delicate moment now spreads its influence into the future with an imperialism more sure than Nepos' unfolding of the whole of time in three volumes. Any reader who is able to see something in these poems can have them, for their survival depends on this, but, in the interest of participating in the power and scope of their fascination, each reader must forbear to possess them. It is this position that the reader enjoys.

Catullus teases Nepos with his book, and in the next poem he teases his readers with intimations of sex, only to turn the tables on them in the final lines, where once again virginity intervenes:[24]

> Passer, deliciae meae puellae,
> quicum ludere, quem in sinu tenere,
> cui primum digitum dare appetenti
> et acris solet incitare morsus,
> cum desiderio meo nitenti
> carum nescioquid lubet iocari,
> et solaciolum sui doloris,
> credo, ut tum gravis acquiescat ardor:
> tecum ludere sicut ipsa possem
> et tristis animi levare curas,
> tam gratum est mihi quam ferunt puellae
> pernici aureolum fuisse malum,
> quod zonam soluit diu ligatam.
>
> Sparrow, plaything of my mistress,
> who plays with you, and holds you in her lap,
> who offers you her fingertip to peck at
> and then provokes sharp bites from you,
> when the shining object of my desire
> is pleased to play some charming game,
> a solace for her suffering, I think,
> to moderate the flames of passion:
> If I could play with you as she does
> and lighten the gloomy troubles of my mind—

that is as pleasing to me as they say
was the golden apple to the swift-footed girl
which loosened her girdle, so long tied.

At the end of this poem, we are told that Lesbia's game with the sparrow is itself the consummation to be desired: it would be as pleasing to Catullus as the apple that brought the end of virginity to Atalanta, and in being as pleasing it denies us the untying of the knot, for the game that suggested sex now becomes its alternative or substitute. Like that "something" which Nepos saw in Catullus' "trifles," but which immediately fades into the suave surface of the urbane tone, the sexuality of those who play with the sparrow never comes into focus.[25] The suggestive ambiguity of Catullus' interest in playing with the sparrow is compared to the ambiguous interest of the virgin Atalanta in the apple: was it a girlish delight in bright things; a desire that fully comprehended the erotic symbolism of the apple; a confused, virginal combination of both?[26] Sexual innuendo is now transferred to Atalanta, whose virginal mind is no doubt incapable of understanding what we know about her reaction to the apple; so the impenetrable and teasing sophistication of Catullus offers us its own compensatory supplement, the penetrable, half-innocent mind of Atalanta, whose confusion we are in a position to observe knowingly.

Like the contradictory gesture with which Nepos is offered the book, the final simile of poem 2 both offers and withholds. These contradictions have to do with the relation between poem and audience, for both the fact that Nepos cannot really have the book that is his and the fact that Catullus does not express a desire to *have* Lesbia dramatize the continuing availability of the aesthetic object to its audience, present and future. Neither Catullus himself nor any particular reader has privileged or preemptive access to the poetry, and this is constitutive of its aesthetic character as well as a guarantee of its persistent freshness. In poem 2, the desire of Catullus is a performing desire which, rather than interposing itself between the audience and its object, suffuses that object with a suggestive sexuality that does not exclude its audience; and yet, at the same time, it provokes and teases us with its elusiveness, its nugatoriness, and, if there is anything of Furius and Aurelius in us, its effeminacy. As in poem 1, the aesthetic object is here constituted as aesthetic by virtue of the peculiar drama of desire and possession between the agents that it assembles.

But the poem I have been describing is to be found in none of the modern texts of Catullus, for editors have detached what they regard as the puzzlingly "inappropriate" simile with which the poem ends in the manuscripts (lines 11–13, now called 2b) to produce a poem that falls into line with one of the most common ways of thinking about Catullus: the superficial Lesbia plays with her sparrow and so assuages her desire for Catullus, who wishes he could do the same himself, but being a man and a great poet he feels too deeply to be so easily satisfied.[27] The truncating of the poem by the editors provides a clear layering of surface and depth, so that the different relations of the characters to the game with the sparrow gives us a reassuring sense of what it is that allows us to say that the trivial is trivial. This truncated version of the poem provides a neat parallel to the usual interpretation of the dedication poem: just as Catullus writes what his culture defines as "trifles," but by virtue of the care he lavishes on them proves himself a dedicated and serious Alexandrian poet, so the intensity of his love for Lesbia transcends its rather trivial object. I doubt that editors would have been so impressed with the problems of the manuscript text at the end of poem 2 were they not so satisfied by the kind of reading made possible by detaching the last three lines.[28] This editorial tradition clarifies one of the roles of Catullus the canonical author, namely, to confirm the distinction between surface and depth, triviality and art, that he seems to put at question. The canonical Catullus is a poet who confronts the prejudices of his own age and culture, unable to appreciate the intrinsic value of art, and affirms or proves what we now know to be its true value. The Catullus that I am describing works with the troubled and suspicious fascination of his culture with what, for want of a better word, we can call *deliciae* to produce a positional drama that has much to tell us about the constitution of what we now call the aesthetic.

## The Anxieties of Publication

As a transition to my next pair of poems, where the relation between reader and poet is framed in the more anxious and violent terms of sexual relations between men, let us consider a passage from one of Pliny's letters (*Ep.* 7.4). Pliny was a great admirer of Catullus and published, evidently with considerable success, "trifles" (nugae) in the Catullan style. Writing to Pontius, he explains how a serious man such as himself came to write hendecasyllabics. It happened that one summer morning he had read to him the work of Asinius Gallus in which the latter compares his father to Cicero. In this work, there is an epigram of the great man to his slave Tiro in which Cicero complains that Tiro had reneged on his promise of some kisses. This sticks in Pliny's mind and, when he retires for his midday nap and finds that he can't sleep, he reflects on the fact that great orators enjoyed and respected this kind of poetry; not one to be left behind, Pliny tries his now unpracticed hand at writing verse and quickly sketches out an account of what it was that had inspired him to write (id ipsum, quod me ad scribendum sollicitaverat, his versibus exaravi). In these verses, he describes how he came across the epigram of Cicero, notable for the same genius that Cicero displayed in his serious works and for showing that the minds of great men rejoice in wit and playfulness. He then describes Cicero's epigram and concludes:

> "cur post haec" inquam "nostros celamus amores
> nullumque in medium timidi damus atque fatemur
> Tironisque dolos, Tironis nosse fugaces
> blanditias et furta novas addentia flammas."

> "After this," I said, "why should I conceal my loves
> and be afraid to make my contribution and confess
> that I know the tricks of Tiro and the teasing
> flirtation and the cheats that add new flames."

This account of the beginning of the path that led him to Catullan hendecasyllabics is itself clearly influenced by Catullus poem 50, which also describes how the poet came to be writing the present poem in a fit of insomnia. The spirit of friendly competition in the writing of verse is common to both poems, for Catullus describes how he and Calvus, having agreed to be *delicati*, spent the day swapping verses, which caused Catullus to become inflamed with Calvus' *lepor*. The poems also share a homosexual theme, with Catullus describing his excitement in the language of love and Pliny confessing to his own homosexual experience.[29] Later in the same letter, Pliny says that his erotic poems have inspired the Greeks to learn Latin, but it would be wrong to dismiss the homosexual element in these poems as literary convention.[30] When Pliny decides to jump on the bandwagon, he asks why he should conceal his *amores* (love, love poetry) and timidly avoid making his contribution (nullumque in medium timidi damus); he confesses that he too knows the tricks of a Tiro, the flirtation (fugaces blanditias) that causes new flames. The logic of the parallel with Cicero's epigram requires Pliny to be saying that he too has been tormented by a provocative and flirtatious boy, but the event that Pliny is describing in this poem, namely, his decision to join in Cicero's "playful game," allows us to understand Pliny's statement that he knows Tiro's tricks as a confession of his own flirtatious abilities. To publish erotic poetry is to play a provocative game with one's audience, adopting the position of the flirtatious Tiro. Pliny's response to Cicero is a kind of blowup of the game that Catullus and Calvus played, a quasi-erotic game of mutual provocation, in which Catullus' tablets function as the bed (c.50.1–2). At Rome it may have been a mark of the great man to feel himself superior enough to the attitudes of common society to be able to play at being the *delicatus*, and Pliny here links himself with Cicero by joining in the game,[31] but the game, like the playing of Catullus and Calvus, has to be questionable, risqué; consider the extraordinary phrase he uses of the way his literary activity snowballs from the incident he has just decribed:

> transii ad elegos; hos quoque non minus celeriter
> explicui, addidi alios *facilitate corruptus.*
>
> I moved on to elegies; these too I finished off
> quite as swiftly; I added others, *seduced by my own fluency/ease.*

The sexual model of the relation between poet and audience can take on a more anxious character, and in poems 15 and 16 Catullus addresses directly the sexual connotations of his poetic teasing as they frame the power relations between poet and reader. These poems explore the poet's vulnerability; the homosexual content of the poems and the phallic nature of the threat presented by the reader indicate that the issue here is the positionality of reader and poet, and that the poet's teasing casts him in the role of the effeminate or subordinate.

The first of these poems consists, like poem 1, in an act of giving, and it plays with the very Roman institution of commendation in the same way that poem 1 played with legal language (habe tibi, 1.8). To commend someone to another is both to draw attention to the commendee's qualities and to entrust that person to the would-be patron, so a potential conflict of interest arises when the commendee is an object of desire.[32] In poem 15 Catullus commends himself and his love to Aurelius, but then begs him to keep his hands off the boy. The twist in the commendation is that the boy is to be protected not from the usual external corrupting influences but from the voracious and indiscriminate penis of Aurelius himself!

> Commendo tibi me ac meos amores,
> Aureli. veniam peto pudentem,

> ut si quicquam animo tuo cupisti,
> quod castum expeteres et integellum,
> conserves puerum mihi pudice,
> non dico a populo—nihil veremur
> istos, qui in platea modo huc modo illuc
> in re praetereunt sua occupati,—
> verum a te metuo tuoque pene
> infesto pueris bonis malisque. (c.15.1–10)
>
> Aurelius, commending to you both myself
> and my love, I ask a modest favor:
> if your heart has ever longed for something
> that you wanted chaste and undefiled,
> preserve my boy for me with modesty,
> I don't mean from the crowd—I have no fear
> of those on the street who pass this way and that
> intent on their own affairs—
> but from you (that's my fear) and your prick
> gunning for boys good or bad.

The basic gesture of this poem is similar to that of poem 1, not only in the combination of giving and withholding, but also in the twist given to a Roman social ritual: the book is dedicated to Nepos, but it is the Muse who is the *patrona*; the boy is commended to Aurelius, but it is Aurelius from whom the boy must be protected. Preceding this poem in the collection is a fragment (14b) addressed to the readers of Catullus' verses, if any should address themselves to his "foolishness" (ineptiae) and not shrink from laying their hands on his work; the poem that follows, addressed to Furius and Aurelius, is directed against those who have misinterpreted his more risky verses. In this context, the problematic act of entrusting in poem 15 looks as if it might be a metaphor for publication: not only do poems 15 and 16 have a common addressee, but the theme of purity or chastity is also shared, for in both cases Catullus is concerned to withhold from Aurelius some core of purity from what has been entrusted to him.[33]

The first ancient writer to use an erotic framework to explore the anxieties and ironies of publication is the archaic Greek poet Theognis. Theognis complains that, although he has given his beloved Kyrnos wings of fame so that the boy will always be present at banquets, lying on the lips of men, Kyrnos deceives him with words (237–54 W). The poet has made his beloved available to all except himself and is deceived by the very medium that he has so effectively used on Kyrnos' behalf. A similar paradox occurs in Callimachus' famous epigram beginning with his programmatic statement "I hate the cyclic [i.e., epic] poem." Callimachus goes on to list other forms of the public (ta dēmosia) that he hates and then concludes: "Lysanie, you are beautiful, yes beautiful—but before the echo has spoken this clearly, someone says, 'Another has you'" (*Ep.* 28). Here the erotic relation provides the same kind of ironic reflection on the poet's alienation from his own words and intentions as it does in Theognis' lines. The pun on *kalos* (beautiful) and *allos* (another), and the association of the echo with the words of another, put Callimachus' words, like his desires, in the public realm, contradicting the literary principles based on exclusivity. As soon as Callimachus moves from hate to love, from criticism to celebration, he finds himself in the world of "ta dēmosia," where he cannot have what he wants: the beautiful boy belongs to another just as certain forms of literary beauty have already been claimed by other authors. Callimachus' sophisticated irony works through juxtaposition and parataxis. We do not know exactly how the final erotic couplet reflects on the foregoing: the two voices, the split between desire and power, the mocking echo, all suggest that these lines stand in an ironic relation to the definitive pronouncements that make up the rest of the poem, and that the poet's relation to "ta dēmosia" is complex. Is it sour grapes or a realistic sense of the possible that prompts Callimachus' renunciation of what is public, in view of the fact that what he finds beautiful belongs to another? As with Theognis and Catullus, the erotic relation in Callimachus' epigram dramatizes the alienation that comes with entering the public world of literature. Callimachus assumes that we don't need everything spelled out for us, that this deadpan juxtaposition says it all to those who know, and so he includes us in his Olympian perspective.[34] For Catullus the relation between poet and reader is more problematic; in late Republican Rome, literature has not yet become the institution it was for the librarians of Alexandria, and to write poetry is still a questionable social activity, so Catullus focuses on his relation not to tradition and to other poets but to the reader. The anxious irony of Catullus is framed in terms of a particular social transaction (commendation), for what concerns him is the peculiar nature of the contract between reader and poet.

Although the literary issues in Callimachus' epigram 28 and Catullus' poem 16 are different, comparison is warranted by the fact that Catullus recalls Callimachus' poem in his own. Callimachus equates his hatred of the cyclic poem to his dislike of the path that "bears the crowd this way and that" (hōde kai hōde, 2); Catullus tells Aurelius that he is not worried about the threat to his boy from the populace:

> istos, qui in platea modo huc modo illuc
> in re praetereunt sua occupati. (15.7-8)

> those who pass by on the street now this way
> and now that, engaged on their own affairs.

Callimachus' rejected path, the way of a debased literary convention that accommodates the masses, now contains the workaday Romans who present no threat to Catullus' boy; the boy himself is derived from the flighty beloved (periphoiton erōmenon, 3) who features next in Callimachus' list of what he hates, providing another metaphor for the literary world he rejects. For Catullus the issue is not the poet's relation to a public tradition, but rather his relation to the audience to whom a poem is entrusted, and he has therefore cast the issue in terms of the very Roman institution of the *commendatio*. The usual threat against which the older man must protect the entrusted boy is not a source of concern here. Instead, it is Aurelius himself who, by virtue of his interest in what is being entrusted to him, provides the potential threat.

But what is this threat in terms of the literary situation? To answer this question, we must consider the following poem, in which Catullus is defending his own sexual purity against imputations of effeminacy by Furius and Aurelius, who have drawn the wrong conclusions from the "many thousands of kisses" (c.16.12) they have read of in his poetry.[35] Here Catullus is concerned with the power relations between poet and reader, and he begins with a phallic threat that reverses the position that Furius and Aurelius, as readers of Catullus' titillating verse, have adopted in relation to the poet who speaks in the style of an effeminate:

> Pedicabo ego vos et irrrumabo,
> Aureli pathice et cinaede Furi,
> qui me ex versiculis meis putastis,
> quod sunt molliculi, parum pudicum.

> I'll bugger you and make you eat it,
> Aurelius you queer and Furius you pansy,
> who read my verses and concluded,
> because they're soft, that I'm not straight. (16.1-4)

Catullus claims that his performance turns his audience into excitable pathics. His verses have charm and bite only

> si sunt molliculi ac parum pudici,
> et quod pruriat incitare possunt,
> non dico pueris, sed his pilosis
> qui duros nequeunt movere lumbos. (8–11)

> if they're a little soft and not quite straight,
> and can incite a tingling, not in boys,
> I say, but in these hairy types,
> whose stiff flanks don't know how to undulate.

The word *durus* (hard, 11) is cunningly given a meaning (stiff/clumsy) that upsets the paradigm implied by Furius and Aurelius when they insinuate that Catullus is a pathic: the hairy types are not flexible enough for the undulations of the pathic, but the poet's verse can still set them twitching.[36] This puts his readers in rather a different position from that assumed by Furius and Aurelius.

The identification of the reader with the pathic in this poem has its precedents. There is a type of ancient graffito of which the following is the most elaborate form:

> amat qui scribit, pedicatur qui legit,
> qui auscultat prurit, pathicus est qui praeterit.
> ursi me comedant et ego verpa⟨m⟩ qui lego.

> The writer loves, the reader is buggered,
> the hearer itches, the passerby is a pathic.
> May bears eat me and I who read eat a penis.[37]

It seems that Catullus' poem reflects a model already present in Roman popular culture. An even closer parallel to Catullus' play with the ambiguous relation between poet and reader is provided by his greatest imitator, Martial (11.90). In Martial's poem, a certain Chrestillus wants Martial to imitate the rough style of the old poets. Chrestillus disapproves of poems "that move on a soft track" (molli quae limite currunt, 1), but Martial turns the tables on his critic's implication by concluding, after he has reviewed the manly kind of poetry that Chrestillus likes, "damn me if you don't know the flavor of prick" (dispeream nisi scis mentula quid sapiat, 8). Depending on whether we take *sapiat* (tastes) literally or metaphorically, we will interpret Chrestillus' approval of the ancient poets' virility in rather different ways, and this raises the important question of how the reader is situated in relation to the poet and the poem. Furius and Aurelius, like Chrestillus, understand the poetry of Catullus to be revealing an effeminacy that puts him in the subordinate position with respect to his male readership; Chrestillus himself adopts the masculine position in relation to Martial by comparing his poetry unfavorably to the "manly" kind that he, Chrestillus, admires. The two poets make a similar kind of move in response, which is to remind the reader that he is the recipient of the poetry. Chrestillus, according to Martial, relishes (as fellator) the prick of the poetry he calls virile, and Furius and Aurelius, as readers, realize the softness of Catullus' poetry, which he as author forces them to adopt; the subjectivity of the poetry is in some sense assumed by the reader, whose pathic excitement puts the author in the dominant position.[38] A more recent example of the same play with the position of the reader is the punning title of John Lahr's biography of Joe Orton: *Prick Up Your Ears!*

This maneuvering reflects a general phenomenon in Roman social life, namely, the obsessive concern with the position of one person relative to another in terms of power and obligation. The poetry of both Martial and Catullus, who repeatedly emphasize the transactional character of the poem, are particularly good examples of this phenomenon. In the case of Martial, this is related to the fact that he is a dependent whose poetry is his means of livelihood, which is not the case for Catullus, who came from a wealthy family. In Catullus the question of the relation between poet and reader is colored not so much by the complexities of dependency as by the new forms of urbanity and sophistication that were being prized in Roman social life. It may be that the sophistication to which the members of Catullus' circle aspired acquired its cachet from being Greek, but the form it takes in Rome is determined by the fact that in its new home it is questionable.[39] The Olympian assumption by Callimachus of a shared sophistication that need never itself become an issue is quite impossible at Rome, where the poet must negotiate the complicated implications of a word like *delicatus*.

Reading poems 15 and 16 in relation to each other reveals that the issue of 16 is not Catullus' sexual morality per se but the position of the reader in relation to the poet's questionable sophistication. Entrusting his *amores* (love, love poetry) to Aurelius, Catullus replays the giving of the book to Nepos with a more anxious tone, for the poet is to some extent in the power of the reader, who, like Furius and Aurelius, is in a position to take the poet at his word. The act of entrusting is paradoxical, then, for the reader must both give the poems their life and maintain their "chastity"; in other words, the poetry needs the provocative relation to the audience that is the essence of its charm, but it also needs a certain sophistication, on the part of the audience, about the nature of the game that is being played. The situation is comparable to that in poem 1, where the smooth and attractive little book whose nugatory nature makes it so available is at the same time the polished literary work that is under the protection of the patron Muse. These two aspects of the poet's detachment from his work are contradictory in respect of the audience: Nepos is offered the book that is then removed from his grasp to the care of the virgin Muse, and Aurelius is begged to keep his hands off what has been entrusted to him.

What is so disturbing about Aurelius for the poet is that he, or rather his penis, is indiscriminate (c.15.10); Aurelius' voraciousness makes no distinctions, which is as bad a quality in a reader as in a lover. If we turn to poem 6, in many ways the reverse of poem 15, we find the same situation with the roles reversed and the poet firmly in control. Here the secretive Flavius is challenged by Catullus to reveal his new *deliciae* (lover, lovemaking, 6.1). Taunting Flavius that his silence can only mean that this new love of his betrays his lack of sophistication (6.2;14), Catullus urges him to entrust his secret to the poet:

> quare, quidquid habes *boni malique*,
> dic nobis. volo te ac tuos amores
> ad caelum lepido vocare versu. (15–17)

> So, whatever you have, *good or bad*,
> tell me. I want to summon to divinity
> you and your love with an elegant poem.

The nature of Flavius' love is immaterial to the poet, who can produce elegance even out of the silence that betrays the inelegance of his friend. Just as the silence of Flavius has not protected him from being pilloried by his sophisticated friend, so his speech would have no control over the poet even if he were to reveal his love. In poem 15, we have the reverse of this situation, for in that poem it is the love of the poet that is threatened by the friend to whom it is entrusted. Between them these poems reveal the two sides of the poem's isolation from the verbal interchange of everyday life: on the one hand, the poet is all-powerful because he speaks for others who are not allowed to speak for themselves, but on the other hand he must entrust his words to others, who may find it as much grist for their mill as he does the "material" that comes from the speech (or silence) of others.

The question we have to address now is that of the substance of the accusations of effeminacy made by Furius and Aurelius (c.16.13). Evidently, these accusations were provoked by reading poems 5 and 7: poem 5 would seem to be the natural referent of "many thousands of kisses" (16.12).[40] It is a poem that has much in common with poem 2 in that the erotic is here associated with foreplay rather than consummation, for the thousands of kisses that Catullus demands of Lesbia, and that seem to be leading to a climax ("and then . . . and then . . . and then . . ."), take us only to a final confusion of kisses that slyly provokes the voyeur/reader:

> dein, cum milia multa fecerimus,
> conturbabimus illa, ne sciamus,
> aut ne quis malus invidere possit,
> cum tantum sciat esse basiorum. (5.10–13)
>
> then, when we've put together thousands,
> we'll mix them up, so as not to know,
> or so no evil man might envy us,
> when he learns there are so many kisses.

Furius and Aurelius read Catullus' apparent lack of interest in "taking" Lesbia as a sign of effeminacy that puts them in a dominant position; his thousands of kisses have that nonpurposive and playfully exquisite character associated with the *delicatus*, or even the impotent.[41]

The eroticism of poems 5 and 7, in which a nonclimactic foreplay is connected with a teasing provocation of the audience, is in sharp contrast to the *deliciae* of Flavius in the intervening poem; Flavius' silence leads Catullus to conclude that he loves some feverish whore (c.6.4–5), and in fact his silence hides nothing:

> non tam latera ecfututa pandas
> ni tu quid facias ineptiarum. (13–14)
>
> you wouldn't display such fucked-out loins
> if you weren't up to something foolish.

The crudeness of Flavius' lovemaking is associated with the obviousness of what is going on; everything about Flavius is blatant, even the squeaking of the bed, which sounds like an ineffective orator:

> tremulique quassa lecti
> argutatio inambulatioque. (10–11)[42]

the broken squeaking of the bed
and its pacing back and forth.

This poem that unmasks and speaks for Flavius, whose crude sexuality consigns him to a silence that is itself blatant (nequiquam tacitum cubile *clamat*, "the vainly silent couch *cries out*," 7), is sandwiched between two poems in which extended foreplay is connected with a provocation of the audience that is a mixture of hiding and revealing. By contrast with Flavius in the central poem of this group, Catullus is telling his *deliciae* (pleasures, whims) to us, and unlike the blatantly phallic activity of Flavius they are both *lepidae* and *elegantes* (compare 6.2). But this telling is erotic and provocative because, again by contrast with Flavius, Catullus is teasing.

In poem 7, where Catullus himself is asked by Lesbia, a propos poem 5, how many kisses will suffice him, he teases his addressee and audience with an archly learned variant on the "numberless as the sands" topos. This is an encore performance, for those who want a reprise of poem 5, in the form of a riddle that withholds its referent (Callimachus, see below) while indulging us in exotic and witty periphrasis:

> quam magnus numerus Libyssae harenae
> lasarpiciferis iacet Cyrenis
> oraclum Iovis inter aestuosi
> et Batti veteris sacrum sepulcrum: (7.3–6)

> as many as the sands of Libya that lie
> in silphium-bearing Cyrene
> between the oracle of blazing Jupiter
> and the sacred grave of Battus:

The poem plays with the desire of the audience to hear it again, as the lengthened and neologistic abstract form *basiatones* ("kissifications," 1) indicates. The innumerability topos is as much an expression of the fact that the audience can never quite be satisfied as it is of the boundlessness of Catullus' love for Lesbia. After the sands come the stars:

> aut quam sidera multa, cum tacet nox,
> furtivos hominum vident amores: (8–9)

> or as many as the constellations in the silent night
> that watch the furtive loves of humans:

These stars, watching the lovers in the silent night, are the audience listening with bated breath to Catullus telling of his erotic life, and they find themselves representing the very impossibility of ever hearing the whole thing. Instead, they may have the dubious satisfaction of knowing what the four lines about the sands add up to: Callimachus, native of Cyrene and descendant of its mythical founder, Battus. Hidden learning is substituted for sexual secrets.

In this group, the poet remains firmly in control, whether he is frustrating the jealous and the curious whose interest he has piqued, as at the end of poems 5 and 7, or offering to make an elegant poem of Flavius' inelegant love, which is what he has already done, in poem 6. Poems 15 and 16 show us how this command might break down when the relation between reader and poet is seen from a different angle: Catullus entrusts his *amores* to the indiscriminate and rapacious sensibilities of Furius and Aurelius, who have no respect for the nature of the game that is being played and see Catullus as the performer who is subject to his audience.[43] Of course, Catullus needs Furius and Aurelius to establish the riskiness of his performance, which depends for its effectiveness on being questionable. Poem 16 is not a defense of poems 5 and 7, nor of the aesthetic qualities they exhibit; still less is it a defense of the poet's morals based on a separation between art and life; rather, it is another move in the game between reader and poet in which the reader finds that the tables have been turned.

I began this chapter by raising the question of the role of sexual stimulation in Catullus' poetics. To take this issue seriously, we do not necessarily have to explain the relation between Catullus' verse and certain physical symptoms. As I have argued, poem 16 needs to be seen as part of a game made possible by the ambiguous and kaleidoscopic potential of the relations between poet, poem, and reader. Both this concern with social transactions and positionality and the fact that the activity of the poet of *versiculi* falls in the category of the questionable, a category that relies heavily on sexual metaphors, are distinctly Roman aspects of Catullus' poetics.[44] The ambiguities of the relations, gestures, and transactions of the aesthetic sphere upset any secure sense of the positionality that is such an important concern of ancient social and sexual life. At the same time, this sensitivity of the Roman context to certain social aspects of the poetic transaction, and the overlapping of Roman aesthetic language with the language of social and sexual relations, allow us to bring into focus aspects of poetry and of the aesthetic relation that have been obscured by modern emphases on the textuality, figurativeness, and even expressivity of poetic discourse.

## Excursus: Poet, Audience, and Slave in Plautus' Pseudolus

One of the earliest and most interesting interchanges between poet and audience is the possibly apocryphal story of Naevius and the Metelli. Naevius had written of the consulship of a member of this powerful family

> Fato Metelli Romae fiunt consules
>
> Either: By destiny the Metelli are consuls at Rome.
> Or: To the ruin of Rome the Metelli are consuls.

The Metelli responded without ambiguity:

> Dabunt malum Metelli Naevio poetae
>
> The Metelli will give the poet Naevius a beating.[45]

The interchange recalls many scenes in Roman comedy in which the clever slave is reminded that he cannot get away with his impudence and trickery forever. Normal power relations, suspended by the license of art and the cunning of the textual, are eventually restored, and in the early days of Roman literature many of the writers (and most of the actors) were slaves, or otherwise of low social status. So the anecdote about Naevius and the Metelli points to some realities about the relation between poet and audience in the early Republic.

In Plautus' *Pseudolus*, the eponymous hero and slave bets his master Simo that he will be able trick the latter into providing the money to free his son's *inamorata*, a prostitute now in the hands of an unscrupulous pimp. Callipho, a friend of Simo who witnesses this scene, marvels at the slave's breathtaking audacity, commenting that he's a real "work of art" (graphicum, 519) if he can bring off this trick; he resolves to postpone his visit to the country so as to be able to watch Pseudolus' show (ludos, 552). Simo suspects that the self-confident Pseudolus is in league with the pimp to defraud him, but Pseudolus denies this:

> aut si de istac re umquam inter nos convenimus,
> quasi in libro quom scribuntur calamo litterae,
> stilis me totum usque ulmeis conscribito. (544–45)

> or if we have ever come to an agreement about this matter
> you can write all over me up to the shoulders
> just like you write letters in a book with a pen.

This is one of many elaborate references to the whipping of slaves in this play, but it takes on a particular significance in the light of Callipho's *graphicum*, a Greek loan-word meaning "worthy to be drawn" (or "written," *graphikos*).[46] In this scene, writing is used to figure both the fascination that Pseudolus' prospective "show" holds for his master's friend and the ultimate power that the master holds over his slave.

The persistent analogy in this play between the project of the slave and that of the playwright and/or actor relates this passage to the ambiguous position of the writer in relation to his audience that I have been describing in this chapter. Having promised both the audience and his master that he will dupe the latter, Pseudolus, who as yet has no plan, compares himself to a poet who has to conjure up what does not yet exist (401–5). Later, he reassures the audience that he is going to deliver on his promises, which he did not make just to keep them amused while the play was going on, and he compares himself to an actor who has to bring on some new device when he comes onstage (562–69). So the scheming slave who undertakes to concoct a plan by which to defraud his master, whom he has warned of his intentions, resembles both the playwright and the actor, who must similarly dazzle the expectant audience. The low status of both actor and playwright is itself reflected in the precarious position of the clever slave who controls the usual Plautine plot. Actors at Rome, as members of an "infamous" (famosus) profession, were subject to certain legal disabilities; even if they were citizens, they were liable to corporal punishment, from which other citizens were protected, and magistrates could summarily have them flogged.[47] This may partially account for the assimilation of the Plautine slave to the actor/playwright.

At the end of the Plautus' play, Pseudolus bribes his master with half of the money he has won from his bet to join him for a drink. Simo suggests that Pseudolus invite the audience as well, but Pseudolus replies, in the last words of the play: "By Hercules, they're hardly in the habit of inviting me, nor I them. (To the audience) But if you want to applaud and show your approval of the cast and the play, I'll invite you for tomorrow" (1332–34). Of course, the audience and the actors belong to different orders of society, but then so do Pseudolus and Simo, and just as the slave and his master go off for a drink together through the manipulation of the slave, so the actor can "invite" the audience for tomorrow's play on a basis of equality. Plautine drama engages the ambiguous relation of actor/playwright to audience through the theme of the clever slave and his improvisational plotting, which manages to defer the beating that the master threatens but must suspend as long as we, like Callipho, have suspended our own business out of curiosity for the "show" we have been promised.[48]

Both the central role of the clever slave and the metatheatrical references to drama in the plays are thought to be Plautus' own contribution to the plays he has adapted from the Greek.[49] It seems that the Romans were particularly conscious of the manipulative or seductive power of art and of its ability to destabilize hierarchical social relations. One might say that the suspicion and fear of art's effect on its audience itself becomes a source of dramatic structures that the Roman audience enjoys in the art it consumes.

CHAPTER 3

# Obscenity Figures

*Catullus, whose name one can't utter without experiencing horror at his obscenities.*

Fénelon

*A few poems which do not lend themselves to comment in English have been omitted.*

Fordyce

As we turn from the erotic to the obscene, many of the issues remain the same because the same ancient model of sexual relations frames the drama of poetic positionality. Though ancient eroticism is often both aggressive and hierarchical, obscenity, both ancient and modern, may involve titillation as well as assault. Because obscene language can be as volatile to handle as the language of eroticism, it provides the poet with a similarly rich opportunity to display his mastery. So some of the poems dealt with in this chapter might also have been considered in the previous one and vice versa. But, in general, obscenity is less concerned with invitation, temptation, and teasing than with usurpation; less with issues of enjoyment and consumption than with the threat of pollution; less with the play of surface and depth than with the violation of boundaries.

In the reception of Catullus, obscenity has always been an important issue. The now infamous words from the preface to Fordyce's commentary of 1961 (the second of my epigraphs) are the last echo of centuries of embarrassment, swelling frequently to outrage, at Catullan obscenity. "A few" turned out to mean thirty-two, which in such a small oeuvre is quite a lot. But Fordyce was out of step with his times and his decision was greeted with universal protest.[1] By 1966 a translation of all of the poems into an English that pulled no punches had appeared in the Penguin Classics.[2] Now Catullus' obscenity is for the most part positively relished, even occasionally enhanced.[3]

Though attitudes to Catullus' obscenity have not always been as extreme as those of Fénelon and Fordyce, it has been customary even for devotees to adopt an exculpatory tone. For Landor, as for many moderns, Catullus' obscenity was a stumbling block and had to be explained. In 1853 Landor is sanguine:

> Tell me not what too well I know
> About the bard of Sirmio . . .
> Yes, in Thalia's son
> Such stains there are . . . as when a Grace
> Sprinkles another's laughing face
> With nectar, and runs on.

But in 1863 ("Written in a Catullus") the problem is more disturbing:

> Among these treasures there are some
> That floated past the wreck of Rome;
> But others, for their place unfit,
> Are sullied by uncleanly wit.
> So in its shell the pearl is found
> With rank putridity around.[4]

It is hard to believe that Landor could really have found his blithe fantasy of Hellenic gaiety an adequate representation of the obscenity in Catullus' oeuvre and his second attempt betrays itself by its awkwardness. More recently, rather than downplaying the obscenity in Catullus, scholars have tended to represent it as a manifestation of some of his more admirable qualities, if perhaps in a less admirable form.[5] A more comfortable variant of Landor's pearl simile is to be found in the dedication poem of Whigham's Penguin translation of Catullus, where Catullus' manuscript, discovered in the bunghole of a barrel of wine, springs from the wine-bung "as from the dung / —the rose" (11).[6] Clearly, Whigham's image is intended to say something about the two sides of Catullus' poetry, the obscene and the tender, to suggest that they are organically connected and so to avoid Landor's embarrassed pleading. In fact, it is a commonplace of Catullan criticism that the beauty and innocence of Catullus' betrayed love is shown up against the obscenity of Lesbia's desecration of that love, especially in poems like 11 and 58, which use obscene language to great strategic effect. Whigham describes the first event in the history of Catullus' manuscript as symbolic of the oeuvre itself, and for him there is a fruitful symbiosis of dung and rose. It may be, as some have argued, that obscenity is simply the concomitant of Catullus' youthful vitality, the flip side of his passionate ardor, or it may be that it expresses his righteous anger at a world that is itself obscene;[7] either way, the main concern of interpreters has been that Catullus should not be stained by his own obscenity.

## Obscenity at Rome

Obscenity is a distinctive feature of Roman culture, not something that is peculiar to Catullus. In both Greece and Rome, obscenity had ritual uses; it appeared, along with the display of *phalli*, as an integral part of various ceremonies performing an apotropaic function, promoting fertility, or both.[8] At Rome the triumph was the occasion for the singing of ribald songs, directed against the victorious general, by the troops; weddings included the "fescennina iocatio" (Catullus 61.120), crude mockery that, like the song of the troops at the triumph, served both to confound the power of the evil eye and to bring the lucky person down to a level where he would not be exposed to what Pliny calls "Fortune the butcher of glory."[9] Both triumph and wedding combine the primal power of obscenity to deflect the emanations of the evil eye with a mockery that is intended to make its object less enviable.[10] Humor is also part of the efficacy of these practices, for humor serves to confound jealousy by deflecting attention. This association of obscenity with mockery and humor in Roman ritual makes it difficult to isolate the function of obscenity itself in these songs: obscene humorous mockery had a complex purpose and its components both complemented each other and overlapped. At this point, it is worth noting that Catullus' obscenity is almost always used in invective, though not all of it is humorous.[11]

Roman authors frequently cite the licit use of obscenity in Roman ritual and ceremony in order to claim for the circumscribed world of their own book or genre a similar license.[12] Theater, belonging to both the world of literature and that of religion (through the festivals), is a particularly useful analogy for obscene poets like Martial, who refers to his poetry as "my theater."[13] Martial himself cites a famous story about Cato that illustrates this attitude to obscenity as something both scandalous and yet licit within its proper context: Cato was attending a theatrical production at the Ludi Florales, a festival in honor of Flora that culminated with prostitutes stripping onstage; on being told that his presence was inhibiting the people from demanding that the actors/prostitutes strip in the customary fashion, Cato left the theater, to great applause, in order that the ancient custom might go on.[14] Obscenity and *gravitas* were at odds, but in this optimistic little anecdote each recognizes and defers to the other in a community that understands what kind of behavior belongs where. The reality was not so tidy: Suetonius (*Iul.* 49.4, 51) refers to the ritual abuse of the general by his troops in passages where he describes the sexual scandals surrounding Caesar, who was abused in very similar terms by his peers. Rome, the "city of abuse" (maledica civitas),[15] was rife with sexual slander even at the highest level of politics, and obscene language was routinely directed at political opponents in epigrams and pamphlets or chanted by mobs of supporters.[16] Suetonius quotes an epigram of Catullus' friend Licinius Calvus, in which Nicomedes of Bithynia is called the "pedicator Caesaris" (buggerer of Caesar); another friend of Catullus, Licinius Calvus, wrote an epigram on Pompey accusing him of being a pathic (*FPL* 18). In extenuation of his own obscenities, Martial (11.20) quotes an extremely obscene epigram against Antony by Augustus. This kind of invective was what Veyne calls the senatorial version of a popular genre in which the intention was to throw the adversary into confusion with a volley of insults.[17] We can read a literary version of this popular genre of public insult called *convicium* or *flagitatio* in Catullus poem 42, where the poet, trying to reclaim some of his writing tablets from an unnamed woman, parodies the insulting chant that might be used to shame a suspected thief into returning stolen property. Several of Catullus' poems contain repeated lines or phrases that recall this insulting chant, and in some form or other popular forms lie behind much of his invective.[18] Roman graffiti, folk customs, and even epitaphs reflect a culture in which the collectivity still feels that it has the right to pass judgment on the behavior of the individual.[19] Furthermore, the Romans prided themselves on a native tradition of *dicacitas*, caustic raillery, of which that great icon of Romanness, Cato the Elder, was a famed exponent.[20]

Our concept of the obscene derives from the Latin word *obscaenus* (or *obscenus*); the Greeks had no special term for this kind of language.[21]

Cicero and others attest to the existence of words that were normally avoided in polite society because of their obscenity, and they use a range of words besides *obscenus* to refer to them.[22] But Pliny, excusing his own obscene poems, cites a long list of distinguished Romans who, like him, wrote "little poems none too grave" (versiculos severos parum, *Ep.* 5.3.2); included in this list are several contemporaries of Catullus, a number of predecessors, and an impressive array of emperors. Both here and in 4.14 (in which he cites Catullus 16), Pliny presents the writing of risqué verse as an appropriate activity of the well-rounded gentleman, who naturally enough has been to comedies and mimes, and occasionally relaxes and lets his hair down (5.3.2). The welter of precedents suggests that the writing of obscene verse was an activity in which the upper-class Roman might legitimately indulge.

It is unlikely, therefore, that Catullus' use of obscene language would have had the intention or effect of scandalizing the bourgeois, nor does it demand explanations of a psychological nature.[23] And yet obscenity in Catullus is a distinctive kind of diction that establishes particular relations between poet and reader. What's more, in the context of poetry it is particularly significant that Roman obscenity was predominantly concerned with the impure mouth. The mouth in Roman culture was the most important site of purity or contamination: eating, speaking, and kissing—the latter as much a social as a sexual activity—all required a pure mouth, but above all speaking, for the Roman's word was sacred.[24] Whether it was used as a threat or as an accusation, obscene language frequently concerned itself with this crucial bodily site of contact with the social world, of the traffic between interiority and exteriority, and of the exchange between what is taken in and what is given out. This preoccupation of Roman obscenity with the mouth makes it a particularly rich source of figuration for poetry and especially for a poetry such as Catullus' that is so concerned with the relations and positions implied by the poetic act. In this chapter, I describe how obscenity *figures* in these poems, first of all by exploring the implications of an obscene figure (irrumation) for the agency of the poet and then by considering some of the special complications that arise for the speaker who handles obscene language and for the reader who responds to it. The poet who must stain without being stained, and the reader whose response to obscenity is bifurcated between disgust and prurience, are both realizing something about the volatile nature of obscene language that poetry is best able to illuminate; conversely, these problematic aspects of obscenity enable the poet to play with the ambiguous nature of poetic positionality.

I end this chapter by examining another issue in Roman obscenity, distinct from the concern with the impure mouth and yet related to it, namely, the concern with the proper hierarchies, articulations, and relations within and between bodies. Here Catullus articulates the Roman use of obscenity to enforce social conformity with an exploration of the nature of poetry itself, which is constructed out of an obscene and promiscuous nexus of relations between words. The poems that I cite here pillory familial or amical associations and understandings that result in obscene relations. Ironically, though, the audience that mocks these friends and relations is committed, as readers of poetry, to the enjoyment of the very anatomies they are mocking. The interference between the reader's relation to the poem as the fictional utterance of a speaker and as a set of formal structures produces contradictory relations to its obscenity.

In the course of the chapter, I also examine some of the ways in which the obscene poems position the activity of the scholar (who is also a reader), and in which the scholar's project and strategies may overlap with those of the obscene speaker.[25]

### Irrumation and the Silent Victim

Richlin 1983, in the most comprehensive treatment of Roman sexual humor, takes the god Priapus as the model for the persona of the author who uses sexual material. Statues of Priapus, an ithyphallic god of fertility, were set up in gardens both to promote fruitfulness and to guard against theft; the god's massive, erect penis performed both functions, the latter by threatening to assault the thief sexually. A poetic genre developed around these statues in the Hellenistic period; in the Roman form of this genre, the statue of the god frequently threatens the potential thief with the attention of his prominent member.[26] Priapus' threats reflect a type of revenge that was in fact taken by aggrieved males in the ancient world, and Catullus' threat at the beginning of poem 16 had some basis in reality: according to Cicero, Clodia herself had a certain Vettius raped by a couple of her henchmen because he had insulted her.[27] The priapic stance is manifested by the most characteristic word in the Roman sexual vocabulary, which is also the most common obscenity in Catullus, the verb *irrumare*.[28] Although we know the meaning and etymology of this word, it is quite literally untranslatable.

Commonly used as a threat or insult, the word denotes an action that is not specifiable in English except by extension of other terms ("fuck the mouth," "oral rape").[29] The fact that the nearest English slang equivalent to a threat of *irrumatio* would be "Eat it!" shows that in English the action, even when degrading to the person who performs it, is all on the side of the fellator; the Latin word reflects the importance of the "priapic" model of phallic aggression. Naturally, the currency of this word as threat or insult may have blunted its literal force over time—as with the modern "Fuck you!"—but it is characteristic of poetry to revive literal meanings and play on them.[30] How, then does *irrumatio* figure in Catullus?

The original meaning of *irrumare* would have been "to put in the teat" (ruma/rumis). Adams 1982, 126, comments that this etymology "reflects the popular obsession among Latin speakers with a similarity felt between feeding and certain sexual practices." But in the light of his copious examples of the standard joke by which *irrumatio* was spoken of as a means of silencing someone, we might draw a further implication from the etymology. *Irrumatio* is, after all, the means by which the mother silences the noisy baby, and in its metaphorical sense as sexual threat it is intended to reduce the victim to a status comparable to that of the baby (*infans*, i.e., not speaking) in relation to the all-powerful adult who silences it.[31] What is originally an expression of love and concern becomes an expression of contempt, not satisfying the recipient but rather forestalling him (the victim is nearly always male). In poem 21, Catullus casts Aurelius, who is continually making advances towards Catullus' boy, as "the father of hungers" (pater esuritionum). But Catullus will forestall Aurelius at the same time as he "satisfies" his hunger:

nam insidias mihi instruentem
tangam te prior irrumatione. (7–8)

for as you plot mischief against me
I will assault you with an *irrumatio*.

Aurelius' hunger stands both for his appetite for the boy and for his poverty, and because Aurelius is poor Catullus is in a position to mock (*irrumare* in the weak sense) his rival; if Aurelius were not poor, the boot would be on the other foot and it would be Catullus who would be silenced (irrumatus): "But if you did that when you were full, I would be silent" (atque id si faceres satur, tacerem, 9). What pains him, Catullus claims, is that his boy might learn from Aurelius to hunger and to thirst

(10–11); so the fear that the boy might learn to reciprocate Aurelius' lust is phrased as concern that he might have to share Aurelius' poverty.[32] Catullus' strategy, namely, to make the hunger that constitutes Aurelius' threat a metonymy for the poverty that enables his own preemptive strike, is itself a form of *irrumatio*, and one peculiarly appropriate to a poet: *irrumatio* becomes a figure for the poet's power to assign his own meanings to those who, perforce, are silent while he speaks.

In poem 37, Catullus launches himself at the inmates of a certain tavern who seem to think that they are the only ones with pricks:

> solis putatis esse mentulas vobis,
> solis licere, quidquid est puellarum,
> confutuere et putare ceteros hircos. (3–5)

> you think you are the only ones with pricks,
> that you alone are allowed to fuck all the girls
> and to think of the others as goats.

To this he answers:

> an, continenter quod sedetis insulsi
> centum an ducenti, non putatis ausurum
> me una ducentos irrumare sessores?
> atqui putate: namque totius vobis
> frontem tabernae sopionibus scribam. (6–10)

> Because you boors sit all in a row,
> a hundred or two hundred, do you think that I
> won't dare to irrumate two hundred sitters all at once?
> Think it over: for I'll cover the front
> of your whole tavern with penises.

The marshalled ranks of the boors become waiting prostitutes (*sedetis*, 6),[33] lined up for Catullus to service. The poet's *irrumatio* of the rivals (11–16) consists in giving his own interpretation to the self-satisfied comradeship of the ensconced gathering, a way of silencing the rivals who now no longer express their own meanings. He follows this up with a threat to scrawl penises all over the front of the tavern: the irrumated victims, unable to speak for themselves, now bear written on their collective front the expression of Catullus' masculinity, rather than their own. Covering the "brow" of the whole tavern with penises, Catullus figuratively makes good on his threat to irrumate all two hundred in one sitting.

The aggression of this priapic threat is poetic. It plays on the fact that the poet takes his silent victims in his own sense; that they appear in his poems as he chooses to understand them, and that their own words, gestures, and intentions may be alienated from them through his words. To put it graphically, the mouths that should express their owners' meanings and appetites now serve the poet's will and pleasure.[34]

In Catullus' most elaborate play on *irrumo*, the victim is silenced because to speak out against the perpetrator would be to acknowledge his own humiliation:

> Gellius audierat patruum obiurgare solere
>   si quis delicias diceret aut faceret.
> Hoc ne ipsi accideret, patrui perdepsuit ipsam
>   uxorem et patruum reddidit Arpocratem.
> Quod voluit fecit: nam quamvis irrumet ipsum
>   nunc patruum, verbum non faciet patruus. (c.74)

> Gellius had heard that the uncle was usually censorious
>   if one did or said anything naughty.
> Lest this should happen to him he worked over
>   his uncle's wife and rendered the uncle an Harpocrates.
> He did what he wished, for even if [or however much] he should
>                                                                 irrumate
>   his own uncle now, his uncle won't say a word.

Thanks to Gellius' precautions, his uncle cannot play the traditionally censorious avuncular role without also playing the cuckold, and this leaves him frozen in the posture of statues of the outlandish Egyptian god Harpocrates, his finger on his lips.[35] Because Harpocrates is represented as a boy, the generational status of the two characters has been reversed. Gellius has turned the stock figure of the uncle into a statue, stock still and ridiculous; like the inmates of the salacious tavern, who are both silenced and made to bear Catullus' meanings, the uncle is displayed in a gesture of silence that nevertheless signifies Gellius' *irrumatio*. The last four lines produce a rich play on the distinction, casually introduced in line 2, between saying and doing, for we cannot be sure whether the irrumation of the uncle is constituted (in a manner of speaking) by the adultery, or whether it is an additional (and literal) indulgence that Gellius allows himself now that he has secured his uncle's compliance. No matter how much the nephew expresses his contempt for the uncle (*irrumet* in the weakened sense), the latter won't say a word, because silence is the usual concomitant of a literal *irrumatio*. The nephew is a poet in action, turning the uncle's potential censoriousness into an advertisement of his cuckoldry and triumphing over him by playing with the literal and the figurative.

Catullus' most graphic scene of *irrumatio*, surprisingly enough, features himself as the victim. The perpetrator in this case is the praetor Memmius, with whom Catullus had served in Bithynia, and who has appeared in poem 10 as the *irrumator praetor* who had prevented his staff from enriching themselves in the customary way. In poem 28 Catullus addresses his friends Veranius and Fabullus, who seem to have had as lean a time of it with their Piso as Catullus did with his Memmius:

> Pisonis comites, cohors inanis,
> aptis sarcinulis et expeditis,
> Verani optime tuque mi Fabulle,
> quid rerum geritis? satisne cum isto
> vappa frigoraque et famem tulistis?
> ecquidnam in tabulis patet lucelli
> expensum, ut mihi, qui meum secutus
> praetorem refero datum lucello?
> O Memmi, bene me ac diu supinum
> tota ista trabe lentus irrumasti. (c.28, 1–10)

> Retinue of Piso, empty-handed cohort,
> with your convenient and lightweight baggage,
> excellent Veranius and you, my Fabullus,
> what are you up to? Have you endured enough
> cold and famine with that good-for-nothing?
> Do your accounts show any profits under your
> expenses, as do mine, for with my praetor
> I entered on the profit side what I paid out.
> O Memmius, how thoroughly and lengthily, how leisurely
> you irrumated supine me with all that beam of yours.

"Despite the graphic detail . . . Catullus does not mean that a sexual act took place." Adams includes lines 9–10 in his examples of the metaphorical and weakened use of *irrumare*, implying simply "ill treatment."[36] But this passage need not be describing a real sexual act for *irrumasti* to retain something of its literal force. The graphic detail in these lines cannot simply be reduced to emphasis ("I've *really* been abused"); rather, it takes its force from the context of the previous three lines. Catullus has just told his friends that he enters his losses in Bithynia as gain, whether because he has no more room on the expense side of the ledger and no profit to enter, or because he has in some way made the best of a bad job—chalked it up to experience, for instance. In the opening lines of the poem, Catullus greets his friends as the empty-handed staff (*cohors*) of Piso, and then teasingly refers to their light and comfortable baggage; for the soldiers (*cohors* in its military sense), light packs would, of course, be welcome.[37] This double perspective characterizes the description of Memmius' *irrumatio* of Catullus, for the thoroughness of Memmius and the leisurely detail that postpones the word *irrumasti* recover the pleasurable aspects of this sexual act. This is not to say that the "graphic detail" is not, in the social code of the metaphor, a mark of Memmius' complete unconcern for his subordinates; what has happened is that the excess of the social abomination has had to appear as gain on the literal, sexual side of the verbal ledger. But gain for whom? The question is moot, for though ancient thought about sexuality tended to attribute pleasure only to the active participant in a sexual act, it is the mouth of the speaker that enjoys the assonance and alliteration of lines 9 and 10, and that recalls and stretches the name of Memmius in the words "bene me ac diu" (9). Although there are Latin poems in which the sexual mistreatment intended as a threat or punishment is actually welcomed by the victim, either a fellator or a *pathicus*, the distribution of roles remains stable because the victim has been doubly insulted.[38] In this case, the speaker is himself the victim and, paradoxically, the victim of this silencing act is the speaker. More radically, Catullus' thorough description of the leisurely *irrumatio* causes the language of aggression to teeter over into the language of pleasure, so that the usual distribution of roles is smudged as the poet speaks the aggressor's pleasure.

Catullus goes on to comment that his friends have evidently been stuffed with quite as large a prick as he has (nihilo minore verpa / farti estis, 12–13), a sarcastic reference to the hunger they had to endure with their abusive praetor. Because stuffing is a form of feeding whose excess bypasses the satisfaction of the eaters in the interests of the feeder, the distribution of the usual feeder/eater roles is here sarcastically reversed.[39] If the poem begins and ends with sarcasm, a stable form of verbal play in which the negative is expressed as a positive (aptis, expeditis, farti), the center is more labile: Catullus accuses Memmius, and by the very intensity of his accusation comes to speak the language of pleasure. *Irrumatio*, as I have been arguing, is elsewhere used by Catullus to figure an interference in the self-expression of another, an imposition by the perpetrator of his meanings onto the victim. But when the poet represents himself as the object of *irrumatio*, the aggressive intentions of the perpetrator may themselves be preempted. In this case, it is hard to detach the language of pleasure from the language of outrage. What exactly do the detail, the assonance, and the alliteration of lines 9–10 express? In what way does the thoroughness of Catullus' description relate to the thoroughness of Memmius' *irrumatio*? Has the speaker humiliated himself by this confession of his degradation or dazzled us with his virtuosity? Does *lentus* (leisurely) express Memmius' pleasure or Catullus' outrage, and how do these expressions relate to the speaker/reader's pleasure in dwelling on the sounds and rhythms of these lines? Does it, in fact, make any sense to ask in what tone these lines are spoken? The bookkeeping metaphor of line 8 raises the question of the stability of the notions of profit and loss, and therefore of perspective, in the context of writing. One interpretation of line 8 is that Catullus, having run out of space on the loss side of his ledger, simply continues to enter his losses on the other side, under gain; the alternative is that Catullus actually considers his loss to be, from another perspective, gain. I have suggested above that in lines 9–10 the extreme expression of Catullus' humiliation turns into, or becomes indistinguishable from, the description of pleasure—a free-floating, textual pleasure that is hard to attribute definitively and exclusively to Memmius or to Catullus and the reader who dwells on his words. The bookkeeping metaphor suggests a standard of determinacy against which the mysterious fluidity of the textual can be measured.

In this poem, the poet, who is the victim of *irrumatio*, escapes the role to which this act would assign him by taking it in a different sense. Speaking the language of Memmius' contempt, Catullus foregrounds the pleasurable materiality of his own poetry, and the intensified language of social contempt tips over into the language of sexual pleasure, producing a more ambiguous distribution of roles than Memmius' sarcastic "stuffing" of his underlings Fabullus and Veranius. As so often in Catullus, the peculiar properties of poetry are realized in the context of a sexual transaction that upsets the standard cultural model.

In poem 28, Catullus flirts with the position of the fellator, that is, not the *irrumator*'s victim but the man who enjoys and actively seeks to perform fellatio, but elsewhere the fellator is cast as silent and secretive. As Veyne 1983 has argued, Roman invective is often an exercise of the power of the collectivity, which increasingly finds itself flouted by those who withdraw from its surveillance into privacy. In the poetry of Martial, the revelation of sexual secrets becomes one of the most common activities of the invective poet; one might argue, in Foucaultian fashion, that the category of secret and deviant sexual proclivity is constituted by the Roman poet as an arena for staging the power of the collectivity against the private and the individual.[40]

In 12.35, Martial accuses an apparently candid Callistratus of being a fellator:

> Tamquam simpliciter mecum, Callistrate, vivas,
>   dicere percisum te mihi saepe soles.
> Non es tam simplex quam vis, Callistrate, credi.
>   nam quisquis narrat talia plura tacet.

> Callistratus, you're in the habit of telling me that you've been
>                                                        buggered,
>   to give the impression that you're candid with me.
> You're not as candid, Callistratus, as you want to be thought.
>   For whoever tells such things is silent about more.

*Tacet* (is silent) here alludes to the fellatio of Callistratus at the same time as it accuses him of secrecy and duplicity about his proclivities.[41] The same association is made in Catullus' poem 80:

> Quid dicam, Gelli, quare rosea ista labella
>   hiberna fiant candidiora nive,
> mane domo cum exis et cum te octava quiete
>   e molli longo suscitat hora die?
> Nescioquid certe est: an vere fama susurrat
>   grandia te medii tenta vorare viri?
> Sic certest; clamant Victoris rupta miselli
>   ilia et emulso labra notata sero.

> Gellius, what reason should I give why those rosy lips
>   become whiter than winter's snow,
> In the morning when you leave home and when the eighth hour
>   stirs you from your nap when the days are long?
> Something is certainly up: does rumor whisper truly
>   that you devour the great erection of a man's mid part?
> It must be so; the broken loins of lovesick Victor shout it,
>   and so do your lips marked by the whey you've milked.

Emerging from his home in the morning and after the midday siesta, Gellius carries a secret on his lips, which speak what they keep silent. His lips carry the mark of the censor, the *nota* (see *OLD* s.v. 4), placed in the census against the name of a citizen who had disgraced himself and was no longer considered fit to be enrolled among the knights.[42] In this case, the innocent white lips of the victim become candid in spite of themselves, speaking what they hide, namely, the *irrumatio* that the poet is simultaneously revealing and performing.[43] Catullus in fact appropriates the role of the *irrumator* from Victor, an ironic name because his loins "shout" only insofar as they betray the signs of having been "broken" by the ministrations of Gellius.[44] The victorious shout of the *irrumator* is mentioned only to be transferred from Victor to the poet who wields the pen.

*Irrumatio* in Catullus draws attention to a potentially aggressive aspect of poetry itself, which puts words into people's mouths; it speaks for everybody and everything while all else is silent (or mouthing its words), and it makes its subject matter take on the meanings of a single voice.[45] But even when the poet is himself the object of *irrumatio*, he may, so to speak, enter it on the side of profit, for poetry allows him to speak from several positions at the same time.

## Staining Without Being Stained

It is, I think, misguided to eliminate the sheer aggression from Catullus' obscene invective by trying to justify it as a measured response to immorality and deficiencies of character. When Catullus complains, in poem 41, that Ameana is asking him a preposterous sum to sleep with her and doesn't seem to have consulted her mirror, he is insulting both Ameana and her lover Mamurra; to turn this poem, as have several of its commentators, into a moral tale about self-knowledge, in which the strength of Catullus' language (Ameana is called "fucked out") reflects the fact that he hates self-delusion, is taking the desire to endorse everything this poet says too far.[46] However, it may be part of the strategy of a poem to separate the obscenity of the victim from the speaker who points it out. Take a poem like poem 98, which implicitly raises, and plays with, the problem of staining another with obscenity without being stained oneself; this poem, a vitriolic attack against the foulmouthed Victius, motivates its own obscenity by attacking the speech of another:

> In te, si in quemquam, dici pote, putide Victi,
>     id quod verbosis dicitur et fatuis.
> ista cum lingua, si usus veniat tibi, possis
>     culos et crepidas lingere carpatinas.
> si nos omnino vis omnes perdere, Victi,
>     hiscas: omnino quod cupis efficias.

> Of you, if of anyone, could be said, stinking Victius,
>     what is said of windbags and idiots.

> With that tongue you could, if need arose,
>    lick assholes and rough rustic boots.
> If you're altogether set on destroying us all, Victius,
>    gape: you'd accomplish all that you desire.

The tongue of Victius, chatterbox extraordinaire, is *obscenely* indiscriminate, but Catullus goes further and courts the danger of losing his metaphorical superiority, or the superiority of metaphor. Playing on the double meaning of *putidus*, "stinking" or "tiresome/affected in speech," the poet establishes his own speech as figurative by contrast to the gushing of the foul-smelling Victius, who only has to gape to destroy us all.[47] The repetition "omnino . . . omnes . . . omnino" reflects the verbosity of Victius without duplicating it, for in the poem the verse and the sound patterning serve to place these words wittily. This distinction between speakers whose respective styles are reflected in the same words allows Catullus to court the irony of using *culos* (assholes) while talking of another's foul mouth, and to court this irony and get away with it is a large part of the poem's wit. It is all a question of who is controlling metaphor.

This poem was the subject of controversy during the early history of our text of Catullus, a period thick with the atmosphere of *odium philologicum*.[48] It is worth pausing to examine this controversy because it provides us with a good example of the way in which the poetry and its strategies may be duplicated by the scholarship that serves it. Scholarly invective, even where it is not obscene, harnesses aggression in the cause of objectivity and therefore runs into a problem structurally analogous to that of staining without being stained. But the early editors of Catullus were not squeamish about their language. The cause in the name of which these editors exercised their own powers of vituperation was the cause of purity and wholeness, for an uncontaminated text had to be retrieved from the corruption of the manuscript.[49] Of course, the content of some of the poems in the manuscript was anything but pure, and in those cases the scholars working on the text were spurred on to particularly inventive insults. The second of Poliziano's *Miscellanea*, published in 1489, is a fascinating case of the interplay between poem and scholarship. The issue of *Miscellanea* 2 is the meaning of the word *carpatinas* (c.98.40), in fact the transliteration of a rare Greek word for a peasant shoe made of undressed hide. Parthenius, evidently ignorant of this word, had emended to the neologistic *coprotinas* formed from the Greek *kopros*, "shit." Poliziano explicated *carpatinas* and then castigated the benighted scholars (tenebriones) who replaced it with *cercopythas* (from *kerkos*, "prick") or *coprotinas*, nonexistent words "drawn from the pigsty, not the school";[50] he himself, by contrast, brings authorities from Greek literature "as though from a storehouse."[51]

Poem and commentary become continuous in Poliziano's invective, which assails Parthenius as an empty windbag, like Victius, and associates him similarly, if a little less closely, with rustic squalor. The fact that the early editions of Catullus had the name of the victim as Vectios, whom they may have identified as the grammarian Vectios Philocomus,[52] makes Poliziano's doubling of Catullus' invective quite appropriate. But superimposed on this Catullan vituperation is a claim to have vindicated the purity of Catullus' language, and in fact this is the issue over which Poliziano identifies himself with the vituperative speaker of the poem! The scatological animus of Catullus' poem is now motivated as a protest at the filthy mouth of Parthenius and his ilk, who, by virtue of their deficient scholarship, are deprived of access to a higher language. In Catullus' poem, the alien Greek phrase stands for the world of a pure language—the object of scholarship—which allows those who command it to descend, in its defense, into vituperation without compromising the purity of their tongues. Unfortunately, there are parallels to Poliziano's polemics in the scholarship that deals with Roman sexual material today.[53]

Poliziano is himself the object of a wittier and more obscene attack for his rejection of the reading *cercolipas*, a neologism printed by Muretus in 1554. The latter is compounded from the Greek words for "tail" and "fat," and is evidently supposed to mean "prick," as does the uncompounded *kerkos* (tail) in some passages; Muretus reads "trepidas . . . cercolipas" or "trembling pricks." This reading turns up in an epigram by Marullus attacking Poliziano (identified as Ecnomus):[54]

> Lingere carpatinas vult Vection Ecnomus, ipse
>   ut possit trepidas lingere cercolipas.
>
> Ecnomus wants Vectios to lick peasant boots, so
>   he himself can lick trembling pricks.

Poliziano is given a double motivation for avoiding the more obscene reading: literally, he wants the trembling pricks to himself, so he fobs off Vectios with the peasant boots; metaphorically, he wants to humiliate ("irrumate") himself, so he adopts an inferior reading. Behind the metaphorical meaning lurks the more sinister, literal meaning! The speaker who can handle double meanings in this way is able to suggest that nothing is what it seems, even Poliziano's motive for avoiding the obscene reading. Marullus' epigram, like so many of Martial's, recruits the lyric's potential for ambiguous utterance to penetrate the private and secret motivations of those who are not what they seem; the victim who has been skewered by an ambiguity as satisfying as this has nowhere to hide, for language itself speaks his duplicitous being.

## Compromising Positions, Bifurcated Sensations

Obscenity is a volatile phenomenon that stirs mixed emotions, and the disgust that it is intended to evoke is often mingled with fascination. Marullus' epigram takes us into the murky world of the scholar's relation to the obscenities that scholarship is often called upon to explicate. But Marullus himself takes his cue from the speaker of Catullus' poem, whose obscene invective he duplicates; the issue raised by that poem, the problem of staining without being stained, is an issue that is played out again in the scholarly invective whose vituperative animus supposedly serves the objective investigation of a higher language. But what of Marullus' insinuations about the scholar's potentially prurient interest in obscene material? I will turn now to two poems that deliberately put the addressee and reader (and, implicitly, the investigating scholar) in a compromising position, beginning with the poem that contains Catullus' most mysterious and cherished obscenity, which even Fordyce couldn't bring himself to omit, *glubit* in poem 58.[55] Catullus' most striking use of obscenity is also his most frustrating; the meaning of *glubit* is still as disputed as the reading at poem 98.4 used to be, but curiosity is that much more intense because the poem is about Lesbia and because the obscenity, if such it is, is very deliberately featured by the poem's structure of suspense:

Caeli, Lesbia nostra, Lesbia illa,
illa Lesbia, quam Catullus unam
plus quam se atque suos amavit omnes,
nunc in quadriviis et angiportis
glubit magnanimi Remi nepotes.

Caelius, our Lesbia, that Lesbia,
Lesbia herself, whom alone Catullus
loved more than himself and all his dear ones,

> now, at the crossroads and alleyways,
> peels the descendants of greathearted Remus.

The whole poem depends on the word *glubit*, which has to balance the weight of the repetition of Lesbia's name and to deliver on the expectation of the enormity that Caelius is called on to witness. Unfortunately, we do not know what *glubit* means. One obscene use of this agricultural word, meaning originally "to strip the bark," has survived (Ausonius *Epigr.* 79.7), and a considerable bibliography has grown up around Catullus' meaning. Suggestions run from "fleeces (of their money)" and "strips (of their clothes)" to various sexual acts, specific (masturbates, fellates) or general (retracts the foreskin).[56] Not to know precisely what it is that Lesbia is doing in the traditional haunts of prostitutes is to be deprived of the resolution that the poem's form demands. By carefully embedding *glubit* between polysyllabic compounds, Catullus emphasizes its bare semantic force;[57] by making it the focal point of a poem that stutters with expressive incapacity, he invests it with authenticity. Whatever the slang connotations of the term, the primary meaning, "peel," implies both revelation and, especially in the context of this poem's suspense, release. But what is being revealed and what kind of release are we to experience?

That so much ink has been spilled on this single word is not surprising. Friedrich Lenz has asked, a propos Weinreich's reference to the "ambiguous" (schillernde) meaning of the word, "Is Catullus supposed to content himself with ambiguity in crying out his utter disgust?"[58] For Lenz, recovery of the obscene force of this word is recovery of the truest voice of Catullus, wrung from him by Lesbia's betrayal. But Lenz goes on to say that the word must refer to a very precise event that triggers Catullus' desperate outburst in the first place. The word does double duty, then, both expressing Catullus' feelings and describing the behavior of Lesbia that has justified those feelings. *Glubit* is the perfectly motivated obscenity: it accuses at the same time as it reveals. Our prurient interest can be satisfied by the same word that expresses our outrage, and we can recover the essence of Catullus' hurt at the same time as we peer into Lesbia's sex life.[59] Lenz's argument that the word must have a specific obscene meaning is overdetermined, but so is the poem's structural suspense, which postpones Catullus' outburst as it arouses our curiosity about Lesbia.

Poems 58 is usually read as an expression of anguish, a key point in the novel of Catullus' relationship with Lesbia.[60] But this is to ignore the communicative rhetoric of the poem: *glubit* satisfies an aroused curiosity as much as it releases a postponed cry of pain. Structurally and rhetorically, poem 58 has much in common with one of Catullus' most playful poems, 56, which also buttonholes its addressee and promises to set him on his ears:

> O rem ridiculam, Cato, et iocosam,
> dignamque auribus et tuo cachinno!
> ride quidquid amas, Cato, Catullum:
> res est ridicula et nimis iocosa.
> deprendi modo pupulum puellae
> trusantem; hunc ego, si placet Dionae,
> protelo rigida mea cecidi.

> Cato, what an amusing and laughable matter,
> worthy of your ears and laughter!
> Laugh as much as you love Catullus, Cato:
> the matter is amusing and just too funny.
> Just now I caught a little boy banging his girl [or, "the boy
> of my girl, masturbating"]
> Immediately [or "in tandem"], so please Dione [Venus' mother],
> I beat him with my own stiff weapon.

It is ironic that two poems that so emphatically have something to tell should generate so much argument as to what it is they are telling. Is *puellae* a dative of direction or a genitive of possession? Is the boy humping his girl or is the boy of Catullus' girl masturbating?[61] Inquiring minds want to know! Obscenity in poems 56 and 58 is intended to provoke the reactions of laughter and outrage respectively, but our distance from ancient Latin turns us into inquiring minds, peering hard to descry the sexual escapades of our subjects. The accidents of history and of the transmission of knowledge have served to intensify the complexity of response that these poems solicit.

The structures of poems 56 and 58 are remarkably similar: in each case, the punch line releases a tension that is built up by the repetition of proper names. In poem 58 Lesbia, the name that Catullus has *given* to his beloved, and therefore a name that makes a claim as much as it refers, is placed between the names of speaker and addressee and held there to prepare the maximum contrast with the obscenity. The obscenity acquires its metaphorical meaning by common currency and not, like "Lesbia," by Catullus' fiat. So the speech habits of others invade Catullus' diction at the same time as Lesbia's promiscuity is revealed. If the obscenity of poem 58 defiles the name and the naming that postpones it, the obscenity of poem 56 is intended to infect the insistently named addressee with laughter; the repeated naming that establishes a relation between the names of the principals—as though *Catullus* were a diminutive of *Cato*—both reflects the infectiousness that is promised and suggests the resistance that has to be overcome.[62] Even if the Cato addressed here is the poet, critic, and neoteric guru Valerius Cato, and not the severe Stoic suicide M. Porcius, the very name has a life of its own and in itself connotes censoriousness; the collocation "Cato Catullum" is comically improbable if sonically effective.[63] So the obscene anecdote that concludes is a story both of sexual misdemeanor punished and of its opposite, the infectiousness of sexual desire. We laugh because the story of infectious desire triumphs over the story of punishment, because *protelo* ('in tandem, straightaway') absorbs "pro telo" (instead of a weapon), and in the process the oxymoronic "Cato Catullum" becomes a ripple of shared laughter.[64]

Poem 56 is not confessional, and we would be inclined to distinguish it from poem 58, in spite of the similarities, for that reason. The sexual anecdote in 56 is part of a transaction between addressee and speaker, and the infectiousness of laughter that Catullus solicits from Cato is both reflected and caused by the infectiousness of sexual desire in the anecdote. In poem 58, Catullus is expressing his outrage and suffering, but isn't there a relation between the sexual relief that Lesbia provides the sons of greathearted Remus and the revelation promised by the first line and delivered by the last? The vocative *Caeli* is the beginning of a long suspension that stresses the exclusive relationship between Catullus and his Lesbia; the revelation of Lesbia's sexual availability coincides with the release of the structural tension for both reader and addressee.[65] Paradoxically, the suspension expressing the speaker's outrage at Lesbia's sexuality also introduces a rhythm of tension and resolution that determines the curious reader's relation to Lesbia's sexuality quite differently. In the last line, the speaker releases Lesbia from the grip of his stuttering incomprehension to show her servicing all and sundry; the reader's outrage at Lesbia's fault is effected by a structural resolution that also makes the reader complicit with the "sons of greathearted Remus." If Catullus did order the poems as they appear in the manuscript, then he may have intended to establish a relation between these two obscene revelations, the one so pleased with itself and the other so tortured. The sexual content of the anecdote in poem 56, which stresses the irresistible mimetic infectiousness of desire, reinforces the communication of laughter that is the point of the telling. Resistance, implied by the name Cato, is swept aside just as the punitive, censorious model is absorbed by the mimetic. In poem 58, however, Lesbia's "peeling" of the sons of Remus subverts the outrage that is being communicated, for it reinforces and sexualizes the structure of the reader/addressee's experience of the poem's revelation, of its rhythm of tension and release. In this respect, poem 58 is *like* poem 56. Obscenity in both of these poems figures in the creation of a bifurcated response to the poems' communicative insistence: outrage is compromised by the satisfaction of a prurient curiosity and by the infectiousness of desire. As in poem 98, the form of the poem's utterance contaminates the position of the inquiring scholar, who finds it hard to separate the objective search for truth from less reputable motivations that the poem brings to the surface, in this case prurient curiosity, and in the case of poem 98 *odium philologicum*.

## Obscenity and Closure

Poems 56 and 58 are good examples of the power of obscenity to produce closure; the extremity of obscene diction is emphasized in both cases by contrast to dignified mythological names (*Remi*, 58.5; *Dionae*, mother of Aphrodite, 56.6). The shock of the contrast effectively closes poems that have promised us something big from the start. Poem 97 starts with obscenity and works its way to a hair-raising climax:

Non (ita me di ament) quicquam referre putavi,
    utrum os an culum olfacerem Aemilio.
nilo mundius hoc, niloque immundius illud,
    verum etiam culus mundior et melior:
nam sine dentibus est. hoc dentis sesquipedalis,
    gingivas vero ploxeni habet veteris,
praeterea rictum qualem diffissus in aestu
    meientis mulae cunnus habere solet.
hic futuit multas et se facit esse venustum,
    et non pistrino traditur atque asino?
quem siqua attingit, non illam posse putemus
    aegroti culum lingere carnificis?

So help me God, I thought it made no difference
    whether I smell the mouth or asshole of Aemilius.
The one is no cleaner, the other no dirtier,
    in fact the asshole's cleaner and better,

for it has no teeth. The mouth has feet half a yard long,
   and gums like an old wagon-box.
What's more it gapes like the cunt of a pissing
   mule split open in the heat.
This guy fucks lots of women and thinks he's charming,
   and he's not consigned to the mill and the ass?
If any woman touches him, wouldn't you think she could
   lick the asshole of a sickly executioner?

This is one of three consecutive poems dealing with one of the most common themes of obscene Roman literature, the impure mouth.[66] Commentators cite Greek epigrams in which addressees are told that their anuses and mouths are interchangeable, but the citations only serve to contrast Catullus' opening with these "parallels."[67] The confusion between the two orifices is here emphasized by the insouciant indifference with which Catullus contemplates the prospect of smelling them, and this has no parallel in the Greek poems. But if Aemilius' two ends are indistinguishable, those of the poem are not: the opening's entertaining of alternatives contrasts with the accumulation of disgust in the final line, where each of the four words conveys some revolting aspect of the depths to which Aemilius' hypothetical girlfriend would sink. The formal difference between the beginning of a poem, where anything is possible, and the end, where there is nowhere else to go, is thematized by the relation of the speaker to Aemilius' body: casually indifferent at first, horrified at the end. But it is a third person who finally takes over the job of approaching Aemilius' body: the woman who can bring herself to touch Aemilius brings mouth and anus—confusingly equivalent smells to begin with—into intimate and polluting contact with each other. This is a particularly compelling version of ring composition and poetic closure; as we pronounce the final line, filling our mouths with obscenity, we duplicate the behavior of the hypothetical girlfriend of Aemilius. In the figure of the girlfriend, the poet transfers the stain of obscenity onto the mouth of another, who is contrasted with the insouciant persona of the poet at the beginning of the poem; this figure in turn stands for the reader, whose tongue lingers over the end of the poem, its anus in fact.

Poetic closure coincides again with an obscene act in poem 88, where Catullus addresses one of his favorite victims, the incestuous Gellius:

Quid facit is, Gelli, qui cum matre atque sorore
   prurit et abiectis pervigilat tunicis?

> quid facit is, patruum qui non sinit esse maritum?
>     ecquid scis quantum suscipiat sceleris?
> suscipit, O Gelli, quantum non ultima Tethys
>     nec genitor nympharum abluit Oceanus:
> nam nihil est quicqum sceleris, quo prodeat ultra,
>     non si demisso se ipse voret capite.
>
> Gellius, what is the man who gets the itch with his mother
>     and sister, and stays up with them all night naked?
> What is the man who doesn't allow his uncle to be married?
>     Do you know what enormity he undertakes?
> He undertakes, Gellius, a crime such as remotest Tethys
>     does not purify, nor Oceanus, father of the nymphs:
> for there is nowhere beyond this for crime to go,
>     not if he were to suck himself with his head bent.

As in poem 97, this poem ends with a breathtaking obscenity that provides an extremely powerful sense of closure. But the formal tightness of the ending depends on a paradox, namely, that Gellius' crime cannot go any further even if he were to fellate himself. The extreme limit of crime is this reflexive act that produces a sexually self-contained body, and, as the poem closes with the ultimate enormity, it produces an image of its own self-containment. Gellius' crime of incest is such that the ocean itself will not wash it away;[68] but Oceanus and Tethys, the parents of the nymphs, were themselves brother and sister: extremity, again, is replication. As the speaker gropes for something different, something extreme by which to measure the enormity of Gellius' crime, the poem turns in on itself; even the question in line 4 repeats obsessively the same sounds while preparing us for something other. Poetry being a highly self-reflexive mode of discourse, the obscenity that closes this poem could be read as a figure for poetic discourse itself. But the fact that poetic textuality is figured by an obscenity produces a bifurcated sensation in its readers: as readers of poetry, we are committed to this body that excites itself, and we desire the closure that sends us back to the beginning again; but, as witnesses of Catullus' denunciation of Gellius, we are expected to turn away in disgust from this limit of monstrosity.

## Obscene Relations, Interchangeable Bodies

The body of Gellius is the ultimate in impurity, for not only is his mouth sullied by contact with his penis but his self-consuming body has also lost its differentiation. Aemilius, with his confusion of mouth and anus, provides an obvious comparison, but Egnatius, the Spaniard who cleans his teeth with his own urine (c.39), is a similar case. An interesting extension of the body in which pure and impure are confused or fused is provided by the complementary and chiastic bodies of Vibennius and his son:

> O furum optime balneariorum
> Vibenni pater et cinaede fili
> (nam dextra pater inquinatiore,
> culo filius est voraciore),
> cur non exilium malasque in oras
> itis? quandoquidem patris rapinae
> notae sunt populo, et natis pilosas,
> fili, non potes asse venditare. (c.33)

> O best of bathouse thieves,
> father Vibennius and pathic son
> (for the father has the dirtier right hand,
> the son the more voracious asshole),
> why don't you go into exile in evil
> climes? Since the father's thefts
> are known to the populace, and your hairy
> buttocks, son, won't sell for a cent.

The father steals and the son sells;[69] their respective activities are represented by different parts of the anatomy and together they produce a perverse anatomy in which hand and anus exchange qualities, for one might as easily call the thieving hand "insatiable" and the anus, venal or otherwise, "dirty."[70] To confuse the right hand, pledge of *fides* (trustworthiness), with the anus is to confuse the pure with the impure, as does the body of Aemilius. But categories are further confused by the pun on *natis* (buttocks) and *nati* (son), for we expect the latter after *patris* in the same metrical position of the previous line: familial position is replaced with body part. In the hierarchy of the body, buttocks and anus are related to the right hand as impure to pure, and, in the hierarchy of the family, son is related to father as powerless to powerful; but this symmetry only accentuates the contamination of the higher category (family) with the lower (body). In the second line of the poem, a similar collapsing of hierarchical systems occurs when the father is hailed as "Vibenni pater" and the son as "cinaede fili": both son and *cinaedus* (pathic) occupy the negative position of a dyadic relationship. If *cinaede* replaces the name that is demanded by symmetry with "Vibenni pater," and the son remains nameless throughout, it is because the indiscriminacy of the son's sexual subordination contaminates the filial subordination that would give him a name. The father appropriates what is not his own and the son has no sense of what is "proper" to him, though, paradoxically, this appears as a form of voraciousness. Son and father are both complementary and interchangeable; as a unit they are obscene because they produce a confusion of categories and a promiscuous profusion of relations that could also be described as poetic.

Consider by comparison the family unit of Furius and his father and stepmother (c.23), a happy little trio with amazing digestions:[71]

> Furi, cui neque servus est neque arca
> nec cimex neque araneus neque ignis,
> verum est et pater et noverca, quorum
> dentes vel silicem comesse possunt,
> est pulcre tibi cum tuo parente
> et cum coniuge lignea parentis. (23.1–6)

> Furius, who have neither servant nor cashbox
> nor bedbug nor spider nor fire,
> though you do have a father and stepmother,
> whose teeth could eat even flint,
> you get on well, you and your parent
> and the wooden wife of your parent.

The stepmother is always a sinister figure in the Roman family; she is to familial relationship what stone is to food and what wood is to body.[72] This anti-family has bodies that are "dryer than bone" (12), a sign of health,[73] though in this case it results from poverty (14). Catullus, who reveals at the end of the poem that he is refusing Furius' request for a loan, is ironically casting the latter's poverty as happiness. The poem ends with Catullus assuring Furius that he is "satis beatus," which means both "happy enough" and "rich enough."[74] This paradoxically happy misery is expressed with a particularly graphic account of the fact that Furius is not polluted by his own bodily discharges:

> A te sudor abest, abest saliva,
> mucusque et mala pituita nasi.
> hunc ad munditiem adde mundiorem,
> quod culus tibi purior salillo est,
> nec toto decies cacas in anno,
> atque id durius est faba et lapillis;
> quod tu si manibus teras fricesque
> non umquam digitum inquinare posses.

> You have no sweat and no saliva,
> no mucus or nasty snot in your nose.
> To this cleanliness add something cleaner,
> that your asshole is purer than a saltcellar,
> nor do you shit ten times in the whole year,
> and *that* is harder than beans and pebbles;
> if you were to rub it and chafe it in your hands
> you would never be able to dirty your hand.

The curious thing about this body is that the anus *could not* pollute mouth (via saltcellar) or hand;[75] it is not so much a body without impurities as a body without relations, a body whose parts are interchangeable and not related or complementary to each other through the usual distinctions between purity and pollution. The description of this perverse cleanliness, however, is disgusting in the extreme because what is absent has nevertheless been conjured up quite graphically and with considerable relish. Once again, the obscenity of the body being described is related to some capacity of poetry itself that the reader experiences with mixed sensations.

When Catullus speaks of Furius' family, he tells him "est pulcre tibi cum tuo parente . . . ," which means either "you get on well with your father [and stepmother]" or "you're a fortunate fellow, and so is your father [and stepmother]." We might say of the family of Furius that the "good fortune" of its several members—their similarly dry and efficiently digesting bodies—substitutes for a relation between them; in other words, one sense of "est pulcre" competes with another.[76] The family "body" is as dysfunctional here as in the case of Vibennius and his son, but in the opposite way.

Catullus fobs off the importunate Furius with his "happy" family; it is interesting to see the ironic use of the happy family theme recur with a similar phrasing in Catullus' attack on Caesar:

> Pulcre convenit improbis cinaedis
> Mamurrae pathicoque Caesarique.
> nec mirum: maculae pares utrique,
> urbana altera, et illa Formiana,
> impressae resident nec eluentur;
> morbosi pariter, gemelli utrique,
> uno in lecticulo erudituli ambo,
> non hic quam ille magis vorax adulter,
> rivales socii puellularum.
> pulcre convenit improbis cinaedis.

> The shameless effeminates agree quite nicely,
> Mamurra the pathic and Caesar too.
> No wonder: stains, equal in each case,
> one from the city, the other from Formiae,
> are deep ingrained and can't be scrubbed away.
> Equally perverted, twinned and reversible,
> both quite learned on the same little bench,
> one no less greedy an adulterer than the other,
> rival comrades of and for the girls.
> The shameless effeminates agree quite nicely.

"Pulcre convenit" (there's a nice agreement) works like "est pulcre" in poem 23: the "agreement" is both a relationship and a similarity between the two principals. Here, and even more emphatically, one sense interferes with the other, for the implications of sexual relationship in *convenit* (*OLD* s.v. 1c) make the fact that Caesar and Mamurra are both *cinaedi* somewhat inconvenient but, as we shall see, not disastrous.[77] The poem plays persistently on the notion of the pair, which appears in several, sometimes paradoxical, forms and produces a perverse unit out of the friends.[78] *Rivales socii puellularum* translates both as "rival comrades for the girls," meaning that the two men compete for the favors of women, and as "rivals of the girls," meaning that they compete against women for the favors of other men. If, further, the two men are *morbosi* (perverted) and *adulteri* in the same bed, then they are participants in a threesome and so rivals in both senses at the same time.[79]

Calling the two men *gemelli*, Catullus not only claims that they are twins but also that they are both "double in form."[80] Suetonius tells us that Caesar was called "the man of all women and the woman of all men,"[81] so the word may be echoing a common insult, in which case the two men are both identical to each other and different within themselves. The poem creates an endlessly adaptable pair, whose similarity in no way prevents them from a form of intercourse that is usually predicated on difference.

With respect to the body politic, the obscene confusion of the pairing in this poem reflects a political scandal in which the hierarchy and competition that should work to control the behavior of individuals has broken down.[82] Catullus' invective against Mamurra and Caesar is directed against the "nice little understanding" that closes this pair off from the control of the society on which they prey. The private understandings and arrangements that challenge the power of the collectivity, as Veyne would put it, are displayed by the public performance of Catullus' language.

In poems 33, 23, and 57, familial and political order, with their rigid hierarchies, positions, and articulations, are reflected and perverted in the order of and between bodies. As we have seen, there are also relations within the society of the poem—poet, poem, and reader—to be expressed through the figure of the obscene body and its functions, charged as it is with notions of domination and subordination, purity and contamination, and focused as it so often is on the mouth as the site of these relations. Although pleasure is seldom a factor in Roman obscenity, when obscenity enters the fluid and often paradoxical world of the textual, as it does in poem 28, pleasure puts in a disruptive appearance that unsettles the rigid positionalities of Roman social relations.

CHAPTER 4

# Urbanity
## The Poetry of Exclusion

In Chapter 2, I described the overlap between the erotic and the poetic in terms like *venustas* and *deliciae*, an overlap that allows Catullus to explore an important dimension of the relation between poet and reader. This chapter is concerned with *urbanitas* and the overlap between social style or manners and poetics. The concepts of social style and manners function essentially as a means of separating outsiders from insiders, of excluding and including, so here too Catullus adopts a relational or positional model for his poetry. But scholarship has generally taken a different direction with Catullus' urbanity, trying to elicit an ethical component from the poetry by elaborating the principles of urbane behavior and their derivation from aesthetic principles: good poetry is like proper behavior, and we can read off the principles of one from the other. Speaking from the position of the urbane Catullus, scholars have shown themselves to be members of Catullus' circle by virtue of their ability to grasp the ethical implications of the Catullan poetic style, which is something that has to be tested on the pulse: to expound the values of this style, one has to adopt it imaginatively and describe how it functions.

I pursue a different critical project in relation to Catullus' urbanity, one that requires us, first of all, to stop *believing* in the poet. My question is not "What is Catullan urbanity?" but "How does Catullus lay claim to urbanity?" In his urbane performances, Catullus positions himself in relation to those he excludes. The urbane style appears as it condemns the inurbane; it is appropriated. Because the terms that convey correct social style or manner are indefinable, a person who is authorized to assign or exemplify them stands, like the poet, in a unique relation to the common language, and must vindicate the right to this position by continually proving that he or she can outperform others. The strategies of the arbiter of urbanity are very much those of the poet. But before turning to the strategies of urbanity in Catullus' poetry, let us briefly consider the status of the concept of *urbanitas* in Catullus' time and in its modern afterlife.

## The Power of the Indefinable

The English word "urbanity" belongs to a set of concepts involved in the aestheticizing of social life whose ideology has recently been described by Terry Eagleton. When Eagleton speaks of the Earl of Shaftesbury's aristocratic conflation of the moral with the aesthetic, it is hard not to think of Catullus: "To live 'aesthetically' for Shaftesbury is to flourish in the well-proportioned exercise of one's powers, conforming to the law of one's free personality in the casual, affable, taken-for-granted style of the stereotypical aristocrat."[1] This thought seems familiar to the reader of Catullus, partially because the Earl of Shaftesbury knew Catullus and partially because Catullus' modern critics have, consciously or not, absorbed the ideas of Shaftesbury. What Eagleton reminds us is that this conflation of the aesthetic and the moral has had an important ideological role to play in the naturalization of political order, the diffusion of power through the unconscious textures of everyday life. Shaftesbury's conflation of ethics with aesthetics revolves around the concept of manners, through which, as Eagleton puts it, "the human subject introjects the codes which govern it as the very source of its free autonomy" (41). The indefinability of Catullan urbanity and related concepts corresponds to the necessarily irreducible character of their modern offspring; as Eagleton points out, the aestheticizing of morality ensures that the law that guarantees the cohesion of society is "beyond all reason, as gloriously pointless as a poem," which renders it immune not only to rational analysis but also to rational criticism.[2] As long as the poem is taken to exemplify the style whose beauty is an index of its ethical rightness, it remains beyond rational analysis or criticism, for all we can do is taste it and find it good. But Catullus' poetry never simply exemplifies style; rather, it claims its stylishness against others who might lay similar claim, and it is only through this relation that the style appears. If the danger of an aesthetic morality is that it renders social relations beyond questioning, then it is important for us to understand aesthetic qualities in relation to the social dynamics that create them.

Scholars who set out to describe or define the Latin word *urbanitas* often find themselves invoking indefinables from modern cultures, not necessarily their own; the locus classicus is Austin's note on *Pro Caelio*, 6.25:

An adequate translation of *urbanitas* is impossible. It is not only an abstract idea, but an attitude of mind; it represents all that seemed to a Roman gentleman to constitute "good form" in manners, *ton*, the opposite of the boorish clumsiness of those *rustici* who had not the advantage of living in the *urbs*; it was something instinctively and naturally Roman (cf. *ad Att.* vii.2.3 "est, quam facile diligas, *autochthōn* in homine urbanitas"). P. de Labriolle, *Les Satires de Juvenal*, p.351, compares it to the conception of *politesse* in France during the seventeenth and eighteenth centuries, "le produit exquis, la fleur de leur civilization". The essence of such "good form" was sparkle, subtlety, wit, elegance: the unforgivable sin was to be clumsy, stupid, dull.[3]

Austin is right to say that an adequate translation of *urbanitas* is impossible, for *urbanitas* is acquired from mixing with the right people and living in the right places, and it is a concept whose purpose is as much to exclude as to define, hence the importance of negatives in Austin's treatment of this word ("the opposite of . . . ," "the unforgivable sin . . ."). Like "gentleman" and *politesse*, *urbanitas* is a concept on which a particular culture prides itself and which therefore needs to be untranslatable.[4] As we shall see, this concept was also indefinable for the Romans who used it. A German scholar describing the sophistication of Catullus' circle finds himself invoking a number of untranslatable, and sometimes naturalized, foreign words:

Hier war man wie er elegant, charmant, witzig und frech; hier pflegte man wie er in einem laessigen "understatement" seine ganze Ueberlegenheit ueber allen als toelpelhaft empfundenen Ernst kundzutun.

Here [sc. Rome] one was, like him [Catullus] elegant, charming, witty and impudent; here the custom was to announce, like him, in a careless "understatement" one's complete superiority to all that one saw as cloddish seriousness.[5]

One begins to get the idea. Syndikus's polyglot description reminds us that the existence of a composite European sophistication derives from the common Latin culture of educated westerners. But the familiarity and the deeply ingrained authority of these terms makes Catullus' Roman urbanity seem a little too entrenched; one must remember that *urbanitas* was itself a term that was undergoing changes in meaning at the time, and that urbanity as a style of behavior and a social value was still somewhat experimental.[6] What these passages suggest is that both the term and the behavior it denotes are intended to create an excluded and despised opposite, and that any examination of the concept of *urbanitas* must consider it functionally rather than as a bundle of qualities.

Ancient attempts to define *urbanitas* often echo the embarrassment that overtakes Cicero when pressed on this word by Brutus in his dialogue of that name (*Brut.*, 170ff.). But perhaps embarrassment is the wrong description, because Cicero uses *urbanitas* in the first place to pinpoint what is lacking in the Italian orators, and the very vagueness of the term serves to emphasize the absolute nature of the gulf between metropolis and province. If *urbanitas* could be defined, then the authority of the Roman to pronounce on such matters would be diminished. So the Italian orators, Cicero states, have everything one could ask for in a speaker except that their speech "is not, as it were, tinged with a certain urbanity." And what is this urbanity? Cicero replies that he doesn't know, but he knows that it exists (171); it is "a more urbane resonance" (resonat urbanius) that rings in the words of "our" orators, and it is the "native flavor" (sapor vernaculus) by which Granius prevailed over the provincial Tinca, even though the latter had a ready wit. But Granius was himself of municipal origin, and it might seem paradoxical that some of the figures who prided themselves most on their *urbanitas*, and chided its lack in others, were provincials like Cicero and Catullus. No doubt the process of acculturation and of acceptance into Roman aristocratic society for these outsiders was oiled by their championship of this quintessentially aristocratic quality.[7] Compare the rather awkward performance of Cicero to the following poem of Catullus, in which the aristocratic Lesbia is championed against the claims of a certain Quintia, who may have come from Catullus' native Verona:[8]

Quintia formosa est multis. mihi candida, longa,
    recta est: haec ego sic singula confiteor.
totum illud formosa nego: nam nulla venustas,
    nulla in tam magno est corpore mica salis.
Lesbia formosa est, quae cum pulcerrima tota est,
    tum omnibus una omnis surripuit Veneres. (c.86)

Quintia is beautiful to many. To me she is fair, tall,
    straight: these particulars I readily concede.

> But the whole that is beauty I withhold; she has no charm,
> > no grain of salt in all that body.
> Lesbia is beautiful, and, loveliest in all respects,
> > alone she's robbed all others of their charms.

Catullus concedes to Quintia all the identifiable qualities one might desire in a beautiful woman, but withholds two of those indefinable ingredients of *urbanitas*: *venustas* (charm) and *sal* ("salt," i.e., wit).[9] The latter term, as Quintilian observes, means "funny" (*ridiculum*) in common parlance, but Quintilian goes on to say that Catullus can't be complaining that there's nothing funny in Quintia's body, and he concludes

> Salsum erit igitur quod non erit insulsum, velut quoddam simplex orationis condimentum, quod sentitur latente iudicio velut palato, excitatque et a taedio defendit orationem (6.3.18).

> So that will be witty (*salsum*) which is not dull (*insulsum*), like some simple seasoning of the speech, which is detected by the private judgment as though by the palate, and stimulates the speech and protects it from tedium.

All this is part of a discussion of *urbanitas*, which is identified, rather unhelpfully, as speech that displays a taste of the city (*gustum urbis*) and, more helpfully, as "a discreet culture acquired from association with the learned" (*sumptam ex conversatione doctorum tacitam eruditionem*). What these examples reveal is that *urbanitas* and related words are not just difficult to define, but essentially indefinable because of the kind of work they do.[10]

In the time of Catullus and Cicero, the application of the word *urbanitas* is undergoing an expansion; its earlier applications to, literally, life at Rome or to a certain crude Roman humor are being joined by a more general reference to a person's metropolitan sophistication. Rome is becoming self-conscious, especially in the persons of the provincials who have come to Rome to display and exploit their own cultivation in the center of culture. Cicero's use of the word shows that it is at the center of developments in ideals of behavior and attitude in the second half of the first century. In some passages, Cicero regrets the disappearance of an ancient *urbanitas*, harking back to a native Roman tradition of caustic wit that hardly opposed itself to *rusticitas*;[11] when Tacitus refers to a crude practical joke as *vernacula* (home-bred) *urbanitas* (*Hist.* 2.88), he recalls that tradition.[12] In the *Pro Caelio*, *urbanitas* is introduced in order to distinguish different kinds of abuse: "if it is hurled more insolently, it is called insult; if more wittily, urbanity" (si petulantius iactatur, convicium; si facetius, urbanitas nominatur; *Cael.* 6). Here it retains the older association with Roman causticity, though it now serves the purpose of making a distinction between crude and sophisticated.[13] But later in the same speech (14.33), Cicero asks of Clodius whether he would have Cicero deal with him with old-style severity (severiter et graviter et prisce) or more indulgently (remisse et leniter et urbane). The word is now used in opposition to the older tradition, whose characteristic wit it denotes in the passages cited above; it now implies some relaxation of a more traditional severity, a deflection from the straight and narrow Roman path.[14]

In a letter to Appius Pulcher (*ad Fam.* 3.8), the ex-governor of Cicero's new province, Cicero specifically alludes to new developments in the meaning of *urbanitas*. Appius has evidently taken Cicero to task for not showing him the proper deference, and Cicero writes to exculpate himself. Among Appius' grievances is the fact that Cicero failed to send the usual deputation to the Senate praising the administration of the ex-governor. Cicero responds that he had not wished to put the provincials to unnecessary expense, and furthermore that he did not believe Appius to be the sort of person to be concerned about such deputations:

Primum te, hominem non solum sapientem verum etiam, ut nunc loquimur, urbanum, non arbitrabar genere isto legationum delectari, (3.8.3)

First, I did not think that you, a man not only wise but, as we now say, urbane, would take pleasure in that kind of deputation,

For Appius not to be concerned about the outward tokens of respect that were the bread and butter of the Roman politician, and to which Cicero himself was greatly attached, he would have to be exhibiting a new, more ironical sense of self; and for Cicero to get away with his excuse, he would have to be offering Appius a new and desirable kind of self-image.

With Cicero's letter to Appius, we come close to the mechanism of Catullus' *urbanitas* as I describe it in this chapter. Cicero is using the word in a sense that appears to be new (he is writing in 51 B.C.E.) to maneuver himself out of an awkward situation. Not only has his behavior, as he claims, been *elegans* ("correct" and perhaps "graceful") in its reconciliation of the demands of the provincials with those of Appius' *dignitas*,[15] but he has left Appius looking clumsy in his recriminations against Cicero, and this at least partially by virtue of the finesse with which he sidesteps Appius' complaint. In other words, Cicero's appeal to the standards of *urbanitas* is itself a maneuver that displays his elegance. I argue that *urbanitas* in Catullus' work is best understood as a performance, and a performance that always involves some kind of aggressive, or at least competitive, relation with another. Urbanity, then, is a position, for the urbane speaker claims his possession of that quality by drawing a line that shows, as it *excludes*, in what respect he has this *je ne sais quoi*.

## Theft and Reclamation

The Catullan collection situates the poet as the arbiter of elegance of his circle, in which capacity he is more often than not exposing those who fail to meet his standards.[16] Cicero gives us a sense of the watchful censoriousness of the connoisseurs of appropriate and sophisticated behavior at Rome when he speaks of the need to be constantly on guard against committing trivial faults of demeanor, unnoticed by the many, but detected by the observant, just as the slightest faults in tone are heard by the truly musical (*De Off.* 1.40–41). Here is Catullus playing the censor in poem 12:

> Marrucine Asini, manu sinistra
> non belle uteris: in ioco atque vino
> tollis lintea neglegentiorum.
> hoc salsum esse putas? fugit te inepte:
> quamvis sordida res et invenusta est.
> non credis mihi? crede Pollioni
> fratri, qui tua furta vel talento
> mutari velit . . . est enim leporum
> differtus puer ac facetiarum.
> quare aut hendecasyllabos trecentos
> exspecta, aut mihi linteum remitte,
> quod me non movet aestimatione,
> verum est mnemosynum mei sodalis.
> nam sudaria Saetaba ex Hiberis
> miserunt mihi muneri Fabullus
> et Veranius; haec amem necesse est
> ut Veraniolum meum et Fabullum. (c.12)

> Asinius Marrucinus, your left hand
> you put to no good use, in wine and joking

> you steal the napkins of your careless friends.
> You call this wit? Deluded dolt:
> The trick is sordid, tasteless as can be.
> You don't believe me? Trust your brother
> Pollio, who'd wish your thefts undone
> at any price . . . for that's a boy stuffed full
> of charms and witticisms.
> So then, expect three hundred angry verses,
> or give me back my napkin, not
> that it concerns me for its value,
> it's a souvenir of friends of mine.
> Fabullus and Veranius sent as a gift
> from Spain napkins of Saetabis;
> these napkins I must hold as dear
> as my Veranius and Fabullus too.

Like many of Catullus' squibs, this is a performance exhibiting the very qualities that the unfortunate victim is pilloried for lacking. Asinius' *ineptia*, the bad timing that makes this exhibition of wit out of place, is the occasion for Catullus' adroit compliment to Asinius' brother and for his neat acknowledgment of the gift from his friends. The poet's opportunism makes a silk purse out of the sow's ear of Asinius' inopportune joke.[17] Of course, the clumsiness of Asinius is a matter of context: to filch people's napkins when they are off their guard and at their ease (*neglegentiores*) is to misread the situation. Catullus neatly creates this misreading by describing the circumstances of Asinius' theft as "in wine and joking"; Asinius thinks that it is he who is making the joke, but Catullus has the word *ioco* refer to the very conviviality that Asinius has violated.

It is Asinius' own brother who provides the evidence that there is a right and a wrong way to play the fool.[18] But if Asinius' brother stands as evidence that it can be done correctly, Catullus himself provides the example, for in describing Pollio as "a boy stuffed full of charms and witticisms" he sets the crude colloquialism "stuffed full" (*differtus*, 9) in the midst of the language of urbanity and gets away with it.[19] Catullus has himself performed the trick that Asinius could not pull off, exemplifying the wit that consists in the piquant interruption of a context (see Quintilian above) with his grossly physical word.[20]

To reveal only at the end of the poem that the napkin that Asinius stole has a sentimental value is a sneaky move, but Catullus' timing in this poem has a purpose, and that is to raise and deflect the charge of *ineptia* (tastelessness) from his own complaint. It is hardly urbane to make such a fuss about a napkin, and Catullus even encourages us to think that it may be a little materialistic (12). The urbanity of the poet's performance here lies in the graceful turn with which he avoids *ineptia*, whose spectre he has himself raised, just as the urbanity of the poem as a whole depends on the elegant exploitation of Asinius' ineptitude. In fact, the end of the poem is a clever and devastating theft of the napkin from Asinius himself, in the sense that the napkin has now come to represent the circle from which Asinius is excluded. Catullus has deftly turned the tables on the thief.

Poem 12 is one of a number of poems in the polymetrics in which the poet sets himself up as an arbiter of elegance, including and excluding people from the circle of the *urbani* with sovereign confidence. In general, this aspect of the collection has been seen as the Roman contribution to Catullus' basically Alexandrian literary program, expanding the aesthetic values of the Alexandrians—particularly their concern with the careful cultivation of small-scale forms—into the social sphere, and laying claim to a new set of values instantiated by the lifestyle of the neoteric poets. Marilyn Skinner puts this view well:

His concern with standards of propriety ventures beyond the domain of literature to embrace a wide range of social usages. Here the artist's instinct for what is right and fitting becomes a touchstone for true refinement. The fastidious, cultured poet-critic is pressed into service as an *arbiter elegantiae* and a censor of conduct. His profession therefore takes on a new social importance, rivaling the ancient stature of the *vates* [poet-prophet] as spokesman for the now-moribund ancestral value system. In the ironic jargon of Catullus' circle, poems may be *nugae* and the craft of letters a *ludus*, but, beneath the surface frivolity, the discipline of art inculcates abiding principles of good taste which can be developed into a general code of behavior.[21]

Poem 12 becomes something like an Alexandrian literary manifesto translated into social terms, "another in the series of pieces preoccupied with *lepor* [charm], attempting to define what is and is not cultivated behavior" (59). But it is hard to see how this poem could be seen as an attempt to define anything. In fact, I would argue that the essential *in*definability of *lepor* is what makes Catullus' brilliant little performance possible. Asinius thinks that his behavior is witty, and by the end of the poem we are none the wiser as to why it isn't, nor as to what distinguishes it from his brother's *lepores* and *facetiae*, or the company's *ioci* (2); instead, we have witnessed a dazzling series of maneuvers that have shut

Asinius out of the elegant world it has created. There could be no "abiding principles of good taste" or "general code of behavior" for this society because improvisation and competition are the essence of its style of intercourse. The stability of the terms of approval and disapproval that are used by Catullus' circle misleads commentators into supposing that there are essences to be discovered "beneath the surface frivolity," though these terms are essentially about surfaces. When Skinner says that, at the end of poem 12, Catullus reveals that Asinius' "theft was loutish—because it unknowingly violated the intimate private relationship between Catullus and his *sodales*" (60), she bypasses the strategic function of the revelation within the poem, which is to make the theft loutish. Catullus' explanation of why he cares about the napkin, and the role this explanation plays in the discomfiture of Asinius, are manifestations of *lepor*, but it is surely digging too deep to say that "the social ideals of *lepor* and *venustas* [grace, attractiveness] are now given a broader dimension by indirect association with a relationship marked by thoughtful recollection and deep mutual sympathy" (60). Why "*deep* mutual sympathy" and "*thoughtful* recollection"? The diminutive form of Veranius' name in the last line brings out the fact that Fabullus' name is already a diminutive, of *faba* (bean);[22] the companions are affectionately assimilated to the status of things, like the napkins that Catullus must love as much as their donors. *Venustas* attaches to this kind of superficial effect as much as to the relationship that it reflects.

I am suggesting that we restore its surface to Catullus' *urbanitas* and that we cease believing in him, in order to understand how the poem creates the impression of a "loutish transgression of intimacy" on Asinius' part. Skinner's treatment of poem 12 exemplifies a common tendency of scholarly discourse on Catullus, in which to write about Catullus is to confirm the gold reserves that guarantee the value of these "trifles" (*nugae*). In this view, the napkin mediates between surface and depth: trivial yet important, it is the site where the deft instinct for what is right, manifested in the poem's aesthetic polish, is made to resonate with deeper moral issues of thoughtfulness and "deep mutual sympathy" in the circle of Catullus' friends. But suppose we see this napkin, alienable and yet not alienable, as the focal point of a struggle for the ownership of discourse; the issue, then, is not what the napkin signifies but who makes it signify and how. Catullus takes the napkin back by substituting his own meanings for those of Asinius. The piquant social opportunism of Asinius' theft is outbidded by Catullus' own counterperformance, which leaves Asinius deprived of the meaning that he wanted to give the napkin, now endowed with meanings that he has made possible, but which exclude him. "You can't handle this stuff," the poem seems to say.

At this point it is worth looking at a comparable situation in one of Cicero's letters (*ad Fam.* 7.32) in which the issue is the ownership of wit. Volumnius has informed Cicero that, in his absence from the city, the bons mots of all and sundry, even the appalling Sestius (who reappears in Catullus c.44), are being attributed to him. Cicero replies that Volumnius is not discharging his duty as superintendent of Cicero's salt mines (the source of his *sales*, "witticisms"). The city, he goes on to say, is so full of dregs that there is nothing so banal (akuthēron) that someone won't think it charming (venustum). Volumnius is begged to see that nothing save the cleverest witticisms are allowed to pass for Cicero's. The whole passage is itself an example of what Cicero calls *eutrapelia* (badinage),[23] the quality in Volumnius' letter that identified it as coming from Volumnius Eutrapelus, and not another Volumnius with whom Cicero was in correspondence (7.32.1). As in Catullus' poem, the question of true wit is tied to the issue of ownership: if Sestius' witticisms can pass as Cicero's, then his ownership of his *sales* is at stake, and if the city cannot distinguish between the banal and the witty, then Cicero's own personality may be eroded in his absence. Cicero's witty—if rather labored—performance establishes the grounds of mutual recognition between himself and Volumnius, the grounds of a sure sense of self, and this recognition of identity depends on the exclusion of others. Like Catullus, Cicero uses the depredations of another on what is his own to establish the circle of the likeminded.

Catullus and Cicero lived during a period in which individuality and individual style were becoming increasingly important.[24] Poem 12 of Catullus, like the letter of Cicero, reflects the competitive context in which personal style is established or vindicated. The true progeny of Catullus' poem are not Martial's attacks on napkin stealers (8.59, 12.29) but his many poems against plagiarists, especially 1.38, where he tells the unfortunate Fidentinus, who is reciting Martial's poems as his own, that he recites them so badly that they have truly become his.[25] Though Catullus' poem is not specifically about plagiarism, it is similar in that Asinius is lambasted for poaching on what Catullus now proves to be his own preserve. Rather than reflecting or exemplifying values, this poem establishes them by means of a manuever that cannot then be eliminated to reveal a pure ethical residue.

Let me broaden the context by comparing the napkin of poem 12 with the perfume of poem 13. Both of these poems are about dinners and what people bring to them.[26] Figuratively, the napkin that the Roman guest brings to a dinner links the society that is created by the occasion to the other worlds of the guest who owns it. Poem 12 has Catullus reclaiming what he brought to the gathering by creating another society from which the thieving dinner companion is excluded. In the next poem, Catullus invites Fabullus to dinner and describes their respective contributions to this potluck:

> Cenabis bene, mi Fabulle, apud me
> paucis, si tibi di favent, diebus,
> si tecum attuleris bonam atque magnam
> cenam non sine candida puella
> et vino et sale et omnibus cacchinnis.
> haec si, inquam, attuleris, venuste noster,
> cenabis bene; nam tui Catulli
> plenus sacculus est aranearum.
> sed contra accipies meros amores
> seu quid suavius elegantiusve est:
> nam unguentum dabo, quod meae puellae
> donarunt Veneres Cupidinesque,
> quod tu cum olfacies, deos rogabis,
> totum ut te faciant, Fabulle, nasum.

> You will dine well, my Fabullus, at my place
> in a few days, if the gods favor you,
> if you bring with you a good and a large
> meal, not forgetting a lovely girl
> with wine and salt [or wit] and all kinds of laughter.
> If, as I say, you bring all this, my charming friend,
> you will dine well; for your Catullus'
> purse is full of cobwebs.
> But in return you will receive pure love,
> or anything more pleasant and more elegant:
> for I will give you perfume, which the Venuses
> and Cupids gave to my girl,
> and when you smell that you will ask the gods,
> Fabullus, to make you into one big nose.

Instead of taking back what has been appropriated by another diner, Catullus is here giving what belongs to another (Lesbia) to his own dinner guest. I described Catullus' napkin in c.12 as the site of a struggle over the control of discourse, but what of Lesbia's perfume? First of all, the perfume acquires its aroma from the preposterous balance of contributions to the impending dinner: Fabullus, the guest, is to bring all the usual ingredients of a good party and Catullus, the host, will provide the costly but inessential garnish. On Catullus' home turf, the concepts of hospitality and of successful entertainment are open to redefinition: Fabullus will trade in all his other senses to boost his sense of smell.[27] Catullus' invitation transforms giving into taking as the host strips his guest down to his nose, dramatizing a specialization of the senses that is part of any aesthetic transaction.

The dinner is the site of urbanity par excellence, a place both of sharing and of competition, as these poems make abundantly clear.[28] In the case of Catullus' impending dinner, the items that will be enjoyed by the participants stand in a competitive relation to each other: the chaotic list of things that Fabullus must bring is answered by the distillations that Catullus has to offer: "pure love" (meros amores, 9) and perfume.[29] Fabullus will bring a beautiful girl, but Catullus will provide the essence of the relation of his girl to the Venuses and Cupids. The perfume is generously overdetermined: a commodity that has a real, though nonculinary function for the dinner, it also suggests a substitute food—the gods, after all, consume the *aroma* of our sacrifices—as well as the essence of sex appeal.[30]

There has been much discussion about the perfume that the Venuses and Cupids have given to Lesbia (if indeed she is the *puella*). Is there a sexual double entendre here (vaginal secretions)?[31] Is this simply an elegant way of referring to "the alluring fragrance of [Lesbia's] person"?[32] Or are we to understand it as perfume and no more? That the Venuses and Cupids should have given the perfume to Lesbia does seem to associate it with her allure. If there is a sexual allusion in the perfume, then there is also a possibility of double entendre in Fabullus' predicted response, for the nose and the penis are related in Roman culture as they are in others.[33] I am not suggesting that Catullus is offering Lesbia sexually to his guest; rather, I would put it like this: smelling the perfume is to enjoying Lesbia as smelling the aroma of food is to eating—if you are human you are tantalized, but if you are a god you are satisfied. Fabullus will be both tantalized and apotheosized by his experience.

The ambiguous status of the perfume, which has so provoked the curiosity of commentators, is consistent with the unorthodox character of the invitation, which subverts the usual relationship between host and guest; neither guest nor reader gets quite what he or she wants, though both are seduced into accepting Catullus' terms. Catullus' provocative invitation raises the issue of what can and what can't be shared: Fabullus' "lovely girl" (candida puella) takes her place in a list of conventional requisites against which the perfume is pitted, and the perfume is the mode of Fabullus' indirect enjoyment of Lesbia, of her mediated availability. On the one hand, the perfume is a particularly personal and intimate offering to the guest, but, on the other hand, it distinguishes the mode of Lesbia's availability to Fabullus from that of the girl that he will provide. Like the napkin of poem 12, then, the perfume is the instrument both of inclusion and exclusion; what is more, Fabullus, an insider to the world of the napkin from which Asinius is excluded (c.12), finds himself in the next poem a guest who is regaled with an essence that is an absence. Where Asinius the prankster thief has and yet doesn't have what belongs to Catullus, Fabullus the guest is and yet isn't invited to share in the host's most intimate world. In this respect, Fabullus is like the reader, whose satisfaction is defined in relation to the exchange he or she has been persuaded to make, an exchange whose inequality must be compensated by a shift in value and a specialization of the senses.

In general, Catullus' urbanity is better understood as something more like a game than "a disposition, a way of thinking, almost an aura."[34] As I argued at the beginning of this chapter, *urbanitas* is essentially undefinable, so that the urbane speaker can only lay claim to it through acts of inclusion and exclusion. Catullus' poetry is created in a society that is defining itself in terms of new kinds of social games, and the poetry itself plays a role in the development of this new form of self-definition; this accounts for the fact that the poems explore aspects of the relational dynamics of the lyric genre analogous to the dynamics of certain social games. So poem 12 reminds us that the poem takes language back from other potential users to prove that it belongs here and always did ("You can't handle this stuff").[35] Poem 13 tells us about the curious, and somewhat competitive, relation between host and guest—that is, poet and reader—constituted by a poem: we are invited in only to be shown that we will gladly accept any terms the poet cares to impose, even, perhaps especially, if he persuades us to trade what we do have for what we can't have, our own world for a whiff of his.[36]

Besides poem 12, Catullus wrote two other poems reclaiming his property from a thief, poems 25 and 42. In poem 42, he summons his iambics to assail the woman who has stolen his writing tablets, denouncing her publicly and repeatedly as a "filthy whore" (putida moecha, 11, 12, 19, 20). Because the woman has no shame, Catullus is eventually forced to change his tack and address her as "modest and upright" (pudica et proba, 24). Clearly the theft is here implicated with a struggle for the control of discourse, and in this poem the poet appears to lose the struggle, for the target of invective who does not recognize the rules of the game escapes his power. In poem 25, a conciliatory tone is adopted from the beginning, but it is sarcastic; the singsong meter and the mimicking effect of the diminutives indicate that the language is parodic:[37]

> Cinaede Thalle, mollior cuniculi capillo
> vel anseris medullula vel imula oricilla
> vel pene languido senis situque araneoso,
> idemque, Thalle, turbida rapacior procella,
> cum diva +mulier aries+ ostendit oscitantes,
> remitte pallium mihi meum quod involasti,
> sudariumque Saetabum catagraphosque Thynos,
> inepte, quae palam soles habere tamque avita.
> quae nunc tuis ab unguibus reglutina et remitte,
> ne laneum latusculum manusque mollicellas
> inusta turpiter tibi flagella conscribillent,
> et insolenter aestues, velut minuta magno
> deprensa navis in mari, vesaniente vento. (c.25)

> Thallus, you queer, softer than the down of rabbits
> or goose's marrow or the teeny earlobe,
> or an old man's languid penis, or a cobweb,
> Thallus, sometimes more grasping than a violent storm,
> when the goddess . . . shows them yawning,
> return that cloak of mine you pounced on,
> and my Spanish napkin and Bithynian cloths,
> which foolishly you tout as family heirlooms.
> Unglue them from your hands and send them back,
> or whips will brand you, scribbled with your shame
> across your fleecy little flanks and softest hands,
> until you seethe and toss just like a tiny ship
> caught in a blustering sea, not with your usual pleasure.

Thallus is a paradoxical mixture of limp passivity and voraciousness, and Catullus' response to his theft is a kind of chant in which the tones of threat and endearment are mingled.[38] The wit of the poem lies in the appropriation of the tone of Thallus, or of a cooing lover of the same. As in the case of the unfortunate Asinius, Catullus' performance is itself a form of theft, because Thallus' language is stolen and turned against him. But Thallus' crime is not just theft, for he has brazenly displayed Catullus' property as though it were part of his heirloom, rather as Asinius tried to involve Catullus' property in a display of his own *sal*. In response, Catullus threatens to set the delicate body of Thallus on fire in a novel way; the phrase "insolenter aestues" (you will burn/seethe unwontedly, 12) announces that he has turned the tables on the thief, whose characteristic writhings will take on an unaccustomed form at his hands in recompense for the fact that he displays as his own what he stole from Catullus. The word *aestues* combines the senses of sexual excitement, burning pain, and turbulent motion; not only does it give Thallus' customary (solitus) but immoderate (insolens) desire an unaccustomed sense, but it also makes him both a manifestation and a victim of the storm that figures his own rapacity (procella, 4). The aggressive turbulence of Thallus' rapacity is turned against him as his seething (aestues, 12) comes to signify the bobbing of a boat on a turbulent sea, which in turn describes his writhings under Catullus' lash.

Thallus' name is Greek (young shoot, branch), which probably means that he is to be thought of as a freedman. Certainly, freedman status would make his display of (stolen) ancestral property appropriately out of place (inepte, 8). "Thallus" may also suggest "phallus," both aurally and semantically, and this gives an extra bite to the comparison of Thallus' softness with the languid penis of an old man (3).[39] Furthermore, the name features the "l" characteristic of diminutive formations, a letter that was thought to signify softness.[40] Characteristically, Catullus here plays with words that look as if they might be diminutives in a context rife with them.[41] The fact that some of the very words that convey violence and aggression in this poem have the look of diminutives (procella, 4; flagella, conscribillent, 11) is part of the poem's strategy of using Thallus' tone against him. Thallus' storm of rapacity is neutralized by the assimilation of the word for "storm" (procella) to the language of pathic softness, and the punishment described in line 11 seems to be generated by Thallus' own proclivities; in fact, the word *flagellum* (whip) is commonly and figuratively used in Latin for the young shoot of a vine or other plant—in other words, it means the same as the Greek *thallos*.[42]

As in poem 12, Catullus here perpetrates a form of theft against the accused thief; in this case, it is Thallus' display of the stolen items "as heirlooms" that provokes him to appropriate the language of Thallus' softness and make it serve his own purposes. But there may be a closer parallel to poem 12, for the diminutives that belong to the style of the pathic are also an important component of the language of the *urbani*;[43] Thallus' language, like Asinius' would-be *sal*, has been stolen from the *urbani*, or so the poems would have us believe. By mimicking the language of the pathic—holding it in suspension—Catullus becomes the urbane speaker who gets away with what Thallus can't, and again the *ineptus* is cast as a thief in order to reflect the *urbanus'* control of language.

Combining preciosity with violence, Catullus threatens to cover Thallus' body with scribbles (conscribillent, 11), a form of writing that reflects both the anger of Catullus and the sinuous softness of Thallus.[44] *Conscribillent*, a compound of the intensive *cum* and a diminutive form of *scribo*, echoes the Greek word *catagraphos* (figured cloths) in line 7, a word similarly formed from a preposition (kata) and the verb "to write" (graphein). Thallus' body, then, is to become a "written" artifact that parodies the patterned material from Bithynia that he has stolen from Catullus, and this artifact can only be displayed to Thallus' shame (11). What has been stolen from Catullus is an aesthetic object with "graphic" associations;[45] in claiming it back, Catullus makes of the very body of the thief a display of his own writing by robbing Thallus of his language. The napkin of poem 12, the perfume of poem 13, and the *catagraphi* of poem 25 (with their parodic substitute, Thallus' body) are all objects implicated in a struggle for control and ownership, whether through the relation of thief to victim, joker to dupe, or host to guest. In each case, Catullus redefines the ground of the relationship in the process of constituting these objects as aesthetic, giving them an aura that derives from their stubborn resistance to appropriation. The situations in these poems figure the inherently aggressive relation toward language's other potential users on the part of the poet who claims the power to manipulate language and to make of it an aesthetic object.

Catullus' greeting of Ameana, the girlfriend of Mamurra whom the province (Gallia Cisalpina) unaccountably considers a rival to Lesbia, is another case of the poet taking back something that has been stolen, in this case the very primacy of Lesbia:

> Salve, nec minimo puella naso
> nec bello pede nec nigris ocellis
> nec longis digitis nec ore sicco
> nec sane nimis elegante lingua,
> decoctoris amica Formiani.
> ten provincia narrat esse bellum?
> tecum Lesbia nostra comparatur?
> o saeclum insapiens et infacetum! (c.43)

> Hail, girl with a nose none too neat,
> nor a pretty foot, nor jet-black eyes,
> nor tapering fingers, nor a dry mouth,
> nor indeed too elegant a tongue,

girlfriend of the Formian bankrupt.
Does the province call you beautiful?
Is our Lesbia compared to you?
O tasteless, witless age!

Taking the opinion of the province at face value, the poem lists the attributes that this paragon of beauty must possess, but only to find each of them lacking.[46] What might have been a succession of insults becomes instead a withholding of the standard litany of praise. But a mere list of attractive attributes cannot account for the allure that transcends its components, or for the piquancy (sal) that attracts the truly sophisticated (compare c.86); those intangibles are lacking in Ameana as surely as the tangibles that are listed. It is the sly tone of Catullus' greeting, a wry puzzlement resisting the pull of the standard litany of beauty, that itself provides the something else which is lacking from the list of what Ameana lacks. As Catullus cancels out each attribute that would warrant the province's opinion of Ameana, he mimics the squandering of the spendthrift Mamurra, Ameana's lover. But this squandering (decoctio) becomes in Catullus' mouth a decoction of elegance, and in the process he himself exemplifies the elegant tongue that Ameana lacks.[47]

## Making Language Perform

The urbanity that I have been describing is competitive, establishing the position of the urbane speaker against others, even, in the case of Fabullus, those who have been invited into the poet's world. As a *je ne sais quoi* that is defined as much by those who lack it as by those who possess it, *urbanitas* is often displayed in the context of a struggle for power. In poem 25, we have heard Catullus adopt the tone of another as part of a claim to mastery; in poem 4, the speaker purports to mediate the autobiography of a yacht, reporting its speech in a tone that is best described as patronizing and at the same time the height of urbanity. Clearly, there can be no struggle for power transpiring between the yacht and the speaker of this poem, but it is the amused and playful sovreignty of the speaker in relation to the speech he reports that distinguishes the tone of the poem:

Phaselus ille, quem videtis, hospites,
    ait fuisse navium celerrimus,

neque ullius natantis impetum trabis
nequisse praeterire, sive palmulis
opus foret volare sive linteo.
et hoc negat minacis Hadriatici
negare litus insulasve Cyclades
Rhodumque nobilem horridamque Thraciam
Propontida trucemve Ponticum sinum,
ubi iste post phaselus antea fuit
comata silva; nam Cytorio in iugo
loquente saepe sibilum edidit coma. (1–12)

That yacht, which you are looking at, my friends,
says that it was the fastest of ships,
and that the speed of no "swimming timber"
could surpass it, whether oars
were the medium of its flight or sails.
And it denies that the threatening Adriatic
shore denies this or the Cyclades,
or noble Rhodes, or bristling Thrace,
or Propontis, or the vicious Pontic Bay,
where that soon-to-be-yacht was once
a long-haired wood; for on Mount Cytorus
its speaking hair would often whisper.

The double negatives (3–4, 6–7) and the epicisms (impetum trabis, 3) have a somewhat pompous and comic effect, but whose speech do they reflect? Wilamowitz heard the patter of a professional cicerone in the verse,[48] but I think the anonymous poet of *Catalepton* 10 understood something important about the social dimensions of the poem when he wrote his parody.[49] In that parody, the yacht is replaced by a mule driver who is displayed at the end of the poem sitting in his retirement on a magistrate's curule chair. The parody is a satire mocking the pretensions of an upstart who has attained high office and whose past looks ridiculous in the trappings of high culture; displaying the muleteer to the guests, the speaker also displays his own superiority in the exquisite fit between the Catullan original and the sordid details of the muleteer's career. The effect of the reported speech is familiar to anyone who has heard some wit report what was said by a social inferior by translating the latter's vulgarisms into the language of high culture.[50] In Catullus' poem, the social dynamics are not explicit, but the play with literary circumlocution depends on a gap between the (supposed) speaker of the direct speech and the speaker who reports it.

It has been argued that the yacht is characterized as the running slave so popular in comedy:[51]

et inde tot per impotentia freta
erum tulisse, laeva sive dextera
vocaret aura, sive utrumque Iuppiter
simul secundus incidisset in pedem. (18–21)

and thence through many violent seas
it bore its master, whether the wind
came from the left or right, or whether Jove
fell following on both the sheets [lit., "feet"] at once.

If the running slave is behind these lines, then the effect is comic, and the relation of the speaker to the yacht for which he speaks one of condescending amusement, even victimization. The urbanity of the poem lies in its indirection, in the lightness with which the speaker guides garrulity into amusing channels much as adults sometimes incorporate the babbling of a child, or the antics of a dog, into some scenario that it is incapable of understanding.[52] Catullus gives us only half of the scene; whatever it is that is being glossed, rephrased, commented on, and reported has to be imagined by the reader, so that the elegance of the language is always the elegance with which the speaker handles the speech of an inferior. The garrulous boasting of the yacht falls into a perfect circle that takes us from the present back to its origin in a wood and then forward again to its present retirement, and this elegance of structure is like the itinerary that the clever sailor realizes out of the random bluster of the wind. Sailing is in fact the perfect metaphor for the skillful harnessing of the speech of another by the poem's speaker.[53]

The classic interpretations of poem 4 have downplayed the gap between the positions of speaker and yacht. Copley 1958 makes of the poem a parable of the New Criticism. Reacting against the treatment of this poem as a set of problems about the yacht (real or not? how big? whose? etc.), about its precise itinerary and the possible autobiographical elements of the poem, Copley (12–13) urges us to focus on the world of the poem itself:

[Catullus'] *phaselus* is very much alive, and in a curious and subtle way, her life is made more real to the reader by the poet's device of having her tell her story not in person—but through a narrator, thus suggesting that her language was not one to be heard and understood by everyone but only by those who had lived on and with her.

In Copley's hands the intermediary speaker becomes the lover who speaks the "poetry" of his mistress, and this privileged, intimate, and respectful relationship becomes the model for our own hearing of the poem, which must eschew speculations about the realities behind the poem that bedeviled earlier scholarship:

It is for this [the "poetry" of the ship] that [Catullus] created the world of his poem; and only if we accept that world, seeing and hearing exactly what the poet's words require us to see and hear, adding nothing to it, inferring nothing from it, will we grasp the meaning of the poem and know its delights. (13)

Copley doesn't seem to hear the garrulity that, according to Wilamowitz, interposes itself between sightseers and sight, still less the patronizing amusement with which the yacht's story is "reported." For Copley, the intermediary who makes available to us the poetry of the ship is transparent, or perhaps I should say inaudible.

After Copley's New Critical warnings, the biographical interpretation of poem 4 was reintroduced in more respectable terms by Putnam 1962, who read the poem, together with poems 31 and 46, as an indirect expression of Catullus' own feelings on returning to his home from service in Bithynia. According to Putnam, Catullus has created a speaking yacht in order to symbolize "the speed of desire" (14), and the guests "suspend disbelief—in order to become willingly involved in the strength of the poet's emotion" (14). Again, the relationship between poet (or speaker) and yacht, which is the essence of this interpretation, is direct: the yacht "*is* [its master's] emotion" and the *hospites* (guests) are to visualize the yacht "not as the poet's pawn but as the possessor, through the poet, of a life all its own" (14). But if the *hospites* are expected to suspend their disbelief in the speaking yacht, then the witty and parenthetical use of the poetic cliché of whispering foliage in lines 11 and 12 will be lost on them. The interpretations of Putnam and Copley are parables of reading that depend on the yacht being an object of absorption: the poet speaks the poetry that he has absorbed from the yacht and that we, in turn, activate by our exclusive absorption in the world of the poem (Copley); or, the yacht absorbs the emotion and desire of the master, so that we can become absorbed in that emotion as we suspend our disbelief in the yacht's power of speech (Putnam). For Putnam and Copley, the fusion of speaker and yacht, and the generous self-effacement that makes it possible for one to be projected onto the other, are a function of the symbolic nature of poetry, which demands an absorbed reader. These readings elide the difference between speaker and yacht, and therefore the difference *within* the language of this poem.

The poem ends with a vocative that is set, paradoxically, into the reported speech of the yacht:

> nunc recondita
> senet quiete seque dedicat tibi,
> Gemelle Castor et gemelle Castoris. (25–27)

> now it's growing old
> in quiet retirement and it dedicates itself
> to you, twin Castor, and to Castor's twin.

In the final line, the doubling of speakers is accompanied by a play on twinness, sameness in difference, and a singular (*tibi*, not *vobis*) plurality. By using the second person, the speaker performs the speech act that he reports, and this doubling coincides with a periphrasis for the name Pollux ("Castor's twin") that emphasizes the fact that language allows the same thing to be said in different ways. At the beginning of the poem, our attention is drawn to two double negatives that also associate the redundancy of language—the fact that a positive can be expressed by a double negative—with a form of linguistic doubling, namely, indirect speech:

> neque ullius natantis impetum trabis
> nequisse praeterire, sive palmulis
> opus foret volare sive linteo.
> et hoc negat minacis Hadriatici
> negare litus . . . (3–7)

> and that the speed of no "swimming timber"
> could surpass it, whether oars
> were the medium of its flight or sails.
> And it denies that the threatening Adriatic
> shore denies this . . .

Because the reported speech is not actually the speech of either yacht or speaker, language is held at arm's length, so to speak, and "performs." But what enables this performance is the patronizing relation of one speaker to another.

As most commentators have noted, the places that the yacht cites to verify its boast are the stops on the journey from Bithynia to Italy in reverse sequence (6–12), ending with the *Pro*pontis and the Pontus. What is not usually remarked is that this reversed geographical sequence is followed by the reversed temporal sequence that takes us from the "after" of the yacht as human artifact to the "before" of the longhaired tree. This in turn is followed by a logical "before" in the form of *nam* (for), which introduces the whispering foliage. One could say that the propulsion carrying us from one point to the next in this passage is neither sail nor oar but metaphor, creating a sequence of different categories of priority (Pro-pontis, antea, nam) leading to the central metaphor that endows the yacht with the power to speak. At this point in the poem (10–12), the yacht's speech is no longer being reported, and its nature as a human artifact, both poetic (in the metaphor of whispering foliage) and vehicular, becomes the focus. The yacht is, pace Putnam, very much the pawn of the poet, and, as a product of the human power to transform nature into the servant of human purposes, it is endowed with speech in order to facilitate a certain game with language.

To whom do we attribute the linguistic play in the following lines?

>     ultima ex origine
> tuo stetisse dicit in cacumine,
> tuo imbuisse palmulas in aequore
> et inde tot per impotentia freta
> erum tulisse, (15–19)

>     from its first origin
> it says it stood upon your peak,
> and dipped its palms into your sea
> and thence through many violent seas
> it bore its master,

*Imbuisse* (dipped) and *palmulas* (palms) may both be taken literally or metaphorically: the yacht "dips its palms" or "initiates its oars" in the sea. Because of the relation between speaker and yacht, wordplay is here associated with the superior knowledge of one speaker to that of another: the yacht says more than it knows, allowing the speaker to wink at us as he reports what it says.

If we think of the relation between speaker and yacht in this poem as facilitating a particular kind of detached urbanity of speech, we can see the similarity between this poem and Catullus' attack on Thallus, in which the poet holds Thallus' own language in suspension, both putting it in quotation marks and speaking it himself. In both cases the urbanity of the speaker has to do with the easy power with which he treats the (putative) speech of the other, reminding us of Horace's characterization of the *urbanus*:

>                    urbani, parcentis viribus atque
> extenuantis eas consulto. (*Serm.* 1.10.13-14)
>
>                    the urbane man, sparing his strength
> and contracting it on purpose.

Poem 4 is the sound of the urbane speaker rationing his strength, a sound that can best be heard against another speaker.

In Chapter 2, we saw how the overlap between Roman aesthetic language and the language of social or sexual attractiveness allows Catullus to dramatize dimensions of the poetic act or relation that might otherwise be invisible; this overlap helps us to understand the position of the poet within the larger society of speakers and the continuity between the relations established by the poem and those that pertain in other activities. Similarly, in this chapter, we have seen that we can understand much about the society created by a poem if we think in terms of activities like stealing, reclaiming, inviting, and reporting, activities around which Catullus' performance has revolved in these poems.

## Play and Frustration

Throughout this chapter, I have been citing examples of the tendency in modern Catullan criticism to search for depth beneath the urbane surface of the poems. Poem 50 has been a crucial poem for this project because it has been read as a narrative of the same transformation of superficial urbanity into profound seriousness that criticism has itself performed on Catullus:[54]

> Hesterno, Licini, die otiosi
> multum lusimus in meis tabellis,
> ut convenerat esse delicatos:
> scribens versiculos uterque nostrum
> ludebat numero modo hoc modo illoc,
> reddens mutua per iocum atque vinum.
> atque illinc abii tuo lepore
> incensus, Licini, facetiisque,
> ut nec me miserum cibus iuvaret
> nec somnus tegeret quiete ocellos,
> sed toto indomitus furore lecto
> versarer, cupiens videre lucem,
> ut tecum loquerer simulque ut essem.

at defessa labore membra postquam
semimortua lectulo iacebant,
hoc iucunde, tibi poema feci,
ex quo perspiceres meum dolorem.
nunc audax cave sis, precesque nostras,
oramus, cave despuas, ocelle,
ne poenas Nemesis reposcat a te.
est vemens dea: laedere hanc caveto.

Yesterday, Licinius, at our ease
we played a lot in my notebooks,
as we had agreed to be frivolous:
playing in this meter, then in that,
swapping verses, joking, drinking.
And I left you, Licinius, inflamed
with your charm and witticisms,
so that I could not eat (poor me!)
but tossed all over the bed, my passion
uncontrolled, longing to see the light of day,
so that I could speak and be with you.
But when my limbs, worn out with toil
were lying on the bed, half-dead,
I made this poem for you, my friend,
that you might understand my suffering.
Now see you don't get bold, I beg you,
dear, not to reject my prayers
lest Nemesis exact a penalty from you.
She's an imperious goddess, don't provoke her!

The structure of the poem has been taken to distinguish two levels of poetic activity: on the one hand, the play of the *delicati* producing their "little verses," and on the other the solitary pain of the "author" Catullus from which "this poem" (16) emerges. Skinner interprets the poem as a description of the creative process in which emotion recollected in tranquillity transforms the ephemeral into the enduring:

It is a process which begins ... in the raffish, bohemian atmosphere of the *otiosi* and the free-wheeling activity of the *ludus poeticus*. As the operation continues, however, the author is compelled to withdraw within himself and undergo no little effort in order to transform the afternoon's ephemeral *versiculi* into an enduring *poema* which will stand as the public profession of his sensibility.[55]

Skinner's narrative is the story of the poetic process, but it contains another story about the reader's access to the circle of the *urbani*: initially excluded from the "free-wheeling" activity of the poetic game, the reader finally gains access to the fruition of that game in the "enduring *poema*" that makes a public profession of the poet's sensibility; the *versiculi* (little verses) are not only ephemeral, they are also inaccessible. An implicit hierarchy of *poema* and *versiculi* gives the audience that has witnessed Catullus' distress the privileged feeling of having access to what Quinn calls the "point at which playing with verse ceased to be just an amusing pastime."[56] Paradoxically, we would gain entrance to the poem precisely where the poet "withdraw[s] within himself," because that is when the poet waxes both confessional and professional. But what the poet confesses is frustration, a frustration that dovetails nicely with that of the reader who has been denied access to the *versiculi* that cause the excitement. What he professes is a desire (preces nostras, 18), but a desire that is never specified. We can no more articulate the "public profession" that Catullus is making than Catullus can articulate what he wants of Calvus.

What is the cause of Catullus' frustration? Away from Calvus and the exchange of verses, he is plagued by an excess of energy that has nowhere to go: the turning of the *versiculi* (from *vertor*, "I turn") swapped by the poets becomes the insomniac twisting of Catullus in his bed (versarer, 11). But when the friends were together the back and forth in which their agreement found its expression was ambiguous, both erotic and artistic. Because of the ambiguity of the word *delicatus*, there is something of a paradox in the expression "as we had agreed to be *delicati*" (3), but that is the point: the agreement of the friends could manifest itself only in a game. Away from the game, Catullus finds himself "inflamed" (incensus, 7) by Calvus' *lepor*, and plagued by a desire to which he can give no name, by an ambiguity that was both generated and absorbed by the responsive play. Separated from the responsive game that had inflamed him, the confessional Catullus longs to be with Calvus again (simulque ut essem, 13) and begs him not to spurn his entreaties (18). But was he ever *with* Calvus? The emphasis in the description of their day together is on alternation and responsiveness, anything but simultaneity. Catullus' desire mirrors that of the interpreter, for it is the desire to stop the play and fix its meaning, to say what lies beneath it. But can the object of this desire be articulated? Only Calvus' response could satisfy our curiosity about Catullus' entreaties, and that response, which might in any case simply continue the ambiguous game of the *delicati*, and so displace Catullus' desire, is closed to us. So the *poema* through which the ephemeral *versiculi* of the friends are supposed to be translated into something more lasting and public contains within it the request that returns it to the back and forth of the poetic game; we know that a tacit agreement is in place because we have been excluded, and, like Fabullus in poem 13, we are invited only to be reminded that all we can have is the flavor of what we can't have.

In the poems I have cited in this chapter, Catullus dramatizes the fact that poetry takes language back from other users (real or potential), as William Carlos Williams reminds us in "This is Just to Say." I have been arguing that the stylistic quality that goes under the general rubric of *urbanitas* cannot be detached from the strategies by which it is claimed, that it is more like a game than a substance. In poem 50, Catullus' own frustration and desire, in the suspension of the game between the two poets, mimics the feelings of the reader who wants to ask something of the urbane text that will elicit a pronouncement. The appropriation of the reader's own questioning of *lepor*, and the insertion of that questioning into the game of the *delicati*, is the ultimate theft of language.

CHAPTER 5

# The Wronged Lover and the Poet's Isolation

The urbane poet, as we have seen, engages in strategies of exclusion and appropriation to dramatize his privileged position. He performs his special relation to language and his control of discourse through a series of aggressive maneuvers. But this privileged position isolates the poet from the reciprocal structures of linguistic intercourse. Further, reciting before an audience, the poet adopts a persona in which, for the time of the performance, he is trapped. For the duration of his performance the reciting poet falls out of circulation and seems to exist in another world, separated from the audience before him.

In this chapter, I read the situations of the lover as dramatizations of the situations of the poet. A special group of Catullus' Lesbia poems, written in the elegiac meter, consists largely of accusations against Lesbia for betraying her lover, accompanied by protestations of the poet's fruitless fidelity to an unreciprocated love from which he is unable to tear himself away. I focus particularly on the poems in which Catullus parades his inability to break off an unreciprocated love, and those in which he expresses doubts about the sincerity of Lesbia's amorous protestations. The former, I argue, engage the drama of the performing poet's isolation and immobility before his audience: the special status of the isolated performer who must sustain the illusion of his persona before an audience is reflected by that of the lover trapped in an unreciprocated love. In the latter poems, the doubts expressed about Lesbia's sincerity engage the drama of the separation of poetic speech from what is spoken outside the poem.

# THE WRONGED LOVER AND THE POET'S ISOLATION

In previous chapters, I describe the Roman social attitudes that underly various kinds of language that Catullus uses; in this case, I examine the norms implied by the language of aristocratic obligation that Catullus summons to describe his relationship with Lesbia, norms against which the peculiar position of the lover-poet is measured. The language of aristocratic obligation assumes a society of equals whose alliances are capable of constant realignment, and this contrasts radically with the isolated world of Catullus' unequal relationship with Lesbia. By removing this language to a new and perversely inappropriate context, Catullus draws attention to the peculiar status of language in a poem that is recited before a silent audience of people who share, but do not exchange, that language.

As throughout, I am also concerned here with the construction and canonization of the author Catullus by modern scholarship, and particularly with the relation of the reader-scholar to the betrayed lover.

## Lesbia and Catullus: Surface and Depth

Catullus the wronged lover is a self-righteous figure who foreshadows by a few years the Caesar who could cite his wounded *dignitas* (standing, esteem) as a pretext for crossing the Rubicon.[1] Unlike Caesar, Catullus hesitated, repeatedly and rhetorically, to break with the offending party, and this is a large part of the reason why his protestations of violated innocence have received a better hearing than have Caesar's.[2] Like Caesar, Catullus the self-righteous adulterer demands to be treated as a special case, and that is precisely what the reader of lyric poetry is itching to do. The fact that Catullus' accusations, suspicions, and protestations engage aspects of the generic, that they give a narrative or dramatic content to the privileged position of the lyric poet, may explain why the self-righteous Catullus has been treated with such sympathy and reverence.

The third part of the Catullan collection (cc.69–116), in elegiac metre, contains a number of poems parading Catullus' doubts about Lesbia, of which this is one:

iucundum, mea vita, mihi proponis amorem
    hunc nostrum inter nos perpetuumque fore.
di magni, facite ut vere promittere possit

>           atque id sincere dicat et ex animo,
> ut liceat nobis tota perducere vita
>           aeternum hoc sanctae foedus amicitiae. (c.109)

> A delightful love, my life, you offer me,
>           this one we have, you say, will be eternal.
> Great gods, grant that she may be able to promise truly
>           and to say it sincerely and from her heart,
> so that we can live out through our whole life
>           this eternal treaty of holy love.

For me this poem invokes the kind of embarrassed silence that follows a joke that has fallen flat. Like the uproarious laughter of the joketeller at his own wit, the earnest ecstasy of the last couplet seems out of proportion to its occasion. By the end of the poem, the promising word *iucundum* (delightful) has been drained of all its promise of geniality,[3] the impulse of the moment has bogged down into a Roman contract, and the passionate exclamation "my life" fades into a lifetime of contractual obligation. After exclaiming that Lesbia offers him a "delightful love" (iucundum . . . proponis amorem), Catullus turns this offer into a promise of perpetuity by an adroit change of construction (proponis . . . fore), and then frets over whether she means it. One wonders what has happened to the Catullus who castigated himself for being a drag (c.8.1, compare c.68.137) and who insulted Varus' girlfriend for not allowing him to speak "offhandedly" (c.10.33–34). But not everybody reacts to this poem in the same way, and, for the most part, its readers have been moved by the spectacle of a Roman lover whose love transcends the understanding of his beloved, and who is forced to summon up the most powerful politico-religious terminology in order to express an ideal for which his society has no proper terms.[4] Furthermore, far from judging the persona of this poem by the urbane standard of the polymetrics (cc.1–60), critics tend to use the poem to rescue the poet of the polymetrics from the charge of superficiality. As Copley 1949 puts it:

> It is only when he began to perceive that Lesbia was not viewing their love in the same way as he was that there began for him the long struggle, never successfully concluded, to give adequate expression to his feelings, to explain the nature of the non-physical side of his love—the very side that had made it significant and worthwhile to him.[5]

Catullus' doubting of Lesbia allows Copley to infer the depth of serious feeling that is latent beneath the lighter polymetrics.

*Iucundus* in poem 109 is evidently a fashionable neoteric word:[6] "the sort of word that Lesbia would use," Lyne comments, but also the sort of word that Catullus himself used in poems outside this group.[7] By freighting this word and the impetuous exclamation of the first line with expectations of sincerity and faithfulness, and casting doubt on the Lesbia who speaks it, Catullus allows us to attribute a latent seriousness to the polymetric love poetry. The first line is integrated awkwardly with the second, and this awkwardness, Copley might say, is the sound of Catullus realizing that Lesbia does not view their love in the same way as he does. But different ears hear different things. In the change of construction that turns the offer of a delightful love into a promise of its perpetuity, we can also hear the speaker finding in Lesbia's words what he wants to find, diverting one kind of statement into another. It is the first reading that has become canonical, and with it comes Copley's narrative of a deepening awareness of love on Catullus' part, an awareness that moves, precipitated by Lesbia's infidelity, into emotional, moral, and conceptual territory into which Lesbia cannot follow him. The function of this narrative is to legitimate the triviality of the polymetrics as merely a stage that Catullus passes through, a stage of a subjectivity that has depths as yet unplumbed. It is therefore safe for the reader to be seduced by the polymetrics, for an *iucundum* that has growth potential can be distinguished from one that doesn't: there comes a point when the word, and the carefree love it connotes, splits into a surface (what Lesbia says) and a depth (what Catullus hears).

## The Language of Aristocratic Obligation

The words to which Catullus commits himself at the end of poem 109 could not be more weighty. They are words that conjure up that most Roman quality of *fides* (trustworthiness). In the elegiac love poems, Catullus refers to his relationship with Lesbia as a *foedus* (compact, cc.76.3, 87.3, 109.6) and an *amicitia* (friendship, c.109.6); he protests his own *pietas* (dutifulness, c.76.2,26), *fides* (c.87.3), and *officium* (service, c.75.2); he compares his love for Lesbia to that of a father for his sons and sons-in-law (c.72.4), and, finally, he accuses Lesbia of *iniuria* (wrong, c.72.7) and of being *ingratus* (ungrateful, c.76.6). This language is far removed from that of the polymetrics, and it is used not only in the Lesbia elegiacs but also in the elegiac epigrams addressed to men who have betrayed Catullus, or threaten to betray him.[8] The stunned repetition and circularity in these poems seems to be conjuring with a basic vocabulary that works almost magically, as a charm in whose repetition the speaker trusts.

What kind of language is this? David Ross argued vigorously that only one sphere of Roman life was common to all of these words, namely, the sphere of party politics and political alliance.[9] From this he concluded that the love poems of the elegiacs are as much about the general disintegration of political and social life as they are about a love affair. Marilyn Skinner's work on Catullus' political attitudes (1979a, 1979b, 1982, 1991) supports this connection between the failure of his relationship with Lesbia and the general decay of the "mos maiorum" (ancestral tradition) that manifested itself most spectacularly in the chaos of the political world of the late Republic. But Ross's claim that the language of the Lesbia elegiacs is specifically the language of political alliance has been widely challenged. Probably, it would be more accurate to call this, with Lyne (1980, 25–26), the language of "aristocratic obligation," a language governing the dealings of the Roman aristocracy with each other in general, dealings that include several specific spheres, among them political alliance and marriage.[10] Contractual reliability and reciprocity were of course the key concerns of all of these dealings, and they are reflected in the language.

In a survey of Catullus that rejects Ross's conclusions, Schmidt 1985 argues that the polymetric and elegiac love poems represent the sensual and ethical sides of love respectively. Schmidt (124–27) restates the theory, attacked by Ross, that in the elegiac poems Catullus is casting his relationship with Lesbia in terms of a marriage.[11] Lesbia's betrayal has the status of adultery, then, and Catullus mobilizes the language of aristocratic obligation to express his disappointment. The irony of a self-confessed adulterer demanding marital fidelity of his mistress seems not to have struck Schmidt; addressing this irony, Rubino 1975 argues that Catullus is caught in a schizophrenic "double bind," finding himself forced to invoke the very values that he has rejected and to expect of the woman a fidelity that would have prevented the relationship from coming about in the first place.[12] It is a testimony to the power of the authorial position and to the patriarchal traditions of the discipline of the Classics that the derangement of Catullus' ethical world is so seldom the subject of comment; even Ovid (*Tr.* 2.427–30) remarked on the fact that Catullus "confessed his own adultery" by telling us of his other amours.

When it comes to explaining the strange application of the language of aristocratic obligation to an adulterous affair, scholars have often taken the line that Catullus is prophetic rather than deranged. Ross has Catullus inveighing against the corruption of public life through the *metaphor* of his relationship with Lesbia; others argue that the poet is struggling with the deficiencies of his society's conceptual world or revaluing its ethical language. According to Lyne 1980, and here he follows Copley 1949, Catullus conceived of a "whole love," combining elements of various kinds of relationship recognized in the Rome of his time, which would rectify his society's compartmentalization of heterosexual love (18). Catullus wanted both the permanence of marriage and the romance provided by the courtesans of the demimonde (19). He uses the language of aristocratic obligation because, although it lacked a vocabulary for profound commitment in love, Roman culture did have a language and code of social commitment. This unorthodox application of a specific vocabulary, then, aims to speak what cannot yet be spoken. Minyard 1985, in contrast, argues that Catullus was trying to shift the sphere of applicability of his society's most powerful moral language from public to private life. Seeing that the inherited system of values and the public world in which it was exercised was corrupt, Catullus stripped traditional language of its civic reference and made it reflect the values of "the interior life of feeling and personal relations" (29). This Catullus is engaged in a transvaluation of his society's values.

The interpretations of Minyard, Lyne, and Ross have the virtue of explaining the effect, or intention, of Catullus' *mis*application of the language of aristocratic obligation to sexual love. But this language is deployed with a certain rhetoric and in certain kinds of speech acts, and the interpretation of Catullus' use of a particular vocabulary must account for more than just the presence of a particular terminology. These poems are striking not only for their language but also for their style: many of them can reasonably be called epigrams, and they fully exploit the capacity of the elegiac couplet for symmetry and antithesis. They are often repetitive and circular in form and sometimes, as in the case of poem 76, distinctly awkward in rhythm. What are they doing? According to Lyne, they are analyzing: "The typical Lesbia epigram is therefore *analytical*, endeavoring to isolate what it was that was in the lovers' grasp, what it was that went wrong, what were the feelings that were in consequence generated" (22, emphasis Lyne's). Commager 1965, whose interpretation of Catullus' love poems to Lesbia is modeled on Eliot's dictum that poetry is "an escape from emotion," understands the "strict oppositions" of the epigrams as an attempt on Catullus' part not only "to define certain elusive emotional conditions, but also to control them" (105).[13] But before these poems analyze or control Catullus' feelings, they accuse Lesbia and exonerate the poet, who constantly cites his own virtue with righteous indignation. Catullus appeals to the language of aristocratic obligation, citing his *fides* and Lesbia's *iniuria* in the same way as Caesar appeals to his own *dignitas* and cites Pompey's failure to reciprocate his support of the latter's *dignitas* (*Bellum Civile* 1.7). The difference, of course, is that Caesar is haranguing his troops prior to taking what he claims is the justifiable action of crossing the Rubicon, whereas Catullus can find no action to take because his relationship with Lesbia does not exist in the sphere of activity that is governed by the language of aristocratic obligation. To use this language in its proper contexts is to appeal to a community of equals that recognizes a certain ethical system, witnesses obligations and wrongs, and recognizes the justifiability of certain responses. What is striking about Catullus' use of the language of aristocratic obligation is that it is spoken in a void: the rhetorical gesture has no ramifications because it does not take place, even fictionally, within the shifting network of obligations and reciprocities within which it would have efficacy. Lesbia is irreplaceable and Catullus has nowhere to turn, nor can his sense of wrong be converted into any kind of credit within a society of relations of which his relation to Lesbia is part. So Catullus' application of the language of aristocratic obligation to this irregular amatory attachment produces a rhetoric that has a peculiarly truncated quality.[14] The Catullan lover speaks with great intensity a language that has been deprived of the social context that would render it efficacious; the poet's language, too, acquires much of its energy from the fact that it is withdrawn from the usual social contexts. Catullus the poet uses the oddness of his lover's appeal to the language of aristocratic obligation to dramatize the peculiarity of the poet's relation to the language he shares, but doesn't exchange, with his audience. One might say that Catullus the lover has fallen out of circulation, and this would also be true of the poet who stands apart from his audience to recite his poems to it.

## The Poet on the Threshold

Standing before the audience and maintaining the persona that consigns him to a different level of reality, the poet is on a threshold. Normal discourse is suspended completely but can be resumed as easily as the persona is dropped. Similarly, the Catullan lover makes a spectacle of himself as long as the condition that isolates him pertains; if he should suddenly come to his senses, the pageant will dissolve. In two of Catullus' most famous poems (cc.8, 76), the lover parades his vain and anguished attempts to break away from an unreciprocated love, something his audience both does and doesn't want him to do.

The two poems provide an interesting contrast between the polymetric and the elegiac Lesbia poetry. Here is Catullus' version of the drama of the threshold in the polymetrics:

> Miser Catulle, desinas ineptire,
> et quod vides perisse perditum ducas.
> fulsere quondam candidi tibi soles,
> cum ventitabas quo puella ducebat
> amata nobis quantum amabitur nulla.
> ibi illa multa cum iocosa fiebant,
> quae tu volebas nec puella nolebat,
> fulsere vere candidi tibi soles.
> nunc iam illa non volt: tu quoque inpote[ns noli],
> nec quae fugit sectare, nec miser vive,
> sed obstinata mente perfer, obdura.
> vale, puella. iam Catullus obdurat,
> nec te requiret nec rogabit invitam.
> at tu dolebis, cum rogaberis nulla.
> scelesta, vae te, quae tibi manet vita?
> quis nunc te adibit? cui videberis bella?
> quem nunc amabis? cuius esse diceris?
> quem basiabis? cui labella mordebis?
> at tu, Catulle, destinatus obdura. (c.8)

> Unhappy Catullus, stop being a drag,
> give up as lost what you can see has died.
> The suns shone brightly for you once,
>   when you would go wherever the girl would lead,
> beloved of me as none will ever be.
> That time when all those games went on—
> you wanted them and she was not unwilling—
> O yes, the suns shone brightly for you then.
> Now she's unwilling: stop wanting her, you fool.
> Don't seek what she avoids, don't live in misery,
> but stubbornly hold out and stand your ground.
> Goodbye, girl. Now Catullus stands his ground.

> He won't demand you, won't solicit you against your will.
> But you'll be sorry when you're never asked.
> Poor wretch, what life remains for you?
> Who'll now approach you? Who'll say you're beautiful?
> Whom will you now love? Whose girlfriend will you be?
> Whom will you kiss? Whose lips will you bite?
> But you, Catullus, stubborn, hold your ground.

How do we hear this poem? It is surely hard for anyone now to agree with Tenney Frank that this is "one of the most naive utterances of love in all the range of poetry," or to say with Tyrrell that Catullus "pours forth in burning scazons, which ring like handfuls of earth thrown on a coffin, his agony."[15] Such comments show the intense sympathy with Catullus the wronged lover that has been the mode of much writing on this poet. At the other extreme are those who hear a parody of the comic lover whose futile attempts to extricate himself from his hopeless condition are a source of amusement for the audience.[16] The self-naming and generic self-identification as the unhappy lover (miser Catulle); the ironic comment, in the last line, on the weakening of resolve caused by the speaker's own rhetoric; the coincidence of the word *ineptire* (to be gauche) with the limping final foot from which the meter gets its name;[17] all this indicates a self-consciousness about the persona that is being introduced. And yet the elegant simplicity of the language and the deftness of the modulations and repetitions cast a pathos over the speech that prevent "unhappy Catullus" from being simply a figure of fun.

This prevention is the artfulness of the poem, an artfulness that is reflected in the critical rhetoric of Benedetto Croce:

> There is the beauty of Catullus' poetry. He translates a state of emotion that is still somewhat sketchy, almost childish without altering it, without modifying it, without embellishing it, without adding any complacency to its own naïveté, not even that complacency towards one's own sincerity that makes one want to tell everything, that complacency that makes poets whose taste is less sure and whose character is less firm botch this genre.[18]

Croce's description of naïveté as a systematic prevention of "effect" and of self-consciousness is a brilliant insight into the structural importance of prevention in the poem. The self-conscious, restraining, and ironic voice of the poem is never quite allowed to prevail over the reminiscing, fantasizing voice, which in turn is never quite allowed to become comically "inept." *Ineptia* is "stayed," that is, both prevented and extended, through the poem. What Croce describes is exemplified, for instance, by line 7,

> quae tu volebas nec puella nolebat
>
> you wanted them and she did not refuse.

The redundancy (nec . . . nolebat) might be a function of the reminiscing voice's awkward attempts to spin out its memories, but it might also be a sly insinuation of Lesbia's eagerness, or just the opposite, a rueful admission of her reluctance. All of these possibilities are held in suspension by the seesaw rhythm and the autonomous formality of the verse itself, which prevents us from reading the line in one way rather than the other. The effect of naturalness, of sincerity, of a speaker simply "being there," is a result of the staying of these possibilities.

The metrical form of the poem is itself given conflicting associations: the spondee at the end of the line that produces the characteristic limp of these limping iambics is introduced in the first line by the word *ineptire*, but at other points in the poem (11, 12, 19) the three consecutive long syllables fall on the word *obdura[t]* (stand your ground). Similarly, the emphatic self-exhortation to consider the matter closed (perditum ducas) at the end of line 2 is undermined at the end of line 4, where the same verb conveys Lesbia's pull (puella ducebat). There is a persistent interplay between the impulse to go on and the need to make an end; in fact, the fiction of the poem engages the formal problem of the potentially endless repetition of its stichic form. The speaker's attempt to break with Lesbia involves a struggle between the pull or "drag" of Lesbia's continued fascination (ducebat) and the summing up (ducas) to which he has committed himself. This struggle is articulated with poetry's own division between its commitment to closure and its potential to multiply itself endlessly in repeated lines. Our impression of the immediacy of this poem, which seems to be "spoken as it is being lived" (Veyne 1988, 34), is the experience of a divided impulse within poetry itself; the poem dramatizes the conflict between closure and continuity through the "staying" that produces what Croce calls the sincerity of Catullus.

Catullus' elegiac version of the same scenario could not be more different:

> Siqua recordanti benefacta priora voluptas
>     est homini, cum se cogitat esse pium,
> nec sanctam violasse fidem, nec foedere nullo

>     divum ad fallendos numine abusum homines,
> multa parat manent in longa aetate, Catulle,
>     ex hoc ingrato gaudia amore tibi.
> nam quaecumque homines bene cuiquam aut dicere possunt
>     aut facere, haec a te dictaque factaque sunt.
> omnia quae ingratae perierunt credita menti.
>     quare iam te cur amplius excrucies?
> quin tu animo offirmas atque istinc teque reducis,
>     et dis invitis desinis esse miser?
> difficile est longum subito deponere amorem,
>     difficile est, verum hoc qua lubet efficias:
> una salus haec est, hoc est tibi pervincendum,
>     hoc facias, sive id non pote sive pote.
> o di, si vestrum est misereri, aut si quibus umquam
>     extremam iam ipsa in morte tulistis opem,
> me miserum aspicite et, si vitam puriter egi,
>     eripite hanc pestem perniciemque mihi,
> quae mihi subrepens imos ut torpor in artus
>     expulit ex omni pectore laetitias.
> non iam illud quaero, contra me ut diligat illa,
>     aut, quod non potis est, esse pudica velit:
> ipse valere opto et taetrum hunc deponere morbum,
>     o di, reddite mi hoc pro pietate mea. (c.76)

If a man has any pleasure in remembering the good
    done in the past, in thinking himself dutiful,
having broken no sacred trust, nor in any bond
    abused the godhead to deceive a man,
then many pleasures in a long life lie in store for you,
    Catullus, from this thankless love of yours.
For whatever good a man can do or say to someone,
    that has been said and done by you.
All of which, entrusted to a thankless mind, has perished.
    So why continue to torment yourself?
Why don't you set your mind to it and tear yourself away?
    Stop suffering what the gods don't want you to.
It is hard to give up a long love all at once,
    it's hard, but do it any way you can.
This is your only hope, you must prevail in this,
    do this, whether you can or not.
O gods, if you know pity, or if ever you have brought
    the last aid to people on the brink of death,
look on me in my misery and, if I've lived without sin,
    take this plague and destruction away,
which creeping like paralysis up through my body

> has driven happiness entirely from my heart.
> I do not now ask that she love me in return,
>    or, since she can't, that she become chaste.
> I want to recover and shed this horrible disease.
>    O gods, give me this much for my piety.

The balance of forces and the balance of attitudes with which poem 8 ends is replaced here by a desperate demand for reciprocity from the gods. With its bare, awkward, and deeply Roman language, this poem situates its speaker quite differently in relation to its audience, which is, as it were, hailed from the other side of a chasm. Catullus' liminal state has become unbearable and seems to solicit a response from the audience before which the poet lingers, but this solicitation only emphasizes the convention that isolates persona from audience, rather like the peril of the movie hero whom the audience tries to warn of what lurks around the corner.

The energy that is generated by this situation has provoked a number of modern critics to provide the compensation that Catullus anticipates "in a long life" (in longa aetate, 5). Several of this poem's interpreters have responded to its solicitation by bestowing a blessing on its speaker from the perspective of a Christianity toward which they see Catullus blindly groping in his overwhelming but disappointed love. Few ancient poems have produced such extravagant reactions as Catullus 76, and few are more puzzling.[19]

For many critics, the Catullus of this poem "gets religion," as the poet John McAfee puts it.[20] Buechner ends his description of Catullus' "novel of love" with a ringing peroration on the poet's prophetic transformation of his love for Lesbia into belief in a higher power.[21] Granarolo steers the naturally Christian Catullus of this poem toward the revelation that eludes him:

> Gifted with a tender and passionate soul, but wounded by life and disappointed in his dearest affections, how could Catullus not have been seduced by the peaceful and gentle God who, far from terrorizing humans, wanted to transform their condition entirely and to push his love for them to the terrible, supreme sacrifice, the only means of regeneration?[22]

Marmorale 1957, whose thesis is that Catullus went through a conversion to Bacchic mysticism, reads poem 76 as a prayer for "purification" (80) in which Catullus glimpses, thanks to his initiation, a love that does not need reciprocation (c.76.23–24), a cosmic Eros to which a man turns when the desire to improve himself becomes irrepressible (225). But the most solemn benediction to the career of Catullus is that of Bignone 1945:

And, in fact, in the elegy in which he prays the gods to free him finally from the degrading slavery of this love, there rises, in the midst of the desert of despair, like a limpid stream from an inner source, a profound sense of religion, intimate, pure, sweet and melancholy, that makes us feel how the tempestuous passion has been purified in Catullus by the bath of tears, and how the open-minded, libertine poet has conquered, in the torment of anguish, the profundity and purity of faith in the divine.... Thus, in religious purity, finished the great, burning, tempestuous love of the life of Catullus (366–67).

Bignone, like Granarolo, reacts to the poem with a fantasy that brings the poem, and the life and love of Catullus, to a peaceful rest in the arms of God. But there is little in this poem to suggest the peace of mind Bignone and other critics describe, and in fact Bignone has supplied from poem 68 (57–62) the simile of the stream that refreshes the weary traveller. The Christian interpreter sees into the heart of Catullus from a perspective that was denied the poet himself, finding in other Catullan poems the position from which to answer the desperate cry of poem 76: the savior friend and the paradisal garden in poem 68 take on Christian connotations under the pressure of the desperate appeal to the gods in poem 76, an appeal that is treated as a prerequisite for the Christian revelation. Granarolo's Catullus, being still a pagan, has nowhere to turn but to the cruel deity who does terrorize humans, the Cybele of poem 63, who, far from sacrificing herself, demands of her followers that they castrate themselves. This connection with poem 63 gives a sinister implication to the final lines of poem 76, in which Catullus prays to have this "plague" torn from him. According to Granarolo, the answer to Catullus' cry lies in the problem itself, for he need only let himself be seduced *again*, but this time by the "peaceful and gentle God" whom he could scarcely have resisted.

These responses to the poem are not entirely gratuitous. Almost all commentators have remarked on the extreme stylistic awkwardness of a poem that is sometimes described as an artistic failure: Catullus, it is sometimes said, has not been able to take control of the struggle in which he is engaged; he seems to be speaking for his own benefit, summoning up words in the vain hope that with them will come, paradoxically, the willpower to stop.[23] No available rhetoric seems to avail. The urge to step in and clothe the naked Catullus in some other, more adequate language proves irresistible to some of his commentators. For Granarolo, the cadence of the Lord's Prayer, which is the future of the Latin that Catullus so desperately speaks, is required by the very restlessness of the poem's rhetoric.[24] For others, the afterlife is the only adequate referent for the "long life" (longa aetas, 5) in which Catullus imagines the pleasures of a clear conscience to be stored up.[25] And if this is not a convincing interpretation of the phrase, it is at least a plausible response to the sarcasm of the opening sentence, in which a substitute for the reciprocity lacking in human relationships is sought in the pleasures of memory. If the *benefacta* that Catullus cites are to receive any recompense, it would have to be in another world.

Granarolo and Bignone, who have seen as Lesbia couldn't the beauty of Catullus' soul, speak from the "long life" of Catullus' fame, a time-scale in which Catullus the author will find the joys that eluded the lover. The minds of the interpreters to whom Catullus' words are now entrusted will replace the thankless mind of Lesbia. To speak of this poem as "the most beautiful prayer to the gods from a suffering soul that antiquity has handed down to us"[26] is to respond to the way that it addresses itself to its audience, as from an abyss (antiquity?) from which it can only be rescued by some form of responsiveness. Pity (misereri, 17) is the province both of the gods and of the audience.[27]

The poem's audience finds its position defined in relation on the one hand to the thankless Lesbia and on the other to the powerful gods. There is a congruity between the lack of reciprocity in the lover's relationship with Lesbia and the performing poet's isolation from verbal intercourse with the audience before whom he speaks. Consigned to the position in which he says and does everything before a silent audience, the poet, like the lover, fears that all this may have been entrusted to an ungrateful mind (76.7–9). As poet he must look to the moment when he drops his mask and the audience either welcomes him back with their applause or leaves him looking foolish, which puts the audience in the position of the gods invoked by the lover in this poem.[28] Taking the position of the gods who are asked to rescue the lover from his hopeless obsession and restore him to circulation, the audience also becomes a substitute for the ungrateful Lesbia, rectifying the fact that Catullus' words had been entrusted to her in vain. The love scenario in this poem dramatizes with great urgency the threshold on which the performing poet stands, and it plays out the anxieties of the situation by distributing different aspects of the audience's position between the gods and Lesbia.

## The Rhetoric of Aristocratic Obligation

The distinctive language of the elegiac Lesbia poems—what is best called the language of aristocratic obligation—is featured at the beginning and end of poem 76, where Catullus looks toward forms of reciprocity that might compensate for the lack of reciprocity in his relations with Lesbia. Both the situation of the Catullan lover and that of the performing poet are characterized by isolation, and this is emphasized by Catullus' desperate use of the language of aristocratic obligation, whose deployment in an amatory context is so striking. In order to understand the effect of this language in its new context, we first need to have a sense of the kind of rhetoric with which the aristocratic relationship was usually accompanied, and I would like to reapproach one of Catullus' elegiac poems via a passage from a letter of Cicero.

There is something manipulative about the letter as Cicero created it. Isolated from the give and take of conversations, with its accidents and imprecisions, the written word forces the recipient to take the position assigned by the well-turned sentence and to take pleasure in the structure of a relationship that can no more be changed than can the rightness of the prose. Cicero's letters are masterpieces of this kind of manipulation, drawing a map, in their intricate but grandiose periods, of the landscape of the relation between sender and recipient, and ballasting the prose with the carefully weighted obligations and benefactions that stabilize the relationship. Here is an example:

Breve est quod me tibi praecipere meus incredibilis in te amor cogit: tanta est expectatio vel animi vel ingeni tui, ut ego te obsecrare obtestarique non dubitem sic ad nos confirmatus revertare ut, quam expectationem tui concitasti, hanc sustinere ac tueri possis; et quoniam meam tuorum erga me meritorum memoriam nulla umquam delebit oblivio, te rogo ut memineris, quantaecumque tibi accessiones fient et fortunae et dignitatis, eas te non potuisse consequi ni meis puer olim fidelissimis atque amantissimis consiliis paruisses. Qua re hoc animo in nos esse debebis ut aetas nostra iam ingravescens in amore atque in adulescentia tua conquiescat (*ad Fam.* 2.1).

The advice that my incredible love for you compels me to give is brief: so much is expected both of your spirit and your intelligence that I do not hesitate to beg and entreat you to return to us so strengthened that you can support and safeguard the expectation that you have awakened; and because forgetfulness will never eradicate my memory of your services to me, I ask you to remember that, whatever your improvement in fortune and standing, you could not have achieved this if you had not, as a boy, obeyed my most faithful and loving advice. So your attitude to me should be such that my already declining age should find rest in your love and your youth.

Such passages are ubiquitous in Cicero's letters. The prose unfolds as a set of variations on the relation between first and second persons, a configuration that recurs obsessively in an almost kaleidoscopic series. This is the essential sound of traditional Roman social and political life, and in one of the polymetrics, addressed to Cicero himself, Catullus strips it bare and deprives it of the usual reverberant acoustic:

> Disertissime Romuli nepotum,
> quot sunt quotque fuere, Marce Tulli,
> quotque post aliis erunt in annis,
> gratias tibi maximas Catullus
> agit pessimus omnium poeta,
> tanto pessimus omnium poeta,
> quanto tu optimus omnium patronus. (c.49)

> Most eloquent of Romulus' descendants
> both past and present, Marcus Tullius,
> and of the ones to come in later years,
> Catullus thanks you with the greatest
> thanks; he is the worst of poets,
> as much the worst of poets he
> as you are the greatest advocate of all.

The copiousness of Ciceronian prose is here reduced to the jaunty rhythms of the hendecasyllable. Even the names of the two principals echo each other in a metrical and assonantal jingle that parodies Cicero's resonant configurations (Mar*ce Tulle* and *Catullus* at the ends of lines 2 and 4). In this stripped-down context, the pat symmetry of the superlatives confirms that Catullus is the worst of poets by the very terms that make Cicero the best of orators, and yet this meeting of the media also judges the Ciceronian style (literary and social) in terms of the standards implied by the hendecasyllable and finds it wanting.[29]

The bareness of statement in poem 49, leaving a silence around itself, appears ironic, but what are we to make of the following?

> Nulla potest mulier tantum se dicere amatam
>   vere, quantum a me Lesbia amata mea est.
> nulla fides ullo fuit umquam foedere tanta,
>   quanta in amore tuo ex parte reperta mea est. (c.87)

> No woman can truly say that she was so
>   loved as Lesbia was loved by me.
> No faithfulness in any pact was ever such
>   as was found on my part in my love for you.

Again, the poem consists of the bare statement of a relation, the measurement of a proportion. In this case, though, the statement seems to realize the metrical form perfectly: the "as much" (quanta/quantum) of the pentameters reinforces the reader's sense of what remains of the couplet, so that the love that comes up to the measure of the past is identified with the fulfilling of the metrical form itself in the capping pentameter. The typical Ciceronian relationship is expressed with an obsessive balancing of first and second persons in a reciprocity of action;[30] Catullus' last line, with its chiming *tuo* and *mea*, produces an illusory version of this, illusory because all of the action comes from the same person ("amore tuo," refers not to Lesbia's love but to Catullus').[31] The awkward echo of the previous pentameter in the words "reperta mea est" dissolves the focus on the opposition of first and second persons, as do the elisions on the personal pronouns, frustrating the usual rhetoric of the compact.

Of this poem Fordyce says, "As in 76 and again in 109, Catullus turns, not in self-righteousness but in despair, to the obsessing thought of his own loyalty. In the change of person between l.2 and l.4 and the jingling repetition of *-ta meast* emotion seems to be struggling with the restriction of form." What I question here is that Catullus' loyalty is available as a thought to be turned to in abstraction from a rhetorical context in which, as a speaker, Catullus cites his loyalty. The uneasiness of the poem's form to which Fordyce refers needs to be heard in relation to the kind of rhetoric that is being frustrated. Catullus cites his loyalty because he feels that he has been wronged. What does the wronged Roman aristocrat do? The answer is simple: he gets revenge. Cicero's letters are full of stories and accusations of violated friendship; arrangements and rearrangements of alliance are constantly taking place to the music of *foedus* and *officium*. The betrayal of *officium* on the part of one person drives the wronged victim into the arms of the betrayer's enemies, or so the victim would have it. A good example of this is the letter of Cicero's urbane friend, and Clodia's sometime lover, Caelius, in which Caelius describes how he has been wronged by Appius (*ad Fam*. 7.12). Appius, who owes Caelius big favors, has been consorting with the latter's enemies and has declared a "hidden war" on him; Caelius suspects Appius of intending to renege on a debt, and in response he makes an alliance with Appius' colleague, even though that colleague is not only no friend of Caelius' but unfavorably inclined toward him on account of Caelius' friendship with Cicero.[32] Appius then suborns a certain Pola Servius to charge Caelius under the *lex Scantinia* (for sexual crime), and Caelius replies by charging Appius under the same law. Caelius' letter, which had begun with an apology to Cicero for his complaint against Appius, ends with a typical balancing of reciprocities:

A te peto ut meas iniurias proinde doleas ut me existimas et dolere et ulcisci tuas solere.

I ask of you that you grieve for injuries done to me as you judge that I am accustomed to grieve for and revenge injuries done to you.

All wrongs are embedded in a shifting system of alliances, and they involve not just individuals but networks in which action and reaction are constantly provoking each other. Cicero even describes his divorce of Terentia and remarriage with his ward Publilia as a rearrangement of alliances:

Quibus enim pro meis immortalibus beneficiis carissima mea salus et meae fortunae esse debebant, cum propter eorum scelus nihil mihi intra meos parietes tutum, nihil insidiis vacuum viderem, novarum me necessitudinum fidelitate contra veterum perfidiam muniendum putavi (*ad Fam.* 4.14.3).

As to those for whom, in return for my undying benefactions, my safety and my fortunes should have been most dear, when I saw that, because of their crime, nothing within my walls was safe, nothing free from threat, I thought that I should arm myself with the loyalty of new relations against the betrayal of the old.

To return to Catullus' citation of his own loyalty in poem 87, what strikes us here is the immobility of the aggrieved speaker and the paratactic isolation of the two audiences addressed. The repeated protestation of faithfulness, and the parataxis of the two audiences they imply (the general public and Lesbia), bespeak the isolation of this compact, which is not part of any network; what we hear in the symmetry and repetition of the couplets is the frustration of a voice that can only rearrange the same pieces and repeat them, a voice that has to address each audience afresh because there is no world that connects them. The jingle between lines 2 and 4 deprives the poem of any sequentiality or consequentiality. Catullus' use of the language of aristocratic obligation is perverse because he gets stuck in the pose of outrage, making an absolute of values that are essentially to do with the arrangement and rearrangement of alliance; he has fallen out of circulation.[33] Although Catullus the lover would probably not be expected, like Caelius, to appeal to his audience to mourn and avenge his wrongs as their own (in fact, it has!), or, like Cicero, to announce his intention of forming new alliances, his citation of loyalty gives the impression of being all dressed up with nowhere to go. The formal unease of the poem, the weak echo of one couplet by another, and the impotent parataxis all reflect a relationship that has no world: to use the language of aristocratic obligation about an affair with a married woman is to deprive oneself of the social context that makes sense of that language. Roman socio-political alliance was fluid, its fluidity presupposing a society of equals whose freedom and equality were expressed by the constant possibility of realignment. Relationships in this society of equals must be based on reciprocity, and the sanction that backs the expectation of reciprocity is the interchangeability of members of the group. All this, of course, is foreign to the world of Catullus' love. Using the language of aristocratic obligation to denounce Lesbia, and expressing his desperation through the truncation of the rhetoric that usually accompanies that language, Catullus fuses the situation of the lover with that of the performing poet, isolated in his performance from the world of his audience.

There are passages in Cicero's letters that look quite similar to some of Catullus' complaints, for instance this one from a letter to Pompey:

Ad me autem litteras quas misisti, quamquam exiguam significationem tuae erga me voluntatis habebant, tamen mihi scito iucundas fuisse; nulla enim re tam laetari soleo quam meorum officiorum conscientia; quibus si quando non mutue respondetur, apud me plus offici residere facillime patior. Illud non dubito, quin, si te mea summa erga te studia parum mihi adiunxerint, res publica nos inter nos conciliatura coniuncturaque sit (*ad Fam.* 5.7.2).

But although the letters that you sent me contain little sign of your goodwill toward me, I want you to know that they were welcome; for nothing tends to give me such joy as the knowledge of my own services; and if they are on occasion not reciprocated I am happy to let the preponderance of service remain with me. I do not doubt that if my utmost devotion toward you should fail to tie you to me, the Republic will reconcile us and unite us.

The pleasure that Cicero, faced with the unresponsiveness of Pompey, takes in the knowledge of his own *officia* (services) makes one think of the opening of poem 76, where Catullus summons up the prospect of the pleasure he will be able to take from the thought of his own *pietas*.

Both authors use financial metaphors, but here lies the difference between them, for Catullus complains that all his kindnesses to Lesbia, deposited in an ungrateful heart, have been lost (c.76.9), whereas Cicero declares that he happily puts up with the fact that the preponderance of *officium* is retained by him. *Officium* here is a currency that is retained *from* Pompey by Cicero; alternatively, Pompey's unresponsiveness has the effect of increasing the value of the *officium* banked with Cicero, who cites his retention of *officium* in an almost threatening way.[34] Cicero's final sentence is typical in its emphatic use of pronouns to nail into place a relationship between the two protagonists, but it reminds us also that the relationship is embedded in a larger context: as long as there is a Republic, Cicero's *officia* will retain their value and their claim on Pompey.

Catullus himself uses the word *officium* in poem 75, but here the careful balancing and symmetry produce a complete stasis:

> Huc est mens deducta tua mea, Lesbia, culpa
>   atque ita se officio perdidit ipsa suo,
> ut iam nec bene velle queat tibi, si optima fias,
>   nec desistere amare, omnia si facias. (c.75)

> My mind, Lesbia, has been led to such a state by your fault,
>   and has so destroyed itself by its own dutifulness,
> that it can no longer like you if you become perfect,
>   nor cease to love you if you stop at nothing.

Because the world of the poem is Catullus' mind, *officium* makes no claim on Lesbia and has no objective status within a social world. Where Cicero is happy to let the preponderance of *officium* rest with him because this gives him a claim on Pompey, the accumulation of *officium* in Catullus' mind seems to work like a poison. Though *culpa* (fault) and *officium* should be correlative (Cicero's "quibus si non mutue respondetur"), they have here become parallel, a rearrangement that is reflected on the formal level because the complementary components of the couplet, hexameter and pentameter, are parallel in sense (Huc ... atque ita ...). The concepts have been wrenched by this parallelism from the configuration in which they mutually define each other.

The first couplet of poem 75 breaks down into two parallel paradoxes, for Lesbia's *culpa* performs a *deductio*, or ceremonial accompaniment, and Catullus' mind is destroyed by its own *officium* (in the sense of "function").[35] Again, this parallelism obstructs a potential conjunction, for in the realm of aristocratic social life the dependent's ceremonial accompaniment of his *patronus* to the forum (known as *deductio*) is categorized as an *officium*.[36] The two facts described in the first couplet are never compounded in a single result as we are led to expect they will be (Huc . . . atque ita . . . ut . . .), for in the second couplet two kinds of feelings that in the language of aristocratic obligation should mutually imply each other (*benevolentia* and *amor*) are respectively prevented and maintained by Lesbia's *culpa* and Catullus' *officium*. A rhetoric of outrage that moves toward a conclusion is undermined by parallelisms and branchings (nec . . . si . . . nec . . . si . . .) that turn the poem into an elaborate pattern, a network of correspondence and antithesis that dissolves any sense of direction.[37] The significant point is that this pattern is assembled out of elements extracted from their original configurations in the language of aristocratic obligation, in which, for instance, *culpa* and *officium* are not two factors that affect a mind but correlative aspects of a relationship between two people as witnessed by a community of peers and potential replacements. Catullus' mental immobility is expressed as a solipsistic parody of the inescapable reciprocities of interpersonal relations in Cicero's letters. This reflects the fact that the poet acts his role before an audience bound together by the language they share, but do not exchange, with him. In lyric poetry, it is the isolation of the poet from the reciprocal contexts of linguistic interchange that allows the poetic texture to accumulate its density. The texture of this particular poem is assembled out of terms abstracted from their usual social configuration, so Catullus' amatory distress dramatizes the isolation of poetic speech by truncating and distorting the rhetorical gestures appropriate to the reciprocal contexts of aristocratic society.

But the significance of the Catullan lover's unorthodox mobilization of the language of aristocratic obligation is not restricted to the generic drama. In light of the increasing fragility of aristocratic political and social relations in the closing years of the Republic as Rome heads toward civil war, the Catullan lover's irrational dedication to an irreplaceable beloved is also a fantasy of absolute commitment possible only in some other world.

## Catullus and Lesbia: Inside and Outside the Poem

What of Lesbia? What is her role in the dramatizing of the poet's position through the fiction of the love affair? In poem 75, she is present only insofar as her *culpa* works on Catullus' mind, rendering it unable to move one way or the other, but in poem 109, which I cite at the beginning of this chapter, her words haunt the poem as its outside. Cited inside the poem, Lesbia's words are put into question by the intensity of the lyric context: "Great gods, make it that she can promise truly, / and say that sincerely and from the depths of her heart" (c.109.3-4). The prayer displays the sincerity of the speaker as it questions Lesbia's; it distinguishes the intensity of speech within the poem from the linguistic life outside the poem, which has been broken off to create this intensity.[38] Certainly, it is pointless and misguided to speculate, as some have done, about what Lesbia actually said and meant, since there may be no real situation, and certainly none that we could recover, to which the poem is referring.[39] Nevertheless, the poem does allude to what lies outside it, and defines its own discourse against the putative speech of another. Lesbia, fickle and false, plays a strategic role in these poems in relation to Catullus the poet, whose extravagances of language we are expected to accept just as we must suspect Lesbia's.

"I love and I hate": several of the elegiacs (cc.72, 75, 85, 92) are concerned with this paradox, which has become an emblem of the Catullan experience.[40] Knowledge of Lesbia's insincerity, we are told in poem 72, is the very thing that causes Catullus to experience his puzzling conflict of emotions:

> Dicebas quondam solum te nosse Catullum,
>   Lesbia, nec prae me velle tenere Iovem.
> Dilexi tum te non tantum ut vulgus amicam,
>   sed pater ut gnatos diligit et generos.
> nunc te congnovi: quare etsi impensius uror,
>   multo mi tamen es vilior et levior.
> qui potis est, inquis? quod amantem iniuria talis
>   cogit amare magis, sed bene velle minus. (c.72)

> You once said that you knew Catullus alone,
>   Lesbia, and that you would not exchange me for Zeus.
> I loved you then not only as the mob loves a girlfriend
>   but as a father loves his sons and sons-in-law.
> Now I know you: and so I burn for you even more,
>   nevertheless you are much cheaper and lighter to me.
> How can this be, you ask? Because such an injury
>   compels a lover to love more, but to feel less affection.

Commentators are generally agreed that Catullus has not quite succeeded in his attempt to describe an experience that was new in antiquity, though they are almost unanimous in their conviction that he actually felt what he is trying to describe.[41] Catullus' knowledge of Lesbia, which is both disillusionment and enlightenment, is supposed to guarantee the truth of the paradox that whereas he loves *impensius*, that is, more heavily and at more expense, Lesbia is both cheaper and lighter to him. Because the Lesbia who questions Catullus' words (qui potis est . . . ?, 7) is the same person whose own words he has seen through, the potential objection is overridden. Lesbia is allowed to question his words just as he has questioned hers (dicebas quondam, 1); his answer is simply to restate what he has already said in an antithesis that neatly divides the final pentameter and closes the poem with epigrammatic finality.

In its most famous formulation, the love/hate theme again raises and overrides an objection, but this time from a curious reader:[42]

> Odi et amo. Quare id faciam fortasse requiris.
>   Nescio, sed fieri sentio et excrucior. (c.85)
>
> I love and I hate. You ask, perhaps, why I do that.
>   I don't know, but I feel it happen and I suffer.

In a sense, this is an anti-epigram: "Odi et amo" is proposed as a paradox to be expounded, a riddle to which the epigrammatist holds the key, as the leisurely invitation to the reader indicates.[43] But the point is that there is no point, and the poet abdicates his position of control: the polysyllable *excrucior* (I suffer) prevents the epigram from snapping shut and places at the point where the speaker's power would be felt most the expression of his suffering and passivity. The epigram aborts and turns into a confession; we accept the paradox because it has forced the poet to relinquish the power of the epigrammatist. And yet, if the addressee is not only the personification of the epigram's demand for a point but also the curious reader of love poetry, then the pentameter identifies the fulfillment of form with the inscrutability of the poet's experience for the reader. As love poetry, the poem frustrates by retiring into an epigram, whose point is now the incompatibility between the reader's demand and the poet's experience. We believe Catullus' claim because it is a truth that cannot be shared, a truth of closure; it satisfies us in the same way as does the closure of the poem.

With reference to Lesbia's extravagant protestations, however, the audience is invited to share in the proverbial experience of all men:

> Nulli se dicit mulier mea nubere malle
>   quam mihi, non si se Iuppiter ipse petat.

> dicit: sed mulier cupido quod dicit amanti,
> in vento et rapida scribere oportet aqua. (c.70)

> My woman says that she would marry no one
> rather than me, not if Jupiter himself would woo her.
> She says it: but what a woman says to an eager lover,
> one should write on the wind and the rushing water.

Here Catullus questions the sincerity of Lesbia's recourse to the poetic hyperbole of the lover, or at any rate, he takes her at her word and then doubts it.[44] In poem 85, the inability of the speaker to satisfy his questioner is itself taken as a sign of the truth of his claim. In that case, the contradiction marks true feeling, but here the hyperbole indicates insincerity. Two different kinds of self-evidence are adduced to support these evaluations: in poem 85 the self-evidence of blind (nescio) feeling (sentio), and in poem 70 that of the proverbial.[45] But whereas the self-evidence of blind feeling closes the audience out of the experience whose truth it must acknowledge, the proverbial is shared with the audience as a truth that it confirms from its own experience. This differentiation of the audience's relation to the author from its relation to Lesbia is something that I have already described in the case of poem 2 (page 43 above), where the transparent and penetrable mind of Lesbia playing with the sparrow (and of Atlanta picking up the apple) is offered to the knowing audience at the same time as that audience is teased with Catullus' own impenetrability.

But the asymmetry between Catullus and Lesbia as speakers is not always maintained, and in one particularly interesting poem Catullus' exposure of Lesbia is made conditional on his own self-exposure:[46]

> Lesbia mi dicit semper male nec tacet umquam
> de me: Lesbia me dispeream nisi amat.
> quo signo? quia sunt totidem mea: deprecor illam
> assidue, verum dispeream nisi amo. (c.92)

> Lesbia always speaks ill of me nor is she ever quiet
> about me: damn me if Lesbia doesn't love me.
> By what proof? Because I'm the same: I curse her
> endlessly, but damn me if I'm not in love.

In this neat and elegant epigram, the generic demand for a point (quo signo?, 3) is amply fulfilled when the poet's claim to knowledge is wittily vindicated by the self-evidence of introspection. And yet, as in poem 85, there is a subtle interplay between the confident power of the speaker of the epigram and the weakness of the confessional lover. The epigrammatist has power over the words of his victim, using the analytical and rhetorical force of this form to turn the tables neatly on the badmouthing Lesbia. But in order to do this, he must confess his own unreliability. The epigram is highjacked by confession when the words "damn me if I'm not in love" (dispeream nisi amo), which echo the first pentameter and nail the proof into place, turn out to be a declaration of love for the victim of the epigrammatic point. *Dispeream* (lit., "may I die") is spoken in two very different ways: in the second line, it has the triumphant tone of one who has seen through the behavior of another, but in the final line it has the ardor, or perhaps exasperation, of the confessional lover. The position of the speaker who unmasks the feelings of another, and therefore presents that person as a spectacle, is no longer transcendent, for at the same time as the speaker is unmasked the experience of the other is recognized. Furthermore, this poem unravels Catullus' declaration "I love and hate" because, in the act of unmasking Lesbia's true feelings for him, Catullus must admit a possibility that has been excluded, namely, that although he speaks ill of her he really loves her, which of course means that there is no paradoxical combination of love and hate. In this case, revealing the mendacity of Lesbia means questioning the poet's own veracity. Here the words of the two principals are treated equally and subjected to the same evenhanded irony, so that the privileged position of the speaker, who elsewhere unmasks hyperbole as lies but speaks paradox as unquestionable truth, can no longer hold. The audience of this poem is now free to suspect the words of Catullus as interested speech in the same way as it has learned to suspect the words of Lesbia.

Taken as a cycle, these poems dramatize the special status of poetic utterance through the fiction of the unreliable mistress; they distinguish a place where words are intensely meant from one where they are casually spoken on the spur of the moment. But Catullus leaves us room to question the position that the poem adopts on whatever is uttered outside its privileged precincts. I began this chapter with a poem in which Catullus reacts to a protestation of Lesbia: "It is a delightful love you offer me, my life" (c.109.1). On its own, this first line conjures up a very different scenario from the solemn contract that Lesbia is supposed to be undertaking at the end of the poem. By the second line, this exclamation of Catullus has become Lesbia's promise ("You promise that this love will be delightful and eternal") and the poem progressively weights her promise with solemn resonances until Lesbia's utterance cracks under the strain. The implication is that the words of Lesbia cannot take the pressure that this speaker puts on language. But as Lesbia's putative promise comes into focus in the first couplet, Catullus' own happy exclamation disappears, and with it the trace of a passionate interchange between lovers: we sense that one context has been betrayed by another. Again, Catullus leaves us in a position to question the strategy by which poetry positions its own utterances in relation to the contexts from which it has broken off.

The same could be said of poem 70, which ends by stating that Lesbia's protestations, like those of all women speaking to their lovers, should be written on wind and water. But because the words "scribere oportet aqua" (ought to be written on water) close this epigram, whose elegiac meter has long associations with inscription on stone, we might wonder whether *oportet* (ought) implies a self-reproach.[47] The unreliable woman of the proverb is speaking to her "desiring" (cupido) lover, and the water in which her words should be written is *rapida* ("snatching," from *rapio*), like the eager lover himself. In a sense, then, her words are already written in rapid water, namely, that of the lover's desire. *Rapida* is metrically identical to *cupido* and comes in the same position of the line (second and third foot); this connection between the two words reminds us that the suspicious judge was the complicit lover who inspired Lesbia's passionate outburst in the first place. The poem breaks the integrity of the context of Lesbia's words, for the water that is the volatile element of the lover's desire in which the woman speaks her words can only appear in the poem as the negative of the stone of inscription (and proverbial wisdom) implied by the context into which her words have been transcribed. These last words, then, remind us of what poetry cannot do, of a writing that it cannot transcribe, of a kind of speech that must be lost when poetic speech begins. The poem covers up this acknowledgement with the opposite claim that the words spoken before the poem began, and outside its precinct, are unworthy of transcription.

The poems with which I have been concerned in this chapter, poems of moral outrage, disillusionment, and desperation, dramatize the two kinds of liminality in which the poem is situated. On the one hand, the poems of immobility, thwarted reciprocity, and desire for rupture reflect the isolation of the poetic speaker before the audience in the special temporality of a performance that is always drawing to a close. On the other hand, the poems of suspicion and disillusionment bear the traces of interchanges and contexts from which poetic speech has severed itself as it lays claim to its special status.

CHAPTER 6

# Gazing at the Golden Age
## Belatedness and Mastery in Catullus 64

Among the poets of Catullus' circle, one learned and virtuosic epyllion (little epic) seems to have been required as proof of the poet's powers, and the spirit of rivalry can be felt in the magnificently extravagant performance sometimes known as "Peleus and Thetis."[1] Catullus seems to be testing not only his own powers but those of poetry or art itself as he conjures up a mythical age lost forever to the experience of a belated humanity that can only represent that time when gods and humans intermingled. Most of the poem consists in a description of a work of art, an *ekphrasis* of the coverlet on the wedding couch of Peleus and Thetis, which provides the opportunity for a brilliant display of the representative powers of poetry. The central figure on the coverlet, itself the object of the admiring gaze of the countrymen invited to the wedding, is the abandoned Ariadne, gazing after the ship of the absconding Theseus. I argue that the gaze—satisfied, frustrated, or interrupted—is the main thematic thread of the poem, and that this theme reflects the problematic relation of a belated poet and his audience toward the beautiful but lost world of myth on which they long to feast their eyes.

But first, a synopsis of the poem. Catullus begins with the voyage of the Argo, the first sea voyage, which he interrupts at the point where the nymphs expose themselves to gaze at this novel phenomenon and Peleus and Thetis fall in love. Here the poet pauses to address the heroes:

o nimis optato saeclorum tempore nati
heroes, salvete, deum genus! o bona matrum

> progenies, salvete ite[rum] . . .
> vos ego saepe, meo vos carmine compellabo. (22–24)

> O heroes, born in a time of the ages all too desirable,
> greetings, race of gods! O righteous offspring of mothers,
> greetings again. . . .
> Often I will hail you with my song.

When the long-awaited day of the wedding of Peleus and Thetis comes, the countrymen desert their fields to gaze at the palace and its rich preparations, among which is the marriage couch covered with an elaborate tapestry of scenes from long ago (50–51). The main scene on the tapestry features Ariadne on the beach, gazing (52) after the absconding Theseus, her clothes fallen from her body in her distracted state (63–67). Catullus now tells the story of how Ariadne got to be in this position, how she fell in love with Theseus at first sight (91–93), helped him to kill the Minotaur, and eloped with him. We then return to the deserted Ariadne, who delivers a long speech of recrimination of Theseus (132–201), ending with the prayer

> sed quali solam Theseus me mente reliquit
> tali mente, deae, funestet seque suosque. (200–201)

> but with the same mind with which Theseus deserted me,
> with that mind, goddesses, may he kill himself and his dearest.

Ariadne's curse comes true. Theseus' father, Aegeus, had been reluctant to let his son set off to face the Minotaur; he had not yet satisfied his eyes with gazing on him (219–20). Aegeus made Theseus dye his sails black for the journey, but charged him to change them to white the moment he saw his homeland on his return. Theseus forgot to change the sails and Aegeus, watching out for his son from the citadel, saw the black sails and threw himself off the battlements (241–45).

We now move to another part of the tapestry where Bacchus, who has fallen in love with Ariadne, is approaching with his companions; the apotheosis of Ariadne is implied but not described. Back at the wedding, the countrymen of Thessaly, having satisfied their gaze on the tapestry, make way for the gods (267–68). The gods arrive, and also the Fates, who sing a mixture of wedding song and prophecy, celebrating Achilles, the son to be born from this marriage. Closing the poem, Catullus regrets that the depravity of the modern age has caused the gods to withdraw themselves from the light of day (384–408).

My synopsis is intended to bring out the thematic importance of the gaze as well as the self-consciously virtuosic handling of structure. The figure of Ariadne, frustrated gazer and enticing spectacle, dominates the poem, featuring both as a projection of the poet's alienation from the time of the heroes that he hails in his song and as a field for the representational powers and voyeuristic indulgence of the latecomer poet. Myth itself casts the poet in a similarly ambiguous position, for it exists both as a distant, lost world and as a compendium of marvels to be appropriated by the poet at will. For the Roman poet, the heroic age is situated in Greek literature, which makes him doubly belated, and yet this poem confidently displays its representational mastery, appropriating Greek myth as a lavish spectacle to be enjoyed by the belated Roman. Politically and militarily, the Romans had become masters of the Greeks, and, in spite their awe of the cultural achievements of the defeated, the Romans confidently appropriated the earlier civilization's prestigious legacy.[2] No doubt Catullus' boisterous confidence with respect to hallowed Greek material has contributed to the suspicion in which the critical tradition has held this poem.

## The Critical Tradition

For Catullan criticism, the poem has been something of an embarrassment; precious and mannerist in style and bizarre in form, it offers us a feast for the senses while apparently denying us the kind of formal synopsis and thematic coherence that would allow us to fix our minds on higher things. Though it is ostensively about the wedding of Peleus and Thetis, more than half of this poem is taken up by the story of Ariadne, introduced because it features on the embroidered coverlet of the wedding couch. To absolve Catullus of wanton self-indulgence, the poem has sometimes been called an experiment in Alexandrian narrative.[3] At its most extreme, this emphasis on the poem's Alexandrianism takes the form of arguing that it is an imitation of a lost Greek poem (or two), but even in more temperate versions of this argument the existence of Greek models and parallels has helped to give this sumptuous poem a respectable pedigree.[4]

Of the literary criticism on this poem, much has focused on the search for a unifying theme that would enable the reader to resist its seductive sensuality. The first major treatment of the work's unity,

Klingner 1964 (originally published in 1956), makes it quite clear that a solid grasp of the poem's carefully concealed unity is the condition under which we can enjoy its surface: "Once one has assured oneself of [the poem's unity], one can abandon oneself with that much more clear a conscience to the enjoyment of the variety and colorful changes that determine the first impression the poem makes on the reader, and that make the unity so difficult to recognize" (213). Klingner found the poem's unity in the theme of the union of gods and mortals, whose dark counterpart is the story of the abandoned Ariadne. Since Klingner, there have been two main lines of interpretation of the poem as a whole. The first takes the moralizing end of the poem for its starting point: Catullus' lament that the gods, disgusted with a criminal humanity, no longer mingle with us as they did in the Golden Age becomes the key to the poem's unity. For the most part, proponents of this line of interpretation stress the irony in Catullus' presentation of a (morally) better Golden Age. The influential article of Bramble 1970 explores the ironies of Catullus' presentation of the Golden Age by following up "clues," apparent to the learned, in Catullus' mythology: the Golden Age, Bramble argues, is seen by a disillusioned Catullus as already corrupt.[5] The other line of interpretation seeks to reunite this poem with Catullus' lyric oeuvre, and particularly the love poetry; it stems from the conviction that this poet whom the experience of love taught to find his own voice must, in some way, be talking about that experience in his most ambitious poem. The integrity of Catullus, as well as that of his oeuvre, is at stake, and so the betrayed Catullus has been cast as the abandoned Ariadne, which brings into play the moral issues of the elegiac love poetry.[6]

In the scholarship that exemplifies these approaches, I have found little that engages my experience of reading this luxuriously beautiful and strange poem, and in fact I suspect that the attempts to divert attention from the poem's distinctive surface to a moralizing message, or to neutralize this surface by referring it to Alexandrian literary principles, are strategies of avoidance. What is being avoided is the sensuality of the poem, which has to be redeemed by being made to subserve weightier themes.[7] The protestations that the poem is more than mere frivolity, artificiality, entertainment, virtuosity, or experimentation, with which interpretations routinely begin, suggest that the scholars concerned are eager to prove that they have not been seduced by the poem's surface. Jenkyns 1982, 94, has spoken appropriately of "a kind of aesthetic puritanism" in this connection, a puritanism that has had the unfortunate effect of obscuring Catullus' fantasizing relation to myth in this poem.

## Myth, Gaze, and Body: The Boscotrecase Panels

By way of introducing a different model for understanding the poem's relation to myth, I would like to consider a work of Roman visual art representing stories from myth. The relation between contemporary painting and Catullus' poem has been remarked on before, and certainly the almost obsessive transitions between levels of reality in the poem's imbricated structure remind one strongly of Campanian wall painting.[8] But I have chosen this particular ensemble, the two remaining panels of a set of three from a room at Boscotrecase, because in these panels the relation of the spectator to the world of myth is engaged through the spectacle of the human body. In all sections of Catullus' poem, the female body features as an object of fascination (the Nereids, Ariadne, the Fates, Polyxena), and clearly it plays an important role in Catullus' visualization of the world of myth.

The panels (now in the Metropolitan Museum, New York) are narrative paintings of Polyphemus and Galatea and of Perseus and Andromeda respectively; they are particularly relevant to Catullus' poem because, like the poem, they establish thematic relations between two mythological scenes, both of them erotic. Klingner's influential analysis of Catullus 64 is based on the kind of thematic parallels and contrasts between the myths that Karl Schefold had found in ensembles of Roman painting.[9] The Boscotrecase panels have recently been studied from this perspective by Eleanor Leach 1988, who begins by pointing out the similarity in the compositions of the two paintings:

Each composition centers about a lofty seaside crag that has been detached and brought forward from its background by dramatic highlighting of angles and planes. Thus focused, our attention falls next upon the principal figures set off by the crags: Polyphemus and Andromeda. Comparing the two panels, we notice that their placement of the principal masculine and feminine figures is in reverse. The position of the savior, Perseus, hovering on the wings in the one panel, is analogous to that of Galatea floating on her seabeast in the other. In each case the secondary action appears in the upper right-hand corner; the Cyclops stoning the ship of Odysseus has its counterpart in the meeting of Perseus and Andromeda's royal father. The one panel thus contrasts a peaceful foreground with an outbreak of savage violence [Polyphemus watching Galatea / stoning Odysseus's ship], while the other lets us anticipate a violent physical contest in the foreground with a royal marriage as its outcome (364–65).

Leach performs a subtle "interassociative reading" of these two panels: she points out that the violence of the secondary scene in the Polyphemus panel reminds us that the apparently peaceful scene between Perseus and Andromeda's father in the other panel is the prelude to violence, for Andromeda is already engaged, and Perseus will have to fight again after freeing Andromeda. Furthermore, there is a play in these paintings on the contrasts between heroic nature and civilization:

The tension between major and minor incidents in each panel shows us the contrast between an uncomplicated love romantically sought by sword or song in a natural setting, and the deception or violence of a harsher civilized reality perilous to illusions of innocence and good faith (367–68).

This is a fruitful line of approach which, by showing us the sensibility that unites art and literature, tells us much about the Roman attitude to mythology. But it needs to be supplemented by a study of the way that these panels solicit our gaze as they provide images from a mythology that is, above all, a world of fantasy.[10] Leach points out that the placement of the main masculine and feminine figures in the two paintings is reversed. But to the (implicitly male) viewer, this is not simply a matter of spatial disposition. Andromeda, her arms open and shackled to a rock whose shape opens up to echo the availability of her body, is central to the composition in a way quite different from the figure of the Cyclops, twisting toward the semi-naked form of Galatea on her sea beast, and almost nailed to the center of the composition by the tall column that rises behind him from the rock on which he sits. The column behind Polyphemus and the fanning, slightly cavernous rock behind Galatea are not just allusions to the respective sexual organs of the male and female figures, they also relate to the gaze of the spectator in contrasting ways and so sexualize that gaze. In the Andromeda painting, the other figures frame her: the sea monster rising from the bottom left and Perseus floating in from the top left channel our gaze at the chained Andromeda, a gaze that is gathered into the shadowed concavities of the rock behind her. The group of Perseus and Andromeda's father on the top right, and a female figure, either a nymph or Andromeda's mother, on the bottom right complete the symmetry. By contrast, the Polyphemus painting is much less static in composition. Its main movement is a diagonal from Galatea on the left, below the seated Polyphemus, to Polyphemus himself, in another story, throwing boulders at the ship of Odysseus, cut off by the edge of the panel, on the right above the seated central figure. If the Andromeda painting is about availability, the Polyphemus painting is about frustration. The eye settles easily on the central figure of Ariadne, but it cannot settle at all in the Polyphemus painting, for the central figure cannot be isolated from the diagonal movement, and this movement itself ties together two stories of frustrated desire, one of which revolves around blindness. The tension between the figures of Galatea—even more enticingly presented than Andromeda—and Polyphemus exists on both narrative and visual levels, for as we look at Galatea our gaze is distracted by the larger and more prominent Polyphemus, who in turn expresses a hopeless longing. Above Polyphemus on the right, his blinded self lifts a boulder to throw at a ship, half of which is cut off from our view.

Between them, the two paintings create a contrast in the visual experience of the viewer, and the choice of these particular mythological themes makes an issue of our own spectatorship and of our desire for the fantastic world of mythology. The story of Andromeda becomes one of wish fulfillment, of the conjuring up of desirable images about which the viewer can float with a sensation of omnipotence represented in the painting by the figure of Perseus. Perseus and the sea monster may be about to fight, but their visual function in the composition has nothing to do with conflict; rather, the exuberant lifting of the monster's head from the sea and the exhilarating fall of Perseus from the sky serve to focus our relationship to the figure of Andromeda. By contrast, the deformed Polyphemus, whose harsh world is tangentially and frustratingly related to the heroic story of Odysseus, and to the erotic world of the sea nymphs, is a poignant image of our own alienation from the world of myth.

## The Figure of Ariadne

In the Boscotrecase panels, the figure of Polyphemus duplicates the viewer's removal from the represented world, whereas the figure of Andromeda suggests the availability of that world to the omnipotent viewer. Catullus' Ariadne, frustrated gazer and enticing spectacle, combines these two opposing relations to the world of myth. But in recent years it has been more common to find in the figure of Ariadne reflections of Catullus' own experience of betrayal at the hands of Lesbia.[11] Commenting on Wiseman's version of this identification, Griffin 1985 cites the following lines:

> non flavo retinens subtilem vertice mitram,
> non contecta levi velatum pectus amictu,
> non tereti strophio lactentis vincta papillas,
> omnia quae toto delapsa e corpore passim
> ipsius ante pedes fluctus salis alludebant. (64.63–67)

> not keeping the delicate headband on her golden hair,
> nor swathed in the light dress touching her breasts,
> her milky nipples no longer bound by the smooth halter,
> all of which fallen completely from her body in all directions
> the waves of the sea played with before her very eyes.

As Griffin points out, Catullus is quite separate from his Ariadne here, "savouring the spectacle of her distress which is soon to be consoled" (98). One is reminded of a common type of scene in Roman wall painting: a male figure (Pan or a satyr) has come across a sleeping woman (nymph or Baccant) and has lifted her clothes to feast his eyes on her naked body; the woman has woken and turned on her side; as the man gazes at the woman's front, sometimes partially clothed by a band covering her breasts, the spectator is treated to a naked rear view. Several Pompeian paintings show the abandoned and sleeping Ariadne revealed in this manner.[12] Griffin's "savouring" is a good word for what is going on here: the incantatory rhythm of the first three lines, with their subtle variations of grammatical structure, seems to hold Ariadne in a soft focus as the camera turns around her in slow motion; the repetitive emphasis on the lightness of the clothes that have fallen to the ground (subtilem, levi, tereti) allows the viewer the pleasures of transparency as well as nudity. The language of film immmediately suggests itself in connection with this passage, which includes a closeup (Ariadne's nipples, 62) and even the thoroughly filmic shot of the water playing with the fallen clothes.

Recent discussions of spectatorship in cinema have emphasized the way that the camera produces particular kinds of relations between the viewer and the viewed that are quite as significant as the relations between the images; it has also described how visual pleasure is implicated in certain kinds of relation to the female body.[13] Feminist film theory provides a useful framework for understanding the role of Ariadne in this poem. Kaja Silverman has argued that the classic cinema's viewer is excluded from the point of the film's discursive origination; devices such as cutting and framing remind us that the reality reflected by the film has been seen by another, absent eye that has presented to our eyes an *impression* of reality.[14] This exclusion is particularly disturbing for the male viewer, whose subjectivity is constructed through identification with discursive power, or the phallus. Classic film deals with this situation, which is a projection of earlier fears of castration, by simultaneously transferring the viewer's weakness onto the female characters and making the female body the site of receptivity to the male gaze. Catullus' Ariadne, whose distracted and abandoned state renders her an object of the male gaze, fits this model exactly. But Catullus also provides us with the figure of the "castrated" viewer in the countrypeople who abandon their agricultural work to gaze at the wedding preparations, leaving the earth deprived of their phallic ministrations:

> non humilis curvis purgatur vinea rastris,
> non glebam prono convellit vomere taurus,
> non falx attenuat frondatorum arboris umbram, (39–41)

> The low vine is not weeded by curved hoes,
> the ox does not tear up the clods with the driven plough,
> the pruners' sickle does not thin the shade of the tree,

The rhetoric of this passage is recalled in the lines describing the semi-naked Ariadne:

> non flavo retinens subtilem vertice mitram,
> non contecta levi velatum pectus amictu,
> non tereti strophio lactentis vincta papillas, (63–65)

The similar use of negatives in these two passages establishes a connection between the suspended work of the awed rustic gazers and the abandoned state of Ariadne that exposes the delights of her body. As a result of the rustics' removal to the palace, the countryside is neglected, but this is expressed in an ironic allusion to the Golden Age theme that cultivation was unnecessary: nature returns to its original state, and even the necks of the beasts of burden grow soft again (mollescunt colla iuvencis, 38).[15] In this ironic Golden Age, the expected visual pleasures of a generous and abundant earth are replaced by the spectacle of a spreading rust:

> squalida desertis rubigo infertur aratris. (42)

> A rough rust appears on the abandoned ploughs.

It is the body of Ariadne that provides the positive visual spectacle of abundance that should accompany the Golden Age negatives and compensates for the ineffectuality of the male gazers.

The gold of this Golden Age is to be found not in the country but in the city, where the palace shines with a literal gold and silver (44), drawing the farmers from their tasks, a fact that is quite alien to the morality of the Golden Age topos. There is more to this than an ironic comment on the morality of the age of heroes: the perversity of the reference to Golden Age topoi and the anachronistically urban setting make this passage a self-conscious reflection on the representation or conjuring-up of a Golden Age. The literalization of the metaphor of the Golden Age emphasizes the attractive power of gold, which draws the farmers away from their work on the earth; the absence of work, epitomized by the rusting of the plough, points us to the gold that is elsewhere, not in a renewed countryside but in the visual pleasures of the town. Migrating to the city, the farmers reverse the movement of the urban poet who, drawn by another kind of attraction, calls up a rural Golden Age. What is most striking in this use of the Golden Age topos is the disjunction between the absence of work and a vision of abundance; in this case, they occur in different places, country and town respectively. All this, then, produces a very self-conscious presentation of the Golden Age whose unconventionality draws attention to the mutual curiosity of town-dwellers and countrypeople about their counterparts, a curiosity that motivates the topos in the first place.[16]

The figure of Ariadne does double duty: as a frustrated gazer, she duplicates that longing for a lost world that suffuses the poem, but as a female body she provides, in her abandoned longing, the available abundance of the Golden Age. She both opens and closes the rift that separates the belated viewer from his or her fantasies. In the figure of Ariadne, the desiring gaze itself becomes an object of visual satisfaction, displayed on the female body that exposes itself in its preoccupation with gazing. This satisfaction rectifies the unfortunate way that the farmers' desire to gaze is registered on the body of the earth, which they have neglected in order to gawk at urban opulence.

## Virtuosity and Wonder

Enclosing all of the longing and gazing in the poem is Catullus' relation to the heroic age that he is conjuring up with his voice, the longed-for age (nimis optato . . . tempore, 22) when the gods appeared to humans, for afterward human depravity caused them to shun our sight:

> quare nec talis dignantur visere coetus,
> nec se contingi patiuntur lumine claro. (64.406–7)
>
> Therefore they no longer deign to visit such gatherings,
> nor do they allow themselves to be touched by the bright light.

Human impiety begins traditionally with the voyage of Argo, the first ship, which dared to ignore the natural divisions of the earth and made possible a new scale of human greed and violence. The voyage of the Argo is both the moment of supreme cooperation and mingling between gods and mortals and the beginning of their separation. But if this impious voyage began the process that took the gods from our sight, it was also a display of virtuosity and daring that caused the nymphs to expose themselves in wonder to human eyes:

> illa rudem cursu prima imbuit Amphitriten;
> quae simul ac rostro ventosum proscidit aequor
> tortaque remigio spumis incanduit [V] unda,
> emersere freti candenti e gurgite vultus
> aequoreae monstrum Nereides admirantes.
> illa, atque [haud] alia, viderunt luce marinas
> mortales oculis nudato corpore Nymphas
> nutricum tenus exstantes e gurgite cano. (11–18)
>
> The Argo first initiated the untried Amphitrite [a nymph] with
>                                                              sailing;
> and as soon as it ploughed the windy sea with its beak
> and the wave churned by the oars grew hot with foam,
> from the white flood of the sea the Nereids
> raised their faces, wondering at the miracle.
> On that day, and no other, mortal eyes saw
> the nymphs with bodies bared,
> standing out from the hoary foam up to their breasts.

The lascivious detail "nutricum tenus" (up to the breasts) reminds us of the way that Ariadne is (or will be) observed in the passage I quoted above, and in fact the word *nutrix*, meaning "nurse," and here signifying "breast" by analogy with the Greek *titthos* ("breast," cognate with *titthe*, "nurse") calls to mind the "lactentis . . . papillas" ("suckling" or "full of milk") of Ariadne. I will return to the interesting neologism *nutrix* in a moment. What strikes one about this passage is that the expected relation between sea and sailors has been reversed: the Argo "initiates" the sea and is itself described as a *monstrum* for the sea nymphs, who appear in familiar guise as objects of prurient interest and as potential mothers. Sailing is here a novel experience for the sea rather than the sailors. This paradox is sharpened by the word *imbuit*, used of the Argo's initiation of the sea; the primary meaning of this verb is "drench" or "wet," and so one might expect the sea to be its subject not its object.[17] The reversal has been made possible by the feminization of the sea, which appears as the nymph Amphitrite, and by the sexualization of the act of sailing (proscidit, 12). Not only does the ship initiate the sea, it also seems to conjure up the nymphs, who appear as soon as the prow has cut the surface and the water has been twisted into foam by the oars (tortaque remigio spumis incanduit unda, 13). Quinn 1970 remarks: "*torta* suggests that the flecks of foam (*spumis*) produced by the twisting action of Argo's oars are actual curls (and the oars, if we like, the curling tongs)" (303).[18]

The voyage of the Argo is like the voyage of the poet into a myth that he brings to life, penetrated, like a woman's body, by his desire and conjured out of the froth of a language by the will to beauty (in this case, hairdressing). Athena builds the ship, or rather weaves it (pinea coniungens inflexae texta carinae, 10) as a curiously wrought artifact like the poetic style of the poem itself, causing the desirable figures of an imagined Golden Age to arise and reveal themselves, their bodies stripped (nudato corpore, 17) in bare wonderment. Virtuosity—the miraculous ease of Athena's fabricating—is the *monstrum* that attracts wonder, and in the figures of the nymphs Wonder itself appears to us, an hypostasized version of our own wonder in a form that projects its own desirability. The emerging of the nymphs from the water is also the emergence in the Latin language of the desirable world of Greek art, for the breasts of the nymphs are an allusion, a neologism appearing in the Latin language to give us a glimpse of Greek (see above).[19]

## Frustration and Compensation

The rustic guests come from the country bearing gifts and, on their faces, a smile that gives their joy away. Everything about these yokels is up-front:

> dona ferunt prae se, declarant gaudia vultu. (34)

> They bring gifts in their hands and declare their joy in their faces.

The house too declares its joy as it meets the gaze of the visitors:

> tota domus gaudet regali splendida gaza. (46)

> The whole house rejoices resplendent with royal treasure.

And yet the house and the guests cannot meet on equal terms, for the house beams in gold and silver; its spacious vistas do not so much open up for these people as recede:

> ipsius at sedes, quacumque opulenta recessit
> regia, fulgenti splendent auro atque argento. (43–44)

> The king's own quarters shine with silver and gold
> As far as the palace in its opulence receded.

Opulence recedes with the halls, for opulence is precisely what these viewers cannot have. What they can have is an image, but an image of desiring itself, of Ariadne watching Theseus recede. Paradoxically, they feed on this image:

> quae postquam cupide spectando Thessala pubes
> expleta est, sanctis coepit decedere divis. (267–68)

> Once the youth of Thessaly was satisfied in its eager
> gazing it began to make way for the sacred gods.

This conception of gazing as a fierce kind of desire that needs to be satisfied in an almost physical way, itself an idea that has the flavor of the heroic age (*Od.* 4.47), finds a tragic instantiation in the story of Aegeus, father of Theseus:

> quandoquidem fortuna mea ac tua fervida virtus
> eripit invito mihi te, cui languida nondum
> lumina sunt gnati cara saturata figura . . . (218–20)

> Because my fortune and your burning courage
> take you from me against my will, although my tired eyes
> have not yet sated themselves on the dear face of my son . . .

Aegeus has the departing Theseus' sails dyed (obscurata ferrugine Hibera, 227) to signify his grief. If he returns safe from the Minotaur, Theseus is to change his sails to white as soon as he catches sight of the hills of his homeland, so that his father may know the good news as soon as possible. But Theseus, sailing blithely away from the angry gaze of Ariadne to the eager gaze of his father watching from the citadel (241), forgets to change the sails and causes his father's suicide. The dyed sails represent a loss within the household; conversely, the colored coverlet on the wedding couch of Peleus and Thetis draws attention to the hope of that house for future offspring. But whereas the coverlet offers visual satisfaction to the guests, for whom the opulence of the house recedes before their gaze, the visual interest of the stained sails only obstructs the purity of the gaze of father to son in which the former would saturate his eyes. It is the breaking of this gaze before saturation that is the beginning of the story told by the coverlet, on which the rustics feast their eyes. The gaze, at first frustrated or interrupted, then satisfied, thematizes in the fictional world the double relation of the poet and his readership to the world of myth.

## Ariadne, Victim of Art

Watching Theseus recede, Ariadne delivers a tirade ending with a curse, which, we are told, Jupiter will bring about (200–201). The fulfillment of this curse is not represented on the tapestry, but it is described by Catullus: the father anxiously watching for his son's return compensates, in the experience of the reader, for the unreturned gaze of Ariadne after the deserter. The relation between the reciprocity and symmetry of the story as completed by the narrator and the unreciprocated gaze of Ariadne is established by the lines that round off the story of Theseus and Ariadne:

> sic funesta domus ingressus tecta paterna
> morte ferox Theseus, qualem Minoidi luctum
> obtulerat mente immemori, talem ipse recepit.
> quae tum prospectans cedentem maesta carinam
> multiplices animo volvebat saucia curas. (246–50)

> So entering the funereal house Theseus, wild
> from the death of his father, was struck with grief
> such as he had brought on Ariadne with his unmindfulness.
> She, looking out sadly then at the receding ship,
> turned many sorrows over in her wounded mind.

The neat reciprocity of the story as completed by the narrator is juxtaposed to the distraught figure of Ariadne as seen by the guests, a juxtaposition that draws attention to the different satisfactions of description and narrative. The viewer's pleasure is always to some extent at the expense of the figures in the picture, who are unconscious of the whole, narrative or compositional, into which they fit; it is a pleasure that depends on our oscillation between entering the particular scene and knowing the whole story. In this case, there are two kinds of resolutions of which the abandoned Ariadne is unaware, one narrative and the other compositional. Catullus provides the compositional, or visual, resolution to the scene of the abandoned Ariadne in the balancing tableau of the riot of Bacchus and his attendants, represented on another section of the tapestry (250-64). We are given two different kinds of completion to the yearning, frustrated gaze of Ariadne: on the one hand, Theseus sails off the tapestry into the world of narrative resolutions, where the unreciprocated gaze of Ariadne and the dissipated energy of her anger are gathered into an economy of poetic justice; on the other hand (at parte ex alia, 251), there is the Bacchic riot, drawn to Ariadne (te quaerens, 253) as she watches Theseus draw away from her, and balancing the desolation of the Ariadne tableau with its jostling gaiety. Through the figure of the helplessly immobile Ariadne, the poet's versatility and virtuosity are displayed while the reader's mobility is confirmed.

Curiously enough, the immobile Ariadne is actually compared to a Bacchant:

> saxea ut effigies bacchantis, prospicit, eheu,
> prospicit et magnis curarum fluctuat undis, (61-62)

> Like a stone image of a Bacchant, she watches, alas,
> she watches and seethes with the great waves of her sufferings,

Ariadne is Bacchic in the intensity of her gaze and the turmoil of her feelings, but she lacks the crucial element of any Bacchic figure, movement. Though gazing, Ariadne's only action, is in itself hardly Bacchic, the empathetic words of the observer—"she watches, alas, / she watches" (prospicit, eheu, / prospicit)—create the same feeling of trapped motion as does a sculpture of a Bacchant.[20] These words are spoken not only of Ariadne but also of the *figure* of Ariadne in the tapestry, trapped by the medium itself in a moment of unbearable yearning; the pathos of the observer's words fuses the narrative level (Ariadne's longing) with the visual level (the figure's suspended animation), and so creates a mode of existence equivalent to that of Myth, in which Ariadne stands, the epitome of the abandoned woman, ready to be cited. Jenkyns appositely compares Keats' invocation to the lovers forever about to kiss in the *Ode on a Grecian Urn*; but it is not just the freezing of a transient moment that links these two poets at this point, for Catullus, like Keats, has realized a mode of experience for his Ariadne that corresponds to her artistic status (Ariadne the mythical *exemplum*); the sympathy of the viewer (eheu) is sympathy for what "Ariadne" is within Myth and for *how* she is within Myth. Catullus' simile draws our attention not to how Ariadne looks but to how we feel looking at her representation, projecting back onto the level of narrative what we feel in looking at the representation. Because it is the viewer who endows the representation with the frustrated will to transcend its own medium, the figure of Ariadne presents the poet and his audience with a projection both of their impotence and of their power. Just as they long for a time they have missed and call upon its figures (c.64.24) across an unbridgeable gap, gazing at a represented world they can never enter, so Ariadne longs for a Theseus disappearing across a sea on whose fringes she must remain. But if the audience fears that it will become trapped in its frustrated and longing gaze at a lost world, then the antidote to this fear is to remind itself of its power to project life into, for instance, the statue of a Bacchant, to create the pathos of another's motion trapped in stone. The comparison of Ariadne to the statue of the Bacchant also reminds us that, as we can move freely in the space in which the Bacchant can't, so we can track to another part of Catullus' coverlet to find Bacchus and his thiasus swooping in to claim her (at parte ex alia, 251). Our position is rather like that of Venus in Horace's Europe ode, telling the abducted heroine to dry her eyes because she has a glorious future (c.1.27.66–76).

In the end, Ariadne is abandoned by Catullus, for he does not recount the story of how Bacchus came to console and deify her, although the god is sighted, coming from another part of the visual field across which the eye of the viewer passes. Leaving Ariadne behind, the viewer encounters a real Bacchic scene, dominated by noise, and we are reminded of the fact that noise is as inaudible in a tapestry as movement is imperceptible:

pars obscura cavis celebrabant orgia cistis,
orgia quae frustra cupiunt audire profani. (259–60)

Some thronged in worship of the sacred objects hidden in their
                                                                         baskets,
the rites that the uninitiated desire to hear in vain.

As with the immobility of the Bacchic statue and the figure of Ariadne, the silence of this noisy scene for those who view it is given a narrative projection: the uninitiated are frustrated in their desire to hear the rites.[21] In the context of the poem's distinction between a time when the gods were visible to human sight and a present when moral decline has caused the gods to avoid us, we are the profane, for whom the rich verbal music of Catullus' lines expresses our vain desire to hear:

> plangebant aliae proceris tympana palmis,
> aut tereti tenuis tinnitus aere ciebant;
> multis raucisonos efflabant cornua bombos
> barbaraque horribili stridebat tibia cantu. (261–64)

> Others were banging tambourines with their long palms,
> or stirring a faint ringing from the rounded bronze;
> many blasted a rough booming from their horns
> and the barbarous pipe screeched an uncouth melody.

The inconsolable and immobile Ariadne, at the center of all of the transitions that carry the spectator smoothly over the surface of the poem, is herself, though she does not know it, about to pass from one man to another. And this point is crucial to the significance of the lamenting Ariadne—a figure of great importance in Western art, music, and literature—for the passage of Ariadne from one man to the other becomes the myth of the comforts and compensations of art.[22] Through her abandoned performance of her abandonment, Ariadne is elevated to the status of diva by the appreciative Bacchus; her lament, expressing the emptiness of (Theseus') words and rhetoric, becomes a display of their power. To begin with, this lament expresses the despair and disillusionment of one who has been deceived by false promises of bliss:

> at non haec quondam blanda promissa dedisti
> voce mihi, non haec miserae sperare iubebas
> sed coniubia laeta, sed optatos hymenaeos,
> quae cuncta aerii discerpunt irrita venti.
> nunc iam nulla viro iuranti femina credat,
> nulla viri speret sermones esse fideles;
> quis dum aliquid cupiens animus praegestit apisci
> nil metuunt iurare, nihil promittere parcunt:
> sed simul ac cupidae mentis satiata libido est,
> dicta nihil metuere, nihil periuria curant. (139–48)

> But these were not the promises you once gave me
> with flattering voice, nor this what you told me to hope for
> but a happy marriage, the wedding that I desired,
> all of which the airy winds tear into nothing.

> from now on let no woman believe the oath of a man,
> let no woman hope that the protestations of a man are reliable;
> when their lustful mind craves to get something
> they have no fear to swear or promise anything:
> but as soon as the desire of their lustful mind is satisfied,
> they have no fear of what they have said, they care nothing for
> perjury.

Ariadne has experienced the emptiness of rhetoric (blanda . . . voce, 139–40); she has fallen into the gap opened up within desire by the male orgasm (145–48), and the discontinuity that she has experienced is final, the emptiness of her environment complete. She laments, but she knows that words are futile in the deserted and unresponsive nature that reflects her abandonment (164–66, 184–87). And yet Ariadne's lament is the great set-piece of rhetoric, whose elaboration is a function of the extremity of her situation; it is the aria of Ariadne (one of the founding figures of opera) that makes her a diva when the pleasure-loving god Bacchus comes looking for her (c.64.253), seduced by her lament. Paradoxically, this lament over the emptiness of words and the discontinuity of human pleasure is a celebration of rhetoric that effects Ariadne's smooth transition from one lover to another. In her lament, Ariadne dramatizes her situation from every angle, moving around this situation with the same thoroughness as the eye of the observer that records her clothes slipping from her body in lines 63–67. The lament is introduced by a passage that frames it with a variety of shots of Ariadne against different backdrops, lingering over the tone of her voice, her facial aspect, her clothes, and what they reveal:

> saepe illam perhibent ardenti corde furentem
> clarisonas imo fudisse e pectore voces,
> ac tum praeruptos tristem conscendere montes,
> unde aciem [in] pelagi vastos protenderet aestus
> tum tremuli salis adversas procurrere in undas
> mollia nudatae tollentem tegmina surae,
> atque haec extremis maestam dixisse querellis,
> frigidulos udo singultus ore cientem. (124–31)

They say that often in the fury of her burning mind
she poured out shrill laments from the depths of her heart
and then in her sorrow she scaled steep mountains
from which she could cast her gaze over the sea's expanses;
then she ran into the incoming waves of the restless sea,
raising the soft folds of her dress and baring her thigh,

and grieving she said these things in her last lament,
forcing cold little sobs from her tearful face.

Ariadne then begins her lament by turning her despair into melody:

sicine me patriis avectam, perfide, ab aris
perfide, deserto liquisti in litore, Theseu?
sicine discedens neglecto numine divum
immemor a! devota domum periuria portas?' (132–35)

Have you left me thus, faithless man, abducted from my father's altars
faithless Theseus, have you left me on the deserted shore?
Thus do you leave me, disregarding the power of the gods,
ah heedless, and take home your accursed perjury?'

There is something similar about these two passages, the one primarily visual, the other auditory. In the introductory passage, a system of parallels and contrasts plays across the boundary between human and natural: "the depths of her heart" from which Ariadne pours her voice contrasts with the "steep mountains" that she climbs; similarly, the tremulous water into which she runs is cognate with the cold sobs that come from her wet mouth. The beginning of the lament, an intricate melodic theme and variation, catches the narrative completion of Theseus' story in the melody of Ariadne's abandonment, for Theseus heedlessly bringing home his perjury is presented as a melodic variation of his abandonment of Ariadne (sicine ... sicine ... ?). These effects contradict the ruptures that provoke Ariadne's lament, both the rupture between Ariadne and her deserted environment and that between Theseus and herself; these are effects that are quite common in literature, but in this context they draw attention to the fact that Ariadne exists in a work of art, just like the tapestry on which the wedding guests see her figure, and that in a work of art there are no discontinuities. The two passages weave a seamless texture out of the rhetoric that expresses Ariadne's abandonment and isolation. Perhaps the most virtuosic element of Catullus' poem is its dazzling and unpredictable handling of transitions, between the various levels of the poem, between one story and another, and between the senses addressed; this element of Catullus' art suggests an affinity with the illusionistic wall painting of the contemporary second style.

Ariadne is both fictional figure and artist; her voice is heard both as lament and as poetry. Paradoxically, Ariadne's lament establishes a connection between the experience of extreme rupture and discontinuity, dramatized by the intensity of her rhetoric, and the smooth transitions allowed by the poetic medium.[23] In his Europe ode (c.1.27), a poem that features the distress of another abandoned woman from myth, Horace goes further than Catullus and makes overt irony of his heroine's distress: Europe's lament culminates in a prayer for death; the listening Venus smiles and, when she has enjoyed herself enough (ubi lusit satis, 69), tells Europe that she is the wife of Jupiter and should learn to enjoy her good fortune, for she will give her name to part of the world (c.1.27.66–76). "Ubi lusit satis": Venus cuts Europe off and returns her to the mythological toybox from which the poet took her; *lusit* reminds us that it's all a harmless bit of mythology, of poetical *lusus*, at the same time that it endows Europe with pathos as the object of Venus' trifling (lusus). Horace's turn to geography, which is the presence of myth for those who are belated, moves—like Catullus' "at parte ex alia" (251)—from the drama of an event to the picturesque tableau of myth laid out as a kind of map. This double perspective on the fable, as both drama (which we may wake into life or reenact) and component of "mythology" (a list of resonant names, a series of picturesque tableaux, a storehouse of exotic marvels) can be referred to the opening of Catullus' poem. There the age of heroes is both a time that the poet calls upon across a rift in history and a box of marvels and decorations that is his to open. It is this kind of double seeing, inherent in the status of myth, and not immaturity on the poet's part, that accounts for the combination of pathos and preciosity in the poem.

## The Power of the Spectator

The double seeing that I have been describing is an effect that springs from, and accentuates, the experience of the spectator who can shift his or her relation to the spectacle at will. When the wedding guests leave, making way for the gods, Catullus lavishes a long, gorgeous, and stunningly virtuosic simile on the dispersal of the guests;

> hic, qualis flatu placidum mare matutino
> horrificans Zephyrus proclivas incitat undas,
> Aurora exoriente vagi sub limine Solis,
> quae tarde primum clementi flamine pulsae
> procedunt leviterque sonant plangore cachinni,
> post vento crescente magis magis increbescunt,

> purpureaque procul nantes ab luce refulgent:
> sic tum vestibuli linquentes regia tecta
> ad se quisque vago passim pede discedebant. (269–77)

> Then, as the West Wind, roughening the calm sea
> with a morning breeze hurries the tumbling waves,
> when Dawn rises at the threshold of the wandering sun,
> and the waves, pushed by the gentle breeze, slowly
> advance and their laughter sounds as they break lightly,
> and then as the wind gets up they grow bigger and bigger,
> and swimming far off they gleam with crimson:
> so the guests, leaving the royal forecourt, dispersed
> in all directions to their several homes with wandering feet.

The content of this simile inverts the scene of Ariadne on the shore on which the guests had been feasting their eyes: now the wave brings to shore a bounty of sounds and images rather than bearing away an object of desire, and morning begins with a crescendo, not a sudden awareness of loss. But all this is to describe the *dispersal* of the guests, and the careful marshalling of the crescendo toward a climax of light and sound is then applied to the random scattering of the crowds.[24] Further, the *comparandum* is actually part of the *comparatum*, for the manner in which the crowd disperses homeward does not echo anything in the description of the incoming waves, rather it completes that description, with the division of a mass into individual streams (now of people) disappearing up the shore. The distinction implied by the qualis . . . talis structure is dissolved by this continuity overlaid on the comparison. Above all, the application of the simile contradicts our expectations: after being told that the guests gave place to the gods, and then being launched into a set-piece simile beginning "Then, as . . . ," we naturally suppose that what is being described is the arrival of the gods. Not only are we disappointed but we experience the arrival of the gods as an anticlimax after this magnificent picture of movement.

Like the opulent recession of the house, this voluptuous retiring of the guests before the arrival of the gods expresses the poignant pleasures of an age that compensates for its belatedness, in relation both to the heroic age and to Greek literature, with a celebration of its own representational powers. The simile, like the description of Ariadne's seminakedness, overlays a sensuous experience on action that it in some sense contradicts. Catullus' emphasis here on the retiring of the guests before the gods' arrival is odd in view of the fact that he glorifies the heroic age as the time when gods and humans mingled. According to the moralizing school of interpretation, Catullus is implying that there never really was an heroic age, or that it was already debased.[25] But perhaps, by diverting the poetic effect we would expect for the arrival of the gods to the glorious retiring of the guests, Catullus makes of the very distance between humans and gods an aesthetic experience characteristic of those who nostalgically conjure up the world of myth.

A more striking example of the interference between the action narrated and the vision of the spectator is the extraordinary overlaying of gazes in the following passage, where Ariadne falls in love with Theseus at first sight:

> hunc simul ac cupido conspexit lumine virgo
> regia, quam suavis exspirans castus odores
> lectulus in molli complexu matris alebat,
> quales Eurotae praecingunt flumina myrtus
> aurave distinctos educit verna colores,
> non prius ex illo flagrantia declinavit
> lumina, quam cuncto concepit corpore flammam
> funditus atque imis exarsit tota medullis. (86–93)

> Immediately the royal girl caught sight of him with
> longing look (the girl whom a chaste bed redolent with sweet odors
> nurtured in the soft embrace of her mother,
> as the myrtles fringe the banks of the Eurotas
> or the spring breeze brings out various colors),
> she did not turn her burning eyes from him
> before she caught the flame throughout her body
> to the depths, and her inmost marrow was all ablaze.

The passionate gaze of Ariadne at Theseus is here suspended as we linger over the virginal bed of Ariadne, feeding our senses unhurriedly while she catches on fire. Ariadne seems to project with the intensity of her gaze (*cupido . . . lumine, flagrantia . . . lumina*) the fire that will return from Theseus to inflame her; we are reminded of certain ancient theories of vision according to which, as Konstan explains, "the eye is a kind of lantern emitting a current of fire, which transmits the motion of any illuminated object in its path back through the body and into the soul, and this results in visual sensation."[26] Konstan points out that Catullus has substituted this natural description, based on the ancient theory of the physics of the gaze, for Apollonius' arrow of Cupid (*Arg.* 3.286–88). But the agency of Ariadne is suspended as we savor the breathing of her bed and the wafting of scents, emanations quite different from the current of fire that streams from her gaze. The description shifts its focus from scent, which cannot be represented in a picture any more than in a poem, to sight, via the grammatical ellipsis "odores . . . quales myrtus," and this introduces the variegated colors of spring in the following line. This slippage, and the dissolve from one sense to another, is the play of the spectator's fantasy in the suspension of Ariadne's fierce gaze. The scents that in this context *are* the virginal passivity of Ariadne allow the fantasizing, or poetical, transition from mother's embrace to the analogically containing fringe of myrtles and on to the *aura* ("breeze" and also "fragrance") that picks out (educit, 90) the various colors of the spring flowers. *Educit*, with its connotations of child-rearing, suggests an analogy between the colors of the flowers picked out by the breeze and the emerging charms of the nubile Ariadne. In the suspension of the narrative at Ariadne's desiring gaze, which marks her emergence into a potentially assertive womanhood, the poem plays back a soft-focus, slow-motion scene of Ariadne in her virginal bed. The power of the viewer is asserted over the agency of the main fictional character, and the flow of light, or fire, passing between the mythical figures is interrupted by the breeze that figures the presence of the viewer, empowered to "pick out" the budding charms of the young Ariadne.

## Seeing the Fates

The poem ends, apart from a short moralizing coda, with the song of the Fates at the wedding feast of Peleus and Thetis. This song is very puzzling, for it focuses on the son who will be born to the couple, and specifically on his "outstanding merits and famous exploits" (egregias virtutes claraque facta, 348), which consist in the massive slaughter he inflicts at Troy. That Achilles' achievements should be attested by the mourning of mothers (349) is disturbing enough at a wedding, but the fact that the career of Achilles, as told by the Fates, culminates in the cruel sacrifice of the virgin Polyxena at his grave (362–70) is even less appropriate to the occasion. In other versions of this wedding, it is Apollo or the Muses who sing, and it is clear that Catullus has gone out of his way to produce this incongruous effect. This passage is crucial for those who interpret the poem as an ironic reflection on the Golden Age,[27] and it is similar in effect to the story of Theseus and Ariadne, which also casts an ironic light on the virtues of the heroic age. Certainly, the song is strange, and its strangeness, I think, is due to the disturbing physicality of this combination of epithalamium and prophetic chant. Beginning with a voluptuous description of the wedding night (328–32), the song proceeds, through the slaughter by Achilles that chokes the Scamander with corpses, to the sacrifice of Polyxena, visualized in very physical terms (362–70). But Catullus' own epithalamia remind us that the wedding, an occasion that precedes the spilling of blood, is not so far removed from the world of war.[28]

As seers, the Fates are able to truncate time, juxtaposing scenes temporally distant from each other and widely different in character. But as a spectacle, they are themselves subjected by the poet to the same kind of kaleidoscopic seeing. The unsettling physicality of this final section of the poem begins with the very vivid description of the Fates themselves. As Jenkyns 1982, 141, points out, the application to old women of language that more commonly suggests youth and beauty is a feature of this rather detailed description:

> cum interea infirmo quatientes corpora motu
> veridicos Parcae coeperunt edere cantus.
> his corpus tremulum complectens undique vestis
> candida purpurea talos incinxerat ora,
> at roseae niveo residebant vertice vittae,
> aeternumque manus carpebant rite laborem. (305–10)

> Meanwhile shaking their bodies with a tremulous motion
> the Fates began to give voice to their soothsaying songs.
> A white dress hugging all of their shaking bodies
> covered their ankles with a purple border,
> and pink bands rested on their snow-white heads,
> and their hands duly pursued their endless task of spinning.

Jenkyns draws attention to the tightness of the robes on these aged bodies and to the use of red and white, characteristic of descriptions of a girl's complexion. I would go further and argue that the Fates, singing and shaking their limbs, are here grotesquely reminiscent of the dancing girls who put on erotic shows at the banquets of rich nobles.[29] The context is right, for the Fates are introduced immediately after the gods have sat down before the lavish banquet (303–4).[30] But as well as singing and dancing, these old women are working, and there now follow ten lines containing a detailed description of the eternal labor (310) of spinning. The Fates, who can see everything, are themselves the object of a way of seeing that mixes what would otherwise be separated in time or place: they are young and old; dancing and working (singing might appropriately accompany both activities); sexy and repulsive; goddesses and entertainers; dancing girls and spinning Roman matrons. What we experience here is the uncanny quality of the old woman, who is both fascinating and disturbing to the Romans, as is clear from the gloating, almost hysterical quality of much of the *vetulaskoptik* (invective against old women) so common in Roman literature.[31] Catullus' description of the Fates exemplifies this attitude to the old woman as a paradoxical, uncanny sight.

If the Fates themselves have a sensuality that anticipates the wedding night of which they sing, so does their work:

> atque ita decerpens aequabat semper opus dens
> laneaque aridulis haerebant morsa labellis,
> quae prius in levi fuerant extantia filo:
> ante pedes autem candentis mollia lanae
> vellera virgati custodibant calathisci. (315–19)

> and all the time the tooth cleaned and smoothed the work
> and bitten tufts of wool stuck to the dry lips,
> tufts that before had protruded from the smooth thread:
> but at their feet soft fleeces of white wool
> were held in wicker baskets.

The soft wool bitten off by the monosyllabic tooth and still hanging on the dry lips, the soft white wool in the baskets woven from twigs—these tactile contrasts are brought to mind when the Fates sing of the coming night:

> adveniet fausto cum sidere coniunx,
> quae tibi flexanimo mentem perfundat amore
> languidulosque paret tecum coniungere somnos,
> levia substernens robusto brachia collo. (329–332)

> the spouse will come, with the lucky star,
> to drench your mind with a love that sways the soul,
> ready to join her langorous slumbers with yours,
> stretching her smooth arms beneath your strong neck.

Both the diminutive form and the sound of *languidulos* (langorous) recall "laneaque aridulis" (316), and the whole of line 316, with its bites and its lips, acquires a curious eroticism from the association. The postcoital sleep of the newlyweds is described in terms of the same hard/soft contrast that dominates the lines from the spinning passage. As with Ariadne, then, the "seeing of" the Fates, those uncanny and paradoxical figures, by others is overlaid on the subjective "seeing of" the Fates, namely, their vision of erotic happiness and slaughter.

The aging female body is visualized again in the song of the Fates celebrating the future exploits of Achilles:

> illius egregias virtutes claraque facta
> saepe fatebuntur gnatorum in funere matres,
> cum incultum cano solvent a vertice crinem,
> putridaque infirmis variabunt pectora palmis. (348–51)

> his outstanding virtues and famous deeds
> will often be confessed by mothers at their sons' funerals,
> when they loose their unkempt hair from their heads,
> and bruise their crumbling breasts with infirm hands.

Here the standard emblem of mourning, women beating their breasts, is visualized in a most disturbing fashion: the breasts are decaying, possibly crumbling, and the hands are weak or shaking. The topos usually cashes in on the visual, erotic potential of such a scene by describing the disfiguring of beautiful breasts, which must therefore be visualized in their pristine nakedness.[32] Here the reverse is the case, for the verb used to convey the bruising is one of aesthetic enhancement, the same verb that is used to describe the tapestry (priscis hominum *variata* figuris, "variegated with the ancient figures of men," 50).[33] In fact, the breasts of the mothers are the medium in which the deeds of Achilles are recorded, deeds acknowledged (fatebuntur, 349) by the acts of mourning. This puts the breasts of the bereaved mothers in the same category as the tapestry, which also proclaims the prowess of heroes (c.64.51), and the first thing that strikes the eye on the tapestry is the body of Ariadne, whose nakedness is the sign of Theseus' desertion. So from the half-naked bodies of the nymphs that mark the wonder of the first sea voyage to the sacrifice of Polyxena in honor of the dead Achilles, it is the woman's body on which the exploits of the heroes are registered and whose vulnerability compensates the viewer's debilitating longing for what has passed.

The sacrifice of Polyxena with which the song of the Fates ends is itself a kind of wedding, for the sacrificed virgin was to be the bride of Achilles in the underworld, but it is not only with the wedding and its erotic violence that this sacrifice is associated; compare

> denique testis erit morti quoque reddita praeda,
> cum teres excelso coacervatum aggere bustum
> excipiet niveos perculsae virginis artus. (362–64)

> finally the booty rendered even to his corpse will witness [his virtues]
> when the rounded mound piled with a high earthwork
> will receive the white limbs of the slaughtered virgin.

to

> qui [sc. divi] postquam niveis flexerunt sedibus artus
> large multiplici constructae sunt dape mensae. (303–4)
>
> after the gods had relaxed (folded) their limbs on the white seats
> the tables were built up generously with many courses.

The architectural generosity of the feast spread for the gods is a mark of honor that is echoed by the similarly piled-up tomb of Achilles, and the limbs of the gods relaxed on the white chairs are grotesquely brought to mind by the white limbs of the struck Polyxena, whose headless body falls as her knees crumble (summisso poplite, 370; compare 'flexerunt artus,' 303). The relaxation of the gods on their chairs is also associated, via the echo of *flexerunt* in *flexanimo* (330), with the postcoital relaxation of the wedding couple. Of the wedding song of the Fates, one might truly say "all things speakable and unspeakable were confused," which is Catullus' indictment of his own godforsaken age (omnia fanda nefanda . . . permixta, 405). What is so disturbing, and at the same time strangely voluptuous, about the Fates and their song is the simultaneity of vision, the mingling of modalities, the dissolution of boundaries and of temporal succession. In the final moralizing tirade, it is the breakdown of succession in the family, with the generations losing their proper relations (400–405), that marks our own impious age. But the mode of seeing is quite different; the rhetoric of moral indignation gives us a firm perspective on the mingling, a mingling that is itself credited with causing a clear periodization of history. The lament for the rupture in our history that retired the gods from intercourse with humans provides a relief from the intensity and simultaneity of the vision of the Fates; it leads us out of the kaleidoscopic vision and blurred physicality of the preceding section, restoring our focus and allowing the magical world that the poem has conjured up to fade into the distance.

I have not so far addressed the question, much disputed in the criticism, of Catullus' attitude to the age of heroes. This question has always been cast in moral terms: does Catullus believe in a more virtuous past, or does he in fact describe the heroic age as already containing the seeds—even displaying the full flower—of the moral decadence of his own time? To what extent is the mythical part of the poem a reflection of the moral problems of contemporary Rome? By now it should be clear that I do not believe that Catullus casts the relation between the contemporary world and the world of myth in moral terms; the mythical world is a fantasy world that engages the reader's desire to visualize, and the reader is far too invested in the contemporary world's power to represent and manipulate the scenes of myth to be in a position to judge its relation to his or her own world in moral terms. The issue that Catullus engages for the spectator/reader is one of the representative adequacy of contemporary art when confronted with the potentially debilitating fact of its belatedness.

I have suggested that the moralistic periodization with which the poem ends leads us out of the phantasmagoric seeing of the song of the Fates. Bryson 1990 has provided a helpful model for understanding the ideology of representation in Campanian painting, a model that, not surprisingly, works very well for this poem:

Wealth and representation function here as cognate terms, so that to adorn the chamber with *xenia* and *trompe l'oeil* is to display not only one's wealth but the very principle of that wealth: the outstripping of necessity and limitation. But visual ideology organises this excess of wealth and of representation by creating visual structures that permit the return from even remote regions of unreality and simulation, back to the limits of the given world: the movement is not one of headlong flight from the real, as with Trimalchio, but of carefully graduated transitions and liaisons between reality and representation (52).

The luxuriousness of Catullus' poem, its virtuosity, its imitation of visual art, its play with frames and with different modes of representation, all suggest that it is celebrating the same kind of representational power as the wall paintings. The mythical world, associated here with a great technological feat (sailing), is the object of a visual longing that is richly satisfied by the representational virtuosity of the poem, at the same time as the poem thematizes the desiring gaze in its narrative, producing a complex interplay between viewer and viewed, between the act of representation and the action represented. The matter of Catullus' epyllion is Greek myth, so the Roman reader is doubly removed from the world of heroes, both temporally and culturally; and yet counterpointing this removal is the position of the conquering Roman as the confident consumer and appropriator of Greek culture.[34] If this poem reflects its context, it does so not so much through the issues of morality and the breakdown of social order as through the peculiar character of Roman cultural consumption. Again, Bryson has relevant words about Campanian *xenia* (still life):

There seems no reason to doubt that the Campanian *xenia* sincerely invoke the earlier, still religious, Greek ethos of hospitality; but they then move in to explore the Roman aesthetic of secondariness, belatedness and excess in relation to Greek culture and art. They are not just pictures of food, but Roman pictures of Greek pictures of food; not just representation, but representation raised to a higher power, where Greek art is absorbed into Roman patterns of luxury consumption. In this doubling or multiplying of mimetic distance, the *xenia* participate in the lavishness of the Roman economy; they provide images of consumption itself as it moves in the Roman world between the poles of simple need and exuberant—delirious—excess (53).

By casting this story from Greek mythology in terms of gazing, longing, and appetite, Catullus presents us with a world that is the object both of alienated longing and of confident indulgence; in this double relation he displays his true Roman genius.

CHAPTER 7

# The Ruse of the Victim
## Poems 10 and 11

My subject in this chapter is again Catullus' display of his own mastery and, more specifically, his situating of poetic capabilities against other kinds of discourse, a procedure that serves to allow poetic power to make a strategic appearance *within a poem.* In poems 10 and 11, confrontations between Catullus and a woman are set in a metropolitan Rome that sends out its elite to govern and plunder the provinces and its armies to conquer the most remote parts of the world. Having tried to articulate imperial power with gender relations, the speaker of these poems finds that the ambiguous position of the women in relation to empire unravels his strategy, but it is at the very point where the Catullan persona confesses his weakness and vulnerability that the power of the poet appears. The poet's staging of his persona's victimization is a means of locating the exorbitant position from which the lyric poet speaks; poetic discourse claims a transcendent status for itself when the poet's distinctive position emerges from a situation of complete powerlessness in relation to the contexts of the speaker's social world.

Lyric poets have a tendency to pose as victims: of cruel mistresses, of faithless lovers, of an uncomprehending world, or even of their own sensitivities and uncompromising aesthetic standards.[1] Catullus is probably the first major poet to make his status as victim a focus of his persona, and this accounts for the protective, at times conspiratorial, intimacy that has developed between him and his readers. He has attracted the sympathies of his readers as victim not only of Lesbia but also of misguided readers, unfaithful friends, censorious old men, and even his own candor and self-knowledge. From the Roman point of view, there could be no one more powerless than the victim of a woman. In poem 10, Catullus recounts his social discomfiture at the hands of a "little whore" who catches him in a mendacious boast that was supposed to impress her; in the next poem, he entrusts the words of a bitter farewell to Lesbia to his "friends" Furius and Aurelius. The latter poem ends with Catullus telling Lesbia that she has destroyed his love as the passing plough cuts a flower at the edge of a field.

As in poem 64, gender and empire are implicated with each other in the two poems discussed in this chapter. Like Ariadne, the women in poems 10 and 11 are ambiguously positioned in relation to the imperial, associated both with Roman speakers and with the foreign world that the empire does, or would, dominate. This conceptualization of the female as both same and other is, as Hallett 1989 has shown, typical of Roman elite attitudes. In all three poems (64, 10, and 11), the contradictory status of the woman is an essential aspect of their structure, but the convenient availability of the mythical figure of Ariadne to negotiate the problem of imperial Rome's cultural belatedness contrasts with the much more troublesome presence of the women in the two poems I now address. This troublesomeness is mainly a function of the triangular relationships in these poems, in which the speaker tries to use the woman to settle agenda between himself and other men as well as vice versa.

On the face of it, these two poems appear to have very little in common. Poem 10 exudes the urbanity of the self-deprecating raconteur:

Varus me meus ad suos amores
visum duxerat e foro otiosum,
scortillum, ut mihi tum repente visum est,
non sane illepidum neque invenustum.
huc ut venimus, incidere nobis
sermones varii, in quibus, quid esset
iam Bithynia, quo modo se haberet,
et quonam mihi profuisset aere.
respondi id quod erat, nihil neque ipsis
nec praetoribus esse nec cohorti,
cur quisquam caput unctius referret,
praesertim quibus esset irrumator
praetor, nec faceret pili cohortem.
"at certe tamen," inquiunt "quod illic
natum dicitur esse, comparasti
ad lecticum homines." ego, ut puellae
unum me facerem beatiorem,
"non" inquam "mihi tam fuit maligne,
ut, provincia quod mala incidisset,

non possem octo homines parare rectos."
at mi nullus erat neque hic neque illic
fractum qui veteris pedem grabati
in collo sibi collocare posset.
hic illa, ut decuit cinaediorem,
"quaeso," inquit "mihi, mi Catulle, paulum,
istos commoda: nam volo ad Serapim
deferri." "mane," inquii puellae,
"istud quod modo dixeram me habere,
fugit me ratio: meus sodalis—
Cinna est Gaius—is sibi paravit.
verum, utrum illius an mei, quid ad me?
utor tam bene quam mihi pararim.
sed tu insulsus male et molesta vivis,
per quam non licet esse neglegentem."

My friend Varus took me from the forum,
as I idled there, to meet his girlfriend;
a little whore, I noticed on the spot,
but not without charm or beauty.
When we got here, various subjects
came up, amongst which, what was the news
from Bithynia now, and how it was doing,
and what sort of profit I had made there.
I answered with the truth, there was nothing
for the natives, nor the praetors nor their staff,
no reason to come back slicker than one had set out,
especially for those whose praetor screwed
them over and didn't give a damn for his staff.
"But surely," they said, "you obtained for yourself
some litterbearers, we're told it's the
local product." I, wanting to make myself
seem uniquely fortunate to the girl, said,
"Things weren't so bad; just because
I drew a bad province doesn't mean
I couldn't scrape up eight stout men."
In fact I had no one, here or yonder
who could shoulder the burden
of an old cot's broken leg. At which
she said (just like her, the cow),
"Please, Catullus, my friend, let me borrow
them a while, I need a ride to Serapis' temple."
"Hold on," I said to her, "when I told you
I *had* them, well, I forgot: my friend
Cinna (Gaius Cinna, I mean) *he's* the one
who bought them. But, whether his or mine,

who cares? I use them as though I'd bought them myself.
But you, you're a bore and a drag to have around
if a man can't be careless with his talk."

Poem 11, by contrast, is a bitter notice of divorce to Lesbia:

> Furi et Aureli, comites Catulli,
> sive in extremos penetrabit Indos,
> litus ut longe resonante Eoa
>     tunditur unda,
> sive in Hyrcanos Arabasve molles,
> seu Sagas sagittiferosve Parthos,
> sive quae septemgeminus colorat
>     aequora Nilus,
> sive trans altas gradietur Alpes,
> Caesaris visens monimenta Magni,
> Gallicum Rhenum horribile aequor ulti-
>     mosque Britannos,
> omnia haec, quaecumque feret voluntas
> caelitum, temptare simul parati,
> pauca nuntiate meae puellae
>     non bona dicta.
> cum suis vivat valeatque moechis,
> quos simul complexa tenet trecentos,
> nullum amans vere, sed identidem omnium
>     ilia rumpens;
> nec meum respectet, ut ante, amorem,
> qui illius culpa cecidit velut prati
> ultimi flos, praetereunte postquam
>     tactus aratro est.

> Furius and Aurelius, Catullus' companions,
> whether he reaches the furthest India,
> whose shore is echoing all its length
>     to the crashing eastern wave,
> or the soft Arabs or the Hyrcani, or
> the Sagae or the Parthians who fight with bows,
> or the lands which the seven-mouthed Nile,
>     overflowing, colors,
> or whether he strides across the high Alps,
> viewing the monuments of great Caesar,
> the rough expanse of the Gallic Rhine,
>     or the Britons at earth's end,
> prepared as you are to attempt with me
> all this, whatever the will of the gods
> commands, pass on these none too pleasant
>     words to my girl:

> let her live and flourish with her adulterers
> whom she embraces three hundred at a time,
> truly loving none, but again and again
> > breaking their manhood;
> and let her not look to my love, as before,
> which has fallen by her fault like the flower
> on the edge of the field, touched
> > by the passing plough.

In one respect these poems, exhibiting two contrasting aspects of Catullus' persona in the collection, appear to conflict in their values, for whereas the "Catullus" of the incident recounted in 10 castigates the woman for not allowing him to exercise *neglegentia* (carelessness), the distraught lover of 11 charges Lesbia in the most bitter terms with a destructive heedlessness. The word *neglegentia* has a powerfully negative sense in relation to such central Roman values as *pietas, fides, constantia,* and *gravitas* (dutifulness, reliability, constancy, seriousness), and in such a context it implies carelessness and lack of responsibility. Of course, the Roman elite, and particularly the young sophisticates of Catullus' circle, claimed, when off duty, the freedom to exercise the conversational irresponsibility and playfulness that were such important ingredients of *urbanitas*.[2] However, the speaker of the last lines of poem 10 is the object of irony, and his appeal to the standards of urbanity is quite unwarranted in view of the fact that—as the "Catullus" recounting the anecdote admits—he was caught in an opportunistic (i.e., anything but *neglegens*) lie (16–17, 21–23). The question we might now ask is whether there is any relation between the indifferent heedlessness of Lesbia, embracing her three hundred lovers, and the pseudo-urbane carelessness of the lie of "Catullus." In the following pages, I argue that there is such a relation, mediated by the imperial ethos that infects all of the dramatis personae of these poems in some way. Imperial power underwrites loose talk in the metropolis, and it is against the background of this loose talk that the distinctive capacities of poetry are enabled to appear.

## Poetry and Lying: Poem 10

The self-deprecating "Catullus" who so engagingly recounts his social embarrassment in poem 10 has earned the affection of centuries of readers.[3] But the strategy of the poem's persona is disturbingly like that of the teller of the tendentious joke in Freud's *Jokes and Their Relation to the Unconscious* (1960); for Freud, the tendentious joke is a response to the failure of an aggressive move toward an object of desire. Balked in his attempt to impress Varus' girl, "Catullus," like Freud's joke teller, addresses his joke to a potential rival (his male readership), with whom he shares, in laughter, the pleasurable release of impulses that have been checked by the girl. The reader who laughs at the discomfiture of "Catullus" is also expected to enjoy his insults against the girl, one of which is sexual (cinaediorem, 24); the joke and the insult together produce an equivalent of Freud's tendentious, or sexual, joke. It is only recently that some of Catullus' female readers, refusing to be charmed by this anecdote, have examined the manipulative strategies by which the poet engages his readers as well as the structure of the Roman status system that the poem reflects.[4]

The poem begins by soliciting the complicity of the speaker's audience in the imperial attitude of the metropolitan male to the woman who will eventually be his nemesis. Catullus, idling in the forum, is taken by his friend Varus to inspect the latter's girlfriend.[5] Referring to her as a *scortillum* (little whore, 3), Catullus marks her as the province of the men, making his visit partially analogous to his expedition to Bithynia with the praetor. But Catullus' impression of the girl as he reports it to his audience is far more favorable than his impression of the province as he reports it to Varus and the girl:

> scortillum, ut mihi tum repente visum est,
> non sane illepidum neque invenustum. (3–4)
>
> a little whore, as I noticed on the spot,
> but not without charm or beauty.

Whereas the prostitute is included in the circle of the *urbani*, the province is measured against the standards of urban refinement and found wanting (9–11).[6] Yet Catullus' ability to see charm in a prostitute is but the other side of his ability to speak in such a casual manner of the disappointing Bithynia; they are both a measure of his urbane detachment and disinterestedness, and of course it is the potential availability of the prostitute to the man and of the province to the imperial staff that underwrites this nonchalance. The complicity of the urbane conversational tone with the imperial ethos is made quite clear by the parallel between

> huc ut venimus *incidere* nobis
> sermones varii, in quibus quid esset
> iam Bithynia, . . . (5–7)

> When we got here, various subjects
> *came up*, amongst which, what was the news
> from Bithynia now . . .

and

> "non," inquam, "mihi tam fuit maligne
> ut, provincia quod mala *incidisset*,
> non possem octo homines parare rectos." (18–20)
>
> "Things weren't so bad; just because
> *I drew* a bad province doesn't mean
> I couldn't scrape up eight stout men."

The casual and easy ranging of metropolitan conversation reflects Rome's imperial status, with the luck of the imperial draw here related to the chance topics of urbane conversation by a repetition of the same verb.[7] When Catullus makes his false claim to have turned to good account his stay in the wretched province, he is attempting to turn a conversational profit out of an unpromising topic, and the source of this profit is to be Varus' girlfriend (16–17).

As a prostitute who has been dubbed *venusta* and *lepida*, the girlfriend of Varus is in an ambiguous position, as both the province of the men and a participant in their metropolitan attitudes. Replying to Catullus' complaints of the poverty of Bithynia and the meanness of the praetor, she chimes in with Varus:

> "at certe tamen," inquiunt "quod illic
> natum dicitur esse, comparasti
> ad lecticam homines." (14–16)
>
> "But surely," they said, "you obtained for yourself
> some litterbearers, we're told it's the
> local product."

The choral response and the "but surely" (at certe tamen), which suggests a continuation of something begun by Catullus, draw us into a discourse that all three speakers share. An equation is made between what is said about Bithynia in the metropolis and what Catullus can be expected to have acquired (*quod* illic / natum *dicitur* esse, *comparasti*). Something of the same spirit pervades Cicero's words to his friend Trebatius in Britain:

in Britannia nihil esse audio neque auri neque argenti. id si ita est, essedum aliquod suadeo capias, et ad nos quam primum recurras. (*ad Fam.* 7.7.1)

I hear that in Britain there is neither gold nor silver. If that is the case, I urge you to capture a chariot and return to us as quickly as possible.

The litterbearers in Catullus' poem are no more real than the chariot in Cicero's offhand joke; as the subject of "illic natum dicitur esse" (is said to have been born there, i.e., "is the local product"), the phrase "ad lecticam homines" is abstract and means "the institution of litterbearers," but as the object of *comparasti* (you bought) it is concrete (men who bear litters). The men whom Catullus is supposed to have acquired never really emancipate themselves from the metropolitan chatter in which they are born, as the clash between abstract singular and concrete plural (quod . . . nat*um* . . . homin*es*) indicates. In this context, Catullus' lie is simply a continuation of the metropolitan attitude in which the reality of the litterbearers is not an issue: the conversation is buoyed up by the imperial ethos much as a litter for whose occupants the litterbearers do not really exist.[8] To this extent, Catullus' castigation of the girl for being the bane of urbanity is justified.

But the celebration of imperial privilege is only one level of the conversation recounted in this anecdote. When Catullus tells his lie about the litterbearers, he explains his motive to his readers:

> ego, ut puellae
> unum me facerem beatiorem, (16–17)
>
> I, wanting to make myself
> seem uniquely fortunate to the girl,

While singling out the girl from the choral duo as the audience of his response, Catullus simultaneously singles himself out from the other men on the governor's staff. The erotic agenda, which is to separate the individual from the group, is overlaid on metropolitan presumption, which depends on a group complicity.[9] In this respect, then, Catullus' castigation of the girl at the end of the poem is quite unjustified.

Implicitly, Gaius Cinna, who is offhand in the matter of ownership (27–32), is contrasted to the girl (sed tu, 33), whose behavior is *insulsa* (gauche) and *molesta* (boorish) because she exposes Catullus' offhanded lie. But this contrast judges her in terms quite inappropriate to the way she has been treated. The sharing between men epitomized by Cinna's putatively loose attitude to ownership, and the related complicity of the metropolitans that is one level of the conversation between Catullus, Varus, and his woman, these alliances have been violated by the attempt of Catullus to single himself out from other men in the eyes of the girl.

So, how is the erotic related to the imperial in this poem? Complicity within the male imperial world has already broken down because of the praetor's neglect of his staff, and of its right to profit from the provincials. In this context, the lie of Catullus functions as a means to recoup his losses in Bithynia in another province, so to speak, and he accomplishes this by singling himself out from the other men, just like the praetor who didn't give a damn for his retinue (nec faceret pili cohortem, 13; unum me facerem beatiorem, 17). When Catullus calls the praetor an *irrumator* (12), he indicates that, in breaking faith with his fellows in their communal exploitation of the provincials, the praetor has reduced them to the status of the sexually dominated. The role of Varus' woman in this context is to act as a kind of secondary province, to be the means by which an individual man singles himself out to compensate for the imbalances that have occurred within the male imperial group. In light of the connection I make in Chapter 3 between irrumation and silencing, the speaker's mendacious volubility toward the woman is a particularly appropriate compensation for the praetor's maltreatment.

The woman, then, has two different kinds of status. As an urban(e) sophisticate, she shares in the metropolitan world and is expected to be complicit in the *neglegentia* that confirms the solidarity of the group and the sovereignty of its discourse, for what the members of the group agree to allow each other is a reflection of what they are allowed over others. But as a woman she is expected to confirm the uniqueness of the particular man who singles himself out in her eyes. This conflict of positions is the standpoint from which we should see her embarrassing request for the loan of Catullus' putative litterbearers. What is puzzling about this request is that we cannot be sure whether we are to believe that she intended to embarrass Catullus or that she spoke quite innocently, in other words, whether her response is naive or sly.[10] To try to decide this question would be a mistake, because this moment is one in which two conflicting but related actions meet; the naive response, in which the woman would be behaving appropriately to one of her positions, is an impudent and cunning transgression in the context of her other position. As a gullible woman whom Catullus is out to impress, she is expected to believe him, and perhaps her request reflects her gullibility; but as a member of the loose-talking metropolitan sophisticates, she must recognize that this is just talk, and that to treat it otherwise would be an act of aggression. This undecidable moment reveals the contradictions in the structure of the poem's world, and when Catullus describes the woman's response as appropriate to a *cinaedus* (pathic, 24) he reflects her ambiguous status: to insult her with an expression that normally refers to an effeminate man is to remind us that her naive femininity in one position functions as shameless behavior in the other. Like the irrumating praetor, she has broken ranks.

The woman's request for the loan alludes to a fact that undermines the presumption of the metropolis with respect to the outside world. The litterbearers, whose reality has now become an embarrassing issue for the boastful metropolitan, are required for a visit to the temple of Serapis. Particularly popular among the demimonde of Rome, the cult of Serapis was one of the Egyptian cults that were repeatedly (and unsuccessfully) repressed in the 50s and 40s.[11] So the request that upsets the presumption of the metropolitan is accompanied by a reminder: that the flow of influence in the imperial world goes both from and *to* the metropolis, and that this flow provides forms of practice that challenge the dominant culture.

Ultimately, though, the standpoint from which the anecdote is told is not political. "Catullus" (the character in the anecdote) is certainly exposed, but we must remember that the anecdote is itself a performance that presupposes a position of confidence for the teller of the anecdote. This position is adopted when the narrator confesses to the audience that he did not possess the litterbearers in question:

"non" inquam "mihi tam fuit maligne,
ut, provincia quod mala incidisset,
non possem octo homines parare rectos."
    at mihi nullus erat nec hic neque illic,
fractum qui veteris pedem grabati
in collo sibi collocare posset. . . . (18–23)

"Things weren't so bad; just because
I drew a bad province doesn't mean
I couldn't scrape up eight stout men."
    In fact I had no one, here or yonder
who could shoulder the burden
of an old cot's broken leg. . . .

The relation that the teller adopts to the "Catullus" in the anecdote can be seen in the contrasting use of negatives. The double negative of the lie expresses the easy confidence of one who can presume and therefore need not boast; after this, the hyperbolic description of his lack of litterbearers undermines this show of power quite devastatingly. But it does more than that, for the confession becomes an opportunity for a display of poetic power that quite glories in its own capabilities. The comic image of the minimalist litterbearer that Catullus doesn't even have (21–23) turns absence into a presence both supremely visual and aural (collo . . . collocare, 23). Catullus' poetic ability to make something out of nothing is confirmed by the same words that undermine "Catullus'" claim to have made something out of nothing in Bithynia. The confession's ironic echo of the double negative of the false claim (nullus erat neque hic neque illic, 21) suspends the claim over an abyss, foregrounding the pure artifice of language. Telling this anecdote against himself, Catullus reveals his control of a layer of discourse itself traditionally associated with the lie, namely, poetic discourse.[12]

## Poetry and Severance: Poem 11

In the final lines of poem 11, the insulting words of severance that Catullus charges his friends to deliver to Lesbia shade off into a pathetic picture of his own ravaged love, which is like the flower that falls, touched by the passing plough. Insult is replaced by another kind of verbal power, for the flower image, carefully detached from the insult in a trailing relative clause that takes up the last three lines of the poem, transmutes Lesbia's destructive heedlessness into a delicate beauty preserved in the frame of the verse itself:

> qui [sc. meum amorem] illius culpa cecidit velut prati
> ultimi flos, praetereunte postquam
>    tactus aratro est. (22–24)

> which [sc. my love] has fallen by her fault like the flower
> on the edge of the field, touched
>    by the passing plough.

Lesbia's callous heedlessness destroys Catullus' love quite incidentally; he is not even the object of her attention. But the coincidence of the end of the poem with the words "tactus aratro est" (touched by the plough) brings together the incidental severing of Catullus' love by Lesbia with the deliberate cutting off of the poem by the poet. A further kind of cutting, the final elision (aratr[o] est), savors the touching of words at the very point where they meet with silence, an artistic touching that is diametrically opposed to the brutal heedlessness of the plough.[13] The rare hypermetric elision between lines 22 and 23 (prat[i] ultimi) prepares for this association of worldly events and places with poetic ones by identifying the edge of the field where the flower is touched and falls with the edge of the metrical line. As at the end of poem 10, the foregrounding of poetic effect depends on the victimizing of the persona, whether by himself or another; the emphasis of the persona on his own nullity tips over into the poetic. In the first poem (c.10), nothingness becomes productive in the medium (poetry) that knows no negative, and in the second (c.11), the brutal indifference of Lesbia toward her lover is made to serve the precise artistic purposes of closure.

But the revelation of poetic power is set, as in poem 10, into an elaborate anatomy of power relations in other dimensions, particularly those of gender and empire. The images of the plough and the flower at the end of the poem are important in this connection. As an object of aesthetic beauty, the flower is here opposed to the plough, an agent of ruthless civilizing power, and the same opposition appears in one of Catullus' epithalamia:[14]

> Ut flos in saeptis secretus nascitur hortis,
> ignotus pecori, nullo convolsus aratro,
> quem mulcent aurae, firmat sol, educat imber;
> . . . . . . . . . . . . . . .
> sic virgo dum intacta manet dum cara suis est. (c.62.39–41,45)
>
> As a flower is born hidden away in fenced gardens,
> unknown to cattle, torn up by no plough,
> which the breezes soothe, the sun strengthens, the rain nurtures;
> . . . . . . . . . . . . . . .
> so is the virgin while she remains untouched,
> while she is dear to her people.

This epithalamium takes the form of a competition between a chorus of girls and a chorus of boys who contest the status of marriage. The girls' choir compares the flower to the untouched virgin because it is happily innocent of the ministrations of agriculture, but in the response of the boys agriculture becomes a metaphor for the beneficial effects of marriage (c.62.49–58); as the boys present it, the bride's removal from her virginal world is a civilizing process that enhances her status. The plough that the girls declaim as an agent of gratuitous violence is a traditional image for male sexuality, and it plays a symbolic role in both the ceremonial founding and eradication of cities.[15] Through her association with the plough, Lesbia, who deflowers the innocent love of Catullus, is aligned with the often violent forces of civilization. However, the problem of communication with Lesbia is put in the context of empire building by the lengthy citation of Furius' and Aurelius' protestations that they would accompany Catullus to the remotest parts of the world, some of which had been the object of the farflung military campaigns of 55 B.C.E..[16] In this context, Lesbia is seen as a threatening monster on the edge of the empire, that is, beyond the pale of civilization, and also, by association with the plough, as a manifestation of the ruthless indifference that characterizes Roman imperial might. This double position, both inside and outside the male imperial circle, is the same as that of Varus' mistress in the previous poem; here, too, the fictional action breaks down because of an ambiguity in the position of the woman.

The imperial scenario is introduced by Catullus because it provides the appropriate hyperbole for the problem of "getting through" to Lesbia,[17] and it casts this problem in terms of the confrontation of the civilized with the savage: Lesbia's unbridled lust is as threatening as the peoples on the boundaries of the empire. Her sexual rapacity also brings to mind the indifferent and uncontrollable violence of nature, for her repeated and loveless exhaustion of her lovers (19–20) recalls the relentless beating of Ocean against the shores of furthest India.[18] Like Ocean, Lesbia lies outside the civilized world, which she clasps in a violent embrace; but even Ocean was conquered by the Roman army when, in 55, Caesar succeeded in getting through to the terminally savage Britons.[19]

However, this structure that would set Lesbia against imperial civilization and male companionship collapses because of the similarity between the protestations of Furius and Aurelius and the sexual behavior attributed to Lesbia. The two "friends" profess themselves "ready to brave (temptare) all this with [Catullus]" and also "to make an attempt (temptare) on all these places"; the military sense of *temptare* (*OLD* s.v. 9) is obviously operative in this passage.[20] So the companionship that is proven by this imperial willingness to take on the whole world turns out to be disconcertingly similar to the ministrations of Lesbia, who embraces her three hundred lovers all at once and breaks their loins.[21]

By setting the discourse of male companionship and empire against the discourse of love, Catullus renders Lesbia monstrous at the price of making the empire, and the male friendship it mediates, callous and unfeeling. The imperial context lends Lesbia's behavior a scale that portrays it as threatening the foundations of civilization, whereas the amatory context gives the imperial list through which Furius and

Aurelius protest their friendship an affect that condemns their listing by association with Lesbia's engulfing of her lovers. Finally, Lesbia's amatory callousness claims a symbol of the ruthless violence of civilizing power (the plough) for its own. Bringing together the "friends" and the lover, Catullus allows them to cancel each other out as they merge into a generalized and indifferent violence on whose periphery he locates, very precisely, himself, severed from the *world* of the poem and absorbed into its formal properties.

The whole of this poem is characterized by an indirection of speech in which the words of one speaker are mingled with those of another: citing the protestations of Furius and Aurelius, Catullus charges them to deliver a message to Lesbia, referred to in the third person. The profusely "faithful" friends are pressed into service to deliver a message of severance to the profusely faithless mistress, whose destruction of the poet's love is itself an indirect result of her indiscriminacy. The word *parati* (prepared, 14) indicates that the opening fourteen lines are citing Furius and Aurelius, though exactly what aspects of the passage we are to attribute to the duo and what to Catullus' paraphrase cannot be decided. The scholarly argument over whether the lines are meant as poetic, even romantic, or pompous, overblown, and insincere, cannot be settled one way or the other because the lines contain two voices, just as the woman's request for the litterbearers was spoken from two positions in poem 10.[22] Certainly, the extended list of places that conveys the protestations of Furius and Aurelius gives the impression that they protest too much, and that the imperial world they survey has in some respects been reduced to monuments, real or potential, of Roman might. But there is more in the geographical survey of the first twelve lines than a pompous listing of the places that Roman power might turn into its monuments (10). Beneath this military imperial voice can be heard another kind of imperial voice that evinces a delight in exotic places and finds in the proliferating and mysterious Nile (7–8) an invitation to the mind itself to wander. This second imperial voice is echoed in poem 46, where Catullus describes a mind aflutter with the desire to wander as it contemplates a leisurely return home from Bithynia via the famous cities of the Greek world. Poem 46 ends with a farewell to his comrades on Memmius' staff:

o dulces comitum valete coetus
longe quos simul a domo profectos
diversae varie viae reportant. (9–11)

Farewell, sweet gathering of companions,
who set out together, journeying far from home,
and now diverging roads return you separately.

As in poem 11, the affect of male companionship is related to the prospect of travel, but in this case the scattering of the imperial retinue turns the world into an exciting prospect, a source of stories and descriptions to be recounted when the friends are reunited at Rome (compare c.9.6–8). In the previous poem (c.45), a duet of amorous protestations, Septimius tells his beloved Acme that he prefers her to all the Syrias and Britains (45.22), shrinking the world to the embrace of the two lovers at the same time as he serializes it as the interchangeable, and rejected, career alternatives of the metropolitan male.[23] The opening lines of poem 11 both reduce the world to a rhetorical convenience of the metropolitan and project alternative worlds for the entrapped lover. If the routine protestations of Furius and Aurelius are the beginning of a movement that is completed by Lesbia's betrayal, launching the poem toward the engulfing vortex of Lesbia's imperial sexuality, then the second voice resists that movement by lingering in the expansive imaginative possibilities of the imperial world. Resistance is vain, and the second voice is absorbed by the first.

Something of this same engulfing of one voice by another occurs in the fifth stanza. Here the words with which Lesbia is sarcastically urged to continue her present life absorb and transform some of Catullus' most ecstatic love poetry: "Let her live and flourish with her adulterers" (cum suis vivat valeatque moechis, 17) is a grotesque echo of Catullus' own call to erotic abandon in poem 5 (vivamus, mea Lesbia, atque amemus, 5.1).[24] The heedlessness that Catullus the lover there recommends with respect to the "grumblings of severe old men" (5.2–3) is now exercised by Lesbia with respect to her lovers. Catullus' sarcastic encouragement of Lesbia to carry on as before turns into a parody of his own call to erotic abandon in happier times, and, as with all good parodies, it reveals something disturbing about the original, whose erotic abandon acquires a tinge of solipsistic rapacity in retrospect. Similarly, the woman who in poem 10 took Catullus at his word betrayed, in both senses of the word, the implicit contract on which the conversation depended. As both same and other, the woman inhabits the speech of the man as its otherness, bringing out its hidden implications.

It is the final image of poem 11 that successfully resists the violence and carelessness that threatens to engulf all the agents in the world of this poem, and it does so by realizing a position from which the *neglegentia* of the plough is appropriated to create a form of contact that is both precise and intimate. The "touch" of the plough, ruthless and incidental, coincides with the touching and cutting of words as they meet with each other and with the silence that surrounds the poem. Catullus' description of his victimization draws attention to the power he exerts in relation to the aesthetic object that is defined as the poem closes, thus giving us two very different perspectives on the same event. As in poem 10, where Catullus confesses the bankruptcy of his boast in the same words as those with which he glories in his poetic power to make something out of nothing, a discredited *nelegentia* is turned to poetic profit. Catullus' exposure of the false *neglegentia* of his persona in poem 10 serves to reveal the position of supreme irresponsibility from which the poet as verbal artificer speaks, a position that is beyond shame or embarrassment. In the following poem, the poet carefully locates himself on a tangent to the *neglegentia* of Lesbia, from which position her ruthless carelessness is appropriated to serve the very precise aesthetic purposes of closure. The victimization of the persona in both of these poems enables the poet to situate poetic forms of discourse against other forms; it is striking that metropolitan, imperial, loose talk provides a foil to poetic discourse in both cases, loose talk that is complicit with the two different forms of *neglegentia* against which the distinctive capacities of poetic form appear.

Our two poems would seem to have little in common if we think in terms of levels of intent and intensity. Traditional stratifications of Catullus' poetry would offer no reason to compare, as victims, the self-deprecating, urbane poet with the betrayed lover, because the experience of victimization represented by these poems is utterly different. But the two poems are perhaps the most powerful in the collection when it comes to provoking the reader's desire to bond with Catullus. The poet who can make fun of himself so well, and who can describe the destruction of his innocence with such poignancy, has been read as a lovable poet, and lovable in the very moment of his weakness. But doubtless it is the implication of this weakness with a form of power that wins over readers of these poems, for the poetic power that the poems finally exhibit is one with which the reader, as a reader of poetry, is already implicated.

CHAPTER 8

# The Death of a Brother
Displacement and Expression

In the previous chapter, we saw Catullus position his own poetic power in relation to his victimized persona. This chapter finds Catullus in situations where contradictory claims are made on his poetic expression, and in response to these situations he produces some of his most complex and experimental poetry. The contradictory claims made on the poet raise the issues of where he speaks from and of how the poem is produced, questions that provoke him to explore the various displacements through which poetic expression is mediated. Again, a potential weakness becomes an occasion for displaying some of the distinctive capacities of poetic discourse, in this case the layerings and simultaneities through which Catullus handles the divergent demands on his expression. But the problem of where the poet speaks from is not only a generic matter, it also concerns the complex cultural identity of Catullus, the Roman poet from Transpadane Gaul with Alexandrian affiliations. This conflicted cultural identity is raised by Catullus' reaction to the death of his brother, a motif that unites most of the poems I will be dealing with in this chapter.

Apart from the liaison with Lesbia, the main biographical motif in Catullus' poetry is the death of his brother, somewhere in the Troad. Three poems directly refer to this event, if such it is: the poem spoken at his brother's grave and ending with the famous words "hail and farewell" (c.101), and two poems addressed to friends who have asked him for poetry, which he claims he is unable to produce while his mind is occupied with grief (cc.65, 68). In fact, Catullus does send poetry to these friends, in one case a translation of Callimachus (c.66), and in the other a letter of thanks to a third person who loaned him a house for his rendezvous with Lesbia (c.68.41–160). All of these poems are concerned with displacement, for though his brother's death displaces all other concerns from Catullus' mind, it also prevents direct communication with his brother, so that even the words spoken at the graveside are provisional; the poem produced for his friend Ortalus is a translation that displaces the poet's own expression with the words of another, and the poem for his friend Mallius a letter of thanks to another friend (Allius).[1] In the wake of his brother's death, poetic expression becomes problematic for Catullus insofar as its origin (the poet's mind) is preoccupied and its ideal destination (the brother) is removed. If Catullus can, and must, write from other motives than grief for his brother, then has he not betrayed that grief? Or is there a model of how a poem is produced that will obviate this clash of expressive demands? And if poetic expression does not emanate from a single center, then how can it be sincere? Where does the poet speak from and where (or how) does the poem go?

Clearly, part of the answer to the question of where the poet speaks from involves his cultural identity, and the experience of displacement in these poems extends into the geographical and cultural when Catullus travels to Troy, origin of the Romans' great ancestor, to greet his brother (c.101), and then holes himself up in provincial Verona to mourn him (c.68). Catullus was born and raised in Verona in Transpadane Gaul, a part of Italy anxious to shed its connections to the barbarian world and to be incorporated in the world of Rome, within which its status was rising fast during the late Republic.[2] As an upper-class provincial, he was able to make his name at Rome through literature, a newly, and still partially, respectable calling for a Roman.[3] His professed literary affiliation was with the poets of Alexandrian Greece, and Rome itself, the conqueror of Greece and capital of a growing empire, had for some time been permeated by an Hellenistic cultural influence of which much of its political elite was suspicious.[4] As we shall see, Rome, Verona, and Hellenistic Alexandria are all places from which the poet speaks in the poems dealing with his brother's death, and the relation between these locations, and what they represent, is not always comfortable. But the most famous of these poems (c.101) finds Catullus at Troy, for centuries the most literary of places and now, suddenly, the scene of a personal tragedy.

## Trojan Reunion

When Catullus' brother dies at Troy, Catullus writes a poem, spoken from the graveside, that begins with a reference to that great poem of homecoming, the *Odyssey*, but this new poem is troubled in its sense of place and time:

> Multas per gentes et multa per aequora vectus
>    advenio has miseras, frater, ad inferias
> Ut te postremo donarem munere mortis
>    et mutam nequiquam adloquerer cinerem.
> quandoquidem fortuna mihi tete abstulit ipsum,
>    heu miser indigne frater adempte mihi,
> nunc tamen interea haec prisco quae more parentum
>    tradita sunt tristi munere ad inferias,
> accipe fraterno multum manantia fletu,
>    atque in perpetuum, frater, ave atque vale. (c.101)

> Transported through many peoples and through many seas
>    I come, brother, to these unhappy funeral rites,
> so that I might present you with the last gift of death
>    and might address in vain the mute ash.
> Because fortune has taken your person from me,
>    alas, poor brother, taken unjustly from me,
> Now, for the meantime, receive what is given as a sad gift
>    at the funeral in accordance with the ancient custom of
> our fathers, wet with a brother's copious weeping,
>    and forever, brother, hail and farewell.

Reversing the movement of the *Odyssey* from Troy to home, Catullus arrives "through many peoples and through many seas" (compare Homer, *Od*. 1.1–4) to perform the final rites for the dead.[5] Odysseus is reunited with his wife, but Catullus' reunion with his brother is at the same time a definitive separation. Odysseus' return to Ithaca inaugurates the resumption of tradition; Catullus, it is true, performs the rites of ancestral tradition in this outlandish place, but these rites are only a substitute for the communion with his brother that death has rendered impossible. The moment and the place of this poem are full of contradictions, condensed into the final "hail and farewell," words that both accompany the ceremony and gesture toward a communication that transcends its inadequate formulae.[6] It is toward these simple gestures of hailing and bidding farewell that the poem moves, putting behind it the burden of futile and ironic preliminaries. Both gestures assume a presence that death has in fact removed, and yet the placing of this composite and contradictory gesture at the poem's end aligns the moment of Catullus' address to his brother with the simultaneous appearance and disappearance of the completed poem, which flashes into presence only to merge with silence. The modern German poet Paul Celan, also deeply concerned with remembering the dead, has remarked that "a poem asserts itself on the edge of itself," a description appropriate to Catullus' displacement of the poem's burden to a point both of arrival and of severance, where the rhythm of the poem touches the time that resumes when it ends.[7] It is at this liminal point that the reader of the poem is most conscious of the gap across which the poem speaks, a gap that for most of its readers includes the poet's own death. To read this poem is to address to Catullus the very greeting he addressed to his brother, as the many poems hailing Catullus as brother attest (see chap. 9). So communication across the grave proves possible, but only if the addressee is displaced by Catullus himself, for it is only the poem *as poem* that can overcome the futility of the poem's address to the dead. In this connection, Catullus' "meanwhile" (interea, 7) suggests that the poem is provisional in the sense that it will only activate its system of positions once the poet has died. A written poem is a communication in which one or other of the parties is absent—depending on whether you look at it from the poet's or the reader's point of view—and this is what makes Catullus' address to his dead brother reversible.

The fact that Catullus' poem threatens to make him the recipient of the final "hail and farewell" is not the only ambiguity in the poet's position. It is not clear, for instance, whether Catullus is offering his brother what ancient custom has "handed down" (tradita) to him as a "sad duty" (tristi munere) to the dead or what is "handed over" (tradita) as a "sad gift" (tristi munere) to the dead;[8] the ambiguity of the phrasing points to a situation in which Catullus is both active (as gift giver) and passive (as recipient of a duty). This ambiguity applies also to the logic of the reference to the *Odyssey*, for it is poignantly inappropriate that, reversing the *Odyssey*, Catullus has gone to Troy to be reunited with his brother, and yet it is entirely appropriate that the Roman should find his brother at the home of Rome's great ancestor. If Catullus the brother experiences a tragic parody of Odyssean homecoming, Catullus the Roman distinguishes himself from the Greek Odysseus by returning to the Troy that is Rome's origin.[9] When he follows the ancient custom of his ancestors at Troy, the moment is both familial and national, and, if the Odyssean parallel gives a bitter quality to the family reunion, it also overlays that event with the proud cultural claims of Rome to Trojan ancestry, for the speaker of this poem is not only a grieving brother but also a Roman poet. In fact, Catullus finds that, at the moment of severance from his brother (which perhaps signals the end of his family line, c.68.22), he is also the nodal point in the sustaining of a long tradition. The mythical reference inserts the event into a scale that changes its valences, and on this larger scale the words of this poet of a world-historical Rome are themselves handed down (tradita) so that the modern reader can address the poet. The words of the poem, then, are spoken from several positions that tend to displace each other.

In the paired poems poems 65 and 66, a covering letter to Ortalus and the translation of Callimachus sent as a substitute for poems that grief prevent him from writing, Catullus juxtaposes a quintessentially Alexandrian jeu d'esprit against a very Roman poem about obligations and responsibility. As we shall see, these poems are engaged in a complex, and at times disturbing, dialogue about poetic expression and sincerity.

## Poetry and Expression

The futile attempt, in poem 101, to communicate with his dead brother displaces Catullus' utterance into larger contexts, so that the intimate gesture on the edge of the poem reaches toward the poem's unknown destinations. In poem 65, the duty to mourn his brother conflicts in the poet's mind with obligation to a friend, each demand threatening to displace the other and producing a poem that attempts to find a model of poetic production that will accommodate this double origin. How can he simultaneously do justice to both of these claims? Can he be mindful both of the words of his friend's request and of the personal grief that demands expression? This all depends on how a poem is produced.

The Latin word from which our "express" is derived actually appears in poem 65:

Etsi me assiduo confectum cura dolore
    sevocat a doctis, Ortale, virginibus,

nec potis est dulcis Musarum expromere fetus
　　mens animi, tantis fluctuat ipsa malis—
namque mei nuper Lethaeo gurgite fratris
　　pallidulum manans alluit unda pedem,
Troia Rhoeteo quem subter litore tellus
　　ereptum nostris obterit ex oculis.
　　. . . . . . . . . . .
　　numquam ego te, vita frater amabilior,
aspiciam posthac? at certe semper amabo,
　　semper maesta tua carmina morte canam,
qualia sub densis ramorum concinit umbris
　　Daulias, absumpti fata gemens Ityli—
sed tamen in tantis maeroribus, Ortale, mitto
　　haec expressa tibi carmina Battiadae,
ne tua dicta vagis nequiquam credita ventis
　　effluxisse meo forte putes animo,
ut missum sponsi furtivo munere malum
　　procurrit casto virginis e gremio,
quod miserae oblitae molli sub veste locatum,
　　dum adventu matris prosilit, excutitur,
atque illud prono praeceps agitur decursu,
　　huic manat tristi conscius ore rubor. (c.65)

Even though I am worn out by incessant suffering
　　and grief keeps me, Ortalus, from the learned virgins,
nor is my mind able to bring forth the sweet fruit
　　of the Muses, such are the misfortunes besetting it—
for recently the wave of Lethe's waters, seeping,
　　lapped my brother's pale foot,
whom the Trojan earth of the shore of Rhoeteum
　　crushes, snatched from my eyes.
　　. . . . . . . . . .
　　my brother, more dear than life,
will I never see you again? But surely I will always
　　love you, always sing with sadness of your death,
as the nightingale sings under the densely
　　shadowed branches, bewailing the fate of murdered Itylus—
but still I send you, Ortalus, in my grief
　　these translated [expressa] poems of Callimachus
lest you think that your words, entrusted in vain
　　to the winds, have seeped from my mind,
as the quince sent by the fiancé as a secret gift
　　rolls from the chaste lap of the virgin,
wrapped in the soft clothes of the poor, forgetful girl,
　　it is shaken out when she rises to greet her mother,

and driven headlong in its downward path,
  while a guilty blush spreads across her sad face.

The "translated poems of Callimachus" (expressa ... carmina Battiadae) that Catullus sends his friend Ortalus are substitutes for the original poem that, preoccupied with grief, he is unable to produce. Translation is figured by the metaphor *expressa* as a form of stamping: the translation is an impression made by the original poem. But the Latin word might also mean "forced out" and is commonly used of sounds of pain or sorrow that are elicited by extreme situations (Seneca, *Benef.* 2.5.2). This second meaning is suggested by the wording of the couplet

> sed tamen in tantis maeroribus, Ortale, mitto
> haec expressa tibi carmina Battiadae ... (15–16)

> but still I send you, Ortalus, in my grief
> these *expressa* poems of Callimachus ...

The songs "forced out" in such grief might appropriately be expressions of sorrow; in fact they are just the opposite, that is, translations stamped out from the words of another poet and so bypassing the connection between poetry and the poet's turbulent mind. In the triangular relationship between Catullus, his brother, and Ortalus, the role of the translation is conveyed by the interference between the primary sense of the word *expressa* and its secondary, latent sense. If we put the word in a larger context, a third sense emerges:

> Sed tamen in tantis maeroribus, Ortale, mitto
>   haec expressa tibi carmina Battiadae,
> ne tua dicta vagis nequiquam credita ventis
>   effluxisse meo forte putes animo, (c.15–18)

> But still I send you, Ortalus, in my grief
>   these *expressa* poems of Callimachus
> lest you think that your words, entrusted in vain
>   to the winds, have seeped from my mind,

Here the word *expressa* may also be understood in its sense "extorted" (*OLD* s.v. 4), for the translation Catullus produces in this difficult time is the response to an obligation that he feels toward his friend, who has presumably made a request for poetry. The word *expressa*, then, concentrates three facets of poetic production: expression (the songs forced out by grief), translation (the imitation of literary models), and commission. What is fascinating about this poem is the way in which it intertwines these notions.

How does a poem emerge? The beginning and the end of poem 65 focus on this emergence: in the first four lines, Catullus declares that he is unable to produce a poem, and in the last six he compares the sending of the poem to Ortalus to the falling of a love-token, sent by her fiancé, from a virgin's lap. What can't Catullus do because of his brother's death and why?

> Etsi me assiduo confectum cura dolore
>   sevocat a doctis, Ortale, virginibus,
> nec potis est dulcis Musarum expromere fetus
>   mens animi, tantis fluctuat ipsa malis—
>
> Even though I am worn out by incessant suffering
>   and grief keeps me, Ortalus, from the learned virgins,
> nor is my mind able to bring forth the sweet fruit
>   of the Muses, such are the misfortunes besetting it,

Writing poetry here seems to be like giving birth; Catullus' mind cannot produce the offspring (fetus) of the Muses because his sadness keeps him away from the learned virgins, and also because his mind is itself turbulent with (fluctuat) suffering. In spite of the suggestion of the usual distribution of sexual roles (male poet, female Muse) in the word *virginibus*, it is Catullus' mind that is figured as a womb, and a womb that is unable to conceive, both because of the turbulent flux of suffering and because it is already pregnant with grief (and potentially with dirges for the brother).[10] Further intercourse with the Muses would be fruitless. This account of the metaphorical force of the opening lines has to be supplemented, however, with an alternative interpretation of "to bring forth (expromere) the fruit of the Muses," for *expromere* normally means "to bring from store," and *fetus* can mean "fruit" as well as "offspring."[11] The storehouse, unlike the womb, is not exclusive about what it can store, and as a metaphor for the mind that produces poetry it has quite different implications. The ambiguity as to how poetry is produced prepares for the anxiety of the word *expressa*, which represses one metaphor implying self-expression and responsiveness (squeezed out) under another implying craft (stamped).

These alternative models for the poetic mind, storehouse and womb, are fused in the image of the lap of the virgin from which the apple falls in the final simile.[12] On the one hand, the shaking of the apple from the lap in which the lover's gift has been stored is an appropriately undignified version of taking the fruits of the Muses out from storage: the words of Callimachus are "stamped" (*expressa*) by Catullus' translation, and sent to Ortalus as the gift of the fiancé is shaken (*excutitur*) from the virgin's lap at the appearance of her mother. Solid objects are passed from one person to another. But the *gremium* of the virgin is also her womb (*OLD*, s.v. 3), where she might appropriately keep the "secret gift" (19) of her lover, in which case the unreliability of the *gremium* is more ominous.

"One should entrust nothing to a woman or a lap" (Nec mulieri nec gremio credi oportet). This Roman proverb is glossed by the epitomizer Festus (second century C.E.) as follows: "The woman's mind is unreliable and flighty, and often what has been put in the lap falls out when one has forgotten about it and rises."[13] The wit of the proverb lies in the zeugma, for one entrusts things to a woman in a different sense than one entrusts things to a lap. But though the connection between the lap and the woman is in one respect metaphorical, there is an obvious metonymical relation between the two. As "lap," *gremium* provides a satirical analogy with the untrustworthy mind of the woman, but as "womb" it points to the source of male suspicion of a woman's trustworthiness: the fear that the product of a woman's *gremium* may not be what the man has entrusted to it. In fact, the first, metaphorical reading covers up for the anxiety of the metonymy, putting the male speaker in a relation of casual superiority to the woman he so wittily dehumanizes. Catullus' final picture of the forgetful virgin's dropping of the apple from her *gremium* hovers between an amusing mishap and a scandal.

But what is the application of this simile? If Catullus sends Ortalus his translation as the girl sends her lover's gift rolling at the arrival of her mother, then Ortalus gets what wasn't really intended for him but happened to be in Catullus' store. The shaking out of the apple, like the pressing out of Callimachus' words in the translation, points to the public, alienable nature of words and poems. But the simile might be applied in a different way: Catullus sends the translation in order to avoid the charge of forgetting the words that have been entrusted to him (*credita*, 17) by Ortalus, of letting them flow (*effluxisse*, 18) from his mind as the virgin lets the apple she has forgotten fall from her lap; according to this reading, the simile realizes the metaphor of pregnancy, especially since *effluxisse* picks up *fluctuat* (4). The words of Ortalus, it is feared, have not "taken" in Catullus' mind; he has somehow been untrue to his friend, an unreliable recipient of the latter's words. The first reading of the simile covers up for the anxiety of the second, just as the satirical force of the metaphorical equation between *gremium* and *mulier* in the proverb covers up the male anxiety at the metonymical relation between them. In a sense, the translation is itself an illegitimate result of Ortalus' words, to which it has no organic relation, for though it is intended to prove that those words were not entrusted to Catullus in vain, it is in fact a product of fidelity to the words of another (Callimachus). This paradox is reflected in the double application of the simile, both to Catullus' discharging of his obligation and to his (putative) forgetting of Ortalus' words. As an alternative to expression, translation allows Catullus to make good on his obligation to Ortalus without interrupting the pregnancy of his mind with grief for his brother, but the appearance of the apple/translation from where it has been stored also carries the alternative implication that the words of Ortalus have miscarried in Catullus' mind, which has not been faithful to what has been entrusted to it.

So the metaphor of pregnancy makes the demands placed on Catullus by the two men incompatible: either he forgets his brother or he lets the words of Ortalus slip from his mind. However, the rolling of the apple from the virgin's lap is not the last thing that happens in the final simile, which ends:

> atque illud prono praeceps agitur decursu
> huic manat tristi conscius ore rubor. (23-24)

> and [the apple is] driven headlong in its downward path,
> while a guilty blush spreads across her sad face.

The virgin's blush is *conscius*, a product of guilt for her forgetfulness and embarrassment at the exposure of intimacy; she recognizes what has been forgotten by the same act as she recognizes her forgetfulness. In fact, the blush is caused by the crossing of two relationships, for the apple that exposes the intimacy of the lovers is revealed by the daughter's spontaneous reaction to her mother's arrival (dum adventu matris prosilit, 22). The blushing virgin is in the same situation as Catullus, whose every gesture produces an interference between two relationships. Here we should remember the confluence of meanings in the word *expressa*, which acknowledges that Catullus is not expressing his grief for his brother at the same time as it excuses the fact that he is not producing poetry in response to Ortalus' words. Both the translation and the apple are sites of an interference between two mutually incompatible relationships, namely, Catullus' relationships to his brother and to Ortalus and the virgin's to her mother and her fiancé (incompatible because marriage means the passage from her mother's protection to her husband's bed).[14] It is the blush, whose liquid spreading is opposed in the last couplet to the bouncing apple, that does justice simultaneously to both relationships. The mindful (conscius) blush compensates for the flux (effluxisse) of Ortalus' words from Catullus' mind as it spreads (manat) over the virgin's face, but it also reverses the association of flowing with death and forgetting in the lines on the dead brother:

> namque mei nuper Lethaeo gurgite fratris
> *pallidulum manans alluit* unda pedem, (5–6)

> for recently the wave of Lethe's waters, *seeping*,
> *lapped* my brother's *pale* foot,

The virgin's blush is the rushing blood of life and of remembrance.[15]

With the figure of the falling apple, Catullus addresses the question of poetic expression and production that is so problematic in this situation of conflicting claims; as an alternative figure of how the poem comes to appear, the blush, which is not produced but rather spreads across a surface, does justice to the simultaneity of these claims. The blush is the poem's self-consciousness, its hidden connections, its simultaneities and unspoken implications; it is a figure for the poem as it is read rather than as it is produced, a figure for the relations that spread across the poem as it is fixed in that moment of attention represented here by the fall of the apple. With the virginal blush, Catullus retreats from the problematic metaphor of expression as pregnancy and birth into this metaphor of the poem as self-consciousness, a metaphor that allows the poem to acknowledge its multiple origins. In its terminal position, and with its associations radiating throughout the poem, the blush, a reaction that expresses the consciousness of another's attention, is Catullus' representation of the poetical itself, displaced from the poet's mind as expressive origin to the interaction between poem and reader. As in poem 101, so here the death of his brother raises for Catullus the problem of where the poet speaks from, a problem that takes the distinctly Roman form of a conflict of *officia* (duties) that is resolved by the figurative use of that peculiarly Roman moral act, the blush.[16]

But with the covering letter to Ortalus comes another poem, the translation of Callimachus' "Lock of Berenice." After the virgin, whose blush is the defenseless revelation of true feeling, we are presented with a scene from the world of the newlywed, described by a sexually sophisticated speaker and permeated with an air of cultivated insincerity.

## The Question of Sincerity

Callimachus' "The Lock of Berenice" (fr. 110 Pfeiffer) is a highly polished and artificial piece of court flattery. It consists of the speech of a lock of queen Berenice's hair, vowed to the gods by the queen for the safe return of her husband and cousin, Ptolemy III, who had set out on an invasion of Syria shortly after his wedding to Berenice. On Ptolemy's triumphant return, the lock was dedicated in a temple of Aphrodite from which it subsequently disappeared, only to be conveniently located by the astronomer Conon as a new constellation. It is the translated lock that speaks from its new home in the sky, explaining the circumstances that led to its present status and protesting its grief at being separated from the queen.

Not only is speech in this poem displaced from a human speaker, but that speaker is itself displaced from its natural location. This displacement is appropriate to the function of the translated poem, which is to allow Catullus' poetic production to be diverted through the words of another, and so to avoid displacing the preoccupying grief of bereavement while making good on an obligation to a friend. The confident professionalism with which the episode of the lock is handled by the Alexandrian court poet could not be further removed from the troubled windings of the covering letter, which seeks to negotiate the disparate claims of grief for the brother and obligation to the friend. Like the stanza on the perils of leisure (*otium*), appended to Catullus' translation of Sappho's famous poem on the symptoms of love (c.50), the covering letter puts the Callimachus poem in a new light, raising the issues of sincerity and obligation in ways that are foreign to the spirit of Callimachus.[17] Not that Callimachus, or rather the lock, doesn't address the question of sincerity: wondering whether the tears of brides are genuine or not, the lock slyly asks Queen Berenice whether it was concern for her *brother* (Ptolemy was in fact her cousin) that caused her grief at his departure:

> et tu non orbum luxti deserta cubile,
>     sed fratris cari flebile discidium? (21–2)

and did you grieve not, deserted, for your lonely bed,
    but for the sad parting of your dear brother?

Coming after the covering letter in which Catullus tells of his bereavement, this winking irony creates an unsettling dialogue between the two texts.[18] What had been intended as a diversion from the poet's preoccupying concerns turns out to engage the very anxieties it was supposed to allay. Vergil, a great reader of Catullus, uses a line from this poem to similar effect in *Aeneid* 6, where the guilty Aeneas, coming across Dido in the underworld, protests:

> invitus, regina, tuo de litore cessi (*Aen.* 6.460)
>
> Unwillingly, O queen, did I leave your shore

echoing

> invita, o regina, tuo de vertice cessi (c.66.39)
>
> Unwillingly, O queen, did I leave your head

What is the relation between Roman *gravitas* and Alexandrian courtliness, between Aeneas' painfully stilted expression of repressed grief and the elegant flippancy of the talking lock? Are Aeneas' protestations that he is a reluctant follower of his great destiny as hollow as the protestations of the lock? Perhaps Vergil follows Catullus here in suggesting that words can never completely be controlled by the intentions of their speaker, being so marked with their own history and its diverse contexts that there is never a clear, univocal answer to the question, "Who is speaking?"

The Greek poem haunts the awkward sincerities of the Roman speakers with its cynical insinuations. According to the most common Roman version of the difference between themselves and the Greeks, the speech of the lock would represent the mendacity of the older culture.[19] But Catullus' juxtaposition is not only a contrast, it is also a progression. What makes the flippant irony about grief for a brother's death in poem 66 unsettling is that there is a temporal progression between poem 65, which ends with the blush of a virgin at the discovery of her fiance's love gift, and poem 66, which concerns a newlywed. The cynicism of the lock speaks from a position of experience relative to the innocence of the virgin at the end of poem 65; it is not clear which poem sites which, for priority, the lock insinuates, may simply be inexperience. However, the translator has the power to resituate the original, and the end of poem

65, the virgin's blush, gives us a context in which to see the shining star that rises at the beginning of poem 66:

> Omnia qui magni dispexit lumina mundi
>   qui stellarum ortus comperit atque obitus
> flammeus ut rapidi solis nitor obscuretur,
>   ut cedant certis sidera temporibus
> ut Triviam furtim sub saxa relegans
>   dulcis amor gyro devocet aereo:
> idem me ille Conon caelesti in lumine vidit
>   e Beroniceo vertice caesariem
> fulgentem clare . . . (1–9)

> He who observed the lights of the great world,
>   who understood the risings and settings of the stars;
> how the brilliance of the swirling sun is eclipsed,
>   and how the constellations retreat at fixed times;
> how a sweet love secretly calls down the moon from her heavenly
>                                                                  round,
>   banishing her to the rocks of Latmia;
> the same great Conon saw me in the heavenly blaze,
>   a lock from the head of Berenice
> shining brightly . . .

In poem 66 we are led from the start to locate the point of radiance, the point from which everything is observed, shining brightly in the sky, where the astronomer whom nothing eludes has pinpointed it. Both the finder and the found emerge out of this long sentence, each supporting the fame of the other, to preside in brilliance over the sentence and to shed the light of fame over the marriage of Berenice and Ptolemy. The agents in this drama are supported by, and support, the sentence's grammatical rise and fall so that the contrast with the previous poem is complete: instead of the almost clumsy attempt to map out the conflicting claims on Catullus in a single sentence, we have the triumphant location of the cast of characters at strategic points in the rise and fall of a sentence spoken from the dominating perspective of the star. The light of the star shines over its world, and the blush, caused by the interference between different relationships, motives, and responsibilities, spreads across its world as a self-consciousness both guilty and mindful.

Although Callimachus' court poem is reproduced by Catullus to obviate the anxiety produced by writing poetry after his brother's death, this poem itself raises the issues of fidelity and sincerity. I have already drawn attention to the lock's innuendos about the tears of brides and the nature of Berenice's concern for her husband/brother (c.66.21–22). The doubt cast by this sexual innuendo on Berenice's sincerity spreads to infect the severed lock's own protestations that it prefers its previous location to its present exalted home. In its most extravagant form, this protestation recalls the imagery of poem 65:

>    namque ego non ullo vera timore tegam,
> nec si me infestis discerpent sidera dictis,
>    condita quin veri pectoris evoluam (72–74)

>    for I will not cover up truth for any fear,
> not even if the constellations tear me apart with their carping
> will it prevent me from rolling out what's stored in a true heart.

The true heart is here figured as a store (condita) from which the truth that it contains is rolled out (evoluam, a verb that can be used of unrolling a papyrus roll). This recapitulation of the imagery of the previous poem turns the tongue-in-cheek protestations of the lock into a parody of the concerns of that poem. Poem 66 speaks for part of Catullus himself, who was in certain respects an Alexandrian poet; furthermore, his claim in poem 65.12 that he will always sing "sad songs" because of his brother's death is not substantiated by our collection.[20] In fact, when Catullus compares himself to the inconsolable Procne grieving for her son (c.65.13), the simile echoes a passage in the *Odyssey* (19.520) in which Penelope tells the disguised Odysseus that she is in a quandary as to whether to continue to respect her marriage to Odysseus or to marry the best of the suitors. The Greek poem insinuates that the Roman protests too much.

But if the Roman Catullus, representing a culture that is never quite at home with itself, stands in a difficult relation to the Greeks, the Alexandrian Greeks themselves are not at home either. The studied insincerity of Callimachus' poem, spoken by a severed lock of hair, is the tone of the imperial culture of the Ptolemaic Greeks, a tone of easy superiority that is concomitant with the Greek culture's disdain for, and alienation from, the Egyptian environment.[21]

Severed from its mistress's head and disappearing from the temple in which it had been dedicated, the lock has left its Egyptian location for the "higher" world of Greek mythology and astronomy, from which it sheds light and fame on its mistress. It claims that Zephyr had wafted it to the temple of Arsinoe—the queen of Ptolemy II, now deified and identified with Aphrodite—and that it had landed in the "chaste lap" (casto . . . gremio, 56) of Venus, a goddess not notable for her marital fidelity.[22] The story of severance, disappearance, and apotheosis is a reflection of the Ptolemaic dynasty's insistence that its heritage is Greek, in spite of its Egyptian home: Alexandria, as Catullus puts it, is "a Greek dweller on the Canopic shore" (Graia Canopitis *incola* litoribus).[23] It is, of course, perverse to describe the lap of Venus as chaste (casto, 56), and the epithet is particularly dubious in view of the fact that Ptolemy II, appropriating the prerogative of his Egyptian predecessors, the Pharaohs, had married his own sister, scandalizing many of the Greeks. "You are pushing the prod into an unholy fleshpot," commented Sotades.[24] The place from which the lock makes its final ascent to heaven is unreal, a mixture of Egyptian and Greek, or rather a place in which Egypt is transformed into Greece; to call it a "lap" is to draw attention both to its artificiality and, in this case, its unretentiveness. The studied and sophisticated insincerity of tone in Callimachus' poem reflects the displacements that characterize the uprooted and inorganic culture of Greek Alexandria.

In the translation that Catullus sends Ortalus, the unretentive *gremium* of Venus, the mythological wind that wafts the lock from there to its apotheosis, and the illustrious shining of the new star all recapitulate, in another key, elements of the anxious world of poem 65. In that poem, the *gremium* of the forgetful virgin produces the shining blush of embarrassment, reflecting Catullus' own concern that his friend may think his words have been entrusted in vain to the winds. As I have argued, the cynical and professional "Lock" not only functions as a contrast to the dutiful covering letter but also speaks for aspects of Catullus' own art that give the lie to his protestations in that poem, a poem that is itself conflicted about the nature of expression.[25] If Alexandria stands for aspects of the poetic enterprise that obviate (self-) expression, and raises sometimes awkward questions about the relation between emotion and artifice in poetry, that is because it also stands for displacement. The confident, virtuosic handling of displacement in Callimachus reflects the cultural confidence of the Hellenistic court in Egypt, but Catullus, both Roman and Transpadane, has a more anxious relation to displacement and to multiple origins, as we shall see.

Looking back at the three poems we have considered so far, we can see how the death of his brother prompts Catullus to explore some of the displacements that are characteristic of poetry. In the case of poem 101, there is a congruity between the frustrated communication between Catullus and his dead brother and the fact that the (written) poem is a communication from one who is absent, even dead. Poem 65 avoids representing the poem as the fruition of a single expressive need to figure its own emergence as a blush, a radiating self-consciousness in which words, images, and themes respond to each other in a way that presumes the attention of another. The relation between poems 65 and 66 reveals the intertextual character of a poem, permeable to other poems (and to various kinds of otherness, such as the history of language) in such a way as to displace the expressive intentions of its author.

## Home, But Which?

In poem 68, Catullus again professes to be unable to accommodate a friend's request for poetry, pleading that his brother's death has ended his youthful indulgence in love and poetry (haec studia atque omnes delicias animi, 26).[26] His brother's death has destroyed all his pleasures and buried his *domus* ("house" here in the sense of "family," 22) and therefore it is the requirement of *pietas* to abstain from poetry. But this reason is displaced by another:

> ignosces igitur si, quae mihi luctus ademit
>     haec tibi non tribuo munera, cum nequeo.
> nam, quod scriptorum non magna est copia apud me,
>     hoc fit, quod Romae vivimus: illa domus,
> illa mihi sedes, illic mea carpitur aetas;
>     huc una ex multis capsula me sequitur. (31–36)

> So you will forgive me if I do not present you with gifts
>     that grief has taken from me, because I can't.
> For the fact that I don't have at hand a supply of books,
>     that is because I live at Rome: that is my home,
> that is my dwelling, there my life is consumed;
>     only one of my many cartons has followed me here.

Catullus now speaks as the learned Alexandrian poet whose *domus* is not the family home in Verona but Rome, where the books are.[27] So Catullus cannot write because he has lost his *domus*, but which one? Between the pleas of incapacity caused by grief and of incapacity caused by the lack of books comes a response to something that Mallius had written in his letter:

> quare, quod scribis Veronae turpe Catullo [Catulle, V]
>     esse, quod hic quisquis de meliore nota
> frigida deserto tepefactet [-factat, R] membra cubili,
>     id, Malli, non est turpe, magis miserum est. (27–30)[28]
>
> So, as for your writing that it is shameful Catullus
>     is in Verona, because here the better class all
> warm their cold limbs in a deserted bed,
>     that, Mallius, is not shameful but to be pitied.

There is some controversy about these lines, which turns mainly on whether *hic* (here) refers to Rome and thus quotes Mallius directly, or to Verona, but there are also textual problems. Two possibilities emerge: either Mallius is telling Catullus that, in his absence from Rome, Lesbia is sharing her bed with the better class of people, or he is teasing Catullus because in provincial Verona the better class of people sleep alone, rather than pursuing the delights of love.[29] However we understand Mallius, Catullus' response is to shift the terms of the situation from the *turpe* (shameful) that conveys the sophisticated urban perspective to the *miserum* (wretched) that reflects grief for the buried house. Mallius should therefore (igitur, 31) forgive Catullus because he cannot provide what grief has taken away. But this shift of perspective is reversed by Catullus' second excuse for not being able to write, which follows immediately. Catullus now sees his presence at Verona in terms of a cultural lack, emphasizing that Rome is his *domus*.[30]

Catullus' inability to write is implicated in the problem of home, which proves to be a complicated one for the Transpadane who has acquired literary fame in Rome at least partially by virtue of his commitment to Greek literature. In poem 101, this issue features in the relation between Catullus' journey to Troy and the Odyssean homecoming: the ironic reversal of Odysseus' reunion with his wife is paradoxically a homecoming for the representative of a race that claimed descent from the Trojans; in poem 68, there is a conflict between Catullus' provincial, Transpadane origins and the site of his literary activity, Rome. It is no coincidence that the poem that precedes this and follows the Callimachus translation is a poem about provincial gossip in Transpadane Italy, in which a speaking door protests its fidelity to its owner much as does Callimachus' lock (c.67). In fact, poem 67 is in many ways a parody of the Callimachean poem, for the world of newlyweds is here clouded with muttered gossip rather than illuminated by mythological fantasy. The translated lock and the door accused of failing to protect its owner's marriage are both in their different ways representatives of problematic homes; they also represent two different kinds of problematic speech—court flattery and small-town gossip—that reflect anxiously on Catullus' complex cultural makeup. These poems are flanked by the two in which Catullus professes inability to write the poetry requested of him by a friend, and together they form a group (cc.65–68) in which anxieties about the origins and destinations of poetic speech are intertwined with concerns about cultural affiliations. But before returning to this group, and particularly poem 67 with its Transpadane setting, let us look briefly at some of the other poems in which Catullus raises his Transpadane origins.

## Catullus Transpadane

For Catullus the relation between the originally Gallic Transpadana and Rome is not only a personal question about his life and career but also a question of cultural legitimacy. The Roman Catullus may feel both embarrassed by his provincial and inurbane connections and proud of his home's rising fortunes and status in the Roman world. The Transpadane centers had recently (in 89 B.C.E.) been given the *ius Latii*, a halfway stage to full Roman citizenship making them equivalent in status to Latin colonies. As Wiseman points out, "Brixia and Verona were no longer *oppida* of the Cenomani and Euganei. . . . The tribal names are not used again: from now on the amalgam of native Gauls and immigrant Romans and Italians call themselves *Transpadani*."[31] The first attested use of the word *Transpadanus* is in Catullus' poem 39, where he pillories the Celtiberian Egnatius, whose habit of smiling constantly to show off his white teeth is particularly obnoxious in view of the fact that Spaniards use urine as toothpaste:

> si urbanus esses aut Sabinus aut Tiburs
> aut pinguis Umber aut obesus Etruscus
> aut Lanuvinus ater atque dentatus
> aut Transpadanus, ut meos quoque attingam,
> aut quilubet, qui puriter lavit dentes,
> tamen renidere usque quaque te nollem. (10–15)

> If you were a city man, or Sabine, or from Tibur,
> or a well-fed Umbrian or a fat Etruscan
> or a Lanuvinan, dark and toothy,
> or a Transpadane (to get to my own people),
> or anyone who cleans his teeth in decent fashion,
> still I would not have you always smiling.

Removed from the world of barbarians, the *Transpadani* are put on a par with the *urbani*, perhaps even proudly contrasted with them. But the new pretensions and anxieties of the *Transpadani* are reflected most clearly in poem 17, where the poet addresses Verona on the occasion of an impending festival in which the citizens will perform ritual dances on a rickety wooden bridge whose stability they mistrust. Catullus joins in the prayers of the citizens for a new bridge, asking in return that they provide him with a welcome spectacle by throwing off the bridge a certain old man who fails to appreciate his young wife.[32] The request of Catullus has long been connected with a Latin phrase, "sexagenarios de ponte deicere" (to throw the sexagenarians off the bridge), which would seem to refer to the ancient and mysterious Roman ritual of the Argei in which straw puppets were thrown off a bridge into the Tiber. The significance of the ritual is debated, but in alluding to it Catullus is claiming a common cultural tradition for Rome and Verona, a claim that would be underlined by his addressing Verona as *Colonia*.[33] During the first century B.C.E., as a result of political unification with Rome and of sharing in the increasing benefits of empire, Italy was undergoing a rapid urbanization that involved a great deal of public building. The hope for the new bridge in this poem would reflect that process, and it places the whole poem in the light of the aspirations of a semibarbarian town to Roman citizenship, finally granted by Caesar in 49 B.C.E. But the condition Catullus places on the fulfilling of the town's wish for a new bridge is that the husband who is unconscious of his wife's charms should be tossed into the muddy lake and leave behind his supine stupor. The husband is called "most tasteless" (insulsissimus, 12), the bridge's rickety limbs "awkward" (inepta, 2), and the young wife "more frisky (delicatior) than a young goat" (15); in other words, Catullus is using the language of *urbanitas* to separate the old Verona from the Verona of its own aspirations, or, alternatively, to express the cultural anxiety of this upstart member of the Roman world. At the same time as this poem lays claim to a cultural community with Rome, by referring to an ancient Roman ritual, it also expresses an anxiety about Verona's perceived lack of metropolitan *urbanitas*.

## Alexandria and Verona

Poem 67, then, needs to be seen in the context of Veronese aspirations and of Catullus' own anxiety about his origins. In many respects, this poem is a Veronese version of "The Lock of Berenice," finding a parodic equivalent of court gallantry in provincial gossip. A door is taken to task by an unidentified interlocutor for its failure to serve its master, whose new wife has evidently been the subject of scandal; the door defends itself and in the process lets us in on further gossip. The apotheosized lock and the door, each professing faithfulness to its owner, could hardly be better symbols of their respective worlds. Their speeches also provide a delicious contrast, for the lock's elaborate and cryptic explanation of its disappearance (c.66.51–70) is answered by the crude directness of the door's protestation that its master's new wife was no virgin when she arrived at the house (c.67.19–36). Further, in the midst of the door's lurid account of the goings-on in its mistress's old home, it pauses to indulge in a bit of mythologizing geography that reminds us of the lock's account of its transportation from the Pantheon to the temple of Arsinoe Aphrodite (c.66.53–68):

> "Atqui non solum hoc dicit se cognitum habere
>   Brixia Cycneae supposita speculae,
> flavus quam molli praecurrit flumine Mella,
>   Brixia Veronae mater amata meae,
> sed de Postumio et Corneli narrat amore,
>   cum quibus illa malum fecit adulterium." (c.67.31–36)[34]

> "But Brixia says that this is not all she knows,
>   Brixia lying beneath the watchtower of Cycnus,
> past whom the golden Mella flows with gentle stream,
>   Brixia, the beloved mother of my Verona,
> but she tells of the lovers Postumius and Cornelius,
>   with whom my mistress committed adultery."

Wiseman 1987, 331, argues that the reference to Cycnus here involves some foundation legend of the newly romanized Transpadane settlements, which needed a respectable mythological pedigree now that they were part of the civilized world. Brixia is called mother of Verona because foundation legends typically expressed the relationship of eponymous heroes as the relationship between the cities themselves. These "mythological fantasies" served the purpose of providing "an acceptable past for towns whose real history was short and uncivilised" (326). Wiseman's comment is particularly interesting because in this poem relations of paternity have gone awry: for instance, though the previous husband of the new mistress of the house was impotent, his father obligingly took his place, ensuring that she did not arrive at her new home a virgin. The door's interlocutor comments:

> Egregium narras mira pietate parentem,
>     qui ipse sui gnati minxerit in gremium. (29–30)
>
> That's an excellent father you describe; how
>     dutiful to piss in his own son's lap!

There is talk of other amours in Brixia, and the door has heard his mistress mention a man whose name he dares not mention, though he gives us a clue:

> praeterea addebat quendam quem dicere nolo
>     nomine, ne tollat rubra supercilia.
> longus homo est, magnas cui lites intulit olim
>     falsum mendaci ventre puerperium. (45–48)
>
> Besides she also mentioned someone I don't dare
>     to name, or he'll raise his red eyebrows.
> He's a tall man, involved once in a lawsuit
>     about pregnancy and childbirth (all concocted).

The mythological aside inserting the upstart colonies into the respectable family of Greek heroes is sandwiched between stories of dubious paternity, and this reflects the dubiousness of the colonies' claims to a respectable mythological past. The closed world of the provinces conjured up by the speech of the door itself, which excuses its own failed stewardship by muttering about what happened in the neighboring town, contradicts the pretensions of the province to participate in the integrated mythological system of the Greco-Roman world. By contrast, the knowing sexual innuendo and courtly flattery of the lock reflect a cultural milieu that is comfortable with its own artificiality, for the pseudo-problem of the disappearance of the lock is there manipulated with great confidence as an excuse for celebrating the mythological and astronomical arts that flourish under royal patronage at Alexandria. In poem 67, the transference of the bride from Brixia to Verona is a parodic counterpart to the translation of the lock in poem 66, and the doubts cast by provincial gossip on the integrity of this transfer reflect on the cultural pretensions of the upstart colonies.

Whatever the correct reading of the end of poem 66, and whoever is speaking, the poem ends with an exclamation that glories in extravagant verbal gestures:

> sidera corruerint [cur iterent, V] utinam! coma regia fiam,
>     proximus Hydrochoi fulgeret Oarion! (93–94)
>
> Let the constellations collapse! May I be a queen's tress again,
>     and let Orion shine next to Aquarius.[35]

By contrast, the end of poem 67 has the door telling that it has heard its mistress speak in a secretive voice (furtiva voce, 41) of a certain man it can't name for fear of reprisals. Obscure provincial mutterings take place in a world far removed from the brilliantly artificial society of Alexandria.

## The Layered Poem

In the next poem (68), speaking from Verona, Catullus ends by taking an urbane, permissive attitude to Lesbia's infidelities, reminding himself that she did not come to him on the arm of her father (as a bride), and that he must put up with her peccadilloes. His pose stands at the opposite pole to that of the scandalmongering provincial door and its suspicious questioner; Catullus, the urban exile in Verona, accepts the fact that the erotic gifts brought to him by the married Lesbia are "taken from the very lap [gremio, 146] of her husband." As in the three preceding poems, the *gremium* is a site of displacement (compare cc.65.20, 66.56, 67.30). In this case, displacement associates Catullus the lover with the addressee of this poem, Mallius, who also receives what has been diverted from another—a poem of thanks addressed to Allius in place of the poetry he requested.

In fact this poem, whose speaker is himself doubly displaced from his home, is pervaded by displacements, as a brief synopsis will reveal: Mallius has written to Catullus asking him to send gifts of the Muses and Venus to comfort him in his loveless state. Catullus replies that the death of his brother has rendered him unable to fulfill this request, so the fact that Lesbia is being unfaithful while he is away from Rome at Verona cannot concern him; further, the lack of books at Verona make it impossible for him to write the poetry that has been requested (1–36). Catullus then writes a letter of thanks to a certain Allius, who made a house available to him and his mistress (Lesbia?). Lesbia stepped on the threshold of this house like Laodamia coming to the house of Protesilaus as a new bride (37–74). But Protesilaus had to join the expedition to Troy immediately after his wedding, and died there. Troy brings to mind Catullus' own brother, buried far from home; after expressing his grief, Catullus turns to Laodamia, swept into a pit of love deeper than the pit dug by Hercules at Pheneus; Lesbia enters the borrowed house with a passion similar to Laodamia's (75–134). Even though Lesbia is not faithful to him, Catullus reminds himself that he has no right to be jealous, seeing that they are not married and that he enjoys nights that have been stolen from her husband. He ends by saying that he has done what he could to requite Allius for his favor, and he wishes happiness on Allius and his girlfriend and on himself and Lesbia (135–60).

At the center of this poem is the memory of the beautiful but ill-omened moment in which Lesbia stood on the threshold of the house borrowed from Allius:

> quo mea se molli candida diva pede
> intulit et trito fulgentem in limine plantam
> innixa arguta constituit solea, (70–72)
>
> where my bright goddess, walking softly,
> entered, placed her shining foot on the worn threshold
> and leaned on her creaking sandal.

In the Roman wedding ceremony, the bride must be carried across the sacred *limen* so that she doesn't tread on it;[36] here the detail lavished on the transgressive but divinized foot of Lesbia makes of her arrival a problematic transference that recalls the delivery of the poem in poem 65, the disappearance of the lock from the temple in poem 66, and the arrival of the bride in poem 67. In this case, the ceremonial passage of the bride to her new home, the ultimate form of legitimate and orderly communication between self and other, is ominously and beautifully suspended from line 72 to line 132, where Lesbia crosses the threshold and conveys herself into Catullus' *gremium* (132) with her gifts stolen from the *gremium* (146) of her husband.

In the myth that is recounted during this suspension of linear progression, the threshold on which Lesbia has stepped becomes a grave or pit (89, 108), and layers of different material are uncovered in the suspension of her transference. The story of Protesilaus and Laodamia brings up the name of Troy, and suddenly this mythological digression becomes an intensely personal lament for Catullus' brother. Ironically, Catullus finds his brother again in the learned myth that divinizes the moment when Lesbia steps on the threshold of Catullus' borrowed house; that to which he compares his relationship with Lesbia turns out to contain a relationship even more proper to him, an irony that confuses our sense of where the poet is speaking from, of what is near and what is far. An outburst of grief for his brother is triggered by the reference to Troy as the communal *sepulcrum* (grave, 89) of Europe and Asia, and the poem at this point turns into a lament for the brother's death, returning to the myth of Protesilaus and Laodamia at the point where Protesilaus leaves for Troy, sweeping her into an abyss (barathrum) of love:

> ... tanto te absorbens vertice amoris
>   aestus in abruptum detulerat barathrum,
> quale ferunt Grai Pheneum prope Cyllenaeum
>   siccare emulsa pingue palude solum,
> quod quondam caesis montis fodisse medullis
>   audit falsiparens Amphitryoniades,
> tempore quo certa Stymphalia monstra sagitta
>   perculit imperio deterioris eri,
> pluribus ut caeli tereretur ianua divis,
>   Hebe nec longa virginitate foret. (68.107-16)

>     ... the current sucking you into so deep a
>   vortex of love had plunged you into an abyss,
> steep as the one the Greeks say, near Cyllenean Pheneus,
>   drains the rich soil of a swamp,
> which once that hero (falsely called the son of Amphitryon)
>   is famed to have dug through the mountain's stabbed heart,
> when his unerring arrows struck the Stymphalian birds
>   at the bidding of a master less than he,
> so that the doorway of heaven might be trod by more,
>   and Hebe not remain a virgin long.

This facetious piece of learned mythological geography is studiedly inappropriate in tone to the pathetic lines that introduce it (105-8), and it inverts the affective direction of the turn at the word *sepulcrum*.[37] The grave and the pit might both be metaphors for the plunging of the poem itself at these points into another level of subject matter and style; by turning into drainage channels, albeit Herculean, this abyss of love unsettles the identification of depth with emotional intensity that it initiated. Whatever the exact literary provenance of the pit to which Catullus alludes, the spirit of Alexandria clearly haunts this passage, reminding us that the poet had pleaded lack of books in the opening letter to Mallius.[38] The pit, like the blush in poem 65, is both a figure and an example of the nonlinear capacities of poetry, drawing attention to the way that subject matter in this poem is stacked to produce a stratified rather than a linear form.

Both the pit and the grave open up in the ill-omened suspension of Lesbia's illegitimate conveyance to the *gremium* of Catullus. If the fact that Catullus will never be married to Lesbia means that, now that his brother is dead, the family is buried (c.68.22) and will not continue, then the poem's accumulative layering may reflect the severing of linear time in the family.

I have read poems 65 through 68 as an interconnected group related not only by common themes but also by a dialogue between aspects of Catullus' cultural identity and the different kinds of expression that are associated with them. The outer pair, spoken in the first person, are experiments with new conceptions of poetic form that will be adequate to the heterogeneous origins and components of poetic expression. The two inner poems present contrasting speakers, both inanimate objects, whose characteristic forms of speech reflect their respective cultural milieux. These poems relate not only to each other, but also to the outer poems, particularly through the amatory or sexual themes that permeate the whole group. The recurring image of the *gremium*, unreliable, unretentive, robbed, and violated, reflects in sexual terms an anxiety about authenticity that ramifies both into the question of how a poem is conceived and delivered and into problems of cultural filiation.

We might conclude by outlining the issues raised by the death of Catullus' brother in these poems. First, if the poet cannot communicate with his brother across the grave, then where does the poem go and who is it for? This issue is reflected in the problems of transference and delivery that permeate these poems in which people are constantly receiving what has been diverted from another. It is an issue that is a problem for any poem insofar as it goes to destinations that are unknown and will perhaps continue to be spoken long after the poet is dead. Secondly, if the death of his brother occupies the faithful poet's mind completely, then how can he write of other subjects and from other motives? We have seen how this problem both raises the anxiety of displacement and at the same time generates experimental models of poetic form and expression; the question of where the poet speaks from is explored with dazzling virtuosity. Finally, the fact that his brother dies at Troy, most ancient and prestigious of places in Roman history, and then sends the poet to the place of his origin, provincial Verona, precipitates an anxious exploration of the poet's complicated cultural affiliations.

CHAPTER 9

# Between Men
## Catullan Literature

Paul de Man begins his chapter on Rilke in *Allegories of Reading* by remarking on the effect that Rilke has had on his readers:

> Many have read him as if he addressed the most secluded parts of themselves, revealing depths they hardly suspected or allowing them to share in ordeals he helped them to understand and to overcome. . . . Rilke seems to be endowed with the healing power of those who open up access to the hidden layers of our consciousness or to a delicacy of emotion that reflects, to those capable of perceiving its shades, the reassuring image of their own solicitude.[1]

He goes on to say that "it is sometimes difficult to discover the memory of the original texts under the abundant confessional discourse that it generates in the commentators" (21). It is part of the role of what we call an "author" to generate discourse in others, and in the case of poets this discourse is often confessional, the responsive echo that proves that the reader has understood, and is worthy of, the poet's confidences. Classical scholarship is not given to the confessional mode, but in the case of Catullus a great deal of writing (novels, poems, and translations), much of it by classicists, is available to tell us what this author has meant to his readers, and it is clear that Catullus is the Rilke of antiquity.[2] Probably the most important poem for this aspect of Catullan reception is poem 101, in which the poet addresses his brother from the latter's graveside; Catullus has himself expressed the pathos of his readership's relation to him.

In his autobiography, Macaulay tells us about his special relationship to Catullus' poetry:

> I have pretty much learned all that I like best in Catullus. He grows on me with intimacy. One thing he has—I do not know whether it belongs to him or to something in myself—but there are some chords in my mind which he touches as nobody else does. The first lines of Miser Catulle; the lines to Cornificius, written evidently from a sick bed; and part of the poem beginning "Si qua recordanti" affect me more than I can explain; they always move me to tears.[3]

Of the poems to which Macaulay refers (cc.8, 38, and 76), two are addressed by Catullus to himself, and in both of these he is attempting to persuade himself to break off the affair with Lesbia that is causing him such pain. The third poem (c.38) is a short and poignant appeal for commiseration in his sickness (metaphorical or literal) to a certain Cornificius, who is rebuked for his lack of sympathy; poem 38 seems to have affected Allen Ginsberg similarly, for its opening (Malest Cornifici tuo Catullo) is the title of an equally poignant poem in which Ginsberg tells Kerouac of his happiness at finding a new lover.[4] Catullus, whose own oeuvre contains its brotherhood of poets, has become the canonical figure for that brotherhood in modern poetry: Swinburne, for example, uses echoes of Catullus' farewell to his brother (c.101) to celebrate the relation between himself and several dead poets.[5] In one Latin poem ("Ad Catullum"), Swinburne addresses Catullus as "brother" and yearns to follow him through the underworld to meet Landor, the British Catullus. More recently, Thomas McAfee has written a cycle of poems under the title *My Confidant Catullus* (1983) in which he discusses poetry and love with the dead poet. And John Cotton 1982, on holiday at Sirmio, communes with the ghost of Catullus as he watches the German tourists and describes his own relish in the particular sensations, natural and gustatory, of the modern site of Catullus' home.

But this idea of brotherhood, absorbed from the Catullan corpus, takes its place in a certain emotional geography in which brotherhood has as its concomitant, or even its motivation, a rejection of the woman. Two of the poems that Macaulay cites (cc.8, 76) are attempts to say farewell to Lesbia, one of them very bitter. Most who have read Catullus in Latin remember the two tags "Odi et amo" (I love and I hate) and "Ave atque vale" (Hail and farewell); between them, these two quintessentially lyric paradoxes distinguish the turbulent and self-torturing ambivalence of Catullus' addiction to Lesbia from the tender and gentle hopelessness of his love for his dead brother. They also make up two sides of the personality of Catullus' oeuvre: the man of violent passions and the "tenderest of Roman poets." The paradox that describes Catullus' feelings for Lesbia characterizes one aspect of the oeuvre, a violence that comprises both sexual passion and bitter hatred, but in contrast the final words of Catullus to his brother have a gestural tenderness and simplicity, a pathos of loss, that is the other side of his oeuvre. At some point, or on some level, most readers of Catullus have absorbed this emotional geography of the Catullan oeuvre, and it has played a large role in the educative purpose that Catullus has served in the classroom. In fact, the phrase "ave atque vale" condenses within its gesture of noble resignation contrasts of a larger scale, such as that between poems 8 and 9, where Catullus' painful and unsuccessful attempt to say farewell to a Lesbia who no longer wants him is juxtaposed to the untainted exclamatory joy with which he welcomes his friend Veranius back from Spain. The latter poem of welcome reminds us of Catullus' own greeting to his family home on returning from his stint on Memmius's staff in Bithynia (salve, o venusta Sirmio ..., c.31.12), and that poem is the complement to Catullus' elated farewell to Bithynia, and to the comrades with whom he set out from Rome in poem 45 (o dulces comitum valete coetus, 45.9). Against these we may put the bitter farewell, entrusted to Furius and Aurelius in poem 11, to a Lesbia whose infidelity has destroyed Catullus' love: "let her live and fare well with her adulterers" (cum suis vivat valeatque moechis, 17). The "ave atque vale" of poem 101 transposes both the tortured bitterness of the farewells to Lesbia and the exuberance of the greetings and farewells to men into an elegiac nobility, to be spoken "for ever" (in perpetuum)[6]

John Cotton's poem "Catullus at Sirmio" (1982) ends with the poet lying in bed in the aftermath of a storm:

> Silence as fragile as the moment
> Holds breath.
> It will last as long,
> To be cherished in the mind,
> Like this Summer,
> When winter shrouds the earth.

This delicate moment transmutes Catullus' "hail and farewell," referred to earlier in the poem, into a fragile poetic epiphany as Cotton reaches the end of his day with the ghost of Catullus. The storm is described in clearly sexual terms and it replaces heterosexual intercourse, which features elsewhere in this poem in the form of fantasies and memories, with the homosocial bond between two poetic sensibilities.[7] Earlier, it was the sight of "the Germanic bum, . . . squeezed out . . . from the bottom of tight shorts" that brought the ghost of the immortal Catullus to trade in his immortality for the position of the living Cotton. Catullus remembers "taking Lesbia from behind" and dreams "of Rome and well-stuffed Ameona [sic, compare "Ameana puella defututa," c.41.1] / Of the Saturn-nippled tits," but Cotton's Catullus speaks a more subtle language when it comes to describing the natural and culinary sensations of Sirmio, and together, at the end of the day, the merged sensibilities of the two poets experience "the storm's consummation." Lying back after "the release of rain," Cotton bestows his "ave atque vale" on the fragile moment, and Catullus slips back into immortality. In this poem, the misogyny that accompanies the communion between men is less overt than in most of what I will be examining in the rest of this chapter (for one thing, Lesbia is not reviled for her "betrayal"), but it remains a good example of the dynamics of gender in the brotherhood of Catullus' readers.

Catullus' intimate words to his dead brother in poem 101 have been echoed in tone and sentiment by many modern writers who have found a "brother" in Catullus, often a brother who, as de Man says of Rilke, has allowed them "to share in ordeals he helped them to understand and to overcome." Here is Swinburne in 1883:

> My brother, my Valerius, dearest head
> Of all whose crowning bay-leaves crown their mother
> Rome, in the notes first heard of thine I read
>    My brother.
>
> No dust that death or time can strew may smother
> Love and the sense of kinship inly bred
> From loves and hates at one with one another.
>
> To thee was Caesar's self nor dear nor dread,
> Song and the sea were sweeter than each other:
> How should I living fear to call thee dead,
>    My brother.[8]

There is something uncharacteristically awkward about the enjambment between the second and third line of the first stanza, forcing us to choose between "mother," the pivot between the opening and closing "brother," and "Rome," the word emphasized by the enjambment. At the beginning of the second stanza, "mother" returns, this time contained in the word "smother," a significant association of ideas in view of the fact that the following line speaks of "a sense of kinship *inly* bred." Clearly, the elective affinity between Swinburne and Catullus is a brotherhood that defines itself against the relation between mother and son. That the relation between men is determined by opposition to the relation between men and women is confirmed by the last line of this stanza, which admits of two different readings: the sense of kinship between the two men is bred by shared "loves and hates," but the phrase also refers to the "Odi et amo" that describes Catullus' violently conflicting emotions toward Lesbia, and the words "loves and hates at one with one another" alludes to this ambivalence of feeling. The same words, then, declare Swinburne's sense of kinship with the passionate loves and hates of Catullus—to be joined, in the next stanza, with shared indifferences—and with the simultaneity of love and hate with respect to a woman. Lesbia and her progeny are the medium through which men communicate, finding themselves at one with one another in the very conflict of their feelings toward her.

When Aubrey Beardsley translates Catullus' poem 101 in 1896, his most significant embellishment of Catullus' words completes the triangle that we have found in Swinburne's address to his ancient brother:

> By ways remote and distant waters sped,
> Brother, to thy sad grave-side am I come,
> That I may give the last gifts to the dead,
> And vainly parley with thine ashes dumb:
> Since she who now bestows and now denies
> Hath ta'en thee, hapless brother, from mine eyes.
> But lo! these gifts, the heirlooms of past years,
> Are made sad things to grace thy coffin shell;
> Take them, all drenched with a brother's tears,
> And, brother, for all time, hail and farewell.[9]

Catullus' *Fortuna* becomes "she who now bestows and now denies," a description that might apply equally to the erratic Lesbia of Catullus' poems, making the intervention of death between the brothers echo with another story. Lesbia the cruel tease who tortures Catullus with her inconsistency is, as we shall see, a characterization that has been accompanied by alarming flights of misogyny in male writers,[10] but it is a woman, A. C. E. Allinson, who provides the best commentary on the buried structure of Beardsley's translation.

In a story called "The Estranger," published in 1913, Allinson interweaves Catullus' mourning for his brother with his betrayal by Lesbia, his disillusionment, and his final, cynical return to her when she summons him back.[11] Catullus and his elder brother, Valerius, had gone their separate ways since they had become men, Valerius' sober life being "the fruit of a wine-red passion for Rome's glory" (10), and the poet's more unbuttoned existence resulting from "the pursuit of an untrammelled individual life, subversive of accepted standards, rich in emotional incident and sensuous perception" (6). Early in the story, there is an idyllic scene from Catullus' childhood in which Catullus, his brother Valerius, and their mother (who died when Catullus was six) spend a day on the shore of the lake. There, the mother tells the boys the story of the Argo, which fills Catullus with desire for strange lands. But as she comes to Medea his mother's voice changes: "Something in her voice made his throat ache, as she went on to tell them of the sorceress Medea; how she brought the leader of the quest into wicked ways, so that the glory of his heroism counted for nothing and misery pusued him, and how she still lived on in one disguise after another, working ruin, when unresisted, by poisoned sheen or honeyed draught" (9–10). Catullus and his brother lie upon the breast of their "Nereid-mother" (10; compare c.64.16–18!) in a moment of understanding between them that remains a persistent bond even after their lives diverge. The woman between them will, of course, change from mother to Medea.

Shortly before his death, Valerius expresses his concern about his brother's affair with Lesbia. Catullus defends Lesbia as the victim of slander, and in response Valerius delivers a familiar paean to Catullus' own innocence: "I know this hot heart of yours is as pure as the snow we see on the Alps in midsummer." When he later sees Lesbia and his friend Caelius in a compromising position, Catullus goes off on a bender in the Subura, falls ill, and recovers to find "a sneering desire for Lesbia's beauty divorced from a regard for her purity." He returns to Lesbia when she sends for him, and Allinson ends the story with these words: "He had blamed death for his separation from Valerius. But what death had been powerless to accomplish his own choice of evil had brought about. Between him and his brother there now walked the Estranger—Life." Catullus' *Fortuna*, who took his brother away from him (c.101.5), has become "the Estranger—Life," but Life as "she who now bestows and now denies," in other words, Woman.

Allinson's story might well be an interpretation of poem 68 of Catullus. There, the relation between Catullus' grief at his brother's death and what Allinson sees as the cynical arrangement between the two lovers is waiting to be made. Thanking his friend for making available a house in which he and the married Lesbia could meet, Catullus launches on the story of Protesilaus and Laodamia, the ill-fated couple who were separated, just after their marriage, by the Trojan War, in which Protesilaus was to die. The mention of Troy produces an outbreak of grief for the poet's brother, who also died in that part of the world (89–100) and with whom, Catullus claims, his house is buried (94). The poem gradually returns to Lesbia, standing on the threshold of their borrowed house, where she had been left at the beginning of the mythical diversion, and Catullus declares that he will put up with Lesbia's infidelities and her married status, being content with what he has.

It has been pointed out that the *domus* (house, household) is an important feature of poem 68: Catullus and Lesbia must meet in a borrowed *domus* (68), because Lesbia has not been led in marriage to his *domum* (144), and this unsatisfactory situation does nothing to alleviate the fact that Catullus' *domus* has been buried along with his brother. In a sense, then, Catullus' liaison with Lesbia does sever the relationship with his brother, which might be maintained through the continuity of the house, but it is a sense quite different from Allinson's.[12] A possible intermediary between Catullus and Allinson is Vergil, who has Aeneas' father echo poem 101 when he greets him in the underworld, inserting the crucial and threatening presence of the Woman:

> quas ego te terras et quanta per aequora vectum
> accipio! quantis iactatum, nate, periclis!
> quam metui ne quid Libyae tibi regna nocerent. (*Aen.* 6.692–94)

> Through what lands and how many seas you have traveled
> to be greeted by me; my son, tossed by such great dangers!
> How I feared that Libya might do you some harm.

Here, the Medea figure (Dido) fails to interpose herself between the two men as Anchises had feared she would, and Aeneas can learn from his father the glorious future of his *domus*.

If Catullus loses a brother in Allinson's story, he gains a father in Thornton Wilder's fascinating *Ides of March* (1948). As the title indicates, this is a novel about Julius Caesar, but its main narrative is carried by the relationship between Caesar, Clodia, and Catullus.[13] Wilder has stretched the traditional chronology so that the deaths of Catullus and Caesar occur within a year of each other. He puts Caesar at the deathbed of the heartbroken Catullus and gives Clodia the role of warning Caesar about the Ides of March. This synchrony allows Wilder to play out the drama of *Weltwende* that is implicit in much of the scholarship on Catullus and, of course, almost synonymous with Caesar. In this drama, Clodia is the perverted genius of the age and Catullus and Caesar its martyrs.

What particularly interests me about this novel is the role of Clodia, who becomes the facilitator of the relationship between Catullus and Caesar. All we know of that relationship from ancient sources is that Caesar was a friend of Catullus' father, and that Catullus wrote some vitriolic poems against Caesar and his proteges but later apologized to Caesar, who accepted his apology and, as an act of reconciliation, invited him to dinner.[14] Wilder does not unlock the mystery of Catullus' enmity towards Caesar, but rather fosters it. Toward the beginning of the novel, Caesar expresses puzzlement at Catullus' hatred (35–36), but what disturbs him more is the poet's inexplicable love of Clodia:

By what strange chain of significances has it come about that this woman who has lost intelligible meaning to herself and lives only to impress the chaos of her soul on all that surrounds her should now live in the mind of a poet as an object of adoration and should draw from him such radiant songs? I say to you in all gravity that one of the things in this world that I most envy is the endowment from which springs great poetry. To the great poets I ascribe the power to gaze fixedly at the whole of life and bring into harmony that which is within and that which is without them. (32–33)

It is later suggested by another character that Catullus' hatred of Caesar has something to do with Clodia, although there is no cause for sexual jealousy on Catullus' part (61); the matter is left inconclusive. But if Clodia's own representation of her history is correct, then it is Caesar who made her what she is, and Catullus is to some extent the victim of Caesar. In a letter to Caesar—the novel is composed of letters and documents—Clodia claims that she has "brutified" herself to avoid importuning Caesar "with this thing they call love," and that it was he who taught her that "living had no character at all and had no meaning" and that "*the universe did not know that men were living in it*" (44, emphasis Wilder's). Clodia is possessed by this Epicurean nihilism, but she sees that Caesar is not, and that there is one more thing that he could have told her but withheld—something that accounts for his own faith in action and work. Clodia, then, plays out the darker side of Caesar's mind and of the age itself, and ends up masterminding the profanation of the Bona Dea ceremony (Wilder has moved this event seventeen years forward) as well as causing the death of Catullus.

Caesar's own attitude to religion is skepticism tinged with intimations of "a mind in and behind the universe which influences our minds and shapes our actions" (38). One of the experiences through which he senses this mystery is poetry; although, like Clodia, he believes that poetry is the medium through which comforting lies and fantasies sap our mental strength, Caesar excepts the greatest poetry, which may be "a voice from beyond man" (39, compare Clodia 78–81). Catullus, tortured by Clodia, herself an emanation of the dark places of Caesar's mind, exhibits both the vulnerability and the transcendental force of poetry, making an attractive quarry for the woman who, according to Asinius Pollio (59–60), searches out the weakest places in her lovers in order to insult them the more thoroughly. But Catullus sees the ruined greatness in his tormentor and produces a poetry that gainsays her nihilism. So Caesar and Catullus need each other: it is the weakness of Catullus the poet to weave self-deceiving fantasies of love around his relationship with Clodia, simultaneously loving and hating the Caesar who produced her; Caesar himself confesses his own weakness: "I am astonished by a weakness that I feel awakening in me, a delirious weakness: oh, to be understood by such a one as Catullus . . ." (36).

The climax of the relationship between Caesar and Catullus is Catullus' death; by its anticipation of Caesar's own murder at the hand of his intimates, this climax becomes a kind of *Liebestod*. At Catullus' deathbed, Caesar gives the poet what he had withheld from Clodia; he alone is able to answer Catullus' cry "that he had wasted his life and his song for the favors of a harlot" (182), and, as Catullus dies, Caesar recites to him the final chorus of Sophocles' *Oedipus at Colonus*. By withholding from Clodia, Caesar has indirectly brought about the circumstances in which he can give to Catullus; this implicit drama eroticizes the mind of Caesar, playing out the ambivalence of his disillusioned but visionary, world-historical mind through the love and hatred of Catullus. Only in response to the suffering of the victimized Catullus, a suffering caused by his own cruel withholding from Clodia, can Caesar make his affirmation of life. Such is the erotics of *Weltwende* as Wilder presents it.

After the narration of Catullus' death, the rest of the novel is taken up by events leading to the assassination of Caesar. It is revealed that Caesar's agents had found documents in Catullus' possession linking him with a plot to overthrow Caesar, but that the dictator had written indulgently to Catullus, blaming his friends and asking him to warn them to desist; Catullus replied defiantly (219-21). Implicitly, then, Catullus plays a role in Caesar's assassination just as Caesar, through Clodia, had driven Catullus to his grave only to cradle him in the final *pieta*. Caesar's death is preceded by a final act of withholding from Clodia, for when Clodia comes to warn him of the conspiracy and supply names and dates, Caesar neither responds to her warning nor tells her that he already knows this information. "I saw her as an old woman sitting by the fire and remembering that she had saved the State" (234); with this patronizing gesture to Clodia, Caesar keeps his date with Catullus and Brutus.[15]

Whether he knew it or not, in the deathbed reconciliation between Catullus and Caesar, Wilder was developing a motif implicit in the traditional biography of the poet. According to the traditional chronology of the poems, poem 11 was one of the last that Catullus wrote, and in this poem two strands of the Catullan biography come together, the relations with Caesar and with Lesbia respectively.[16] Catullus definitively repudiates Lesbia, from whom, so the story goes, he has been estranged for some time; Lesbia has made a request for reconciliation and this is his reply.[17] But the reference in poem 11 to the monuments of "great Caesar" (Caesaris ... monimenta magni, 10) is taken to indicate that the reconciliation between Catullus and Caesar mentioned by Suetonius has already taken place; so this poem, written at the end of Catullus' life, creates a chiasmus in Catullus' relations with Lesbia and Caesar: as Lesbia is finally repudiated, Caesar and Catullus are reconciled.[18]

Reconciliation between men coincides with the insulting of Lesbia in the most recent novel about Catullus, *The Key* by Benita Kane Jaro (1988). The novel is narrated by Caelius, who has been charged by Catullus' father to "explain" his son to him after the latter's premature death. Early in the story, Caelius and Catullus both make love to the same woman in a very steamy threesome, leaving Caelius feeling, as he lies back in postcoital languor, "somehow more than [Catullus'] friend" (14). At the end of the novel, it is revealed that Caelius had had an affair with Lesbia and he asks forgiveness of Catullus' father, now himself at death's door. Old Catullus refuses, but shows Caelius the manuscript of poem 58:

Caelius, my Lesbia, that Lesbia
that dear Lesbia whom Catullus loved
more than himself and everything he owned,
now at crossroads, and in alleyways,
gluts her cunt on the generous sons of Rome.

(Jaro's translation, 229)

Catullus senior's bony finger points to a place where his son had crossed out a word and substituted another:

Caelius, *our* Lesbia, that Lesbia . . .

The old man tells Caelius that though *he* doesn't forgive him, Catullus has already done so (230). In a note in the appendix, Karo explains that she has interpreted *nostra* in line 1 literally, rather than as a poetic form of the first person singular, and that this ambiguity became the basis of her book. The same note deals with the mysterious *glubit* (lit., "peels"), for which Karo has produced the most obscene of all the translations hitherto suggested. Her interpretation of the two problematic words makes the poem simultaneously an act of forgiveness toward Caelius—recalling the earlier threesome—and the most violent insult to Lesbia and to female sexuality.

Lesbia appears again as the facilitator of a relationship between men that is mediated by death in a cycle of poems by James Baxter. "Words to Lay a Strong Ghost" is contained in Baxter's collection *Runes*, published in 1973. These poems "after Catullus" were partially the fruit of Baxter's collaboration with the Catullus scholar Kenneth Quinn;[19] as the title indicates, they are poems in which a disillusioned but obsessed lover tries to come to terms with his love. Catullan motifs are woven through the fourteen poems, whose central figure, Pyrrha, is, like Clodia, both faithless and irresistible. Rivals (referred to as Caelius and Egnatius) are lambasted, moments of joy are celebrated ("In my friend Allius' condemned house"), a budgie is buried ("Pyrrha's eyes are red . . . Because nothing desired can last for long"), and Pyrrha reveals her Horatian connections (c.1.5) in a poem about jealousy ("He'll find out what its like! That mug!").

Baxter follows the trend of modern scholarly opinion in reading autobiography into Catullus' Attis poem (c.63), in which a follower of the goddess Cybele runs away to the wilds and castrates himself;[20] his poem "The Wound" describes the castration inflicted on the speaker by Pyrrha in the form of

Exile from the earth I came from

Pub, bed, table, a fire of hot bluegum
The boys in the bathing sheds playing cards.

Pyrrha plays Cybele to Baxter's Attis, who, "No longer a man," accepts his bondage. This poem, the eighth in the cycle, introduces the theme that will lead to the final poem—spoken "At the Grave of a War Hero"—where life itself (the Estranger!) becomes the great castrator, and "Death . . . the only love affair / Worth having." In the poem that follows "The Wound," Pyrrha is told that the young Caelius who now has her will soon lie impotent beside her in bed,

> hating your cold heart
> And what's below it, the eight-headed
> Sea-rock-monster barking between your thighs.[21]

The castrating Pyrrha who alienated Baxter from the world of his male companions now reunites him with his disillusioned rival.

In "The Streetlight," Pyrrha the castrating goddess has become a vampire, perpetually resurrected in the mind and body of the poet:

> I hate
> And love; I love and hate . . .
> Under the streetlight it's your mouth that's wet with
>    blood:
> I'm your refrigerated meat!

The imagery of castration mutates from refrigerated meat to severed flower, echoing Catullus' simile of innocent love destroyed at the end of poem 11, in the cycle's penultimate poem. The speaker, now a successful man of letters with a family, looks back on his affair with Pyrrha, seeing it with convenient doublethink as both the lost paradise of true passion and the destroyer of his life force:

> I didn't know
> Then how short life is—how few
> The ones who really touch us
>
> Right at the quick—I'm a successful
> Man of letters, Pyrrha—
> Utterly stupid!—a forty-year-old baby
> Crying out for a lost nurse
>
> Who never cared much. The principle
> That should have made me tick went early
> Half underground, as at the paddock's edge
> You'll see in autumn some flower
>
> (Let's say a dandelion)
> Go under the farmer's boots

Like a faded sun
Cut with a spade.

The cycle ends at the grave of Baxter's friend, a war hero who died swimming the Taieri in winter. Baxter tells him

You're out of touch, mate—no gear to fiddle—
  Nobody to fuck, punch, kick a ball at—

But the middle-aged poet envies his friend:

    Yet from here
Death looks to me like the only love affair
Worth having—you rot
In khaki; I in civvies—

Let's say they cut off the toes,
Then the fingers, then the legs at the knees,
Then the hands, then the legs at the thighs,
Then the arms at the shoulders—

Wisdom is the armless legless stump
Howling for its mother!

The great castrator is Life, and Pyrrha her agent, Pyrrha who first alienated the protagonist from the world of his buddies but now brings life's amputee to the grave of his friend, where he dreams of the only love affair worth having and says farewell ("Good luck, mate; goodbye!").

Baxter's cycle is a compendium of misogynist strategies, of which there is no better example than the way he handles the mixture of violence and tenderness in his persona. To the twentieth century reader, it may seem odd that the Victorians regarded Catullus as the "tenderest" of Roman poets, and Baxter has clearly chosen to speak with the voice of Catullus mainly because of the irreverent, earthy, and vernacular tone that modern poets have most prized in him.[22] The affair with Pyrrha is supposed to attest to the reckless abandon of the life-affirming poet, and the vitriol hurled against both the rivals and Pyrrha herself is evidently another manifestation of this same gusto.[23] And yet the tenderness that makes the (feeling, sensitive) poet a victim is equally important even to the modern image of Catullus; in Baxter it is, as one might expect, a tenderness that can only be revealed as already betrayed and destroyed by Woman. So the "forty-year-old baby" who—married and successful—looks back on his affair with Pyrrha is "crying out for a lost nurse / Who never cared much." In the final poem, the systematic amputation that leaves an "armless legless stump / Howling for its mother" represents two quite opposite processes: on the one hand, the now successful man of letters, rotting in civvies, has lost the violent passion associated with the Pyrrha affair and, deprived of his gusto, is being reduced to a mewling child. On the other hand, the vulnerable poet, castrated by the monstrous Pyrrha, is stripped by life's cruelties to the most innocent and helpless of beings. Two opposite self-images are projected, each invested in Pyrrha, and the prevarication of the amputation metaphor reveals the contradictory purposes she is serving.[24]

In Baxter's cycle, Death, "the only love affair / Worth having," brings the two friends together in a celebration of their reckless lust for life, which became a deathwish because Life (read Woman) always betrays you.[25] Wilder's version of this story is more complex because the relation between Caesar and Catullus, which leads to a kind of love-death, is about the repression of love and faith by reasons of state: Caesar wants to inspire the love or hatred that would put him back in touch, and he wants to be forced, by the pitiful victim of an emanation of his own mind, to affirm life. But in both of these cases the woman serves as an alibi for the creative genius, the contradictory nature of whose desires and self-image is disguised by the blame that is put on her.

Catullus' graveside farewell to his brother has been echoed endlessly by his imitators. The constantly revivified gesture seems to transcend the frustrations of its original situation, where the intervention of death makes the words futile. Catullus seems to have anticipated the pathos of his own readers, who find themselves communing through a dead language with a dead poet; in fact, many of these readers have addressed Catullus himself as he addressed his brother, proving, with melancholy relish, that words spoken across the chasm of death are not spoken in vain.[26] As J. C. Squire puts it in his poem, "To a Roman,"[27]

> You died two thousand years ago, Catullus,
> Myriads since then have walked the earth you knew
> All their long lives and faded into nothing,
> And still across that waste men think of you.

Catullus' journey "through many peoples" to his brother's grave becomes an imaginative journey across centuries strewn with the lives of the dead. But Squire speaks to Catullus not only "across that waste" but also across the poems: the years, the poems, and the life reflected in the poems are all clutter behind which Squire sees the essential Catullus, withdrawn into the purity of his own mind from a cruel, cynical world

that is about to fall into ruin. "The poet should be chaste, his verses—":
poem 16 is the authority for Squire's vision of Catullus, uneasy among
his companions, "taking their filth more cleverly than they" but alienated from the debauchery in which he participates. At one point, Catullus grows abstracted as he catches sight of a distant sail, and his
companions realize that he is completely indifferent to them. Lesbia tries
to break down Catullus' inner withdrawal:

> Disliking, piqued by, that strange difference in you,
>   Contemptuous and curious, she would dare
> And then deny, provoke, and then repel you,
>   Yet could not make you other than you were.
>
> The soft-pressed foot, the glance that hinted heat,
>   The scanty favors always auguring more,
> The haughty, cold indifference, mingling twin
>   Frigidities of the vestal and the whore,
>
> Still could not even more than wound, cloud over,
>   The eager boy in you she so despised,
> The love of fineness, sweetness, loyalty, candor,
>   The innocent country memories you prized.

I suspect that this picture of Lesbia is more or less what Beardsley meant
by "she who now bestows and now denies." Squire's vivid and bitter
portrait, which finds little support in the poems, suggests some personal
agenda, but, besides being a mask for the modern poet, the Catullus in
this poem is also a figure for the reader. Squire's scenes of Catullus with
his companions and with Lesbia might have their origins in the experience of the reading schoolboy who retires from the group into the
world of books, causing the resentment of his fellows and their attempts
to distract him. The experience then becomes the model through which
different scenarios in later life are understood, at the same time as
(paradoxically) a memory of innocent companionship from the schooldays when Catullus was first encountered is preserved against the cynical,
adult world. When Squire's Catullus gazes at the sail while his companions carouse, two different kinds of abstractedness are conflated, one
forward-looking ("A silent sail that cuts the clear horizon") and the
other retrospective ("Watching a distant sail that seems unmoving, /
The symbol of some lost tranquillity"); in other words, the moment
reflects the experience of reading at two different stages of life, both
experiences of abstracted isolation. In the scene with Lesbia, the "innocent country memories" of an "eager boy" who remembers other

kinds of relationship ("The love of fineness, sweetness, loyalty, candor") are a haven proof against the destructive onslaught of Lesbia.

What Lesbia did destroy, according to Catullus, was his love for her, cut like a flower at the edge of a meadow. Here is Squire's appropriation of that image in his poem's two final stanzas:

> A flower in a garden grew, Catullus,
>   Sometime you saw it, and the memory stayed.
> One flower of all the flowers you ever glanced at,
>   A perfect thing of dew and radiance made.
>
> Emblem of youth, plucked, carried away and drooping,
>   Out of the garden; emblem of your lot,
> Perplexed, bewildered, languishing, an alien
>   Who was born to cherish all his world forgot.

The poem returns to its beginning, where across the waste of time men still think of Catullus, just as Catullus remembered the flower across the waste of his life. The flower growing in the garden (not, as in c.11, a meadow) is not only an emblem of Catullus' youth, it is also Catullus' poetry itself, the flower of an anthology, emblem of the reader's youth. Lesbia destroyed Catullus' love as the plough does a flower, but she could not destroy the *image* of the flower; as Squire's reader projects back onto Catullus the sentiment of his own cherishing of images from Catullus' poetry (the yacht in c.4, the flower in c.11)—images carried by the reader into the inhospitable everyday world—the love for Lesbia that the flower represented is bypassed and Catullus and the reader come together. The author Catullus in this poem is a prolepsis of the reader himself, who retrojects onto Catullus' abstraction from his surroundings an image of his own experience of reading, of cherishing "all his world forgot." What piques Lesbia, "that strange difference" in Catullus, is what only the sensitive reader can know; in fact, the "difference" in Catullus is the presence of the modern reader, who still thinks of Catullus across the waste of time, finding in him that which is not of his own time. Lesbia is the threat—generalizable to a jealous and unsympathetic external world—that makes the relationship between reader and author a close one.

Whereas Swinburne calls the dead Catullus "brother" and Squire thinks of him across the ages, G. T. Wright, a translator of Catullus who appends to his translations a poem addressed to the poet (1975), confesses that he is puzzled:

> It's strange to think of Catullus as having my feelings
> Without my background. He'd hardly read anything,

> Not a single line of the Romantic poets or Shakespeare,
>
> didn't even know English, which is almost a prerequisite
> for a poet whose subject is me. Somehow he managed,
> in spite of these classical failings, to blunder into
>
> our song. Funny, unhappy, suspicious, accusing,
> collecting all the arguments against pain
> in tones that change color as you go near them,
>
> he resisted, resisted, and he displayed himself
> refusing to know how powerless he was,
> how will fails, how passion sometimes is
>
> almost entirely agony. A thousand thanks,
> model, Catullus, and lover, for bitter words
> which in a tough season I turned into these.

Like Baxter, Wright has used Catullus to come to terms with an experience of his own ("in a tough season"). He translates poems 51, 5, 70, and 11, making a narrative cycle that begins with the Sappho translation, which many scholars believe is the signature piece of the Lesbia affair, and ending with the poem of divorce, also in Sapphics; in between come the ecstatic "Let us live, my Lesbia, and love" and the disillusioned epigram about the untrustworthiness of what a woman says to an eager lover; like Squire (and Baxter), Wright ends with the flower.

For the exorcistic and therapeutic purpose to which he is put, Wright's Catullus must be both mysteriously kin and yet different. The poet "collecting all the arguments against pain" recalls some of the commonplaces of Catullan scholarship concerning Catullus' use of poetry to control his feelings.[28] But Catullus' main asset for Wright's purposes is a dogged naivete that makes the act of translating him therapeutic. There is then a distance and an imbalance of knowledge between Catullus and his modern translator, which means that Catullus doesn't quite have "our" feelings. Wright's representation of Catullus recalls quite closely that of Robert Bagg in an essay on Catullus and Shakespeare (1965); Bagg finds in Shakespeare's sonnets and Catullus' poetry two different responses to a similar situation: "Both attempt to preserve and express a sense of their own love's goodness in response to a shattering sexual betrayal" (65). For many modern interpreters, Catullus *has* read Shakespeare. Bagg's representation of Catullus emphasizes, by contrast to Shakespeare, Catullus' naivete:

> [Catullus'] sophistication plays through the gaiety and style he requires from his friends and from himself in society, but in all that touches him most

personally, in his vision of love, he is passionately naive, even with a touch of squareness. If we think of naivete as ignorance or renunciation of other possibilities for thinking or acting than one's own, and suffering for it, then naivete abounds in the *Carmina* (64).

In spite of the contrast he draws with the tolerant and flexible Shakespeare, Bagg concludes that "revolutions of sensibility and literary style cannot cheat the human personality of melancholy kinships across the generations, as well as they are famed to do" (95). The quotation from Keats's "Ode to a Nightingale" ("The Fancy cannot cheat so well / As she is famed to do"), reversing Keats's disillusionment with the potential of song to speak to a universal and transhistorical human Fancy, manages to mix into the brew the Romantic poets that Wright acknowledges Catullus had not read.

"Melancholy kinships" with Catullus are made possible for both Squire and Wright by the resistance of Catullus, the resistance to his own environment (Squire) and to the world of the reader (Wright). Catullus' remembering of all his world forgot, against the distractions of his companions and of Lesbia, is what allows Squire himself to think of Catullus across the waste. In the versions of Wright and Bagg, Catullus resists the knowledge that readers of Shakespeare and Keats are saddled with, and this makes him a comforting companion in suffering. The autonomy claimed by the aesthetic, figured here by Catullus' resistances both to his environment and to the knowledge forced on us by history, preserves the poetry against the contexts both of its composition and of the time of reading, so that individual readers can continue to find in it the "reassuring image of their own solicitude," or feel that Catullus has allowed them "to share in ordeals he helped them to understand and to overcome," as de Man says of Rilke.

Catullus resists the translator as well: in the third and fourth stanzas of Wright's poem, the resistance of Catullus mustering all the arguments against pain "in tones that change color when you approach them" associates Catullus' resistance to pain with the resistance of his text to the reader and potential translator. But the text is both elusive and self-conscious, it hides and reveals itself, depending on how you understand the fact that its tones change color when you approach them; the paradoxical quality of Catullus' psyche and text comes to a head in the lines

> He resisted, resisted, and he displayed himself
> refusing to know how powerless he was . . .

The erotic and the textual are fused in this passage, which provides an interesting version of the teasing erotics of poetry described in Chapter 2. Resisting the pain of a disappointed love, and also the approach of the reader and translator, the poetry of Catullus finally renders itself to the poet who approaches it in the "tough season" that establishes his melancholy kinship with Catullus. The final word of the poem, "these," points to a self-evidence that resolves the erotic elusiveness attributed to Catullus' poetry; Wright's translations are the words of Catullus as they "turn" seasonally ("in a tough season"), a natural form of appearance that replaces the elusive changing of color in Catullus' "tones." What precipitates this seasonal, rather than historical, reappearance of Catullus' words is the unhappy experience of love that the "tough season" implies, an experience that fosters a melancholy kinship, making Catullus both double and lover of the translator. The time in which poet and translator meet is one that, separated from the flow of history, is all their own. Wright thanks Catullus "for bitter words," referring to the last poem in his cycle of Catullan translations, poem 11, where Catullus charges Furius and Aurelius (in Wright's translation) to "convey to that girl of mine these few unkind / words." The words that pass between men separated by history, but united in melancholy kinship, are made possible by, and directed against, the Woman.

Catullus, as poet of *Weltwende*, may find himself addressed as kin by the modern reader because he bore witness to the inauguration of our own era. In C. H. Sisson's "Catullus" (1974, 102), it is the poet's anticipation of the imminent coming of Christ that allows Sisson to hail him as "friend," and, as we might expect, this Christian fellowship is accompanied by an unhealthy dose of misogyny:[29]

> Catullus walked the Campus Martius.
> He had seen all he needed to see.
> Lain on his bed at noon and got up to his whore.
> His heart had been driven out of his side
> By a young bitch—well, she was beautiful,
> Even, while the illusion was with him, tender.
> She had resolved herself into splayed legs
> And lubricity in the most popular places.
> He had seen Caesar too—had he not been, once,
> The drunken pathic of the king of Bithynia—
> Returning in triumph from the western isles:
> Nothing was too good for this unique emperor.
> Against these fortunes he had nothing to offer
> —Possibly the remains of his indignation,

A few verses that would outlive the century.
His mind was a clear lake in which he had swum:
There was nothing but to await a new cloud.
We have seen it. But Catullus did not;
He had already hovered his thirty years
On the edge of the Mediterranean basin.
The other, rising like a whirlwind in a remote province,
Was of a character he would have ignored.
And yet the body burnt out by lechery,
Turning to its tomb, was awaiting this,
Forerunning as surely as John the Baptist
An impossible love pincered from a human form.

VALEDICTION

Catullus my friend across twenty centuries
Anxious to complete your lechery before Christ came.

It is interesting to compare this version of the world-historical Catullus with that of Lindsay 1929; far from blaming Clodia's betrayal for the lechery of Catullus, Lindsay sees Clodia as "the furthest and deepest externalization of the Roman energy, all the more preciously fine because the lust that agitates her is too great to continue constructively on earth. Its next stage can but be poetry, the poetry of Catullus." For Lindsay, Caesar caught the moment of creative poise between Lesbia and Catullus "and constructed the Empire." But this is a labile moment and Lindsay's Catullus indeed anticipates the Christianity that was to destroy it when "on Mount Ida [he] thrilled to a new pulsation, a desire to tear the rags of the flesh off and dance on the peaks of madness." Christianity, according to Lindsay, is a poor substitute for the rites of Cybele, and it "merely added to the sheer terror of the phrygian, a complex scheme for pandering to the needs of moral baseness."

Sisson's version is much more in tune with the critical mainstream, which would see Catullus driven into the arms of the gods by an impossible love. This "impossible love" is a forerunner of Christ's, and one must conclude that Sisson describes the torment of the crucifixion as a pincering in order to allude to Catullus lying between the splayed legs of Lesbia. But the Catullus of most of this poem is one who anticipates Christ by exhaustion, so to speak, not so much forerunning and foreshadowing Christ's love as unconsciously awaiting it because he has exhausted the amorous possibilities of his own culture and been betrayed by Lesbia (and Caesar).[30] This Catullus is figured as the yacht of poem 4, retired, after having seen it all, to the "limpid lake" (24) where it is displayed to the visitors. Catullus' mind, "a clear lake in which he had swum," is empty of mystery and possibility, but, in spite of the lechery, it is also pure.[31] Scholars have been much exercised to protect Catullus' purity of heart, but Sisson's poem manages to make Catullus' lechery actually synonymous with his purity, for his mind becomes a pure lake by virtue of the fact that he had "seen all he needed to see"—that is, had burnt himself out in lechery. As a forerunner of Christ, he performs a sanitary role, anxiously completing his lechery and burning out his body so that the new dispensation will not be tainted by the old; it is only "the remains of his indignation" that outlive the century. Sisson's Catullus becomes a friend across twenty centuries by virtue of the world-historical role he plays, sacrificing his body in a *reductio* of ancient carnality that creates the void invoking Christ. In the valediction, the speaker reverses Catullus' journey from Rome to the remote province where his brother dies to hail the Roman Catullus from another remote province (Britain), where he speaks from the perspective of what was then happening in a third (Judaea).

But if Catullus' lecherous and pincered body communes with the sacrificed body of Christ and is so purified, that is because Lesbia's body survives to bear the marks of Catullus' immortal indignation and to represent the flesh that Christianity rejected. Not for Lesbia the purifying fire of lechery:

She had resolved herself into splayed legs
And lubricity in the most popular places.

The liquid mind of Catullus was pure in its exhaustion of possibility, and swimming there he cleansed himself; but Lesbia, slippery (*lubricus*) in the most popular places, is a revolting parody of this expansive liquidity. The Latin derivate "lubricity," standing for Catullus' mysterious *glubit* (c.58.5), is simultaneously euphemistic and obscene, and this says much about the position that Sisson adopts with Catullus. Combining the arch Latinisms "resolved," "lubricity," and "popular" with the direct and monosyllabic "splayed," Sisson identifies himself as a speaker who can handle obscenity without being stained, thanks to his access to the purity of the Latin language, and this linguistic layering supports the purpose of the poem in general, which is to separate Catullus' debauchery from Lesbia's.

The confessional mode is particularly apt to make hierarchical separations between partners in the same transgression. Catullus the adulterer complains of the married Lesbia's infidelity not to her husband but to himself, and we are supposed to swallow this because, after all, we are reading Catullus, not Clodia or Metellus.[32] In Gael Turnbull's "After Catullus" (1983), the married speaker complains about his love for a maddeningly unlikely married woman with whom he is having an affair:[33]

> You ask me?—her?—flat chest, varicose veins and teeth
> in need of care—true, agile hips, smooth belly and snug
> crotch (despite four healthy children)—but slow to come
> and hysterical—gabbling in panic—incoherent phone
> calls—always writing that she'll write another letter next
> time (always next time)— . . .

The poem goes on at some length complaining about the woman and ends with the speaker throwing up his hands at the pointlessness of it all:

> and I,
> at the age of forty-three (know better?)—with wife and
> kids I'm fond of, more than fond—to fall in love—and
> she, hung up on her husband, anyway—

The Catullus "after" whom this is spoken gives the poet an alibi for his speaker's petulant and insulting outburst. With the first words, the reader is drawn into the position of confidant, a position in which the reader accepts the victimhood of the poet. As the speaker complains of the woman's incoherent gabbling, he replicates it with his own stream of exasperated complaints, joined loosely with dashes and interrupted by parentheses. Is the poem's speaker then the object of the poet's irony? Not entirely: the poem creates an artistically satisfying simulation of gabbling incoherence that is in fact an endlesslessly resourceful varying of rhythm and metrical line, and this condemns the woman's verbosity all the more efficiently. The poet ensures that there is an asymmetry between the similar inconsistencies and incoherences of the two adulterers. In fact, in this poem the poetic is marked as the difference between the woman's gabbling and the speaker's rhythmical stream of complaints.

The speaker of Turnbull's poem is addicted, like Catullus, and uses the authority of Catullus to mythologize this addiction. In the dedication poem to his translation of Catullus, Jack Lindsay (1929) addresses his own brother as follows:

> Philip, I know that there are few
> who (in the earth of whisky) spew
> quicker repentance with a quicker

> rush for purer better liquor,
> Phil, than you; and so I write
> your name here, since I cannot see,
> ingenuous with mere delight,
> a rasher case of poetry.

This mythologizing of alcoholic addiction as "a case of poetry" is suggested by Catullus' own mythologizing of his addiction to Lesbia, and the next stanza opens with a welcome to Catullus, who is invited to take Clodia to bed with him again. Were Lindsay to have lived next door to Catullus, he confesses, his love would have been no more true than that of Caelius or Alfenus, for "Others' pain / Cannot but be grotesque and queer. . . ." But Catullus is dead and a poet, and instead of jeering at him Lindsay gives him his love, just as he gives his brother an indulgence that comes from seeing him as "a . . . case of poetry." The poem ends:

> The rage is gone, the tears are shed.
> Past patient doors of death and birth
> I take her to my callous bed
> and laugh with you at all the world.

So Lindsay's callous bed avenges Catullus' pain and rectifies the control exerted by the object of addiction over both Catullus and Phil, leaving Lindsay to laugh at all the world with both of his "brothers."

If Lindsay's poem takes, at least provisionally, a somewhat irreverent attitude to Catullus' pain, we have to wait several more decades for a confrontation with the ancient poet that does not end up appropriating the authority of his voice. Thomas McAfee, in his cycle of poems *Catullus, My Confidant* (1983) has produced something unique, namely, a sustained argument with Catullus in which one poet expresses resentment at what another could get away with. The first poem is titled "Advice from Catullus":

> My friend Catullus, always aware
> Of everything high and mighty and low
> And discordant, tells me to beware of
> People who speak or dress too nicely, and
> People who do the opposite. "Caesar,
> At his best, is comfortable and wise!"
>
> I listen to Catullus and believe him.
> Then he's suddenly dressed like a peacock,
> Perfumed, off on another passionate journey

> To Clodia's. His last words to me,
> As he prepares a speech: "Will I outdo
> Her brother? How is the sound of my voice today?"

In the next poem, Catullus reads McAfee's manifesto and criticizes it ("Write me beautiful women, particular / Ones, or ugly women, particular / Ones"), and in subsequent poems McAfee shoos away the sparrow ("You've made a fool of everybody"), advises Catullus to give up Lesbia, and complains that no head of state would care if *he* wrote epigrams against him. The final poem, "Catullus' Mad Song," returns to the theme of the opening: Catullus has a different face for everybody and everything, in fact "He has no face" and can extricate himself from the most embarrassing of positions with ease,

> And then he wrote a book
> About it all. Somehow
> Instead of the clap, he got religion,
> And richer. Where could I damn him
>
> To that's not worn out or full?

It seems appropriate to end this chapter with these words taking issue with a poet we have taken rather too much to our hearts.

# Conclusion

What have I made of Catullus, the ancient Roman? I have not tried to resurrect him, to make him leap once more across the page, a unique but recognizable individual whom we can welcome into our hearts. Perhaps what that particular genre needs at this stage is an iconoclastic approach that will face us with a much more ambiguous figure, following in the vein of McAfee. At the same time, I have not attempted to situate Catullus specifically in late Republican Rome of the 60s and 50s, engaged in the literary and political agendas of those years, nor have I placed him among the dramatis personae of the contemporary Roman elite, reconstructing his position in its events and issues. In fact, I have tried to shift the focus away from Catullus the individual altogether, situating his poetry more broadly in the culture of his time in order to describe the meeting of the lyric genre with Roman preoccupations and norms.

I have replaced the confessional individual with whom the reader bonds, or on whose behalf he or she pleads, with a poet who explores the terms and possibilities of the poetic license we have given him. Perhaps it is our increasing awareness of how relations of all kinds (social, political, personal) are played out through institutions, conventions, and media that makes this kind of approach to the Catullan corpus appropriate for our postmodern consciousness; we have been very interested recently, thanks to the influence of Foucault, in the way positions are distributed by particular practices. We have also, like the Republican Roman elite, suffered acute anxieties about performance (have our politicians become performers and our performers politicans?). And we have taken a troubled interest in the mechanisms of our entertainment (what exactly are we celebrating and enjoying?). Some of these issues are more directly raised by the Rome of the imperial period, with its actor-emperors, its multimedia mass spectacles, and its demoralized intellectual elite, but they are concerns that were endemic to Roman culture.

The Catullus I have described is one who provokes us to think about what kind of a practice poetry is, about its continuities with the situations of everyday speech, and about why we read it. Provocation may prompt us to vindicate what we already know, or it may push us to uncover what we have forgotten. One of the most common of traditional responses to Catullan provocation has been to confirm that, in spite of deliberately deceptive appearances, his work vindicates its claim to belong to the realm of the poetic, even its most exalted regions. My own response has been to explore with Catullus what one might call the unconscious of the lyric genre, aspects that are so obvious that they are forgotten, such as, for instance, the fact that the poet speaks while his audience is silent.

When we give someone a poetic license, we encourage a certain performance of power, a performance that may be a kind of escapology that we observe (Chapter 7), but that is more likely to cast us in the position of victims, which suggests that to feel the power of speech we must sometimes be its victims. After all, this is a game and we need not locate ourselves permanently in the positions we adopt to play it. If poetry is the medium in which we celebrate language, we must not forget that language is a medium of human relation, and that what we are celebrating through poetry is the complex drama that is enabled by the way we relate through language as (real or potential) speakers.

Throughout the book, I have shown how the experience of certain formal dimensions and relational structures of poetry is engaged by the fictional scenarios of the poems; to take a simple example, the words "hail and farewell" at the end of poem 101 make the contradictory situation in which Catullus finds himself at his brother's graveside congruent with the situation of the reader, for whom closure brings both the epiphany of the poem as an object and the loss of a voice; furthermore, like Catullus, the reader may repeat words that seek to establish a relation across the grave with the poet. Conversely, this poem tells us something about the subject matter that has been implicated in the aesthetic drama. Doesn't the funeral, in which we look one last time at the body of the deceased ("hail and farewell"), enable the gesture by which we join the epiphany of a life to the loss of a living being?

I suspect that many works of different media and genres could be analyzed to show how the fictional content and emotional affect of the work serve to flesh out the drama or affect of the consumer's engagement with a particular aspect of the work's medium, form, or mode of presentation. Some examples may help to indicate the forms that such an analysis would take, an analysis that has already been broached by critics dealing with works whose subject matter is self-referential. For instance, Svetlana Alpers has pointed out that the theme of the outsider looking in at a letter is exploited in seventeenth-century Dutch painting to dramatize aspects of the situation of both painter and viewer.[1] In the case of Vermeer's *Woman Reading a Letter*, it is the painter, or the viewer, who is cast in the role of the onlooker. The painting contains only one figure, a woman standing by an open window absorbed in a letter; we see the light from the world outside the open window, whose glass reflects back to us the image of the reading woman. The woman's absorption in the letter that we cannot read, and her radiation by the light of a world that is inaccessible to us, accentuate the deficiencies of our position: we will never know the meaning of this moment that has become so fascinating to us and can never see what she sees. In the foreground of the painting, there is a table covered by a carpet with a bowl of fruit on it, and in front of the table is a drawn-back curtain. As Alpers points out (202–3), this foreground "bars our entry even as it confirms our presence." But there is more to it than that, for the carpet that is casually thrown over the table is bunched up on the left side, where it has caught the light coming from the window to give us an almost tangible sense of its texture. In fact, the worn texture of the carpet becomes more interesting to us than its pattern or "writing." This part of the carpet in the foreground is juxtaposed to the blank letter in the background, a juxtaposition that very precisely renders the transaction in which we are engaged. Although we are excluded from the object and meaning of the reading woman's absorption, we have caught, and are invited to read, a moment in the life of the world around her that she herself has missed. So vivid is the texture of the worn carpet that we seem to read the very passage of time in this household, its erosions and accumulations brought to our attention by the configuration of this carpet draped carelessly over the table. What Vermeer plays on in this painting is the positionality of the viewer in the genre of the domestic scene, in which the exclusion of the viewer (and painter) from the lived reality of the intimate scene is compensated by access to a perspective on the domestic world that is not available to its inmates. To position oneself within the transaction that compensates inability to read the letter with access to the texturality of the carpet, and all that this transaction implies about one's relation to the depicted world, is part of what it means to position oneself in the aesthetic drama of this painting.

The content of a work may reflect the consumer's situation in a quite literal sense, as we can see in the case of the movie about the haunted house. Whatever this genre may be engaging in the way of anxieties about house ownership, domestic privacy, and history, it also reflects something about the audience's relation to the moviehouse itself, a place inhabited for short periods of time by different audiences who undergo intense experiences during the time they rent their seats.[2] Probably, very few people actually think of the movie theater as a house haunted by lurid events and by the thrills of past audiences, but it is just this unconscious experience into which the theme of the haunted house taps. The ghost story in general engages a different positional drama according to its medium and that medium's particular way of positioning the consumer. One might, for instance, see the literary ghost story as a projection of the position of the reader as a revenant who returns from time to time to haunt the book as a ghostly presence, whereas the book in turn haunts the reader in the intervals between reading where everyday life resumes. I have suggested elsewhere that the plots of certain operas might be analyzed in terms of the drama of the consumer's relation to the medium.[3]

❖  ❖  ❖

At the beginning of this book, I cited William Carlos Williams's "This is Just to Say" as a parable of the drama of lyric position. In a note to his wife, Williams asks her to forgive him for eating the plums she was saving in the icebox; I related this to the kind of theft, or preemption, of language that Catullus celebrates in some of the urbane poems I analyze in Chapter 4. But the poet also returns what he has stolen to a kind of second-order icebox that is the poem itself, through which we can experience vicariously the moment when he opened the door to find the plums in a state of sweet, cold, and delicious preservation. Our rediscovery of language, of simple words like "delicious," "sweet," and "cold," recapitulates the poet's own tempting discovery, but with the crucial difference that we won't be writing him any apologetic notes because, as I argue in Chapter 2, our aesthetic positioning means that we cannot *have* the poem.

Six hundred years before Williams found his plums in the icebox, the manuscript of Catullus was discovered in Verona, a moment celebrated by Campesani in an epigram in which Catullus, returned at last to his native town, speaks to his compatriots. Punning on the word *papirus* ("paper" and "lamp"), he urges his compatriots to celebrate the poet whose manuscript/light had been hidden under a bushel (cuius sub modio clausa papirus erat).[4] It seems appropriate to bring Catullus up to date with a further anachronism, replacing the light under the bushel with the light of the icebox that preserved these poems fresh through the centuries (plus uno . . . perenne saeclo). We open the icebox. The light goes on. The icebox hums and the poems glisten, tempting and inaccessible.

# Notes

## Introduction

1. Williams 1985, 74.
2. Keats 1970, 700–701. In the "Fall of Hyperion" (i.18), we find the words "when this warm scribe my hand is in the grave," which confirms that the speaker of this poem is the dead poet.
3. Culler 1981, 154.
4. The idea originates in John Stuart Mill's 1883 essay "What is Poetry?": "Eloquence is *heard*, poetry is *overheard*. Eloquence supposes an audience; the peculiarity of poetry appears to us to lie in the poet's utter unconsciousness of a listener. Poetry is feeling confessing itself to itself in moments of solitude." Mill 1976, 12.
5. Quinn 1982, 89.
6. The concept of "confessional" poetry was developed by Rosenthal 1967 to describe the poetry of Lowell and others writing in the 1950s and 1960s (Plath, Ginsberg, Roethke, Berryman, Sexton). Rosenthal is a little vague as to what he means by this term: the poetry is treated mainly as a form of self-knowledge on the part of the poets, but the implications of the term for the relation between poet and reader are not explored.
7. Selden 1992 is a brilliant De Manian reading of Catullus, and I am delighted to see that in some respects it reaches, by a rather different route, conclusions similar to my own (particularly on page 488, where Selden speaks of the masochism of the aesthetic relation in connection with c.16). Hubbard 1984 is a very sophisticated reading of c.68 from a similar perspective.
8. Elsewhere, Quinn (1972, 279) rightly compares this aspect of the poems of Catullus to Cicero's letters: "We have, moreover, to imagine the experiments taking place at a time and within a circle where the cult of the elegant, poised, ironic expression of the everyday was assiduously cultivated by a much wider *elite*, including such people as Cicero: for the more personal letters of Cicero to his

friends bear a family resemblance to the lighter poems of Catullus; both represent the Latin of conversation, improved upon—not to make the words sound more impressive or more carefully chosen, but to make them sound more casual and at the same time just right."

9. Cicero, *Pis.* 70–71, says of the poems of Philodemus, "Multa a multis lecta et audita." On the importance of reading aloud in Roman literary life, see Starr 1991. Wiseman 1985, 124–27, has some good remarks on the ambiguous status of the Catullan poem.

10. In a sense, criticism is itself a realization or performance of the text in which the critic attempts to speak the whole poem, to articulate everything that the written poem is saying. In this connection, see the interesting remarks of Quinn 1982, 103–4, on *praelegere*, which he describes as "the authoritative performance of the scholar-critic, the enactment of his understanding of the text."

11. There is a considerable bibliography on the neoterics, some of it skeptical as to the existence of an identifiable group, but Lyne 1978 provides a good account of the evidence for its existence and activity and Ross 1975, 3–8, has a valuable interpretation of the context in which the neoterics emerged. On Catullus' Alexandrianism, see Buchheit 1975 and Clausen 1970.

12. In c.47 Catullus laments that Porcius and Socration, the latter possibly a nickname of Philodemus (Frank 1928, 85), are being feted by Piso, while his friends Veranius and Fabullus "beg for invitations at the crossroads" (7). Catullus berates himself in c.44 for having read a frigid speech of Sestius in order to get a dinner invitation.

13. Veyne 1988.

14. See the review of Heiden 1991.

15. Veyne excludes Catullus from this kind of analysis; unlike the elegiac poets, Catullus produces an *illusion* of sincerity: "The Jealous Man is on stage, and we come in on his monologue.... The poem is set in real time, it is spoken as it is being lived.... That is why this magisterial art gives such an impression of naturalness" (34, re c.8). This poetry is *over*heard by its readership, which judges it by the standards of mimetic truth. This positioning of Catullus in relation to the elegiac poets reflects Catullus' role within the Roman pantheon, which I will address in the next chapter: the perfect balance between artifice and naturalness that Veyne sees in Catullus' art sites the elegiac poets in relation to an unsustainable Catullan poise. Catullus' art is classical insofar as it "snips at nature and sews it back together again without falsifying it" (35), and so, according to Veyne, the elaborate game that the elegiac poets play with the reader becomes what one might call a postlapsarian activity.

16. The complexity and importance of Roman status divisions during the late Republic is succinctly described by Beard and Crawford 1985, 40–49. Interesting studies of particular manifestations of the contradictions between ideology and reality in social status can be found in White 1978, 80–82, and D'Arms 1984.

17. Zanker 1988, 25–31.

18. On writers and equestrian status, see Taylor 1968, especially 472–74, where she discusses the choice between *ambitio* and *otium*.

19. On the highly aristocratic Clodia, almost certainly the woman Catullus referred to as Lesbia, see Wiseman 1985, 15–26. Licinius Calvus, on the evidence of cc.14, 50, and 54 a close friend of Catullus, came from what Fordyce 1961, 134, refers to as "an old and distinguished family."

20. See the remarks of David 1983, 318–23, on provincial orators at Rome.

21. Caelius' letters to Cicero constitute Book 8 of Cicero's *Epistulae ad Familiares*.

22. On the concept of the author, see Foucault 1979, from which I quote below, and Pease 1990, a very useful study of the changing meanings and functions of the word "author" from medieval times to the modern period.

23. Friedricksmeyer 1983, 85note 26.

24. Friedricksmeyer 1983, 1.

25. The lines Friedricksmeyer amplifies are:

cum suis vivat valeatque moechis,
quos simul complexa tenet trecentos,
nullum amans vere, sed identidem omnium
  ilia rumpens. (c.11, 17–20)

26. In one of the most recent studies of Catullus, Martin 1992, 116, describes Catullus' readers as bystanders whose job is "to cheer the verses on." He cites in this connection c.42, in which Catullus repeatedly insults a woman who has stolen his notebooks as a "filthy whore." Gaisser 1993, 212–13, quotes a Latin imitation of c.42 by Leonardo Bruni (early fifteenth century) that enhances and extends Catullus' insults with considerable relish.

27. The adjective *lascivus* (mischievous, playful) is used of Catullus by Propertius (2.34.87), Ovid (*Tristia* 2.427), and Martial (7.35.5).

28. C.16, 6–11. I discuss this poem in detail in Chapter 2.

29. Compare Minyard 1985, 27: "Catullus . . . creates a new reference of feeling for these words [ *fides, foedus, amicitia*, etc.]. Lesbia and her husband, however much married, were not joined in a union ratified by feeling. Therefore, the marriage was not real but an imitation. Respecting it would entail repudiation of the new *fides*, not its realization." Stehle 1986, 220, has some good words on this aspect of Catullan criticism: "The modern audience, though, has collaborated [with the tyranny of the speaker] by providing material for constructing a 'deathless,' 'profound,' 'spiritual' love which obliges the worthy subject to return it. An audience finds poetry that is comfortable and does it violence. Perhaps our eager elaboration of the Catullan claims has denied the poetry a chance to construct the other paths of its good readings."

30. Christopher Hollis's *We Aren't So Dumb*, quoted by Havelock 1939, 74. In the preface to the second edition, Havelock has some very interesting remarks about the motives for constructing an anti-ideological Catullus in the thirties.

31. The more recent elaborations of this position include Rankin 1975 and Minyard 1985, 22–28. Skinner 1982 provides an interesting corrective to the view that Catullus' values were personal, not political.

32. These lines come from "The Cave of Making," Auden 1976, 523.

## Chapter 1

1. Vergil alludes to Catullus in several places, but especially noteworthy are the allusions to c.101, Catullus' graveside farewell to his brother, at *Aen.* 6.692 (Anchises greeting Aeneas in the underworld) and 11.97–98 (Aeneas' farewell to the dead Pallas).

2. The opposition between Martial and Catullus goes back to the Renaissance and Catullus' earliest readers. Muret, for instance, protests that "there is as much difference between the writings of Martial and Catullus as between some wag on the street-corner and the well-bred jests of a gentleman." Cited by Gaisser 1993, 155.

3. Compare Quinn 1972, 256: "To fail to distinguish between Poems 5 and 7 and Poems 48 and 99 is carrying openmindedness too far. We might as soon refuse to distinguish between Catullus and Ovid."

4. See Munro 1938, 227–43, on the relative merits of Horace and Catullus. Munro quotes Fénelon: "How much are Ovid and Martial, with their ingenious and carefully wrought strokes, beneath these unstudied words [odi et amo], where the possessed heart speaks alone in a kind of despair."

5. Havelock 1939, 95.

6. Marchiesi, for example, praises Catullus for writing of love without either weighing it down with the tragic or trivializing it. He accuses Vergil of doing the former in *Aen.* 4. Quoted in Traina 1986, 41.

7. Traina 1986, 6, compares Lucretius' "horror ac divina voluptas" to Catullus' "odi et amo."

8. On Lucretius, see Bollack 1978, 118; on Vergil, Parry 1963.

9. On this ambivalence, see Habinek 1992a.

10. Apuleius, *Apol.* 10, provides our first clue to the identity of Lesbia: "accusent C. Catullum, quod Lesbiam pro Clodia nominarit." Lesbia seems to be linked to Clodius in c.79 (on this poem, see Skinner 1982), but Clodius had three sisters and not everyone agrees that Clodia Metelli is Catullus' Lesbia. The bibliography on Lesbia and Clodia is large (Holoka 1985, 9–11), but see Wiseman 1985, 216–18, and 1974, 105–6, for a skeptical view of the accepted identification and its effect. Deroux 1973 presents the case for the traditional identification quite fully and convincingly.

11. Schwabe repeatedly refers to Clodia Metelli as *quadrantaria* (costing a quarter), echoing the insulting name that Caelius coined for her, taken up by Cicero in the *Pro Caelio* (26, 29). His assessment of Clodia's treatment of Catullus (69–70) is worthy of Cicero himself, and starts modern Catullan scholarship off on its vituperation of a debauched and deceitful Lesbia who corrupted the innocent Catullus.

12. On the strategy of Cicero's *Pro Caelio*, see Wiseman 1985, 75–90.

13. Yeats 1956, 139. The rest of the poem reads:
All shuffle here; all cough in ink;
All wear the carpet with their shoes;
All think what other people think;
All know the man their neighbour knows.
Lord what would they say
Did their Catullus walk that way?

14. The learned associations of the name Lesbia are brought out when Catullus compliments Caecilius' girlfriend by calling her "Sapphica puella / Musa doctior" (c.35.16–17).

15. Adler 1981.

16. Compare, for instance, the remark of Frank 1928, 22, a propos Catullus' comparison of his love for Lesbia to that of a father for his sons (c.72.4): "The simile was not quite correct, but his experience had somehow exceeded the pagan vocabulary of the day." Further examples of this line of thought are given below.

17. The expression is used by Lyne 1980, who argues (1–18) that "traditional Roman society made it socially and psychologically difficult (to the point of impossibility) for gentlemen to find whole love with someone of equal status and circumstances" (17). Catullus aspired to a "relationship that was permanent, reciprocal, solemnized, and loving and sincere" (36) but had to invent new terms (like "foedus amicitiae") to express it. See also Havelock 1939, 90–96.

18. Copley 1949, 36.

19. Jaro 1988.

20. Lee 1990, xi, provides an excellent short summary of the state and history of the text (ix–xi). For a more detailed history of the the text of Catullus, see Goold 1958 and Gaisser 1993.

21. On the rediscovery of the text of Catullus and the early history of the text, see Gaisser 1993.

22. The vicissitudes of the manuscript are told in a poem of Benvenuto de Campesani attached to copies G and R. On this poem, see Skutsch 1970.

23. Goold, cited by Lee 1990, x.

24. Gaisser 1982 is a fascinating study of the work of Catullus' earliest interpreters; Gaisser quotes Poliziano's account of his labors (84–85).

25. See Gaisser 1993, 29–31. Parthenius, who published the first commentary on Catullus in 1485, refers to Catullus' poetry as a vast hydra that he has tackled with Herculean courage (Gaisser 1982, 96).

26. On the question of whether Catullus was responsible for ordering the poems, see *Introduction*, note 51.

27. On the *Poematia* of Sentinus Augurinus, which gave Pliny much pleasure and even awakened his admiration: "Multa tenuiter, multa sublimiter, multa venuste, multa tenere, multa dulciter, multa cum bile" (*Ep.* 4.27.1). On Pompeius Saturninus: "Praeterea facit versus, quales Catullus meus aut Calvus.... Quantum illis leporis, dulcedinis, amaritudinis, amoris! inserit sane, sed data opera, mollibus levibusque duriusculos quosdam, et hoc quasi Catullus aut Calvus" (*Ep.* 1.16.5). Sending a copy of his hendecasyllables to a friend, Pliny describes their variety as a product of the variety of his leisure and of the

changeable exhaustiveness of his character: "Accipies cum hac epistula hendecasyllabos nostros, quibus nos in vehiculo in balineo inter cenam oblectamus otium temporis. his iocamur ludimus amamus dolemus querimur irascimur, describimus aliquid modo pressius modo elatius, atque ipsa varietate temptamus efficere, ut alia aliis quaedam fortasse omnibus placeant" (*Ep.* 4.14.2–4). With the last remark about the purpose of this variety, Pliny indicates that even his leisure is a form of canvassing; the variety of his moods provides an image of the varied audience before which he performs and which his variety solicits.

28. Zanker 1988, 25–31.

29. Cicero, *Pis.* 70–71: "Poema porro fecit ita festivum, ita concinnum, ita elegans, nihil ut fieri possit argutius . . . ita multum ad istum de isto scripsit ut omnes hominis libidines, omnia stupra, omnia cenarum genera conviviorumque, adulteria denique eius delicatissimis verbis expresserit, in quibus si quis velit possit istius tamquam in speculo vitam intueri."

30. For a Lacanian analysis of the narrativity of the Lesbia affair, see Janan 1994.

31. Compare the reconstructions of the love affair in the introductions to the editions of Merrill (1893, xviii–xxv) and Baehrens (1885, 24–30). On Schwabe's importance, see Wiseman 1985, 216–18.

32. See, for instance, Buechner 1977, entitled "Der 'Liebesroman' des Catull," and Bayet 1953, 28: "To regroup them [sc. the Lesbia poems] in a plausible order is enough to retrace what has been called 'the novel of Catullus,' which is much more than a novel: an experience just as naked, but more eternal than that of Adolphe."

The basic narrative of Catullus' life as it was traditionally reconstructed is told so well and with such delicious irony by Havelock 1939 that it is worth quoting in full:

> *We may suppose* . . . that Catullus spent his boyhood at Verona and on Lake Sirmio, a youth of good provincial family, but, *we must assume*, living a life close to that of the Gallic frontiersman. His education, *no doubt* received at Verona, was, *we can readily imagine*, assisted by tutors and grammarians of the district—we hear elsewhere of several who taught in Cisalpine Gaul at about this period—who could teach him that love of Greek poetry so manifest in his verse. At Verona (*it is tempting to assume*), he was introduced to Metellus, the husband of his future love, during Metellus' governorship of Cisalpine Gaul in 62 B.C.E. Armed (*we may imagine*) with letters of introduction, he comes, a young unsophisticated provincial, to the capital, meets Clodia (if he has not met her already), his superior in years and station, and falls violently in love with her. For a period he worships her from afar, expressing his emotion in his more romantic love-lyrics. With her assistance, however, (*it is safe to guess*) he obtains entry, despite his provincialisms, to the most exclusive circles of fashion and politics in Rome, thus achieving personal relationships which he proceeds to reveal in his verse. By the year 60 (*we may perhaps infer*) his love had been declared and consummated at the house of one Manlius Torquatus [poem 68]. . . . It was a fleeting happiness he thus enjoyed. His

brother died (*probably*) next year (59); the loss may well have clouded the rest of his life. Revisiting Verona, *doubtless* to console his parents, he hears of Clodia's infidelities [poem 68]. . . . Her husband however had died, so (*no doubt* about this time) Catullus asked her (*we infer* from one epigram) to marry him. But she preferred a life of pleasurable freedom, at Rome and at Baiae the watering place, enjoying various lovers [*Pro Caelio*], among them one Caelius Rufus soon bitterly recognized and attacked by the poet as his chief rival. *About this time* also (*we must asssume*), responding to advice from elder and grayer leaders of literature like the orator Hortensius and Manlius Torquatus, he essayed a more learned and Alexandrian manner, deserting his earlier simplicity to attempt some longer and more elaborate poems, meanwhile maintaining a running fire of political and personal lampoons directed specially against Caesar, Pompey and Caesar's lieutenants. By 58 his love for Clodia had (*probably*) died; at any rate none of his love lyrics can be shown to past-date this year. In 57 he joined the suite of the proconsul of Asia for that year, visited his brother's grave, and (*if we can assume* the poem on *The Old Yacht* to be autobiographical) sailed home to Sirmio in a private yacht purchased in Asia. This eastern journey (*we may imagine*) encouraged his experiments in mythological verse and romantic idyll in the Alexandrian manner. Meanwhile Rufus, after quarrelling with Clodia, had become involved in a prosecution which she assisted herself; Cicero as defending counsel counter-attacked by blackening Clodia's character as much as he could. Therefore (*we can guess*) that Catullus on his return must have learned these secrets of Clodia's private life revealed in court (56 B.C.E.). The fresh shock (*no doubt*) helped to inspire his last address to her in 55, an address (*perhaps*) provoked by a request from her for a reconciliation. In this poem [11] he stated that his love is already dead. However, its complimentary references to Caesar's conquests in Gaul and Britain *lead us to believe* that in the realm of politics he had by this time accomplished a reconciliation with the dictator of Gaul. He must have died a few months later (80–81, emphasis Havelock's).

33. For instance, Merrill 1893, xxxi–xxxii, and Baehrens 1885, 30.

34. The story is complicated a little by the fact that Catullus' passion for Lesbia is often said to have made a serious poet of him (Schaefer 1966, 109; Baehrens 1885, 24, Buechner 1977, 59). However, during the course of the relationship, as reconstructed, Catullus detaches from its unworthy instigator the latent seriousness that Lesbia has elicited.

35. Segal 1968; Rankin 1972; Skinner 1981, 39–41.

36. For instance, Buechner 1977, 75: "We have followed the drama in which Catullus recklessly and completely abandons himself, experiences the oppression of the weight of his passion, seeks to master the experience of being wronged, to finally beg the gods for liberation. This drama is of boundless universality." Offermann 1977, 298, describes a movement from uncomplicated love to desperation (cc.1–60) and then back again (cc.69–116), but with an audience now endowed with a knowing suspicion of Lesbia.

37. Compare the statement of Ross 1975, 9: "Sophistication and wit . . . may have fascinated his poetic imagination, *but he was no intellectual playboy*, by nature or circumstances, and we can see another very different side of his genius—more serious, traditional and Roman" (emphasis mine). Another version of the collection's turn to the serious is provided by Block 1984, 54, who sees c.65, and the death of Catullus' brother, as the turning point from trivial boudoir love to more serious concerns.

38. Johnson 1982. Heine 1975, in his introduction to the *Wege der Forschung* volume on Catullus, begins by remarking on the dominance of the problem of unity in the recent decades of Catullan studies.

39. Havelock 1939, 85–86, and Kroll 1929, vii.

40. Originally advanced in Quinn 1959, 27–43.

41. Quinn 1972, 256.

42. Macleod's argument that the other poems containing, and attacking, Furius and Aurelius (cc.15, 16, 21, 23) are parodies is used to bolster the claim that "no cheap irony disturbs the venomous anger and the sorrowful regret which infuse the poem [c.11]" (302). There is now no reason to suppose that Furius and Aurelius, who have apparently accused Catullus of *mollitia* (c.16) and tried to seduce his boy (c.15, 21), are really enemies.

43. For instance, Macleod compares *Eclogue* 1.64–66 to the beginning of c.11 and observes that the journey as an escape from an unhappy love is a common motive, but the parallels do not lead him to conclude, as he does with poem 51, for instance, that we are dealing with a parody; in this case, the exaggeration of the gesture reflects an intense reality, emphasizing the fidelity of Furius and Aurelius and the fact that "the journey is that of a desperate and embittered man who will go to any lengths to flee what he has lost" (301).

44. Compare the denial that "a serious poem must be describing a real situation and a funny poem an invented one" (303), to the warnings that we must not take Catullus or Furius and Aurelius seriously because their statements are just the basis of a joke (301) and that the comic features of c.21 preclude any too serious reaction to the poem (299).

45. "The present age is all the more at home with Catullus because the feelings he expressed were those of an individualist clinging, in a disintegrating society, to the one standard which he could feel was secure, that of personal integrity." R. G. Levens (writing in 1954), quoted by Ferguson 1988, 1.

46. When Horvath, restoring a manuscript reading and adducing parallels from Catullus himself, tries to claim that one of the major Lesbia poems (c.68) revolves around a ménage à trois between Catullus, the addressee, and another woman, he draws on himself the wrath of Granarolo (1967, 186–98), who accuses him, at great length, of leveling Catullus to the moral status of his contemporaries.

47. The phrase comes from Tennyson's poem "Frater Ave atque Vale":

There beneath the Roman ruin where the purple flowers grow,
Came that 'Ave atque Vale' of the Poet's hopeless woe,
Tenderest of Roman poets nineteen-hundred years ago.

(Tennyson 1987, 3: 71)

48. Compare Raphael and Macleish 1978, 16; Squire 1923, a poem discussed in Chapter 9; and this passage from Robert de Maria's novel *Clodia* (1965): "Perhaps that was why he could not survive in Rome. He did not enjoy corruption though he could participate in the outer forms of it. He did not understand that innocence and corruption are only two sides of the same coin" (352-53).

49. According to Wiseman, the obscenity with which c.16 begins and ends (Pedicabo ego vos et irrumabo, c.16.1, 16.14) is Catullus' reaction to "those who held his moral standards in contempt," the only way that Catullus could "get his message through to sensibilities so much cruder than his own. What Aurelius saw as a high-class bit of tail was to Catullus something chaste and innocent, to be cherished and protected" (124). So the violence and obscenity in Catullus, far from contaminating the tenderness, are simply other manifestations of that tenderness.

50. Compare Foucault 1979, 150: "These aspects of an individual which we designate as making him an author are only a projection, in more or less psychologizing terms, of the operations that we force texts to undergo, the connections that we make, the traits that we establish as pertinent, the continuities that we recognize, or the exclusions that we practice."

51. Useful discussions of these questions are Minyard 1988, Skinner 1981, and Hubbard 1983, but the search for patterns in the collection, and particularly the polymetrics, has become something of an industry and the bibliography is now very large. Those who uncover patterns and cycles (and the multitude, variety, and intricacy of these might be cause for suspicion) have always assumed that those patterns and cycles must have been arranged by Catullus himself, though it is no less likely that an editor should be responsible. After all, why should an editor be any less ingenious than the critics who have "discovered" these patterns and cycles?

## Chapter 2

1. For the distinction between the disclaimer of Martial (1.4.8), which in the context of the more repressive atmosphere of the empire certainly did involve a distinction between life and art, and this passage of Catullus, see Citroni 1975, 32-33. The distinction here is between what is appropriate to the bard or epic poet (pium poetam ipsum, 5-6) and what is appropriate to the writer of *versiculi*. Richlin 1992a, 12-13, 145-47, has excellent discussions of this poem, pointing out that the separation of life from work is not the issue at hand and stressing the importance of Catullus' ambivalent sexual pose in the poem.

2. Richlin 1992a and Selden 1992 both make excellent cases for a sexual model of the relationship between reader and poet in Catullus. Richlin's book describes the priapic model in Roman humorous poetry (mainly invective and satire), and deals with Catullus specifically on pages 144-56, and Selden discusses Catullus' game with the reader in a framework that is quite similar to mine, though in his version the game is played on the field of interpretation.

3. A selection of English imitations of these poems can be found in Duckett 1925, 10–25.

4. The poems of Catullus are quoted according to the text of Mynors 1967.

5. On Catullus' use of this word, see Seager 1974. The combination of erotic and aesthetic senses in this word is best illustrated by c.35.13–18.

6. The *OLD* covers all of these meanings with appropriate citations, but I will cite a few passages mainly to illustrate the negative or questionable connotations of this word. The basic notion of "inessential/luxury" is supplied by Lucretius' lines: "Navigia atque agri culturas moenia leges / arma vias vestis [et] cetera de genere horum, / praemia, delicias quoque vitae funditus omnis, / carmina picturas, et daedala signa polire" (5.1448–51). Compare Seneca, *Benef.* 4.5.2: "Neque enim necessitatibus nostris provisum est, usque in delicias amamur." Cicero tells Atticus that he won't be attending the Games because he wishes to avoid "omnem deliciarum suspicionem" (*ad Att.* 2.10). Martial complains to a sluggish reader, "Quid prodest mihi tam macer libellus, / nullo crassior ut sit umbilico, / si totus tibi triduo legatur? / numquam deliciae supiniores" (2.6.10–13). Quintilian distinguishes those readers who only consider the old poets, with their natural eloquence and manly strength, to be worth reading from those who are delighted by "recens haec lascivia deliciaeque" (*Inst.* 10.1.43). For the meaning "airs" or "caprices," there is Cicero's "ecce aliae deliciae equitum vix ferendae!" (*ad Att.* 1.17.9). Finally, for a usage quite close to that of Catullus 2, compare Martial's reference to the "delicias lususque iocosque leonum" (1.14.1), the miraculous playing of the lions with the hares at the Games, where the lions tease the hares by catching them in their mouths and then letting them go. Bayet 1953, 20, has described this word very well in a passage that is worth quoting in full:

> Another, equally notable, aspect of the Catullan position is expressed by the word *deliciae*, which covers all the games of love, psychic and physical. It has a nearly unbelievable depth of suggestion, grouping meanings as different as "kindnesses" and "amusements," "caprices" and "enjoyments"; but with the etymological implication of a "temptation" and a pleasurable "seduction." So that the word, titillating in itself, represented both the opinion of commmon morality and a provocative attitude with respect to it.

7. *Delicatus* may not be etymologically related to *deliciae*; the *OLD* gives *lacio* (entice) as the root of *deliciae* but gives the etymology of *delicatus* as dubious. To the Roman mind, though, these words were clearly related; Cicero, for instance, says that, because he wishes to avoid "omnium deliciarum suspicionum," it is inappropriate for him to appear "non solum delicate sed etiam inepte peregrinantem" (*ad Att.* 2.10).

8. When Catullus spends the day playing poetic games with his friend Calvus, it is because they had agreed to be *delicati* (c.50.3), and when Catullus explains to Mallius that his brother's death has chased from his mind all interest in love poetry, the expression he uses is "all toys (*delicias*) of the mind" (c.68.26).

9. See Newman 1990, 30–32, on *nugae* and mime.

10. Chapter 2 of Edwards 1993 is an excellent discussion of the range of associations and moral issues engaged by *mollitia* (softness, effeminacy). The identification of sexual effeminacy with homosexuality in modern times has led several scholars to see the *versiculi* criticized by Furius and Aurelius in c.48, where Catullus tells Juventius of his insatiable desire to kiss him, rather than in cc.5 and 7. Quinn 1970, 145, comments: "Can anyone doubt, after reading Poems 5 and 7, that Catullus is a man?" But for the Roman there was no incompatibility between effeminacy and heterosexual activity. Seneca's diatribe against Maecenas (*Ep.* 114.4,6), in which he accuses him of effeminacy of literary style as of lifestyle, refers, in the midst of a host of other signs of effeminacy, to the fact that Maecenas was a man "qui uxorem miliens duxit, cum unam habuerit," and this immediately after citing the fact that he was accompanied by two eunuchs, "magis . . . viri quam ipse"!

11. Probably the most important of the polymetric poems in this connection are cc.6, 10, 12, 17, 21, 25, 37, 42, 47, and 56.

12. As Veyne (1978, 55) points out, the old Roman sexual morality was a puritanism just as much as was the Christian, only the Roman was a puritanism of virility. The immensely popular pantomime was looked at askance by the moralists because, as Veyne puts it, "the charm of the dance and of song made these men of state and these thinkers tremble, so that they opposed to it the spectacles of the gladiators, more virile, more educational for the citizen" (54).

13. Much of my discussion of this poem focuses on passages and issues that have received attention from previous scholarship, but I treat them in different contexts and from different angles. For an excellent presentation of the main stream of scholarship on this poem, see Latta 1974.

14. Publication, like any other major decision in the life of an upper-class Roman, was undertaken after a consultation with a friend or friends. Several of the letters of Cicero and Pliny reflect this practice; see, for instance, Cicero, *ad Att.* 4.8a.3, and Pliny, *Ep.* 9.25, 2.10.

15. This effect of studied casualness was much sought after in Catullus' time; Cicero, for instance, recommends that the orator adopt a "neglegentia diligens" in the use of short phrases (*Orator* 78).

16. The lightness of the poet's relation to his own work, and the invitation to audience members to make of it what they will (perhaps more than the poet does himself), are constitutive elements of what later becomes the genre of *nugae* or *ineptiae*. Pliny, sending a friend his "hendecasyllables," cuts short his introduction of his work with the words:

> Sed quid ego plura? Nam longa praefatione vel excusare vel commendare ineptias ineptissimum est. Unum illud praedicendum videtur, cogitare me has nugas ita inscribere "hendecasyllabi," qui titulus sola metri lege constringitur. Proinde, sive epigrammata sive idyllia sive eclogas, sive, ut multi, poematia seu quod aliud vocare malueris, licebit voces; ego tantum hendecasyllabos praesto (4.14.8–9).

For an examination of the use of words like *ineptiae*, *ioci*, and *nugae* as titles, see Bower 1974.

17. Richlin 1992a, 162, speaks of Catullus in this poem as a literary Priapus who "pimps his book."

18. The fullest exposition of this poem as an Alexandrian manifesto is given by Cairns 1969. See also Wiseman 1979, Chapter 11. An excellent corrective to the usual focus on the learned, philological aspect of Roman Alexandrianism is provided by Hutchinson 1988, Chapter 6, and especially pages 282–83, where Hutchinson points out the sensuous and seductive aspects of the Roman poets' descriptions of their own work: "The poets fit Callimachus into their own aesthetic language, and use that language to develop their own conception of their poetry, a conception far richer and more insidious than Callimachus' overt conception of his" (283). Hutchinson is speaking here of the elegists, but what he says is also applicable to Catullus.

19. See Latta 1974, 209.

20. Putnam 1982, 32 (especially note 1), has an interesting discussion of words meaning "smooth" or "polished" in Latin. He cites a number of passages that castigate effeminates for their use of the *pumex*, but does not seem to think this nuance of any importance in Catullus. Seneca's "Ite nunc et in istis *vulsis atque expolitis* et nusquam nisi in libidinibus viris quaerite oratores" (*Contr.* 1, *praef.* 10, emphasis mine) tells us something about the implications of Catullus' "pumice expolitum," and to this one might add Persius 1.85–87 (emphasis mine): "Pedius quid? crimina *rasis* / librat in antithetis, doctas posuisse figuras / laudatur: 'bellum hoc.' hoc bellum? an, Romule, ceves?" Richlin 1988, 168, 188–89, has some useful material on the theme of male depilation in Roman literature.

21. "To tease" is one of the meanings of *delicias facere*; compare Plautus, *Cas.* 528, *Poen.* 296. Compare also Martial 1.14.1.

22. The view that Catullus is making an invidious, Alexandrian comparison between Nepos' huge work and his own slim but polished volume is no longer held by most scholars. Three volumes do not in fact constitute a large work, and Nepos seems to have been something of a neoteric himself (Wiseman 1979, Chapter 10). The word *laboriosis* (7), however, does suggest that he is teasing Nepos a bit; it is, as Quinn points out in his commentary, "a word that suggests going out of one's way to make work for oneself" (90); compare Cicero, *Cael.* 1, "vos laboriosos existumet."

23. The fact that the Muse is addressed as *patrona* also has the effect of withdrawing the book from Nepos. Some scholars have suggested emending what is evidently a corrupt text in this line to give the expected reference to Nepos as *patronus* (e.g., patroni ut ergo), but see the arguments against this in Gold 1987, 56–57. I disagree with Gold only in that I see this reference to the patron Muse as a deliberate replacement of the more usual human patron.

24. It has been argued that the sparrow would have been understood by the Romans as a phallic symbol. The evidence for this seems good enough that a suspicion of double entendre should enter the mind of the reader, but this does not mean that the whole poem becomes an elaborate allegory in which every statement has a specific sexual translation. Thomas 1993 is the most recent to put the case for the double entendre and he does so very judiciously. For the most part, those who have seen a sexual meaning in the sparrow have taken the

allegorical path; see Genovese 1974, 121-25; Giangrande 1975, 137-46; Nadeau 1980, 879-90 (discreetly written in Latin!). Against the first two of these, see Jocelyn 1980, 421-24.

25. Catullus' confusion of surface and depth in c.2 is nicely illustrated by his use of the word *solaciolum* (a little consolation, 7). On the one hand, this word belongs to the psychological background of Lesbia's behavior: we watch Lesbia play with the sparrow and conclude that she is sublimating her desire in this game. But the grammar and form of the word assign it to the surface of the scene: Lesbia plays "carum nescioquid" (some dear thing), and she plays a *solaciolum*, the diminutive emphasizing the delight of the observer in what he sees. The potential narrative of frustration and consolation behind Lesbia's game is blocked by the diminutive form of the word that suggests it, and replaced by a voyeuristic delight. The same is true of the "little golden apple" (aureolum malum, 12) whose narrative potential in the myth in which it brings Atalanta's virginity to an end is blocked by the use to which it is put in the simile, where it illustrates Catullus' desire to play with the sparrow.

26. The Alexandrian poets represented Atalanta as having already fallen in love with Hippomenes and so welcoming defeat. They played up the symbolism of the apple as a love token (Fordyce 1961, 91). Pearcy 1980, 152-62, who supports the integrity of 2a and 2b, emphasizes this interpretation of the Atalanta story in order to argue that, for Catullus to see Lesbia playing with the *passer*, and therefore to know that she is in love with him, is as pleasing as was the apple that declared Hippomenes' love to Atalanta. Pearcy has to transpose 9-10 to the end of the poem in order to get around the awkward fact that it is playing with the *passer* that would be pleasing to Catullus.

27. Copley 1949, 22-40, is a classic statement of the thesis that Catullus' experience of love was on a level that could not be reciprocated by the depraved and trivial Lesbia; for an application of this model to c.2, see Williams 1968, 140-43; Bignone 1945, 360; Buechner 1977, 66; Lyne 1980, 51-52.

28. This poem presents a number of textual problems of which the only one that affects my reading is the question of the relation of 11-13 to the rest of the poem. In the ancient manuscripts, 1-13 are presented without a break, and the modern tradition of printing 11-13 as a separate fragment (like 14b, a clearer case) was begun by the renaissance editor Guarinus. Grammatically, there is nothing impossible about taking *possem* in line 9 as conditional with "tam gratum est" as apodosis (could I but play with you, it would be as welcome). Fordyce 1961, who cites this solution of Ellis's (91) along with Ellis's parallels for the indicative in the apodosis (Plautus, *Poen.* 921, Martial 2.63.3), rejects this interpretation because of the inappropriateness of the simile that would result. This supposed inappropriateness seems to be the main stumbling block to taking 1-13 as a single poem. Quinn, who has no qualms about changing "cum ... acquiescet" in line 8 to "tum ... acquiescat," describes Vossius' conjecture *posse* for *possem* in line 9 as "a brilliant attempt to weld 1-10 to 11-13" but "rather too good to be true" (95).

29. Most scholars have noticed that the language Catullus uses of the effects on him of Calvus' *lepos* is erotic (Finamore 1974, 11-19, especially the citations on 11-12). Others have obviously felt uncomfortable with the homosexuality

of this passage, most notably Clack 1976, 50–53, who claims that the erotic language is not addressed to Calvus at all but derives from the fact that Calvus and Catullus had spent the afternoon writing about Lesbia; "Calvus had a number of amusing things to say about Roman ladies in general and Clodia especially" (52). This totally gratuitous diversion of the expression of the erotic effect of one man on another to lockerroom conversation between two men about a woman shows what it takes to save Catullus' honor!

30. Aulus Gellius' anecdote (19.9.7) about the Greeks who taunted Antonius Julianus that the Romans, with their barbarous language, had no erotic poetry of any grace apart from Catullus and Calvus is a good indication of the atmosphere in which upper-class Romans produced homosexual verse. Julianus quotes, by way of response, epigrams by Valerius Aedituus, Porcius Licinus, and Quintus Catulus, all on homosexual themes.

31. The question of Roman attitudes to homosexuality is controversial; MacMullen 1982 disagrees with scholars like John Boswell and Veyne, who have seen a tolerance of homosexuality in ancient Rome. The view that "relations with boys, provided that they were not *ingenui*, were both very common and very lightly viewed" has been supported more recently by Griffin 1985, 25–26. Clearly, no single answer can be given to the question of the Roman attitude to homosexuality; the various statements cited by scholars have to be considered in their context, for at Rome it very much depends on who is talking to whom and in what context. Cicero, for instance, expresses very different attitudes to augury in different works. For our purposes, MacMullen's quotation of Minucius Felix (28.10) to the effect that Romans tolerated all sexual license as *urbanitas* is most apposite. Wiseman 1985, 3–4, reminds us that the "The 'Julio-Claudians' were actually Iulii Caesares and Claudii Nerones, wealthy aristocrats who behaved as such," and that the attitudes of the Roman elite did not suddenly change with the end of the Republic. The sexual attitudes and practices of the emperors, amply documented by Suetonius, may tell us something about those of their republican forbears. Most recently, Richlin 1993 has presented the evidence for homophobia at Rome in a fascinating study of the *cinaedus* that has an excellent discussion of recent controversies about ancient sexuality.

32. A whole book of Cicero's letters, Book 13, consists of *epistulae commendaticiae* in which Cicero praises the commendee and stresses the closeness of his relationship with him, and how important it is for Cicero that the addressee should look out for the interests of the commendee. The particular kind of *commendatio* in Catullus' poem is best illustrated by Cicero, *Pro Caelio* 17, where he speaks of how Caelius' father entrusted (commendavit et tradidit) the young Caelius to Cicero as a mentor. For *commendo* meaning "render agreeable or attractive," see *OLD* s.v. 6.

33. Compare *castum* and *pudice* in 15.4–5 to "parum pudicum" and *castum* in 16.4–5.

34. Veyne 1988, 18–19.

35. This pair features in one other poem of Catullus (c.11), where their long-winded protestations of friendship are answered with a request to take a short and unpleasant message to Lesbia. In c.16 the duo appear as readers who

have judged Catullus from his *versiculi* (16.3), and again a problem arises from the fact that Catullus must entrust his words to them.

36. My interpretation of *pruriat* and "movere lumbos" as referring respectively to the sexual arousal and wiggling buttocks of the pathic and not, as is more usual, to erections is in agreement with Wiseman 1987, 222–24, and Buchheit 1976b, 342–44. Both authors provide ample parallels for these meanings. See also Selden 1992, 485, and especially note 117 on *cevere*. For the sexual stimulation caused by effeminate poetry, see Aristophanes, *Thesm.* 130–34, and Persius 1.19–21, both of whom locate the excitement in the anus. For *movere lumbos* used of the movement of the pathic's buttocks, see Vergil, *Cat.* 13.21, and for *prurire* used of the sexual excitement of the pathic (usque ad umbilicum), see Martial 6.37.3. Notice the use of *prurit* in this sense in the graffito quoted below (*CIL* 4.2360). Richlin 1992a, 248, note 9, remains unconvinced by Buchheit and holds to the traditional interpretation of *prurit* as active rather than pathic.

37. *CIL* 4.2360; compare 13.10017. On this graffito, see Housman 1931. Housman interprets *prurit* in line 2 to mean the same as I have argued it does in Catullus 16.9. Svenbro 1988, 207–218, has recently studied the Greek parallels to this graffito and argues that pederasty is one of the models through which the Greeks understood the relation between writing and reader; according to this model, the reader is cast as the *erōmenē*.

38. For a similar analysis of the relation between reader and author in Catullus 16, see Selden 1992, 485; Batstone 1993, 150–55, is an interesting study of the relation between literal and figurative in this poem that also raises the issue of the position of the reader. An extraordinary passage from Seneca's *Epistles* (46.1–2), in which Seneca describes his encounter with a text of Lucilius, is cited by Habinek 1992b, 196–97, and it provides a fascinating example of the use of a sexual model for reading. The passage begins with Seneca the reader exploring a text that is *levis* (smooth), unlike his own body (and Lucilius'). But drawn on by the text's "sweetness" (dulcedo), Seneca gradually comes to take the feminine position in relation to a text that is "virile", "big," and "taut," and which he swallows whole (exhausi totum)! The process is exactly the same as in Catullus 16, where the effeminacy of the text paradoxically penetrates the reader, except that in this case the reader is actually rejoicing in his passivity.

39. Cato's words about the old Roman attitude to poetry convey an attitude that never completely disappeared: "Poeticae artis honos non erat; si quis in ea re studebat aut sese ad convivia adplicabat, grassator vocabatur" (*Mor.* 2). Cicero's equation of words like *urbanus, festivus,* and *elegans* with effeminacy in his attack on Clodius (*In P. Clod. et C. Cur.,* frag. 22) is a good example of the questionable reputation of these fashionable social values. As Edwards 1993, 96, points out, elite Romans of the late Republic and early principate had to perform a balancing act between urbanity, which always ran the danger of tipping over into effeminacy, and rusticity, which gave virility a bad name.

40. Pace Quinn 1970, 143, who cites c.48 and other homosexual verse. To the Roman mind, a partner of the opposite sex did not preclude effeminacy (see note 7).

41. Petronius' impotent Encolpius makes a distinction between kissing and real sex when he describes his dalliance with Circe as follows: "In hoc gramine pariter compositi mille osculis lusimus, quaerentes voluptatem robustam" (127).

42. *Inambulatio* would seem to be a technical term for the pacing of an orator; see *Rhet. Her.* 3.27 and Cicero, *Brut.* 158. *Argutus* is usually a positive term for speakers and poets (*OLD* s.v. 2 and 6b), but it can also mean "garrulous" (*OLD* s.v. 4).

43. The Greek word *cinaedus* that the Romans used for "pathic" also means "dancer."

44. See Veyne 1979, 16–19, on the problems the Romans had accepting Hellenism and the cultural indulgences with which it was associated. Though Hellenism was always seen as a threat to the Roman duty of "virile tension," it eventually became acceptable to the Romans, even if their ambivalent attitude is reflected in the pervasive theme of the "senator whose private life is nothing but soft but who shows himself nevertheless to be a man of energetic action" (19).

45. On Naevius and this exchange with the Metelli, see Jocelyn 1969.

46. Laevius (frag. 13 in Courtney 1993) compares the writing on a sheet of paper to a back marked by tattoos or a beating: "fac papyrin . . . haec terga habeant stigmata." Unfortunately, we do not know the context of this line.

47. On the status of the actor at Rome, see Edwards 1993, 123–26. Catullus' contemporary (and the dedicatee of his book) Cornelius Nepos declared that to exhibit oneself on stage to the people is considered by the Romans to be inconsistent with respectability, even though the Greeks did not find it a source of shame (quoted by Edwards 1993, 98). Dupont 1985, 95–110, argues that for the Romans the problem with the actor was that his self-display and his creation of a persona were dangerously close to the theatrics of the political arena in which the Roman elite acted their *virtus* to and for the people. This is confirmed by Richlin 1992b, who has shown how close the orator came to the actor in his gestures, use of voice, and even application of makeup; she also shows how this proximity was a considerable source of anxiety to Roman rhetorical theorists striving to distinguish the two: the orator must avoid being too dry and jejune while maintaining a clear boundary between his effects and the effeminate antics of the actor. In contrast, we have stories of Roman nobles dancing at their own banquets: according to Velleius Paterculus (2.83.2), Lucius Plancus danced the role of the sea god Glaucus, naked except for a fishtail and blue paint. Wiseman 1985, 47, who cites these stories (note 111), comments, "When admiration of the professional's art came to mean more than the dignity of his own status, at a private party the sophisticated Roman could let his hair down and act as a *mimus* himself." Martial makes a connection between poets and actors when he describes the poet blowing kisses in response to applause (1.3.7, 1.76.14), a custom associated with actors (see Citroni 1975 ad loc.)

48. Pseudolus himself reminds us that the trickery by which he has outwitted his master is ultimately no protection from the absolute power that his master holds over him. When Simo promises that he will get his revenge sometime,

Pseudolus answers, "Why threaten? I've got a back" (quid minitare? habeo tergum, 1325).

49. For an excellent study of Plautine "metatheater," see Slater 1985, especially 12–18.

## Chapter 3

1. Wiseman 1985, 242.
2. Whigham 1966.
3. Curran 1975 complains, with some justification, that Quinn's commentary of 1970 is still coy and squeamish on sexual matters, although it avoids "Fordyce's crude emasculation of the Catullan corpus." For complaints of unneccessarily indecent interpretations, see Jocelyn 1980 and Witke 1980.
4. Both poems quoted in Gillespie 1988, 86.
5. Typical is the passage from Granarolo, quoted approvingly by Quinn 1959, 106:

> To sum up, the smutty is not something to which Catullus is committed in itself. . . . It is rather a manifestation which we may regret, but which we must describe as such, of his ebullient dynamism, of his rather swaggering and very touchy combativeness, of his overflowing vitality. Extreme in all matters . . . we will seem him bring the same flame to his emotional fevours and to his aesthetic aspirations.

Granarolo 1967, 171, in his turn quotes approvingly Bignone 1945, 384, on the extremely obscene c.97: "One feels that these verses are dictated by a passion of hate that has its own power; that they possess a youthful energy, which as happens in Catullus, will reach the purest of spheres of poetry and of the ideal, once turned to a more worthy sentiment. . . ." Bardon 1970 goes further and claims that Catullus' obscenity is "une forme de tendresse" (73). His chapter on this subject ends: "The coarsenesses of Catullus are a hymn to existence, and his sexual obsession, and the impropriety of his language, reveal a disorderly but powerful impetus toward life, not a perversity. A Catullan obscenity? A soul without sin" (74).

6. Whigham 1966 is rather free with Campesani's poem (attached to the manuscripts G and R) describing the reemergence of Catullus' manuscript; Campesani says that the manuscript was found "sub modio" (under a bushel).
7. Lateiner 1977, 29, takes Catullus' obscenity as, among other things, a response to an obscene age. See the passages quoted on pages 32—33.
8. See Richardson 1974, 214–16, for comparative material from other cultures on this use of obscenity.
9. "Fortuna gloriae carnifex." Pliny, *N.H.* 28.39. For the ritual and apotropaic uses of obscenity at Rome, see Adams 1982, 4–6.
10. The word *fascinum*, meaning "evil spell," came to be a common word for penis because of the efficacy of representations of this part of the body against jealous emanations. Marcadé 1968, 20–26, is a good treatment of the power of obscenity and humor to avert the magic influence of the jealous.

11. Cc.32 and 56 are the only examples in Catullus of obscenity that is not used in invective.

12. Richlin 1992a, 2–13, is an excellent treatment of literary *apologiae*.

13. Martial 1, *Praef*. The etymology of *obscenus*, also written *obscaenus*, is disputed, but one of the candidates is *scaena*, the others being *caenum* and *scaevus*; see Thierfelder 1956, which argues for *scaevus*.

14. Valerius Maximus 2.10.8. Note that prostitutes took the place of *mimae*: "Praeter verborum licentiam, quibus obscenitas omnis effunditur." Lactantius, *Inst.* 1.20.10.

15. Cicero, *Pro Caelio* 38.

16. Adams 1982, 11, and Opelt 1965, 154–57. Skinner 1982 contains interesting material about Roman political invective as it relates to c.79.

17. Veyne 1983, 10. This "folk justice" is described at greater length by Usener 1901.

18. For repetitions, see cc. 23, 24, 29, 36, 57, 103; for graffiti in c. 59 and elsewhere, see Cèbe 1965; for folk custom, c. 17.

19. A point made by Veyne 1983.

20. Saint Denis 1965, Chapter 3.

21. Henderson 1991, 2, who gives a good definition of obscenity: "By obscenity we mean verbal reference to areas of human activity or parts of the body that are protected by certain taboos agreed upon by prevailing social custom and subject to emotional aversion or inhibition. These are in fact the sexual and excremental areas. In order to be obscene, such a reference must be made by an explicit expression that is itself subject to the same inhibitions as the thing it describes." Cicero, *De Off.* 1.35.127, distinguishes between word and thing: "Quodque facere non turpe est, modo occulte, id dicere obscenum est."

22. The locus classicus is Cicero, *ad Fam.* 9.22, but see also Celsus 6.18.1. Expressions like "latine loqui" (to speak in Latin), *simplicitas* (candor), and "verborum veritas" (truth of expression), all used by Martial in his preface to refer to what we would call obscene language, prove that it was possible to present this kind of language in a positive light. Both Propertius (2.34.87) and Ovid (*Tristia* 2.427) call Catullus *lascivus*, which the *OLD* classes under the meaning "free from restraint in sexual matters." The word *lascivus* suggests playfulness rather than effrontery or dirtiness; Martial calls Propertius *lascivus* (8.73.5), and clearly this cannot mean "obscene" in our sense; however, Martial excuses what he calls his "playful directness of expression" (lascivam verborum veritatem) by citing the precedent of Catullus and other writers who are read from cover to cover (1, *Praef.*). On words used to characterize "obscene" language, see Jocelyn 1985, 10–11.

23. Cèbe 1965, 228, takes obscenity to be one aspect of the revolt of Catullus and his circle against conformity, literary and social, a revolt that involves scandalizing the bourgeois. The most sophisticated and valuable psychological study of Catullan obscenity is Skinner 1991, who argues that in the polymetric love poems Catullus turns obscene language against himself, measuring "the extent of his folly in hoping to possess what he was never intended to have" (10).

24. Richlin 1992a, 27–30, 69, 150; Skinner 1982, 198–200; Krenkel 1981.

25. For discussions of obscenity in Catullus, see Richlin 1992a, 144–56; Lateiner 1977; Skinner 1979b, 1982, 1991. I have written about the figurative use of obscene material, particularly with reference to impotence, in Horace's *Epodes* in Fitzgerald 1988.

26. Catullus, frag. 1, seems to come from a hymn to Priapus. On the Roman cult of Priapus, see Grimal 1984, 46–49; on the literary tradition, see Parker 1988.

27. Cicero, *Pro Caelio* 71. For further references to this kind of vengeance, see Jocelyn 1985, 21, note 62.

28. The verb *irrumare* occurs six times: 16.1,14, 21.13, 28.10, 37.8, 74.5. In addition, *irrumator* occurs in 10.12 and *irrumatio* in 21.8.

29. Adams 1982, 125–30, who cites some possibly neutral uses of the word on page 127, including that of a scholiast on Juvenal 6.51: "Quia et irrumantur mulieres."

30. Richlin 1981, disagreeing with Housman 1931, 407–9, argues that *irrumare* never has a weakened sense (for instance, "cheat") in Catullus and Martial. Though I agree that it is neither here nor there whether the use of this verb implies that a particular sexual act actually took place or really is being threatened (see also Curran 1975, 313), I do not agree that the weaker meaning is never relevant in these authors. In some poems (e.g., Martial 2.83, Catullus 74), there is a play on both weaker and literal senses, and it would be as detrimental to the point of the poem to deny the relevance of the weaker sense as it would be to translate the word as "cheat."

31. Richlin 1992a, 148, points out that, because irrumation forces the victim to be silent, it is a particularly appropriate threat against Catullus' critics in c.16.

32. Konstan 1979 argues that the poem connects hunger and lust, though I cannot agree with him that it distinguishes Aurelius' passionate appetites from Catullus' real love.

33. See *OLD* s.v. *sedeo* 1, "awaiting hire," and Adams 1982, 165, for the meaning "ride," referring to intercourse with the woman, or effeminate, on top, a position regarded as slightly abnormal and conceded by the woman as a special favor (but see the interesting remarks on changing attitudes to the "equus eroticus" in Veyne 1978, 53). As Syndikus 1984, 1: 210–11, observes, the inmates of the tavern would not be sitting but reclining; he concludes that the word here has the sense "hanging around" and cites parallels in page 211, note 6.

34. Compare the analogous situation in the graffito quoted on page 50, where the reader who fills his mouth with the words of another is cast as the *irrumatus*. Having uttered one self-destructive wish (ursi me comedant), the reader has filled his own mouth with the agressive intentions of another so that the second humiliating wish (et ego verpa[m] qui lego) is in fact a description of what has already happened. Adams 1982 quotes this graffito as an example of the weakening of the sense of *irrumatio* that results from its being widely threatened but never carried out(!). So the reader here "would surely have treated the imprecation as equivalent to 'I have been fooled'" (129). But the situation is more specific than that, for being fooled here takes a form

that is metaphorically related to the literal sense of *irrumatio*. On this text, see Housman 1931, 406-7; CIL 4.8230 is a less elaborate version of the same topos.

35. Harpocrates is the graecized form of one of the names of Horus, son of Isis and Serapis. He crops up again in c.102, and may have been a proverbial figure for silence in the Roman world; see Otto 1890, 160.

36. Adams 1982, 129.

37. On this poem, and particularly Catullus' play on *inanis*, see Skinner 1979a, 137-40.

38. *Priapea* 51, 64; Martial 3.82.33.

39. Skinner 1979a, 139-40.

40. Foucault 1978 argues that the importance given to the examination of sexual thoughts and actions in the Catholic confessional was a means of extending the workings of power into the most private recesses of the mind. Before this could happen, sex had to be constituted as something secret.

41. Adams 1982, 127.

42. Wlosok 1980 contains some interesting remarks on the role of the censor, stressing the importance of shame in Roman culture.

43. Curran 1966 draws attention to the literary theme of the lover's pallor, a telltale sign that usually elicits questions about the identity of the beloved. Catullus takes the poem in very different directions after leading us to expect the traditional inquiry.

44. *Emulgere* (milk), *serum* (whey), and *labra* ("tub," as well as "lips") reduce Victor to an animal; see Curran 1966, 26.

45. See the remarks on poetry's nondialogic nature in Bakhtin 1981, 285-58.

46. As do Arkins 1982, 16-17, Skinner 1979b, 112, Scott 1971, 23, and Commager 1965, 103. Arkins (12) is on firmer ground when he cites the invective against Aufillena (cc.110, 111) to argue that Catullus has constructed a sexual ethic of his own, for those poems do adopt a rather moralistic tone.

47. Victius has been identified by some with the informer Vettius (see Skinner 1982, 204, and note 21). If he is to be so identified, then his filthy mouth is clearly related to his trade. Skinner cites an epigram of Martial that presents us with a slanderer who was formerly a fellator; his mouth was purer when he fellated (2.61).

48. Gaisser 1982.

49. On the importance of the conception of purity for early humanism, see Jed 1989. Jed (45, note 26) cites an interesting passage from Poliziano's *Miscellanea*: " 'Oarion' synceriter esse apud Catullum (66,94) quod 'Aorion' isti legunt qui bonos violant libros."

50. "Ex hara productos, non schola, vocabula nuda, nomina cassa, et nihili voces." Poliziano is adapting Cicero's words on Piso, the Epicurean (*Pis.* 16.3).

51. "Nos de graeco instrumento, quasi de cella proma, non despicabilis, nec abrogandae fidei proferemus autoritates, quibus et lectio praestruatur incolumis, et interpretamenti nubilum discutiatur." Quoted by Gaisser 1982, 97.

52. See Baehrens 1885, 584.

53. The intemperate review of Richlin's *Gardens of Priapus* by Jocelyn 1985 is an interesting but reprehensible example of modern philological polemic. Jocelyn ends his review, "Students of Greek and Latin literature have always talked to each other about passages relating to sexuality.... The only new development is that attempts are now being made to talk to ill-prepared undergraduates and even to persons totally ignorant of the classical languages. This is not a development to be welcomed." What this says about classical scholarship is not encouraging, and it seems to cast Richlin as the thief who has broken into the private preserve of Classics and on whom the guardian of the preserve descends with all his philological rigor. Jocelyn avoids Richlin's frank translation of obscenities, wary of modern associations, and speaks, for instance, of "the expulsion of fecal gas" where Richlin speaks of "farts"; this comes from someone who professes to find Richlin's "contemporary academic jargon" (such as "cuing" and "metacommunication") amusing! In the name of preserving the purity of his own academic jargon, Jocelyn resorts liberally to the language of insult ("foolish," "grossly perverse," "nonsense," "absurdity," "grossly misunderstood," etc.).

54. Quoted by Gaisser 1982, 97.

55. Fordyce 1961 recognizes that this is an obscenity ("ugly" and "offensive" are the words he uses), but he does not enter the controversy about its meaning. Presumably, the reason he does not omit this poem is that it is a crucial document in the Lesbia story.

56. For "masturbates," see Lenz 1963, Jocelyn 1979, Arkins 1979, Penella 1976; for "has intercourse with," Skutsch 1980; for "fellates," Randall 1979; for "strips (of clothes and cash)," Quinn 1970, 260; for "retracts the foreskin," Kroll 1929, 103. As sexual but deliberately ambiguous, Adams 1982, 168.

57. Randall 1979, 30, argues that "the shaping of the mouth to pronounce it, which resembles the shaping of the mouth for *fellatio*, suggests what Catullus has in mind." Lateiner 1977, 17, claims that the word was chosen for its obscene sound.

58. Lenz 1963, 63. Skutsch 1980, 21, maintains that the exclamatory outrage of the poem precludes *glubit* from meaning "masturbates": "'My own Lesbia, making herself available to anybody, anywhere!' That is the point, and it would be intolerably weakened if not intercourse but a more specific action were meant." But Lenz (64) and Arkins 1979, 86, proponents of "masturbates," both castigate Lesbia for *not* making herself fully available to her men and for robbing them of their semen without giving herself in return!

59. Curiosity about Lesbia's sexual charms finds its way into the scholarship every now and then. Zarker 1972, 108, introduces his research into this subject with the words: "In spite of the eloquent testimony to her literary interests, the *amica omnium* could not have attracted such a devoted following as a result of her intellectual talents alone. Let us see what we can learn about the physical charms of Lesbia." Whigham 1966 examines the word *glubit* in his introduction, and prefaces this section with the words: "Finally, the question has to be faced as to whether [Clodia] did in fact become a public prostitute" (20–21). Whigham spends several pages speculating on this matter.

60. Most recently by Skinner 1991, 8, who has some interesting remarks on the role of social status in the scenario of Catullus' love for Lesbia.

61. Ellis 1889 and Quinn 1972 have the boy "banging" his girl, as does Cerri 1989; the latter cites some parallels for this kind of threesome, and argues that the point of the poem is that the boy is trying to adopt an adult role prematurely and Catullus reminds him of his passive status. Scott 1969 also takes the scenario to be a threesome but understands *puellae* as a genitive and identifies the *pupulus* as Clodius. Kroll 1929 ad loc, Housman 1931, 402, and Adams 1982, 145–46, have the boy of Catullus' girl masturbating.

62. Quinn 1972, 245, describes this poem and c.97 as "calculated provocations of those who let themselves be scandalized. The object is to achieve what Cicero in the *De Officiis* was to hold unforgivable—talking about the unmentionable in so many words (si rerum turpitudini adhibetur verborum obscoenitas)—and to get away with it by sheer exuberance (an irrepressible sense of fun), or elegance of form, or both."

63. Ellis 1889, 197–98, argues for M.Porcius, as do Buchheit 1961 and Scott 1969.

64. "Pro telo" is the reading of manuscript G and is printed by Quinn 1970 and Merrill 1893 in their editions. Scott 1969 supports this reading, though his argument depends on a very indirect allusion to the *Iliad*. Whatever the original text, a pun was surely intended. It would be thoroughly appropriate that Catullus should describe his reaction with a word (*protelo*, "in tandem") that Lucretius uses for the chain reactions in matter itself (2.531, 4.190); elsewhere, I have argued that c.5 has affinities with Lucretius' discussion of love in Book 4 (Fitzgerald 1984, 77, note 4).

65. As in the case of c.56, so here we cannot be sure of the identity of the addressee; if it is M.Caelius Rufus, erstwhile lover and later enemy of Clodia, who gave her the name "quadrantaria Clytemnestra" sometime before 56 B.C.E., then Catullus and his addressee share a similar experience of Lesbia. On the trial of Caelius, at which he was defended by Cicero and prosecuted with the help of Lesbia, see Wiseman 1985, 54–91. A certain Rufus is addressed by Catullus in cc.69 and 77, and some have identified him, too, with Clodia's lover. Austin 1960, 148–49, discusses the identification of the addressees of cc.58, 69, and 77; he denies that the addressee of c.58 is M.Caelius Rufus, arguing that it is the Veronese Caelius addressed in c.100. Syndikus 1984, 279–80, and Lenz 1963, 65, agree with him, but Quinn 1970, 258–59, accepts the identification with M. Caelius Rufus.

66. The word *impurus* almost always implies contamination by oral-genital contact. In Roman invective, people with foul breath were suspected of fellatio, and assimilation of the mouth to other orifices was a common form of insult; Catullus, for instance, refers to mouths contaminated by urine in cc.39, 78b, 97, and 99. Of the three consecutive poems about the "os impurum" introduced by c.97, the second is the attack on the foulmouthed Victius discussed above; the third turns the tables and has Catullus the victim of an implicit accusation of "os impurum" when the beloved Iuventius wipes his mouth after Catullus has stolen a kiss from him. On the relation between the three poems, see Forsyth 1979.

67. *Anth. Pal.* 11: 241, 242, 415.

68. Rankin 1976 speculates that the allusions to incest in Catullus' poetry have to do with his jealousy of Clodia's (alleged) relation with her brother.

69. Ellis 1889, 115, documents the frequency of theft at the baths. Petronius, *Sat.* 92, reminds us that sexual pickups were another feature of this establishment.

70. Martial 2.51.6 has an interesting version of the "culus vorax," which in this case belongs to a certain Hyllus who spends his last denarius on satisfying that part of his body while his unfortunate belly looks on in hunger. Here again one body part has usurped the prerogative of another.

71. Richlin 1988, 358–59, is an interesting treatment of this poem in the context of Catullus' system of food imagery.

72. "Quid ut noverca me intueris aut uti . . . belua?" (Horace, *Epod.* 5.9). The proverbial expression "apud novercam quererere" (i.e., to deaf ears) says it all (compare Plautus, *Pseud.* 314).

73. Kroll 1929, 44.

74. Clearly, Catullus is mocking the traditional Roman ideal of the simple life, which is supposed to bring true happiness; see Syndikus 1984, 160–62. Horace's mention of the shiny ancestral saltcellar at c.2.16.13–14 sounds proverbial for the simple life.

75. The obscene purity of Furius' body, described in insultingly graphic terms, functions as a figure for the futility of Furius' repeated requests for a loan (26–27): he will no more get the loan than he could ever soil his hand by rubbing his own excrement.

76. Cicero's sarcastic representation of the Epicurean god, who is paradoxically incapable of pleasure, gives us a good sense of the smug self-satisfaction that this phrase may convey: "Propone ante oculos deum nihil aliud in omni aeternitate nisi mihi pulcre est et ego beatus sum cogitantem" (*N.D.* 1.41.114).

77. Skinner 1979a, 143, points out that, though Mamurra is identified as the *pathicus* in line 2, the position of the word associates it also with Caesar. The sexual reversibility of this duo indicates that the proper chain of command has broken down.

78. Catullus' poetry is full of pairs: Furius and Aurelius (cc.11, 16); Veranius and Fabullus (cc.12, 28, 47); Porcius and Socration (c.47); Lesbius and Lesbia (c.79); Caesar and Mamurra (c.57); Aufillenus and Aufillena (pursued by Caelius and Quintius, c.100); Cato and Catullus (c.56); Acme and Septimius (c.45); Rufa and Rufulus (c.59); Castor and his twin (c.4). Often this pairing implies a certain smugness on the part of the couple, but the obsessive doubling in the language of poems like c.31 (which climaxes with "hoc est quod *unum* est," 11) suggests that it is a stylistic idiom of Catullus.

79. Ellis 1889, 203, sees a financial metaphor in *socii* (partners in; Cicero, *Rosc. Amer.* 40.117); with respect to the *puellulae*, "Mamurra and Caesar had not only equal shares, but each the shares of the other; what was *proprium* to one was shared by him with the other, and the *totum* thus belonged to both and neither."

80. Schmidt 1976 documents this meaning of the word, which is used of creatures, such as centaurs, that are composite in body. He argues that the word

here refers to the sexual reversibility of the pair of which each can take either position. Lebek 1982 supports Schmidt's interpretation with a possible parallel from the *Anthologia Latina*.

81. *Iul.* 52.3. Compare Cicero on Clodius: "Contra fas et inter viros saepe mulier et inter mulieres vir" (*Dom.* 54.139).

82. Skinner 1979a is an excellent treatment of Catullus' use of the standard language of political pamphleteering to reflect his own ambiguous attitude to the political scene.

## Chapter 4

1. Eagleton 1990, 36.
2. Eagleton 1990, 38. Compare the words of Minyard 1985, 26, a propos Catullus: "The qualities that make a good person are those shown by a good poem."
3. Austin 1960, 53. The only full-scale treatment of *urbanitas* is Ramage 1973, but there is also valuable material in Saint Denis 1965. For an analysis of several of the terms in the semantic field of *urbanitas*, see Monteil 1964.
4. Though sometimes a foreign element is internal to these kinds of concepts. There is an interesting symmetry between Austin 1960's recourse to the French word *ton* in his explication of "good form" and Cicero's wonderfully schizophrenic "*autochthōn* [Greek for 'native'] in homine urbanitas."
5. Syndikus 1984, 12
6. On the expansion of the meaning of *urbanus* during this period, see Saint Denis 1965, 152–55. The volatility of the concept appears, for instance, in Cicero's negative characterization of Clodius as *urbanissimus* (*Pro Caelio* 15.36, compare *In P. Clod. et C. Cur.*, frag. 22). See also Ramage 1973 on *urbanitas*.
7. See the interesting remarks of David 1983, 318–23.
8. It is significant that a number of the writers associated with Catullus came from Cisalpine Gaul, including Cornelius Nepos, Valerius Cato, Cinna, Furius Bibaculus, and Caecilius (c.35); coming from the provinces to the metropolis, where they were making a literary reputation for themselves, they seem to have adopted all the more fervently the city's ideals of sophistication. The Quintia of c.86 may have been Veronese, like the Quintius of c.100; at any rate, in c.43 Catullus' comparison of Lesbia to the overpraised Ameana specifically makes a point about provincial inurbanity.
9. Catullus only uses *urbanus* four times (cc.22.2,9, 57.4, 39.8), but several of his favorite words (*venustus, elegans, lepos, sal* etc.) belong in what Ross calls "the vocabulary of urbane Rome"; see Ross 1969, 105. Catullus' use of *venustus*, a word frequently conjoined with *urbanus* by Roman authors, is examined by Wiltshire 1977, and Seager 1974 deals with *venustus, lepidus, bellus,* and *salsus* in Catullus.
10. Compare Havelock 1939, 101–2: "[Catullus] gives no formula for this urban consciousness; to formulate it might destroy it, since its essence is a kind of tacit agreement between a certain number of people to speak and behave in a certain manner."

11. On the old Roman tradition of caustic wit (dicacitas), see Saint Denis 1965, 49–79. Cicero refers to this "veterem urbanitatem" in *ad Fam.* 7.31.2 and 9.15.2 ("non Attici, sed salsiores quam Atticorum Romani veteres atque urbani sales"; the whole passage is very interesting).

12. Saint Denis 1965, 151.

13. Compare Cicero, *De Off.* 1.104.

14. *Humanitas*, sometimes coupled with *urbanitas* (e.g., Cicero, *ad Fam.* 3.9.1), also has this sense; compare Cicero, *De Off.* 1.40.144, where the man who meditates too deeply at a dinner is described as *inhumanus*, even though this behavior might be quite appropriate on other occasions, such as before arguing a case. The reconciliation of the *gravitas* and *severitas* of the old Roman value system with the *humanitas* that the man of culture was now expected to display was an important issue in the first century B.C.E. (Hellegouarc'h 1963, 288).

15. "Quid a me fieri potuit aut elegantius aut iustius quam ut sumptus egentissimarum civitatum minuerem sine ulla imminutione dignitatis tuae" (Cicero, *ad Fam.* 3.8.2). Here *elegans*, a popular word with the urban sophisticates of the period, means something like "correct"; compare Cicero, *ad Att.* 5.20.6. But its newer resonances may also be operative.

16. See, for instance, cc.6, 8 and 10 (in which Catullus is his own target), 17, 22, 24, 36, 39, 43, 44, 84, 86, 97, 98, and 105.

17. Compare c.6, where Catullus offers to make a "lepidus versus" out of Flavius' *ineptiae*.

18. Catullus has put Asinius' *cognomen* Marrucinus at the beginning of the poem because his inurbane behavior recalls the Italian origins of the Asinii, members of the tribe of the Marrucini, who had been led by Asinius' grandfather in the Social War. See Neudling 1955, 12–13.

19. *Differtus* is the conjecture of Passerat for the *disertus* of the manuscripts (dissertus in manuscript O). Ellis 1889, Merrill 1893, and Kroll 1929 print *disertus*, whereas Baehrens 1885, Mynors 1967, Fordyce 1961, and Quinn 1970 print *differtus*. Fordyce makes a convincing case for *differtus*.

20. This word that disturbs its context is compensated for by the rather precious Greek word *mnemosynum* (souvenir), used of the napkin, a word that stands out in the opposite direction and so balances out the discourse. The Greek word, used by Meleager of a love token that calls to mind a distant beloved (*A.P.* 12.68.7) is found only here in Latin.

21. Skinner 1981, 105. A similar statement can be found in Minyard 1985, 26. Skinner's more recent work on Catullus has been some of the most challenging and interesting on this author, and I use her earlier work as an example of the standard line on Catullus' urbanity only because it is the most eloquently expressed.

22. Similarly, Catullus draws attention to the fact that his own name has a diminutive form when he juxtaposes it with Cato in c.56.3.

23. Aristotle (*Rhet.* 2.12.16) defines *eutrapelia* as "pepaideumenē hubris."

24. Elsewhere, Cicero proudly recounts that Caesar eagerly collects his witticisms, and can now distinguish the real thing from impostors, so finely is his ear attuned (*ad Fam.* 9.16.3–4). Unfortunately, some of these witticisms might

give Caesar offense, and Cicero professes that he would willingly relinquish his reputation for wit if he could disown these remarks, but his style gives him away. Here Cicero is victimized by his own style in an age in which the republican freedom of speech has been lost (9.16.3) because of the very cult of personality that has contributed to the rise of people like Caesar. On the growing concern with personal style in this period, see Selden 1992, who cites Cicero, *De Off.* 110–14.

We might remember that Catullus, who professed to have no interest in Caesar's nature or tastes (c.93), awakened a less disinterested, but ultimately generous, response to his attacks on Caesar from the great man himself. According to Suetonius (*Iul.* 73), Caesar claimed that Catullus' poems against him had cast "perpetua stigmata" on his name, but he invited Catullus to dinner that same afternoon and maintained his friendship with Catullus' father. Tacitus (*Annales*, 4.34.8) reports that Caesar tolerated the insulting poems of Catullus and Furius Bibaculus.

25. On Martial and plagiarism, see Kay 1985, 258–59.

26. Forsyth 1985 shows that cc.12–14 are all concerned with gifts and giving among loving friends, and argues that they constitute a distinct unit between a Lesbia cycle (cc.2–11) and a Furius and Aurelius cycle (cc.15–26).

27. The Roman invitation poem regularly features the theme of the "smart poverty" (Edmunds 1982) of the poet and introduces with it a conflict of values. Its prototype (*A.P.* 11.44) is addressed by Catullus' contemporary, Philodemus, to his patron Piso. Philodemus implies that the attractions for which Piso will sacrifice sows' udders and Chian wine, namely, good friends and sweet poetry, are in fact of greater worth; however, he also tells Philodemus that he will get a richer dinner next time if he is generous with the poet. Dettmer 1989 points out that Fabullus suffered at the hands of Piso when on his provincial staff much as Catullus did at the hands of Memmius (cc.28, 47), and that Philodemus is probably the Socration whom Catullus in c.47 identifies as taking the rightful place of Fabullus in the favors of Piso (see Neudling 1955, 140). She argues that Catullus' poem deliberately evokes Philodemus' invitation in order both to outdo Philodemus and to play a practical joke on his friend. This joke and the joke played on Catullus by Calvus in c.14 are intended, according to Dettmer, to provide examples of what constitutes a witty prank in Catullus' circle and so to contrast with Asinius' tasteless attempt in c.12.

28. D'Arms 1990 points out that there was a significant tension between the egalitarian ideals of Roman conviviality and the hierarchical realities of the Roman dinner.

29. There is considerable controversy as to what *amores* refers to: affection, love poetry, and the beloved (Lesbia herself) are all possibilities that have been advanced. The text at this point is uncertain: manuscript O has "meos amores," but most editors read *meros*. Those who believe that Catullus is offering Lesbia sexually to his guest (Littman 1977, Hallett 1978) would read *meos*, but *meros* has the advantage of trumping Fabullus' contribution of wine with undiluted (merus) love. Marcovich 1982 argues, on the basis of analogies between this poem and Philodemus 23, that "meros amores" refers to love poems.

30. For the ancient practice of anointing oneself with scent at dinner, see the references in Kroll 1929, 29–30, and Xenophon, *Symp.* 2.3, where perfume is called for to make the dinner perfect.

31. This is the view of Littman 1977 and Hallett 1978, refuted by Witke 1980.

32. Quinn 1970, 135.

33. Adams 1982, 35.

34. Skinner 1981, 61.

35. Compare Bakhtin's (1981, 297) admittedly overstated remarks on the monologic nature of poetry: "The poet strips the word of others' intentions, he uses only such words and forms . . . that they lose their link with concrete intentional levels of language and their connection with specific contexts . . . *Everything that enters the work must immerse itself in Lethe, and forget its previous life in any other contexts*" (Bakhtin's emphasis). If we see Fabullus as a figure for the reader, Catullus' poem suggests a more competitive and dramatic situation: what we bring to the poem, and we must bring the mundane linguistic prerequisites, is trumped by what the poet offers us, and even this remains ultimately his own.

36. Bernstein 1985 also interprets c.13 as a poem about poetry: "Catullus has written a programmatic piece to his intended audience: an invitation to read and appreciate his simple, elegant, and witty verse" (130). However, where Bernstein understands the unconventional invitation as involving a description of Catullus' poetic style, I would interpret the peculiarity of the invitation as a reflection of the peculiar relation between poet and reader.

37. Catullus accentuates the singsong effect of this catalectic iambic tetrameter, a meter he uses only here, by allowing no substitutions for the iambic foot. There is an intriguing possibility that the second line of this poem is quoted by Cicero, *ad Quintum*, 2.15.4: "auricula infima molliorem." But the phrase may be proverbial (Quinn 1972, 166).

38. Most of the scholarship on this poem is concerned with the textual crux of line 5, about which there is unlikely ever to be agreement. Unfortunately, this line seems to hold the key to the fictional setting of the poem. The "mulier aries" and "mulier alios" of the manuscripts may well conceal the word *mulierarios*, and the goddess could be Venus. Colin 1954 develops an interesting scenario in which the "effeminates" (mulierarios) are off their guard as they gape (oscitantes) at Thallus, a provocative dancer (the original meaning of *cinaedus*) entertaining the guests, from whom in this moment of weakness he extracts gifts. A more recent attempt to solve the crux by Granarolo 1981 involves reading "cum laeva mulierarios offendit oscitantes"; in this interpretation, the *mulierarii* are "skirt-chasers" who, engaged in their business, are not looking out for Thallus.

39. The ancient theory that the impotence of old men made them more liable to turn to the role of the pathic (Halperin 1990, 23–24) may motivate this simile for the softness of a *cinaedus*, in which the reference is ironic because Thallus' name connotes youth.

40. Jocelyn 1979, 91.

41. See, for instance, c.12.17 (Veraniolum meum et Fabullum), discussed on page 96 above, and c.56.3 (Cato Catullum).

42. Thallus is the name printed in most editions, but the manuscripts, with one exception, read *Talle* in lines 1 and 4. Neudling 1955, 167, suggests that this may be a corruption of *Tallei*, vocative of the *gentilicium* Tallius. If Thallos is the correct name here, Neudling suggests that it possibly belongs to Antonios Thallos, a poet of the *Anthologia Palatina*.

43. Ross 1969, 23–26, 158–59.

44. Plautus, *Pseudolus* 544–45, also compares whipping to writing in a passage examined on pages 56–57.

45. There is no certainty about the meaning of the extremely rare word *catagraphos*. In Pliny (*N.H.* 35.56) it is used of outline drawings, and Merrill 1893, 48, argues that it here means "writing tablets," because these were commonly made of boxwood from Bithynia.

46. Philodemus' poem listing the physical attributes of a beautiful woman (*A.P.* 5.132) provides an example of the kind of poem Catullus is turning on its head. Possibly, the two poems are related by more than this topos: having praised the body of his beauty, Philodemus declares that she is *opikē*, that is, an unsophisticated Italian who "does not sing Sappho," and yet, he says, Perseus was in love with the Indian Andromeda. With Catullus the physical merges with the spiritual in the transition from "dry mouth" to "elegant tongue," and part of what makes Ameana unacceptable is that she is not, like Lesbia, sophisticated.

47. For *decoctus* used of literary style, see Cicero, *de Orat.* 3.103, where it is negative (overripe), and Persius 1.125, where it is positive (mature, condensed).

48. Wilamowitz-Moellendorff 1924, 295–98.

49. Renaissance poets followed the example of the author of *Catalepton* 10 in droves. Gaisser 1993, Chapter 6, deals with many of these neo-Latin compositions.

50. Ezra Pound 1948, 76, has an interesting imitation of this poem called "Phasellus Ille," in which he mockingly adopts the tone of a self-satisfied editor whose mind "was made up in 'the seventies.'"

51. Khan 1967, 169–71, whose argument involves the parody of this poem in *Catalepton* 10.

52. Elegant Romans liked to keep little slave children around, almost like windup toys, to amuse them with their garrulous cuteness. This is the subject of Slater 1974. These children, usually known as *delicia*, amused their owners with their *garrulitas*. Slater, following Birt, suggests that Camerius in c.55 and the "pupulum puellae" of c.56 are *delicia* (and may be the same person).

53. The fact that the speech of the yacht is reported distinguishes this poem from Greek epigrams dedicating to the appropriate deity tools of the trade that are being retired; in those epigrams, it is either the dedicator or the dedicated object that speaks. Fordyce 1961, 96.

54. Besides Skinner 1981, quoted below, see Johnson 1982, 111–12, Hallett 1988, 399, and Quinn 1972, 280. Since Pucci 1961, this poem has usually been read as an important literary manifesto expressing Catullus' deep commitment to an art based on values opposed to conservative Roman ideals; Segal 1970 and Buchheit 1976a both take this line.

55. Skinner 1981, 84–85.
56. Quinn 1972, 280.

# Chapter 5

1. Suetonius, *Jul.* 33; Caesar, *Bellum Civ.* 1.7.7 and 1.9.2.
2. The comparison is made, to Catullus' advantage, by Minyard 1985, 15–29.
3. *OLD* s.v. 2, "delightful to be with, congenial"; *OLD* s.v. 3, "agreeable to the senses."
4. This is the attitude, for instance, of Copley 1949, 24–26. Quinn 1971, 72, comments, "We catch the irony, know it justified and understand as well as Catullus that he was hoping against hope." Konstan 1972, 103, interprets the change of construction for *proponis* as Catullus' attempt to go beyond the traditional associations of *amor* with a light affair "to a new expression for a new thing"; Catullus would make a contract out of words of passion, and for this he must create a new language, which is what he proceeds to do in this poem.
5. Copley makes it clear that this deeper love was latent early in the affair (and in the polymetrics) but did not become explicit until Lesbia betrayed Catullus:

> It would appear that as long as Catullus and Lesbia were happy together, as long as he felt that his feelings were reciprocated, he either was unaware that his love for her possessed any special or unusual characteristics, or felt no need to attempt an expression of them (24).

6. See Ross 1969, 76–80. Syndikus 1984, 124, in contrast, argues that *iucundus* is a more weighty word than has usually been allowed, quoting Cicero on true friendship (*Lael.* 47, 49, 51).
7. Lyne 1980, 36. Fifteen uses of this word are cited in Wetmore 1912, and this is the only use in the elegiac epigrams.
8. Cc.73, 77, 82, 91, 102.
9. Ross 1969, 80–95; 1975, 9–15. Ross follows the arguments of Reitzenstein, whose article "Zur Sprache der lateinischen Erotik," originally published in 1912, can be found (in somewhat edited form) in Heine 1975, 153–80. A detailed study of the Roman vocabulary of political alliance is provided by Hellegouarc'h 1963, who shows, among other things, that the language of politics in Rome often borrowed from the language of love; see, for instance, 142–43 (amare), 180–81 (cupere), 213 (blanditiae), 215 (amplecti-complecti).
10. Lyne 1980, 25–26. Lyne should have added that some of this language (*pietas* and *fides*, for instance) is also used in religious contexts. The wide currency of some of these words is illustrated by the fact that *officium* is used in epitaphs to refer to the dutifulness of wives even in the circles of freedmen and freedwomen (see Williams 1968, 405–6). Lyne's bibliography on the aristocratic social code and its terminology on pages 291–92, note 4, is very full.
11. McGushin 1967 is an earlier version of the argument that Catullus is representing his relationship with Lesbia as a marriage, and on page 92, note 4,

he identifies some of his predecessors in this view. There are some good criticisms of the marriage theory in Dyson 1973, 138–39, who also takes Ross to task on page 138, note 2.

12. Bardon 1970, 118–19, remarks on the opportunism of Catullus' use of moral language, but maintains that "Catulle est la sincerité même."

13. Commager was reacting against what had become the canonical view of Catullus as the quintessential "lyric" poet pouring forth his feelings with spontaneous and simple directness, and he gives some examples of this view on the first page of his article. Eliot's antiromantic view of lyric poetry was itself to become canonical, as Commager's quotation of Graves reveals: "The poem is either a practical answer to [the poet's] problem, or else it is a clear statement of it; and a problem clearly stated is half-way to solution . . ." (93). Quinn 1959, 91–92, had quoted both Eliot and Graves in his section on Catullus' "meditative lyric." More recent versions of Commager's therapeutic theory can be found in Skinner 1988, 340 (Catullus' poetry confronts and orders experience), and Syndikus 1984, 101–2 (the form of the epigrams provides a "purging of all too powerful emotions").

14. Catullus' poems to his friends sometimes have the same truncated rhetoric: c.77, addressed to a Rufus who has betrayed him in some unspecified way (possibly with Lesbia), is trapped in repetitious exclamation.

15. Quoted by Commager 1965, 91.

16. References in Syndikus 1984, 106, note 9. Skinner 1971 reviews the evidence that Catullus presents himself as comic *amator*, but concludes that "the poem's central ironic focus depends on a razor's-edge balance of emotional commitment and intellectual detachment" (305).

17. The poem is written in scazons or choliambics (limping iambics), which are iambic trimeters with a dragging spondee as the last foot.

18. Croce 1950, 68; the translation is from Veyne 1988, 34–35.

19. Marmorale 1957, 162, calls it "the most beautiful prayer to the gods that antiquity has handed to us from a soul that has suffered," and Edna St. Vincent Millay "the most beautiful short poem in any language I know" (both quoted by Commager 1965, 105).

20. McAfee 1983.

21. Buechner 1977, 76, states that, a half century before the birth of Christ, Catullus gave witness to the divine invincibility and to the ethical character of all love: "The union of two people succeeds if they are united in something common that transcends them." He recognized divinity as the protector of his love and, after long wanderings, turned to them in prayer: "Passion has led to insight."

22. Granarolo 1967, 107.

23. Lyne 1980 and Commager 1965 agree that c.76 is a failure, but this is what makes it moving to Commager (98); according to Lyne (33), the poem is aesthetically unsatisfying. Williams 1968 points out that ending a hexameter with four long syllables, as in line 15, is a mannerism affected by Hellenistic Greek poets, but adds that in this poem the effect "signals a determination to accommodate the most simple and direct language, regardless of metrical roughness." The effect has a significance quite opposite to what it would have in other poems

of Catullus, but it is "no less the result of careful artistry than the high polish of routine Alexandrianism" (411).

24. Had Catullus been vouchsafed the Christian revelation, Granarolo 1967 speculates, the pride displayed in this poem would have been chastened and the egocentric prayer "eripite hanc pestem perniciemque *mihi*" would have been changed to "libera *nos* a malo" (107). Earlier (96) he cites Ciaffi, who claims that Catullus' words "si vestrum est misereri" (c.76.17) anticipate the Christian prayer "miserere nostri."

25. See Granarolo 1967, 90, note 1, citing Marmorale and Gigante.

26. Marmorale 1957, cited in Granarolo 1967, 40.

27. Granarolo 1967, 96–103, has an interesting discussion of the idea of divine pity in ancient thought a propos Herescu's claim that Catullus is here the first to attribute the quality of mercy to the divine.

28. Compare Propertius 1.25–26 and Catullus 41.5–6.

29. Syndikus 1984, 248, note 2, lines up some of the critics on either side of the debate as to whether the praise of Cicero is meant seriously or ironically. As one might expect, the tendency in recent times has been to see irony, even parody of the Ciceronian style, in the superlatives; Quinn's commentary, for instance, is generally sympathetic to the ironic reading where Fordyce's is not. Quinn 1970, 235, makes a good presentation of the case for reading "optimus omnium patronus" as criticism of Cicero's indiscriminate and unprincipled advocacy ("best advocate of all and sundry"). Thomson 1967 is probably the most recent argument against the ironic reading, though his theory that the poem is a tactful response to Cicero's own poetical efforts requires us to supply a lot of context to the poem from rather slender evidence. See Selden 1992, 464–67, and Batstone 1993, 155–63, for deconstructive readings of this poem, both of which see it as undecidable.

30. Compare the last sentence of Cicero, *ad Fam.* 7.12, quoted below on page 131.

31. Editors have remarked that "in amore tuo ex parte reperta mea est" seems a clumsy and roundabout way of saying "in my love." Ellis 1889 and Merrill 1893 took it to refer to all of Lesbia's lovers, who did not love her as much as Catullus. Konstan 1972, 105, translates "amore tuo" as "in your love for me" and inteprets the whole of the second couplet as follows: "There never was in any bond a faith so great as I found in your love." Konstan gives its full sense to *reperta* and interprets the poem as being critical of Catullus' self-deception. I think, however, that the elaboration of the phrasing here is intended to produce a false impression of reciprocity.

32. "Homini alienissimo mihi et propter amicitiam tuam non aequissimo." Cicero, *ad Fam.* 7.12.2.

33. Ross 1975, 10, well describes the unorthodoxy of Catullus' position: "When one party in a political *amicitia* had done dirt to another, had committed an *iniuria*—when, that is, political necessity had changed and it became expedient to sever the connection—nothing was easier than to break it off, more often than not coolly and with perfect composure."

34. Hellegouarc'h 1963, 154–55, cites some of the financial metaphors used in connection with *officium*, which he describes as "a sort of coin of exchange."

On the coercive power of *beneficia* and the network of *beneficium, officium, gratia*, and *fides*, see MacMullen 1986, 521-24.

35. The *deductio*, in which the bride was led to the house of the groom, was a fixed part of the Roman wedding ceremony (see Williams 1958). It is therefore ironic here that Lesbia's sexual fault (culpa) is described as escorting (deducta) Catullus' mind.

36. Hellegouarc'h 1963, 161.

37. Line 1 accounts for the problem in line 3, and line 2 for that in line 4, while the alternation of active and passive in the first couplet (deducta, perdidit) is repeated in the second (fias, facias).

38. See the suggestive remarks of Northrop Frye, in Hosek and Parker 1985, 31-37, on the importance for the lyric of the fiction of turning away from our ordinary continuous experience.

39. Examples of such speculation are given by Pedrick 1986, 201, note 15. As Eva Stehle points out in her response to Pedrick's paper, Pedrick herself assumes that real words of Lesbia lie behind the poem insofar as she questions the faithfulness of the indirect speech in c.70 to what it reports (Stehle 1986).

40. To take but one example, the song cycle of Dominick Argento based on poems of Catullus is called "I Hate and I Love," and it begins and ends with c.85.

41. Lyne 1980, 40; Kroll 1929, 244; Commager 1965, 95. See also Copley 1949, 28-29.

42. Bishop 1971, 636-38, discusses the love/hate topos in Hellenistic epigram and concludes that Catullus is closest to the quasi-philosophical treatment of the theme by Euenus (*A.P.* 12.172). I would suggest that a closer parallel to this poem is the epigram by Catullus' contemporary, Philodemus, about Xanthippe's charms; there the poet tells his heart that it will be set on fire: "But from what beginning, or when, or how / I do not know; you will know, poor wretch, when you are smouldering" (*A.P.* 5.131.3-4). Bishop argues that Catullus' epigram follows the form of a philosophical dialogue (statement by *magister*, question by *discipula*, answer by *magister*) and that the epigram fuses erotic and philosophical themes. A more extensive treatment of the love/hate theme both before and after Catullus can be found in Weinreich 1926, 32-83, which concludes that examination of the topos only shows the genuineness of Catullus' experience of the *Urphaenomen* of hate and love. In a sense, Weinreich's study follows the process of questioning and confirmation that the poem itself invites.

43. According to Weinreich 1926, 44-46, this *Antwortformel* is distinctively Roman; in poetry it begins with Catullus, to be taken up and worked to death by Martial. Weinreich takes the formula as a manifestation of the importance of the bond between poet and reader in the time of Catullus.

44. See Pedrick 1986, 201, especially note 15.

45. Catullus' epigram is modeled fairly closely on Callimachus, *Ep.* 25 Pfeiffer, also about the unreliability of lovers' oaths. Evidence of the proverbial character of lines 3 and 4 can be found in Syndikus 1984, 6, note 13.

46. This poem is a variant of c.83, but in that poem it is the husband, foolishly satisfied with Lesbia's denunciations of Catullus, who is the butt.

47. This is the position of Konstan 1972, 104. See also Miller 1988.

## Chapter 6

1. "Epyllion" is a term invented in the nineteenth century to designate the genre of the miniature epic; it has no ancient precedent. See Most 1981, 111, especially note 9. Lyne 1978 argues that the the mannered miniature was the distinctive genre of the neoteric "school" and describes the epyllion as a "brief, highly wrought *epos* which more or less ostentatiously dissociates itself from traditional *epos*, concentrating on unheroic incidentals in the sagas of heroes, or on heroines as opposed to heroes, or on otherwise offbeat subject matter; employing a narrative technique that was often wilfully individual and selective; and yet largely maintaining epic language, metre and style" (172–73).

2. Gruen 1992 passim.

3. A form whose characteristic feature is "the desire to avoid the expected connection, the logical train of thought: to surprise the reader by constant change of view-point, of time scale, of addressee" (Williams 1968, 227). See also Fordyce 1961, 274.

4. Pasquali and Wilamowitz-Moellendorff, cited by Klingner 1964, 161, note 2, both see a Hellenistic original behind this poem. For a more recent study of the poem's Alexandrianism, see Thomas 1982.

5. See also Konstan 1977, 108: "Catullus . . . by a subtle use of imagery and ambiguity, allusions, responsions and startling juxtapositions—in fact through all the devices of Hellenistic mannerism—creates a pervasive tension in the epyllion which is not that of antithesis . . . but of irony. Catullus exposes the contradictions and corruption of life and values of the upper class, at least, in Rome, not so much by contrast with some viable ideal, but rather from within, revealing the failure of Roman culture to meet the moral requirements of his time." Harmon 1973, 331, argues that the poem exposes the seeds of decay in the heroic and old Roman codes, but concludes that Catullus looks back with nostalgia to an age that, for all its faults, "offered at least an approximation of the life for which man's nature yearns." For an argument against the moral interpretation, see Dee 1982, rejected by Schmidt 1985, 77–86, who summarizes the evidence for a moral reading.

6. Putnam 1961 is the first sustained and thoroughgoing interpretation along these lines; Most 1981, 120, sees the poem as a combination of themes from all of Catullus' poetry, "a profound meditation on love and loss, on felicity and despair, on the relations between man and man, and man and god." See also Forsyth 1976, Glenn 1981, and Konstan 1977, 78: "Our epyllion, too, I believe, reflects Catullus' abiding concern with the problem of how private passion, which was tangential to the sphere of traditional morality, could be the basis of an enduring relationship".

7. Typical of the tendency to subordinate the poem's visual opulence to a higher meaning is O'Connell 1977, whose title is "Pictorialism and Meaning in Catullus 64." O'Connell concludes: "In a way that we can recognize as essentially Roman, Catullus employed the Alexandrian fascination with poetic pictorialism to create a poem that is serious and, in its indirect way, ultimately moral in concern" (756).

8. See Bryson 1990, 39–40, on the "Second Style," roughly contemporary with Catullus (from about 60 B.C.E.). Granarolo 1972 argues for a common spirit between Catullus 64 and contemporary wall painting, and there are some excellent remarks on aspects of the second style relevant to Catullus' poem in Martin 1992, 155–56.

9. Granarolo 1972, 430–31, describes the relation between the approaches of Schefold and Klingner. Schefold's analysis of decorative ensembles in Pompeian wall painting has been extended by Brilliant 1984.

10. Veyne 1988, 117–18, situates the world of myth in a time that is the object of longing—*optato*, as Catullus puts it at the beginning of this poem (22):

> Its [sc. Myth's] essence is to call up an oneiric temporality, situated "before" our history and lacking substance. . . . This time without consistency is situated at some inestimable distance from our years, for the unit of measurement is not the same. We feel in some obscure way that we are separated from it less by a form of duration than by a change in being and truth. A nostalgia overcomes us at the idea of this cosmos, so like our own, but secretly so different and as inaccessible as the stars. Its strangeness would be even greater if those places that were myth's theater really existed and if Pelion and Pindus were mountains visible to our gaze. In what dream century was our Pelion criss-crossed by centaurs, and what kind of phantom mountain must it have been to be able to participate in this other form of temporality?

Veyne's description of the strange temporal and spatial relation between our world and the world of myth makes one think of the dreamlike spatiality created by Roman wall painting.

11. Johnson 1982, 159, provides the best formulation of this approach:

> Here in the complex fusion of lyric monologue and lyric narrative, feelings of guilt for past innocence betrayed and feelings of anger and radical inferiority find their focus in Ariadne, in whom the victim of love, the unmanned poet, finds an answering metaphor for his impotence, for his intolerable feminization: Ariadne, the quintessential victim, the woman who, having risked all for love, is betrayed and abandoned and shrieks her outrage and her suffering to the deaf winds and the deserted beach.

12. Examples of the sleeping woman exposed can be found in Marcadé 1968, 34, 42, 43, 51. For representations of Ariadne on Pompeian wall paintings, see Reinach 1922, 111–13, and Richardson 1974, 193.

13. The classic treatment of this is Mulvey 1975. Catullus' description of the distraught, abandoned, and semi-naked Ariadne corresponds to Mulvey's contention that the woman in mainstream cinema is presented as inadequate or castrated. Silverman 1988, 1–41, adds that it is the male viewer's exclusion from the site of filmic production, itself a form of castration, that motivates the presentation of the woman as castrated. The parallels (described below) between the description of the semi-naked Ariadne in lines 63–65 and the description of the countryside unworked by the (phallic) plough, hoe, and sickle in lines 41–43 provide a striking confirmation of Silverman's argument.

In describing in this chapter the relation of the reader (or potential viewer) to the poem and its sights, I assume that this reader is cast by the poet as male. There may certainly be readers who refuse this role or read the poem from different perspectives than what is offered to them (though this is not necessarily true of all women readers).

14. Silverman 1988, 28–32.

15. Two kinds of Golden Age can be distinguished in ancient literature, a soft Golden Age in which the earth produced its bounty without human toil, and a hard Golden Age in which toil and virtue went hand in hand. Reckford 1958.

16. Bryson 1990, 48, shows how this self-conscious attitude to the sophisticated staging of country life in the Villa Rustica of the late Republic manifests itself in the decorative scheme of a wall painting in Boscoreale.

17. The text is a little uncertain here, and Baehrens 1885, 364, reads "illa rudem cursu proram [O] imbuit Amphitrite [O corr]" to get the more conventional disposition of subject and object. Baehrens is followed by Quinn 1970. But Merrill 1893, Mynors 1967, Kroll 1929, and Fordyce 1961 all print "illa rudem cursu prima imbuit Amphitriten."

18. I like this very much, evidently more than Quinn 1970, who rejects the reading of the manuscripts' *incanduit* (grew hot) in favor of the renaissance conjecture *incanuit* (became white), which recalls Homer's *polios* and avoids an echo with *candenti* in the next line. *Incanduit* would confirm the association of the oars with hot curling tongs, but perhaps even the emended text, with *candenti* on the next line, already suggests the same idea.

19. The detail may be learned, but attention to detail has its own erotic or voyeuristic dimensions, as witnessed by this poem on the explicator of Calvus' notoriously thorny *Zmyrna*:

> Uni Crassicio se credere Zmyrna probavit.
>    Desinite, indocti, coniugio hanc petere!
> Soli Crassicio se dixit nubere velle
>    Intima cui soli nota sua extiterint.
>         (Suetonius, *de Gramm.* 18)
>
> To Crassicius alone has Zmyrna agreed to entrust herself.
>    Cease, you unlearned, to seek her in marriage!
> To Crassicius alone has she promised to be married
>    For only to him have her intimate secrets been revealed.

20. Grimal 1984 (3d ed.), 376, compares the appearance of a statue (Ariadne) in the tapestry to the mixing of artistic modes in the *ars topiaria* of the Roman garden, whose aesthetic Catullus reflects:

> It looks as though the poet is describing a setting in the manner of the gardens. . . . And the constant passage from a pictorial art to statuary can only be explained, we believe, within an aesthetic where each genre fails to recognize its own limits, in order to put itself at the service of something other than itself: in this case to create, by all means, this atmosphere of an enchanted and divine world that we have already encountered in the gardens.

Boucher 1956, 200–1, speculates on the sculptural type that Catullus may have had in mind. He points out that there is a maenad in the Capitoline Museum with the same superimposition of erotic grace onto fury as in Catullus' description of Ariadne.

21. Compare Apollonius, *Arg.* 1.763ff.

22. On the importance of the lamenting Ariadne in seventeenth-century music, see Bianconi 1987, 204–19; for Ariadne in literature, see Lipking 1988. It is striking that Richard Strauss's *Ariadne auf Naxos* is probably the most self-reflexive of all operas, and, with its opera-within-an-opera plot, it bears comparison with Catullus' poem.

23. This effect reminds us of the tapestry itself, for the figure of Ariadne on the tapestry might at one time hold our attention, and at another appear as an element in our scanning of the whole composition.

24. The contradiction of movement between *comparatum* and *comparandum* is complemented by an intertextual contradiction, for this simile is modeled on two Homeric similes, one describing the Greeks advancing in waves like breakers crashing on the headland (*Il.* 4.422–60) and the other describing the opposing ranks of the Greeks and Trojans, whose bristling spears are like the sea rippling before the rising West Wind (*Il.* 7.63–64). In both Homeric cases, the simile is describing a *confrontation* between two groups, whereas in Catullus the guests are giving place to (decedere, 268) the gods.

25. Bramble 1970, 29.

26. Konstan 1977, 57. It is interesting to see that Christian Metz has appropriated this ancient theory of vision to explain the process of watching a film; Silverman 1988, 23, cites him as follows: "Watching a film is a constant process of projection and introjection, of sending out 'a sort of stream called the look' so that objects can travel back up the stream in the opposite direction.'"

27. Bramble 1970, 24–27.

28. As the girls' choir of c.62 put it, "What do the enemy do that is more cruel when they have captured a city" (quid faciunt hostes capta crudelius urbe? 24)? The Fates turn from their prophetic song, culminating in the sacrifice of Polyxena, to the epithalamium with the words "*dedatur* cupido iam dudum nupta marito" (let the wife be *handed over* immediately to the longing husband, 374); the italicized word is regularly used for the surrender of a city or the handing over of someone for punishment, but it also seems to belong to the language of the wedding hymn (c.61.58). Both the Roman wedding and the Homeric capture of a city are symbolic rapes. Editors cite Achilles' "oioi Troiēs krēdemna luoimen" (let us loose the veil of Troy on our own, *Il.* 16.100) in connection with

> nam simul ac fessis dederit fors copiam Achivis
> urbis Dardaniae Neptunia *solvere* vincla
> alta Polyxenia madefient caede sepulcra; (c.64.366–68)

> for, as soon as Fate will have given the power to the tired Achaeans
> to loosen Neptune's chains around the city of Dardanus,
> the high burial mound will be drenched with the blood of Polyxena;

Possibly, the sacrifice of Polyxena supplies the erotic violence implied by the Homeric phrase.

29. See Wiseman 1985, 44–48, for details on these entertainments.

30. For *tremulum* used of deliberate, erotic motion, see Martial's description of a dancing girl at 14.203.1 (tam tremulum crisat).

31. See Richlin 1992a, 109–16, 1984.

32. Compare "unguibus ora soror foedans et pectora pugnis" (*Aen.* 4.673).

33. Parallels for such a use of *variare* to aestheticize bruises can be found only in the gallows humor of the characters of Plautus (*Miles* 216, *Poen.* 26).

34. See Gruen 1992. Zetzel 1983 points out that there are references to the story of Medea in Catullus 64 that are taken not from Greek literature but from Ennius' tragedy *Medea Exul*.

## Chapter 7

1. A classic example of the poet as his own victim is Baudelaire in his poem "L'Heautontimoroumenos," which contains the lines:

> Je suis la plaie et le couteau!
> Je suis le soufflet et la joue!
> Je suis les membres et la roue,
> Et la victime et la bourreau!
> 
> Baudelaire 1961, 85

> I am the wound and the knife!
> I am the blow and the cheek!
> I am the limbs and the wheel,
> And the victim and the executioner!

2. The figure of the bane of urbanity, who, like the woman here, takes advantage of the carelessness of others, crops up again in c.12, where Asinius Marrucinus is pilloried for stealing the napkins of dinner guests who are off their guard (neglegentiorum, 3). Cicero exemplifies the positive sense of *neglegens* in a letter to Atticus, where he laments the absence of his friend and the loss of the "sermonis communicatio . . . suavissima" between them; he goes on to say that he misses Atticus' conversation in various spheres, including "in publica[ne] re, quo in genere mihi neglegenti esse non licet" (*ad Att.* 1.17.6). The negative side of *neglegentia* is best exemplified by Cicero's "legum offici rei publicae sociorum atque amicorum neglegentior" (*Verr.* 3.143). Terence, in the prologues to *Adelphoe* and *Andria*, uses *neglegentia* in negative and positive senses respectively; see Martin 1976, 98–99. On *neglegens* in this poem, see Newman 1990, 161.

3. Although one of Catullus' earliest readers, Valeriano (writing in the 1520s), congratulates Catullus on escaping the "greed of harlots" by *pretending* that he had forgotten the litterbearers were not his but Cinna's! Gaisser 1993, 134.

4. Two recent treatments of c.10 (addressed in this chapter) are particularly interesting and provocative challenges to Catullan strategies of audience manipulation, namely, Pedrick 1986 and Skinner 1989. Both treatments emphasize the fact that the woman who engineers "Catullus'" discomfiture in the anecdote recounted by the poem is still the object of the poem's oppression, however much we may be invited to take a critical view of "Catullus." Skinner's subtle and wide-ranging analysis of the social, political, and gender structures that are the subtext of the poem defines both the extent and the limits of the poem's analysis of the dynamics of power in the Roman world. She summarizes her reading as follows:

> In C.10, then, Catullus preaches a short parable about the essential unfairness of the Roman status system. To express the equivocal nature of power, he incarnates it to a small but telling degree in a churlish *alter ego*, permitting him to justify conceit by calling it sophistication and to offend against the social decencies in every possible way. Meanwhile, he assigns to the figure of Varus's *amica* the full burden of protest against the presumptions of the speaker and therefore against the workings of a skewed system.... Yet her triumph must be ephemeral, for as a woman and a plebeian she *cannot* be allowed to have the last word. That is why the text concludes as abruptly as it does, with its withering denunciation of her as *insulsa* and *molesta* (19, emphasis Skinner's).

5. It is interesting that both poems set up a spatial tension between the public world of Roman business and the woman: in c.10 the idling Catullus is taken from the forum by Varus to see his girl, and in c.11 Furius and Aurelius are diverted from (putative) imperial expeditions to deliver a message to Lesbia. See the remarks on *huc* in c.10 by Skinner 1989, 19.

6. At this point, I should say that I find the attitude of the narrator (and indeed of "Catullus") towards Varus' mistress far less negative than does Skinner. Is it a fair representation of this passage to say that Catullus terms the girl "a barely acceptable little tramp" (16)? Certainly, the speaker's attitude is (by modern standards) patronizing, but would an ancient audience have thought that this speaker exhibits "extreme gender and class prejudices" (14), or that he "ruthlessly imposes upon her a stereotyped and trivialized self-image" (14)?

7. As Skinner 1989, 13, points out, *incidisset* "adverts to the practice of determining the specific territorial assignments of former consuls and praetors by drawing lots."

8. Skinner 1989 has some interesting documentation of the decadent associations of the *lectica*: "Young, robust Roman males were not expected to resort to litters, which were normally used only by physically feeble individuals—elderly men, invalids and women." Her claim, however, that the ownership and/or use of a litter would be so outrageous that Varus and his mistress must be facetious in lines 14–16 does not convince me. As she admits, Cicero casually mentions riding a litter to dinner (*ad Q. Fr.* 2.6.3) and does not tender any excuse (though Skinner points out that, at fifty, he could have pleaded age).

9. Nielsen 1987, 155–56, has a good description of the way that the groupings of characters in the society of this poem change as it progresses, finally leaving Catullus and Varus' mistress confronting one another.

10. Scholarly opinion differs as to whether the girl intends to borrow the chariot or is simply calling Catullus' bluff (Skinner 1989, 20, note 5).

11. On the cult of the Egyptian deities Isis, Osiris, and Serapis at Rome, see Latte 1967, 282–84.

12. As the Muses tell Hesiod in the *Theogony* (27), they know how to tell many lies that are similar to the truth. For a rather different version of Catullus' recuperation of the losses inflicted on his persona, see Nielsen 1987, 160: "Catullus has jeopardized his name and his reputation for repartee so that, by challenging the traditional reference to *sal*, he might refine its humor to a higher level of quality."

13. On Catullus' use of "illustrative elisions," see Lee 1962. The verb *tangere* often conveys a more aggressive sense than the English "touch"; compare, for instance, Catullus' "tangam te prior irrumatione" (c.21.8). Both aggressive and gentle senses are operative here.

14. The flower has been interpreted as an ambivalent image of Catullus' narcissistic but aesthetically satisfying love for Lesbia by Stigers 1977, who reads the image through the argument between the boys and the girls in c.62. The literary associations of this image are also described by Putnam 1974 and Celentano 1991. Celentano particularly stresses the relevance of the epic comparison of the young man cut off in the prime of life to a flower, but also quotes, from the other end of the literary spectrum, the proverb "tam perit quam extrema faba" (91, note 29).

15. The ancient custom of ploughing over a destroyed city is illustrated in their note on Horace, *C.* 1.16.20, by Nisbet and Hubbard 1970, 213. This practice is complemented by the use of the plough to mark out territory when founding a city (*Aen.*, 5.755). Vergil uses military and imperial language of ploughing at *Georgic* 1, 98–99, and 104–5.

16. "Caesar crossed the Rhine in the summer of that year and reached Britain in the autumn; in the spring Gabinius had entered Egypt to restore Ptolemy to his throne; and in November Crassus set out on his ill-fated expedition to the tempting East." Fordyce 1961, 124. The word *comites* is applied by Catullus to the members of a praetor's *cohors* at c.28.1 and c.46.9.

17. The verb *penetrare* in the second line of this poem can also be used of ideas or emotions "getting through" to a person (*OLD* s.v. 5).

18. For the identification of the "Eastern wave" (Eoa ... unda, 3–4) with Ocean, see Merrill 1893, 25.

19. Balsdon 1979, 66, points out that the invasion of Britain brought the kudos of extending the empire beyond the ocean.

20. There has been voluminous scholarly debate as to whether Furius and Aurelius are to be thought of as friends or enemies of Catullus, and whether we are to think of the opening as sarcastic or not. In other poems addressed to one or both of this pair (cc.15, 16, 21, 23, 24, 26), Catullus insults or attacks them in ways that seem to go beyond the kind of badinage that he practices with his

friends (e.g., cc.6, 14). My opinion on this subject is similar to that of Sweet 1987, who provides a full survey of opinions on the problem (note 1; see also Fotiou 1975, 150–52, and Friedricksmeyer 1993, 102–5). Sweet argues that the poem sets up a mood of companionship and optimism only to undermine it at the point where the mission of Furius and Aurelius is revealed; on a second reading, "the catalogue now appears as a thinly veiled parody whose language mocks the exaggerated devotion professed by Furius and Aurelius and implies that it is a pompous fake, just as Lesbia's was, and whose length is merely a foil for Catullus' bluntness" (516–17). In Chapter 1, I discuss the attempt of Macleod 1973 to clear this poem of irony and make Furius and Aurelius into true friends of Catullus. The most recent treatment of this poem, Friedricksmeyer 1993, argues that the address to Furius and Aurelius is sincere and marks a reconciliation with erstwhile enemies, whereas the address to Lesbia constitutes a break with an erstwhile lover.

21. Fotiou 1975, 156, draws this and other parallels between Lesbia and Furius and Aurelius, and Sweet 1987, 517, stresses the negative political overtones that emerge from the juxtaposition of the omnivorous Lesbia against the conquering Caesar.

22. Sweet 1987, 513, note 5, surveys the different opinions on the geographical catalog.

23. As Fordyce 1961, 208, points out, these journeys would have been real possibilities in 55 B.C.E., when the expeditions of Crassus to the East and of Caesar to Britain were in the air.

24. The words sent to Lesbia here also echo the only other poem of Catullus in the Sapphic meter, the translation of Sappho c.51, often thought to be the first poem Catullus wrote to Lesbia. The *identidem* of 11.19 would seem to be a bitter echo of *identidem* at 51.3, where it refers to the eager attention of the person who sits opposite Lesbia and seems like a god to the speaker. Yardley 1981 argues that Furius and Aurelius are being commissioned by Catullus to make a formal renunciation of friendship to Lesbia, and that the words "vivat valeatque" are formulaic in this transaction.

## Chapter 8

1. Like most of the recent students of this poem, I believe that c.68 is to be thought of as a unit, though it may be that its two parts, traditionally called 68a (1–40) and 68b (41–160), relate to each other in the same way as do cc.65 and 66. The question of whether it is actually one poem or two connected poems is not that crucial, though Skinner 1972 makes a good case for regarding 68a as "a finished artistic product" (509). The evidence of the manuscripts is quite clear on the fact that the two parts of the poem have different addressees, Mallius and Allius respectively (Most 1981, 116–17; Tuplin 1981, 113–14).

2. Wiseman 1987, 324–34, provides an excellent treatment of the growing pretensions of this part of Italy in Catullus' time.

3. On the status of literature and poetry in the late Republic, see Quinn 1982, 128–30, 136–39.

4. On the complicated relation of the Roman cultural elite to Greek culture, see Balsdon 1979, 30–58, Veyne 1979, and Gruen 1992.

5. On the allusion to the *Odyssey*, see Conte 1986, 32–39. Carrié 1993, 113, points out that epitaphs of soldiers often mention brothers, and that pacts between brothers to see to each other's funeral rites are quite common.

6. Quinn 1970, 440. As Quinn suggests (441), the words "ave atque vale" may have been part of the traditional ceremony (compare *Aen.* 11.97–98, salve aeternum mihi . . . aeternumque vale.)

7. Celan 1970, 143.

8. Quinn 1970, 441.

9. Toohey 1984 (especially 9–11) describes the role of Trojan genealogies at Rome and the racial prejudice or Hellenophobia that may have motivated it.

10. Possibly, *fluctuat* in this context recalls the Greek *kuma* (wave), derived from the verb meaning "to conceive" or "to be pregnant." But if Catullus' mind is figured as a womb, then *fluctuat* could also imply the menstrual flow that would equally prevent conception. "Giving birth" was a fairly common metaphor for artistic creation; see *OLD* s.v. *pario*, 4.

11. Ellis 1889 ad loc suggests that there is an allusion to Pindar, frag. 273 Bergk, where poets are the keepers of the golden apples of the Muses.

12. Possibly, this simile refers to a passage from Callimachus' story of Acontius and Cydippe in the *Aetia*, though not enough is known of that part of the *Aetia* to allow for more than speculation. See Daly 1952.

13. "Proverbium est, quod et illa incerti et levis animi est et plerumque in gremio posita, cum in oblivionem venerunt exsurgentium, procidunt" (Festus 1165, quoted by Kroll 1929, 199).

14. Catullus himself provides a beautiful picture of the moment of transition from mother to lover at c.64.86–93, and a more cynical view in the lock of Berenice's insinuation that the parents are fooled by the bride's false tears in c.66.15–16.

15. Witke 1968, 20–24, has a good treatment of the final six lines of this poem in relation to the theme of renewed life.

16. Cicero discusses conflicts of duties and how to resolve them in *De Officiis* 1.59; see also Aulus Gellius, *Noctes Atticae* 5.13. For an extended treatment of the moral significance of the blush for the Romans, see Seneca, *Ep.* 11, where after praising Pompey because "numquam non coram pluribus rubuit" (4), Seneca goes on to remark that the one thing actors cannot do at will is blush (ruborem sibi exprimere non possunt, 7). In a scene from Terence's *Adelphoe*, a father confronting his son with the latter's misdeed remarks in an aside "erubuit: salva res est" (643). Catullus himself, trying to shame the woman who has stolen his writing tablets, hopes that his *convicium* will squeeze a blush from her iron face (ruborem / ferreo canis exprimamus ore, c.42.16–17). The most famous and highly charged blush in Roman literature is, of course, Lavinia's at *Aen.* 12.64–69.

17. In c.51 Catullus translates one of Sappho's most famous poems (31 LP), much of which describes the physical effects on the lover of the sight of the beloved. He then appends to the Sappho poem a moralizing stanza (probably tongue-in-cheek) on *otium*, which reinterprets the physical symptoms of

love as the restlessness caused by excessive leisure (otio exsultas nimiumque gestis, 14).

18. The irony of these lines has been a problem for those who think that this poem simply reflects Catullus' own bereavement. Kidd 1970, for instance, is forced to read the lines as a statement, not a question, thus: "Besides, in your case, your grief was not just for the loss of a husband: the important factor was the sad parting for a beloved brother" (42). Much of the critical comment on this poem has been concerned with showing how Catullus has found aspects of his own experience in the Callimachean poem. Signs of Catullus' investment in the subject matter have usually been detected in the changes in the emphasis or affect of the original made by Catullus in his translation; Putnam 1960 is a sensitive example of this line of criticism.

19. Sinon, in *Aeneid* 2, is the great figure of Greek mendacity in Roman literature. Cicero speaks of the "ingenia ad fallendum parata" of the Greeks (*ad Q. Fr.* 1.2.4), and, more particularly, he identifies Alexandria, the place from which come the plots of the mimes, as the source of all trickery and deceit.

20. The reading of manuscript V at line 12 was "semper maesta tua carmina morte *tegam*," defended by Ellis 1889, 354–56, as meaning "I will keep close or veil in silence." This reading would obviate the problem that Catullus does not seem to have been true to his word, but see the arguments against it in Clausen 1970, 93, note 11. Wiseman 1969, 17–18, and Block 1984, 50–51, argue that Catullus fulfills his promise insofar as all of the remaining poems are in elegiacs, the meter of mourning.

21. Green 1990, 405. On displacement in Alexandrian literature, see Selden, forthcoming.

22. Catullus' *gremium* is a direct translation of Callimachus' *kolpous* (frag. 110.56 Pfeiffer).

23. Compare Vergil, *Georgic* 4, 287–88: "Qua Pellaei gens fortunata Canopi / accolit effuso stagnantem flumine Nilum." Catullus' *incola* makes a stronger emphasis on the fact that the Ptolemies are not Egyptians than Callimachus' *naietis* (58).

24. Plutarch, *Mor.* 11a, quoted in Green 1990, 82.

25. As Selden 1992 points out, this poem in which Catullus claims that he is unable to write poetry is itself full of poetic figures.

26. Sarkissian 1983 and Hubbard 1984 have interesting discussions of this poem in its entirety, both focusing on Catullus' problematization of the relation between art and personal experience. Sarkissian argues that in c.68 Catullus explores "the conflict between the world a poet can create in his art and the world in which he must live" (39), and that this conflict is related to another between the desperate attempt to cling to what little is left of the relationship with Lesbia and a realization that it is over. A very similar, if more theoretically sophisticated, approach is taken by Hubbard, for whom "the author's textual articulation of personal experience destabilizes itself into two antagonistic patterns of assertion—a 'mystified' self, which sublimates the author's fantasies and anxieties directly into the poetic construct, and a 'demystified' self which reconsiders experience and feeling through rational deliberation" (43).

The nature of Mallius' request has been the subject of some controversy revolving around the meaning of the expression "munera . . . et Musarum . . . et Veneris" (12). Some have argued that we have a hendiadys, meaning "love poetry," others that learned poetry is being distinguished from erotic, and a third group that Catullus is being asked to supply Mallius with a woman, or even his own sexual favors. For a survey of the views on this problem, see Sarkissian 1983, 46–47, note 15. In spite of "tibi . . . *utriusque* petenti" (39), I do not think that Mallius has requested two specific and different kinds of things, but rather that he has two kinds of needs, both of which can be fulfilled by a love poem. Hubbard 1984, 42, has some interesting thoughts on the fact that, in spite of this *recusatio*, Catullus produces a poem about love.

27. The two excuses are usually explained as referring to the "munera Musarum" and the "munera Veneris" (10) respectively.

28. I have changed Mynors's *Mani* to *Malli*. Manuscript V has *Mali* here.

29. Fordyce 1961, 347, argues that the *quod* clause is a regular feature of Latin epistolary style and introduces an indirect quotation; this requires the correction *Catullo* and the subjunctive *tepefactet* for V's unmetrical *tepefacit*. The two alternatives and their respective problems are well described in Fordyce's note.

30. *Carpitur* (35) in the passive is more likely to convey the erosion of life (aetas) than the full enjoyment of it, so when Catullus says of Rome "illic mea carpitur aetas," he expresses an ambivalent attitude to this "home."

31. Wiseman 1987, 331.

32. Wiseman 1987, 333–34, argues that Catullus' family may have been expected by the *coloni* to donate the bridge. Inscriptions from about this time mention Valerii who had been involved in erecting public buildings.

33. On the political aspects of this poem, and especially the significance of the phrase "sexagenarios de ponte deicere," see Cenerini 1989.

34. The text in line 32 is as emended by Voss; the manuscripts have the meaningless "Brixia chinea suppositum specula."

35. Mynors 1967 prints Lachmann's *corruerint* for the *cur iterent* of manuscript V, according to which line 93 would mean "give the stars cause to repeat 'Would that I might become a royal lock.'"

36. Baker 1960.

37. Playing with the very different senses of the verb *fero* in *detulerat* (108) and *ferunt* (109), Catullus brings the emotional and the literary into an ironic juxtaposition.

38. Tuplin 1981, 125–31, argues that Catullus' source for the *barathrum* simile is Euphorion's *Chiliades*.

# Chapter 9

1. De Man 1979, 20.

2. There is an excellent treatment of Catullus' influence on modern, mainly English-language, literature in Wiseman 1985, 211–45, partially focused on attitudes to Lesbia; Wiseman 1975 has the same focus but deals only with novels, of which there have been many. Duckett 1925 is a useful anthology of (English-

language) poetry that is inspired by Catullus, and McPeek 1939 deals with the same subject up to the eighteenth century. The bibliography of Holoka 1985, 286–96, is very useful, and to this one can now add Ludwig 1990 and Gaisser 1993, 193–271, on neo-Latin Catullan poetry.

3. Macaulay, cited by Munro 1938, 233–34.

4. Ginsberg writes:

"Malest Cornifici Tuo Catullo"

I'm happy, Kerouac, your madman Allen's
finally made it; discovered a new young cat,
and my imagination of an eternal boy
walks on the streets of San Francisco,
handsome and meets me in cafeterias
and loves me. Ah don't think I'm sickening.
You're angry at me. For all my lovers?
It's hard to eat shit, without any visions;
when they have eyes for me it's like heaven.

Ginsberg echoes Catullus wittily at the point where he anticipates Kerouac's response: "Ah don't think I'm sickening. / You're angry at me. For all my lovers?" (Irascor tibi. Sic meos amores? 38.6). Ginsberg 1984, 123. For a bohemian homosexual Catullus in a poem featuring the brotherhood of poets, see Lowell's "Words for Hart Crane":

Because I knew my Whitman like a book,
Stranger in America, tell my country: I
Catullus redivivus, once the rage
of the Village and Paris, used to play my role
of homosexual, wolfing the stray lambs
who hungered by the Place de la Concorde.

5. In the poems "To Catullus" (Swinburne 1925, 5.70), "Ave atque Vale; In Memory of Charles Baudelaire" (3.44–51), and "Ad Catullum" (3.155).

6. The title of Pierson Dixon's 1953 novel about Catullus is *Farewell Catullus*, words taken from the letter of condolence sent by Caesar to Catullus senior, though clearly they are also addressed by the author and his audience to the poet himself.

7. The term "homosocial" applies to all of the relationships between men described in this chapter, whose title "Between Men" refers to the title of Sedgwick 1985. Sedgwick uses the expression "homosocial desire" to posit "the potential unbrokenness of a continuum between homosocial and homosexual" (1), and her book charts with great subtlety the shifting relations between homosociality and patriarchy in English literature. I follow Sedgwick (20) in using the schema of the triangle in my analysis of "Catullan" homosociality.

8. "To Catullus," Swinburne 1925, 5.70.

9. Quoted by Duckett 1925, 197–98.

10. Dixon 1953, 73, for instance, has Lesbia "twist and tantalize" Catullus in order to get him to write lampoons for her political purposes. Other examples below.

11. Allinson 1913, 1–36. Wiseman 1985, 221–22, has a short account of her life and career.
12. Ferrero 1955, 99–100.
13. The same trio dominates Pierson Dixon's *Farewell Catullus* (1953).
14. Suetonius, *Jul.* 73.
15. The pun on the name of Caesar's assassin when Clodia tells Caesar she has "brutified" herself in order not to importune him with love (44) suggests that the fruition of their love is displaced onto the final encounter between Caesar and Brutus.

Caesar's patronizing vision of an aged Lesbia reminds us that in the Catullus literature a kind of revenge against Lesbia is supplied by those who have imagined her, post-Catullus, as an old, or degraded, woman. In Arthur Symons's poem "Lesbia in Old Age," the physically decrepit Lesbia says:

Let us live and love,
My Lesbia: yes and I shall live,
A hungering, thirsting shadow of
That love I gave and could not give.
I gave him pleasure, and I sold
To him and all men; he is dead,
And I am infamous and old,
And yet I am not quieted.
Take off your curses from my soul:
(Symons 1913, 17)

Marcel Schwob, in his *Vies Imaginaires* of 1896, kills off Clodia as follows: "She died toward the morning of a stifling night. . . . A fuller had paid her a quarter of an *as*; he lay in wait to take back the money in an alley at the twilight of dawn, and strangled her. Then he threw her corpse, its big eyes open, into the yellow water of the Tiber." (Quoted in Wiseman 1974, 110).

16. The references to Gaul and Britain indicate that the poem cannot have been written before late 55 B.C.E., and there are no references to anything after that date in the poems. It is generally assumed that c.51, the translation of Sappho that names Lesbia, is written at the beginning of Catullus' affair with her and that c.11, the only other poem in the Sapphic meter, marks the end of the affair. See, for instance, Friedricksmeyer 1983.

17. Schwabe 1862, 129, was probably the first to supply this context to c.11, and it was eagerly taken up (compare, for instance, Havelock 1939, 81, Merrill 1893, Kroll 1929).

18. Friedricksmeyer 1983, 75, stresses the reconciliation with the world of men, with Caesar, and with Roman *virtus* that goes with this repudiation of Lesbia. In Dixon's *Farewell Catullus*, Caesar is again a father figure who warns Catullus away from Lesbia. In that novel, Caesar wrongs Catullus by making love to the latter's slave and lover, Poppaea, and Catullus wrongs Caesar with his lampoons. But a letter in the epilogue (273–74) from Caesar to Catullus' father delivers the forgiveness that had been absent from the relation between Catullus and Lesbia.

19. Wiseman 1985, 243–44.

20. See, for example, Forsyth 1976 and Quinn 1972, 250–51.

21. This vision of the "vagina dentata" is conjured up from the Scylla of Catullus 60: "latrans infima inguinum parte" (2).

22. Copley's translation of 1957, for instance, has Catullus writing in the style of e. e. cummings.

23. A violent tough-mindedness is paraded in passages like:

> I'm in the saddle now,
> Riding the tornado—it could break the wings
> Right off my glider. (4)

See also the passage on page 224. It is striking that the novels about Catullus by Hardy 1957 (*City of Libertines*) and Jaro 1988 (*The Key*) both feature an extremely physically violent Catullus.

24. Compare this passage from Pierson Dixon's *Farewell Catullus*: "Since their return from Asia she [Poppaea, Catullus' slave and lover] had made him happy; or nearly, for he was troubled by moments of doubt. He was conscious that his poetic muse was becoming milder, more humane, more scholarly; flashes of wit and stormy passion came more rarely. Were Poppaea and her calming influence the cause? Ought he to break away, renounce contentment and plunge again into the intoxicating life of the capital? There Clodia waited, his Erinys, maddening and elusive. This way lay misery but it was the road to inspiration too" (248).

25. See "Deathwish Drang," Baxter 1973, 18.

26. "One can even identify a whole genre—going back to Landor and beyond—of poems on (or to) Catullus by poets who have translated him . . ." (Wiseman 1985, 242).

27. Squire 1923, 57.

28. To the examples cited on pages 119–120 and 270 n. 13 one could add Bagg 1965, 65: "When each confronts an emotional disaster, not so austerely charged as tragedy, yet nearly beyond each man's powers to master, poetry becomes for both a possible means to extend mastery."

29. Sisson had published translations of Catullus earlier, in 1966.

30. Something of the spirit of Sisson's poem is apparent in Camille Paglia 1991's version of Catullus and Lesbia: "Men and women are suddenly free, but freedom is a flood of superfluous energy, a vicious circle of agitation, quest, satiation, exhaustion, ennui" (131). Again: "Lesbia, the wellborn Clodia, introduces to Rome a depraved sexual persona that had been current, according to aggrieved comment of the Old Testament, for a thousand years in Babylon. Female receptivity becomes a sinkhole of vice, the vagina a collector of pestilence to poison Roman nobility and bring it to an end" (132).

31. One is reminded of what Catullus' brother says to him a propos his adultery in Allinson 1913, 16–17: "I could wish you had not fallen in love with another man's wife, and if he were still living I should try to convince you of the folly of it. But I know that this hot heart of yours is as pure as the snow we see on the Alps in midsummer. That is all I need to know."

32. Compare Friedricksmeyer 1983, quoted page 12.

33. Turnbull's poem could be described as a combination of Catullus 41, in which Ameana is told she is charging too much for a woman of her appearance, with poems like c.8, where Catullus reveals his hopeless infatuation with Lesbia.

## Conclusion

1. Alpers 1983, 202.
2. This was pointed out to me by Jennifer Church.
3. Fitzgerald 1994.
4. Skutsch 1970 points out that *papirus* means both "paper" and "light."

# Bibliography

Adams, J. N. 1982. *The Latin Sexual Vocabulary*. Baltimore: The Johns Hopkins University Press.
Adler, Eve. 1981. *Catullan Self-Revelation*. New York: Arno.
Allinson, A. C. E. 1913. *Roads from Rome*. New York: Macmillan.
Alpers, Svetlana. 1983. *The Art of Describing: Dutch Art in the Seventeenth Century*. Chicago: University of Chicago Press.
Argento, Dominick. 1981. *I Hate and I Love: A Cycle for Mixed Chorus and Percussion*. London: Boosey and Hawkes.
Arkins, Brian. 1979. "Glubit in Catullus." *Liverpool Classical Monthly* 4, no. 5: 85–86.
Arkins, Brian. 1982. *Sexuality in Catullus*. Hildesheim: Olms.
Auden, W. H. 1976. Edward Mendelson, ed., *Collected Poems*. London: Faber and Faber.
Austin, R. 1960 (3d ed.). *M. Tulli Ciceronis pro Caelio oratio*. Oxford: Oxford University Press.
Baehrens, Aemilius. 1885. *Catulli Veronensis liber*. 2. Leipzig: Teubner.
Bagg, Robert. 1965. "Some Versions of Lyric Impasse in Shakespeare and Catullus." *Arion* 4, no. 1: 64–95.
Baker, Sheridan. 1960. "Lesbia's Foot." *Classical Philology* 55: 171–73.
Bakhtin, Mikhail. 1981. *The Dialogic Imagination*. Austin: University of Texas.
Balsdon, J. 1979. *Romans and Aliens*. London: Duckworth.
Bardon, Henry. 1970. *Propositions sur Catulle*. Brussels: Latomus.
Batstone, William. 1993. "Logic, Rhetoric and Poiesis." *Helios* 20, no. 2: 143–72.
Baudelaire, Charles. 1961. *Les Fleurs du Mal*. Paris: Editions Garnier.
Baxter, James. 1973. *Runes*. London: Oxford University Press.

Bayet, Jean. 1953. "Catulle: La Grèce et Rome." *Entretiens sur l'antiquité classique* 2: 3–39. Geneva: Fondation Hardt.
Beard, Mary, and Michael Crawford. 1985. *Rome in the Late Republic*. Ithaca: Cornell University Press.
Bernstein, William. 1985. "A Sense of Taste: Catullus 13." *Classical Journal* 80: 127–30.
Bianconi, Lorenzo. 1987. *Music in the Seventeenth Century*. Cambridge: Cambridge University Press.
Bignone, Ettore. 1945. *Storia della letteratura latina* 2. Florence: Sansone.
Bishop, J. D. 1971. "Catullus 85: Structure, Hellenistic Parallels and the Topos." *Latomus* 30: 633–42.
Block, Elizabeth. 1984. "Carmen 65 and the Arrangement of Catullus' Poetry." *Ramus* 13: 48–59.
Bollack, Mayotte. 1978. *La Raison de Lucrèce*. Paris: Editions de Minuit.
Boucher, J.-P. 1956. "A propos du carmen 64 de Catulle." *Revue des études latines* 34: 191–202.
Bower, E. W. 1974. "*Ineptiae* and *Ioci*." *Latomus* 33, no. 3: 523–28.
Bramble, J. C. 1970. "Structure and Ambiguity in Catullus LXIV." *Proceedings of the Cambridge Philological Society* 16: 22–41.
Brilliant, Richard. 1984. *Visual Narratives: Storytelling in Etruscan and Roman Art*. Ithaca: Cornell University Press.
Bryson, Norman. 1990. *Looking at the Overlooked: Four Essays in Still Life Painting*. London: Reaktion.
Buchheit, Vinzenz. 1961. "Catull an Cato von Utica (c.56)." *Hermes* 89: 345–56.
Buchheit, Vinzenz. 1975. "Catulls Literarkritik und Kallimachos." *Grazer Beitraege* 4: 21–50.
Buchheit, Vinzenz. 1976a. "Catull c.50 als Programm und Bekenntnis." *Rheinisches Museum* 119: 162–80.
Buchheit, Vinzenz. 1976b. "Sal et lepos versiculorum (Catull c.16)." *Hermes* 104, no. 3: 331–47.
Buechner, Karl. 1977. "Der 'Liebesroman' des Catull." *Symbolae Osloenses* 52: 53–78.
Burgess, Dana. 1986. "Catullus C.50: The Exchange of Poetry." *American Journal of Philology* 107: 576–86.
Cairns, Francis. 1969. "Catullus 1." *Mnemosyne* 22: 153–58.
Carrié, Jean-Michel. 1993. "The Soldier." In Andrea Giardina, ed., *The Romans*, 100–37. Chicago: University of Chicago Press.
Cèbe, J-P. 1965. "Sur les trivialités de Catulle." *Revue des études latines* 43: 221–29.
Celan, Paul. 1970. *Ausgewaehlte Gedichte, Zwei Reden*. Frankfurt: Suhrkamp.
Celentano, Maria. 1991. "Il fiore reciso dall'aratro: ambiguità di una similitudine (Catull. 11, 22–24)." *Quaderni urbinati di cultura classica* 27, no 1: 83–100.
Cenerini, Francesca. 1989. "*O colonia quae cupis ponte ludere longo* (Cat., 17): Cultura e politica." *Athenaeum* 67: 41–55.

Cerri, Giovanni. 1989. "Il Carme 56 di Catullo e un' iscrizione greca di recente pubblicazione." *Quaderni urbinati di cultura classica* 31, no. 1: 59–65.
Citroni, M. 1975. *M. Valerii Martialis epigrammaton liber 1*. Florence: La Nuova Italia.
Clack, J. 1976. "Otium tibi molestum est: Catullus 50 and 51." *Classical Bulletin* 52: 50–53.
Clausen, W. 1970. "Catullus and Callimachus." *Harvard Studies in Classical Philology* 74: 85–94.
Colin, Jean. 1954. "L'Heure des cadeaux pour Thallus le cinède." *Revue des études latines* 32: 106–10.
Commager, Steele. 1965. "Notes on Some Poems of Catullus." *Harvard Studies in Classical Philology* 70: 83–110.
Conte, Gian Biagio. 1986. *The Rhetoric of Imitation*. Ithaca: Cornell University Press.
Copley, Frank. 1949. "Emotional Conflict and Its Significance in the Lesbia-poems of Catullus." *American Journal of Philology* 70: 22–40.
Copley, Frank. 1957. *Catullus: The Complete Poetry*. Ann Arbor: University of Michigan Press.
Copley, Frank. 1958. "Catullus c.4: The World of the Poem." *Transactions of the American Philological Society* 89: 9–13.
Cotton, John. 1982. "Catullus at Sirmio." *Ambit* 89: 54–55.
Courtney, Edward. 1993. *The Fragmentary Latin Poets*. Oxford: Clarendon Press.
Croce, Benedetto. 1950. *Poesia antica e moderna*. Bari: Laterza.
Crowther, N. B. "Catullus and the Traditions of Latin Poetry." *Classical Philology* 66: 246–49.
Culler, Jonathan. 1981. *The Pursuit of Signs: Semiotics, Literature, Deconstruction*. Ithaca: Cornell University Press.
Curran, Leo. 1966. "Gellius and the Lover's Pallor: A Note on Catullus 80." *Arion* 5: 24–27.
Curran, Leo. 1975. Review of Kenneth Quinn, *Catullus: The Poems*. *American Journal of Philology* 96: 312–14.
Daly, L. W. 1952. "Callimachus and Catullus." *Classical Philology* 47: 97–99.
D'Arms, John. 1984. "Control, Companionship and *Clientela*: Some Social Functions of the Roman Communal Meal." *Echos du monde classique* 28: 327–48.
D'Arms, John. 1990. "The Roman *convivium* and the Ideal of Equality." In Oswyn Murray, ed., *Sympotica: A Symposium on the Symposium*. Oxford: Oxford University Press, 308–20.
David, Jean-Michel. 1983. "Les orateurs des municipes à Rome: Intégration, réticences et snobismes." In *Les "bourgeoisies" municipales aux 11e et 1e siècles av. J.-C.*, 309–23. Paris: Editions du CNRS.
De Man, Paul. 1979. *Allegories of Reading*. New Haven: Yale University Press.
De Maria, Robert. 1965. *Clodia*. New York: St. Martin's Press.

Dee, James. 1982. "Catullus 64 and the Heroic Age: A Reply." *Illinois Classical Studies* 8, no. 1: 98–109.
Deroux, C. 1973. "L'Identité de Lesbie." In *Aufstieg und Niedergang der Roemischen Welt* 1, no, 3: 390–416. Berlin: De Gruyter.
Dettmer, Helena. 1989. "Catullus 13: A Nose is a Nose is a Nose." *Syllecta Classica* 1: 75–85.
Dixon, Pierson. 1953. *Farewell Catullus*. London: Hollis and Carter.
Duckett, Eleanor. 1925. *Catullus in Poetry*. Smith College Classical Studies 6. Northampton, Mass.: Smith College.
Dupont, Florence. 1985. *L'Acteur-Roi, ou, le théâtre dans la Rome antique*. Paris: Les Belles Lettres.
Dyson, M. 1973. "Catullus 8 and 76." *Classical Quarterly* 23: 127–43.
Eagleton, Terry. 1990. *The Ideology of the Aesthetic*. Oxford: Blackwell.
Edmunds, Lowell. 1982. "The Latin Invitation-Poem: What is it? Where Did It Come From?" *American Journal of Philology* 103, no. 2: 184–88.
Edwards, Catharine. 1993. *The Politics of Immorality in Ancient Rome*. Cambridge: Cambridge University Press.
Ellis, Robinson. 1889. *A Commentary on Catullus*. 2d ed. Oxford: Clarendon Press.
Ferguson, John. 1988. *Catullus*. Oxford: Clarendon Press.
Ferrero, Leonardo. 1955. *Un' introduzione a Catullo*. Turin: Universita di Torino.
Finamore, John. 1974. "Catullus 50 and 51: Friendship, Love and *Otium*." *Classical World* 78, no. 1: 11–19.
Fitzgerald, William. 1984. "Lucretius' Cure for Love in the *De Rerum Natura*." *Classical World* 78, no. 2: 73–86.
Fitzgerald, William. 1988. "Power and Impotence in Horace's *Epodes*." *Ramus* 17, no. 2: 176–91.
Fitzgerald, William. 1992. "Catullus and the Reader: The Erotics of Poetry." *Arethusa* 25: 419–43.
Fitzgerald, William. 1994. "The Questionability of Music." *Representations* 46: 121–47.
Fordyce, C. J. 1961. *Catullus: A Commentary*. Oxford: Oxford University Press.
Forsyth, Phyllis. 1976. "Catullus: the Mythic Persona." *Latomus* 35, no. 3: 555–66.
Forsyth, Phyllis. 1979. "Order and Meaning in Catullus 97–99." *Classical World* 72: 403–8.
Forsyth, Phyllis. 1985. "Gifts and Giving: Catullus 12–14." *Classical World* 78, no. 6: 571–74.
Fotiou, A. 1975. "Catullus 11: A New Approach." *Grazer Beitraege* 3: 151–58.
Foucault, Michel. 1978. *An Introduction*. Vol. 1 of *The History of Sexuality*. Middlesex: Penguin.
Foucault, Michel. 1979. "What Is an Author?" In Josue Harari, ed., *Textual Strategies: Perspectives in Post-Structuralist Criticism*, 141–60. Ithaca: Cornell University Press.

Frank, Tenney. 1928. *Catullus and Horace: Two Poets in Their Environment.* New York: Holt.
Friedlaender, Ludwig. 1936. *Roman Life and Manners under the Early Empire* 2. London: Routledge.
Friedricksmeyer, Ernst. 1983. "The Beginning and the End of Catullus' Longus Amor." *Symbolae Osloenses* 58: 63–88.
Friedricksmeyer, Ernst. 1993. "Method and Interpretation: Catullus 1." *Helios* 20, no. 2: 89–105.
Gaisser, Julia. 1982. "Catullus and His First Interpreters: Antonius Parthenius and Angelo Poliziano." *Transactions of the American Philological Association* 112: 83–106.
Gaisser, Julia. 1993. *Catullus and His Renaissance Readers.* Oxford: Oxford University Press.
Genovese, E. N. 1974. "Symbolism in the Passer Poems." *Maia* 26: 121–25.
Giangrande, G. 1975. "Catullus' Lyrics on the Passer." *Museum Philologum Londiniense* 1: 137–46.
Gillespie, Stuart. 1988. *The Poets on the Classics.* London: Routledge.
Ginsberg, Allen. 1984. *Collected Poems 1947–1980.* New York: Harper and Row.
Glenn, Justin. 1981. "Ariadne's Daydream (Cat.64.158–63)." *Classical Journal* 76, no. 2: 110–16.
Gold, Barbara. 1987. *Literary Patronage in Greece and Rome.* Chapel Hill: University of North Carolina Press.
Gould, G. P. 1958. "A New Text of Catullus." *Phoenix* 12, no. 3: 93–116.
Granarolo, Jean. 1967. *L'Oeuvre de Catulle.* Paris: Les Belles Lettres.
Granarolo, Jean. 1972. "Liens entre le baroque decoratif et la poèsie á la fin de la république romaine." *Euphrosyne* n.s. 5: 429–35.
Granarolo, Jean. 1981. "Encore à propos de la *Crux* Catulle XXV, 5: Essai de solution." *Latomus* 40, no. 3: 571–79.
Green, Peter. 1990. *Alexander to Actium: The Historical Evolution of the Hellenistic Age.* Berkeley: University of California Press.
Griffin, Jasper. 1985. *Latin Poets and Roman Life.* Chapel Hill: University of North Carolina Press.
Grimal, Pierre. 1984 (3d ed.). *Les Jardins Romains.* Paris: Fayard.
Gruen, Erich. 1992. *Culture and National Identity in Republican Rome.* Ithaca: Cornell University Press.
Habinek, Thomas. 1992a. "Grecian Wonders and Roman Woe: The Romantic Rejection of Rome and Its Consequences for the Study of Roman Literature." In Karl Galinsky, ed., *The Interpretation of Roman Poetry: Empiricism or Hermeneutics?* 227–42. Frankfurt: Lang.
Habinek, Thomas. 1992b. "An Aristocracy of Virtue: Seneca on the Beginnings of Wisdom." *Yale Classical Studies* 29: 187–203.
Hallett, Judith. 1978. "Divine Unction: Some Further Thoughts on Catullus 13." *Latomus* 37: 747–48.

Hallett, Judith. 1988. "Catullus on Composition." *Classical World* 81, no. 5: 395–401.
Hallett, Judith. 1989. "Women as *Same* and *Other* in the Classical Roman Elite." *Helios* 16: 59–78.
Halperin, David. 1990. *One Hundred Years of Homosexuality.* New York: Routledge.
Hardy, W. G. 1957. *The City of Libertines.* New York: Appleton-Century-Crofts.
Harmon, D. P. 1973. "Nostalgia for the Age of Heroes in Catullus 64." *Latomus* 32, no. 2: 311–31.
Havelock, E. A. 1939. *The Lyric Genius of Catullus.* Oxford: Blackwell.
Haven, Richard. 1989. "Noises Off: Catullus on Stage." *Massachusetts Review* 30, no. 4: 571–72.
Heiden, Bruce. 1991. "Sermon from Abroad." *Arion* 1, no. 3: 202–8.
Heine, Rolf, ed. 1975. *Catull: Wege der Forschung, 308.* Darmstadt: Wissenschaftliche Buchgesellschaft.
Hellegouarc'h, J. 1963. *Le vocabulaire latin des relations politiques sous la republique.* Paris: Les Belles Lettres.
Henderson, J. 1991. (2d ed.). *The Maculate Muse: Obscene Language in Attic Comedy.* New Haven: Yale University Press.
Holoka, James. 1985. *Gaius Valerius Catullus: A Systematic Bibliography.* New York: Garland.
Hosek, Chaviva, and Patricia Parker, eds. 1985. *Lyric Poetry: Beyond New Criticism.* Ithaca: Cornell University Press.
Housman, A. E. 1931. "*Praefanda.*" *Hermes* 66: 402–12.
Hubbard, Thomas. 1983. "The Catullan Libellus." *Philologus* 127: 218–37.
Hubbard, Thomas. 1984. "Catullus 68: The Text as Self-Demystification." *Arethusa* 17, no. 1: 29–49.
Hutchinson, G. O. 1988. *Hellenistic Poetry.* Oxford: Oxford University Press.
Janan, Micaela. 1994. *When the Lamp Is Shattered: Desire and Narrative in Catullus.* Carbondale: Southern Illinois University Press.
Jaro, Benita. 1988. *The Key.* New York: Dodd, Mead.
Jed, Stephanie. 1989. *Chaste Thinking: The Rape of Lucretia and the Birth of Humanism.* Bloomington: Indiana University Press.
Jenkyns, Richard. 1982. *Three Classical Poets: Sappho, Catullus, and Juvenal.* Cambridge, Mass.: Harvard University Press.
Jocelyn, H. D. 1969. "The Poet Cn. Naevius, P. Cornelius Scipio, and Q. Caecilius Metellus." *Antichthon* 3: 32–47.
Jocelyn, H. D. 1979. "Catullus 58 and Ausonius Ep.71." *Liverpool Classical Monthly* 4, no. 5: 87–91.
Jocelyn, H. D. 1980. "On Some Unnecessarily Indecent Interpretations of Catullus 2 and 3." *American Journal of Philology* 101: 421–24.
Jocelyn, H. D. 1985. "Concerning an American View of Latin Sexual Humour." *Echos du monde antique* n.s. 29, no. 4: 1–30.
Johnson, W. R. 1982. *The Idea of Lyric: Lyric Modes in Ancient and Modern Poetry.* Berkeley: University of California Press.

Kay, Nigel. 1985. *Martial Book XI: A Commentary.* New York: Oxford University Press.
Keats, John. 1970. *The Complete Poems*, ed. Miriam Allott. London: Longman.
Khan, H. 1967. "The Humour of Catullus, Carm.IV, and the Theme of Virgil, Catalepton X." *American Journal of Philology* 88: 163-72.
Kidd, D. A. 1970. "Some Problems in Catullus LXVI." *Antichthon* 4: 38-49.
Klingner, Friedrich. 1964. "Catulls Pelus-Epos." In *Studien zu griechischen und roemischen Literatur*, 165-224. Zurich: Artemis.
Konstan, David. 1972. "Two Kinds of Love in Catullus." *Classical Journal* 68: 102-6.
Konstan, David. 1977. *Catullus' Indictment of Rome.* Amsterdam: Hakkert.
Konstan, David. 1979. "An Interpretation of Catullus 21." In C. Deroux, ed., *Studies in Latin Literature and Roman History.* Brussels: Latomus.
Krenkel, W. 1981. "Tonguing." *Wissenschaftliche Zeitschrift Rostock* 30, no. 5: 37-54.
Kroll, Wilhelm. 1929. *C. Valerius Catullus: Poemata.* 2d ed. Leipzig: Teubner.
Lateiner, Donald. 1977. "Obscenity in Catullus." *Ramus* 6, no. 1: 15-32.
Latta, Bernd. 1974. "Zu Catulls Carmen 1." *Museum Helveticum* 29: 201-13.
Latte, Kurt. 1967. *Roemische Religionsgeschichte.* Munich: Beck.
Leach, Eleanor. 1988. *The Rhetoric of Space: Literary and Artistic Representations of Space in Republican and Augustan Rome.* Princeton: Princeton University Press.
Lebek, W. 1982. "*Gemini* and *Gemelli:* Anthologia Latina (Riese) 457,8 and Catull. 57,6." *Rheinisches Museum* 125: 176-80.
Lee, Guy. 1990. *The Poems of Catullus.* Oxford: Clarendon Press.
Lee, M. O. 1962. "Illustrative Elisions in Catullus." *Transactions of the American Philological Association* 93: 144-53.
Lenz, Friedrich. 1963. "Catulliana." *Rivista di cultura classica e medievale* 5: 62-70.
Lindsay, Jack. 1929. *The Complete Poetry of Gaius Catullus.* London: Fanfrolico Press.
Lipking, Lawrence. 1988. *Abandoned Women and Poetic Tradition.* Chicago: University of Chicago Press.
Littman, R. 1977. "The Unguent of Venus: Catullus 13." *Latomus* 36: 123-28.
Ludwig, Walther. 1990. "The Origin and Development of the Catullan Style in Neo-Latin Poetry." In Peter Goodman and Oswyn Murray, eds., *Latin Poetry and the Classical Tradition*, 183-97. Oxford: Clarendon Press.
Lyne, R. 1978. "The Neoteric Poets." *Classical Quarterly* 28: 167-87.
Lyne, R. 1980. *The Latin Love Poets.* Oxford: Oxford University Press.
Macleod, Colin. 1973. "Parody and Personalities in Catullus (Catullus 50, 55, 58b, 24, 15, 21, 23, 16, 11, 89)." *Classical Quarterly* 23: 294-303.

MacMullen, Ramsay. 1982. "Roman Attitudes to Greek Love." *Historia* 32: 484–502.
MacMullen, Ramsay. 1986. "Personal Power in the Roman Empire." *American Journal of Philology* 107: 512–24.
Marcadé, Jean. 1968. *Roma amor: Essai sur les représentations érotiques dans l'art étrusque et romain*. Geneva: Nagel.
Marcovich, Miroslav. 1982. "Catullus 13 and Philodemus 23." *Quaderni urbinati di cultura classica* 11: 131–38.
Marmorale, Enzo. 1957 (2d. ed.). *L'Ultimo Catullo*. Napoli: Edizioni Scientifiche Italiane.
Martin, Charles. 1992. *Catullus*. New Haven: Yale University Press.
Martin, Ronald, ed. 1976. *Terence: Adelphoe*. Cambridge: Cambridge University Press.
McAfee, Thomas. 1983. *My Confidant Catullus*. Connecticut: Ives St. Press.
McGushin, P. 1967. "Catullus' *Sanctae foedus amicitiae*." *Classical Philology* 62, no. 2: 85–93.
McPeek, James. 1939. *Catullus in Strange and Distant Britain*. Cambridge, Mass.: Harvard University Press.
Merrill, Elmer. 1893. *Catullus*. Boston: Ginn.
Mill, John Stuart. 1976. *Essays on Poetry*, ed. F. Parvin Sharpless. Columbia: University of South Carolina Press.
Miller, Paul Allen. 1988. "Catullus, C. 70: A Poem and Its Hypothesis," *Helios* 15: 127–32.
Minyard, John Douglas. 1985. *Lucretius and the Late Republic*. Leiden: Brill.
Minyard, John Douglas. 1988. "The Source of the *Catulli Veronensis liber*." *Classical World* 81, no. 5: 343–53.
Monteil, Pierre. 1964. *Beau et laid en latin*. Paris: Klincksieck.
Most, G. W. 1981. "On the Arrangement of Catullus' Carmina Maiora." *Philologus* 125: 109–25.
Mulvey, Laura. 1975. "Visual Pleasure and Narrative Cinema." *Screen* 16, no. 3: 8–18.
Munro. H. A. J. 1938. *Criticisms and Elucidations of Catullus*. New York: Stechert.
Mynors, Roger. 1967 (3d ed.). *C. Valerii Catulli carmina*. Oxford: Clarendon Press.
Nadeau, Y. 1980. "O passer nequam (Catullus 2–3)." *Latomus* 39: 879–90.
Neudling, Chester. 1955. *A Prosopography to Catullus*. Iowa Studies in Classical Philology 12. London: Oxford.
Newman, J. K. 1990. *Roman Catullus and the Modification of the Roman Sensibility*. Hildesheim: Weidmann.
Nielsen, Rosemary. 1987. "Catullus and *sal* (Poem 10)." *Antiquité Classique* 56: 148–61.
Nisbet, R. G. M., and Margaret Hubbard. 1970. *A Commentary on Horace Odes Book One*. Oxford: Clarendon Press.
O'Connell, Michael. 1977. "Pictorialism and Meaning in Catullus 64." *Latomus* 36: 746–56.

Offermann, H. 1977. "Zu Catulls Gedichtcorpus." *Rheinisches Museum* 120: 269–302.
Opelt, Ilona. 1965. *Die Lateinischen Schimpfwoerter und Verwandte sprachliche Erscheinungen.* Heidelberg: Winter.
Orff, Carl. 1955. *Catulli carmina: Ludi scaenici.* Mainz: Schott.
Otto, A. 1890. *Die Sprichwoerter und sprichwoertlichen Redensarten der Roemer.* Leipzig: Olms.
Paglia, Camille. 1991. *Sexual Personae.* New Haven: Yale University Press.
Parker, W. H. 1988. *Priapea: Poems for a Phallic God.* London: Croom Helm.
Parry, Adam. 1963. "The Two Voices of Virgil's *Aeneid.*" *Arion* 2: 66–80.
Pearcy, L. T. 1980. "Catullus 2b or not 2b." *Mnemosyne* 33: 152–62.
Pease, Donald. 1990. "Author." In Frank Lentricchia and Thomas McLaughlin, eds., *Critical Terms for Literary Study*, 106–117. Chicago: University of Chicago Press.
Pedrick, Victoria. 1986. "*Qui potis est, inquis?* Audience Roles in Catullus." *Arethusa* 19: 187–207.
Penella, Robert. 1976. "A Note on (De)Glubere." *Hermes* 104: 118–20.
Pound, Ezra. 1948 (2d ed.). *Selected Poems.* London: Faber.
Pucci, Pietro. 1961. "Il Carme 50 di Catullo." *Maia* 13: 249–56.
Putnam, Michael. 1960. "Catullus 66.75–88." *Classical Philology* 55: 223–28.
Putnam, Michael. 1961. "The Art of Catullus 64." *Harvard Studies in Classical Philology* 65: 165–205.
Putnam, Michael. 1962. "Catullus' Journey (*Carm*.4)." *Classical Philology* 57: 136–45.
Putnam, Michael. 1974. "Catullus 11: The Ironies of Integrity." *Ramus* 3: 70–86.
Putnam, Michael. 1982. *Essays in Latin Lyric, Elegiac and Epic.* Princeton: Princeton University Press.
Quinn, Kenneth. 1959. *The Catullan Revolution.* Carlton: Melbourne University Press.
Quinn, Kenneth. 1970. *Catullus: The Poems.* London: Macmillan.
Quinn, Kenneth. 1972. *Catullus: An Interpretation.* London: Batsford.
Quinn, Kenneth. 1982. "The Poet and His Audience in the Augustan Age." In Wolfgang Haase, ed., *Aufstieg und Niedergang der Roemischen Welt* 31, no. 1. Berlin: De Gruyter.
Ramage, Edwin. 1973. *Urbanitas: Ancient Sophistication and Refinement.* Oklahoma: Oklahoma University Press.
Randall, J. G. 1979. "Mistresses' Pseudonyms in Latin Elegy." *Liverpool Classical Monthly* 4: 27–35.
Rankin, H. D. 1972. "The Progress of Pessimism in Catullus, Poems 2–11." *Latomus* 31: 744–51.
Rankin, H. D. 1975. "Catullus and the Privacy of Love." *Wiener Studien* 9: 67–74.
Rankin, H. D. 1976. "Catullus and Incest." *Eranos* 74: 113–21.

Raphael, Fredric, and Kenneth Macleish, trans. 1978. *The Poems of Catullus.* London: Cape.
Reckford, Kenneth. 1958. "Some Appearances of the Golden Age." *Classical Journal* 54: 79–87.
Reinach, Salomon. 1922. *Répertoire de peintures Grecques et Romaines.* Paris: Leroux.
Richardson, N. J. 1974. *The Homeric Hymn to Demeter.* Oxford: Oxford University Press.
Richlin, Amy. 1981. "The Meaning of *Irrumare* in Catullus and Martial." *Classical Philology* 76: 40–46.
Richlin, Amy. 1984. "Invective Against Women in Roman Satire." *Arethusa* 17, no. 1: 67–80.
Richlin, Amy. 1988. "Systems of Food Imagery in Catullus." *Classical World* 81: 355–63.
Richlin, Amy. 1992a (rev. ed.). *The Garden of Priapus: Sexuality and Aggression in Roman Humor.* New York: Oxford University Press.
Richlin, Amy. 1992b. "Making Gender in the Roman Forum." Paper read at the American Philological Association, New Orleans.
Richlin, Amy. 1993. "Not Before Homosexuality: The Materiality of the *Cinaedus* and the Roman Law Against Love Between Men." *Journal of the History of Sexuality* 3, no. 4: 523–73.
Rosenthal, M. L. 1967. *The New Poets: American and British Poetry Since World War II.* New York: Oxford University Press.
Ross, David. 1969. *Style and Tradition in Catullus.* Cambridge, Mass.: Harvard University Press.
Ross, David. 1975. *Backgrounds to Augustan Poetry: Gallus, Elegy and Rome.* Cambridge: Cambridge University Press.
Rubino, Carl. 1975. "The Erotic World of Catullus." *Classical World* 68, no. 5: 289–98.
Saint Denis, E. de. 1965. *Essais sur le rire et le sourire des Latins.* Paris: Publications de l'Université de Dijon.
Sarkissian, John. 1983. *Catullus 68: An Interpretation.* Leiden: Brill.
Schaefer, Eckart. 1966. *Das Verhaeltnis von Erlebnis und Kunstgestalt bei Catull.* Wiesbaden: Steiner.
Schmidt, Ernst. 1976. "Gemelli (Catull, c.57,6)." *Rheinisches Museum* 119: 349–51.
Schmidt, Ernst. 1985. *Catull.* Heidelberg: Winter.
Schwabe, Ludwig. 1862. *Quaestiones Catullianae.* Giessen: Ricker.
Scott, William. 1969. "Catullus and Cato (c.56)." *Classical Philology* 64: 24–29.
Scott, William. 1971. "Catullus and Caesar." *Classical Philology* 56, no. 1: 17–25.
Seager, R. 1974. "Venustus, lepidus, bellus, salsus: Notes on the Language of Catullus." *Latomus* 33: 891–94.
Sedgwick, Eve. 1985. *Between Men: English Literature and Male Homosocial Desire.* New York: Columbia University Press.

Segal, Charles. 1968. "The Order of Catullus, Poems 2–11." *Latomus* 27: 305–21.
Segal, Charles. 1970. "Catullan *Otiosi*: The Lover and the Poet." *Greece and Rome* 17: 25–31.
Selden, Daniel. 1992. "*Ceveat Lector*: Catullus and the Rhetoric of Performance." In R. Hexter and D. Selden, eds., *Innovations of Antiquity*, 461–512. New York: Routledge.
Selden, Daniel. Forthcoming. "Alibis." *Classical Antiquity*.
Silverman, Kaja. 1988. *The Acoustic Mirror*. Bloomington: Indiana University Press.
Sisson, C. H. 1974. *In the Trojan Ditch: Collected Poems and Selected Translations*. Cheshire: Carcanet Press.
Skinner, Marilyn. 1971. "Catullus 8: The Comic *amator* as *eiron*." *Classical Journal* 66, no. 4: 298–305.
Skinner, Marilyn. 1972. "The Unity of Catullus 68: The Structure of 68a." *Transactions of the American Philological Association* 103, 433–39.
Skinner, Marilyn. 1973. "The Unity of Catullus 68: The Structure of 68a." *Transactions of the American Philological Association* 103: 495–512.
Skinner, Marilyn. 1979a. "Parasites and Strange Bedfellows: A Study in Catullus' Political Imagery." *Ramus* 8, no. 2: 137–52.
Skinner, Marilyn. 1979b. "Ameana, Puella Defututa." *Classical Journal* 74, no. 2: 110–14.
Skinner, Marilyn. 1981. *Catullus' Passer: The Arrangement of the Book of Polymetric Poems*. New York: Arno.
Skinner, Marilyn. 1982. "Pretty Lesbius." *Transactions of the American Philological Association* 112: 197–208.
Skinner, Marilyn. 1988. "Aesthetic Patterning in Catullus: Textual Structures, Systems of Imagery and Book Arrangements: Introduction." *Classical World* 81, no. 5: 337–40.
Skinner, Marilyn. 1989. "*Ut Decuit Cinaediorem*: Power, Gender and Urbanity in Catullus 10." *Helios* 16: 7–23.
Skinner, Marilyn. 1991. "The Dynamics of Catullan Obscenity: cc.37, 58 and 11." *Syllecta classica* 3: 1–11.
Skinner, Marilyn. 1993. "*Ego mulier*: The Construction of Male Sexuality in Catullus." *Helios* 20, no. 2: 107–29.
Skutsch, Otto. 1970. "The Book Under the Bushel." *Bulletin of the Institute of Classical Studies of the University of London* 17: 148.
Skutsch, Otto. 1980. "Catullus 58.4–5." *Liverpool Classical Monthly* 5, no. 1: 21.
Slater, Niall. 1985. *Plautus in Performance: The Theatre of the Mind*. Princeton: Princeton University Press.
Slater, W. 1974. "Pueri, Turba Minuta." *Bulletin of the Institute of Classical Studies of the University of London* 21: 133–40.
Squire, J. C. 1923. *American Poems and Others*. London: Hodder and Stoughton.

Starr, Raymond. 1991. "Reading Aloud: *Lectores* and Roman Reading." *Classical Journal* 86: 337–43.
Stehle, Eva. 1986. "Response." *Arethusa* 19, no. 2: 214–20.
Stigers, Eva. 1977. "Retreat from the Male: Catullus 62 and Sappho's Erotic Flowers." *Ramus* 6, no. 2: 83–102.
Svenbro, Jesper. 1988. *Phrasikleia: Anthropologie de la lecture en grèce ancienne*. Paris: La Decouverte.
Sweet, D. R. 1987. "Catullus 11: A Study in Perspective." *Latomus* 46: 510–26.
Swinburne, Algernon. 1925. Reprint, 1968. *The Complete Works of Algernon Charles Swinburne*, ed. Sir Edmund Gosse and Thomas Wise. New York: Russell and Russell.
Symons, Arthur. 1913. *Knave of Hearts*. London: Heineman.
Syndikus, H. P. 1984. *Catull: Eine Interpretation*. 3 vols. Darmstadt: Wissenschaftliche Buchgesellschaft.
Taylor, Lily. 1968. "Republican and Augustan Writers Enrolled in the Equestrian Centuries." *Transactions of the American Philological Association* 99: 469–86.
Tennyson, Alfred. 1987 (2d ed.). *The Poems of Tennyson*, ed. Christopher Ricks. 3 vols. Berkeley: University of California Press.
Thierfelder, A. 1956. "Obscaenus." In *Navicula Chiloniensis: Studia Philologica F. Jacoby Oblata*, 98–106. Leyden.
Thomas, Richard. 1982. "Catullus and the Polemics of Poetic Reference: Poem 64.1–18." *American Journal of Philology* 103, no. 2: 144–64.
Thomas, Richard. 1993. "Sparrows, Hares and Doves: A Catullan Metaphor and Its Tradition." *Helios* 20, no. 2: 131–42.
Tompkins, Jane. 1980. *Reader-Response Criticism: From Formalism to Post-Structuralism*. Baltimore: The Johns Hopkins University Press.
Thomson, D. F. S. 1967. "Catullus and Cicero: Poetry and the Criticism of Poetry." *Classical World* 60: 225–30.
Toohey, Peter. 1984. "Politics, Prejudice and Trojan Genealogies: Varro, Hyginus and Horace." *Arethusa* 17: 5–28.
Traina, Alfonso. 1986 (2d ed.). Introduction to Enzo Mandruzzato, trans., *Catullo i Canti*. Milan: Rizzoli.
Tuplin, C. J. 1981. "Catullus 68." *Classical Quarterly* 31, no. 1: 113–39.
Turnbull, Gael. 1983. *A Gathering of Poems*. London: Anvil Press.
Usener, Hermann. 1901. "Italische Volksjustiz." *Rheinisches Museum* 56: 1–28.
Veyne, Paul. 1978. "La Famille et l'Amour Sous le Haut-Empire Romain." *Annales* 33: 35–63.
Veyne, Paul. 1979. "The Hellenization of Rome and the Question of Acculturations." *Diogenes* 106: 1–27.
Veyne, Paul. 1983. "Le folklore à Rome et les droits de la conscience publique sur la conduite individuelle." *Latomus* 42, no. 1: 3–30.
Veyne, Paul. 1988. *Roman Erotic Elegy*. Chicago: Chicago University Press.
Weinreich, Otto. 1926. *Die Distichen des Catull*. Tübingen: Mohr.
Wetmore, Monroe. 1912. *Index verborum Catullianus*. New Haven: Yale University Press. Reprint, 1961. Hildesheim: Olms.

Whigham, Peter. 1966. *The Poems of Catullus.* Middlesex: Penguin.
White, Peter. 1978. "*Amicitia* and the Profession of Poetry in Early Imperial Rome." *Journal of Roman Studies* 68: 74–92.
Wilamowitz-Moellendorff, Ulrich von. 1924. *Hellenistische Dichtung in der Zeit des Kallimachos* 2. Berlin: Weidmann.
Wilder, Thornton. 1948. Reprint, 1987. *The Ides of March.* New York: Harper and Row.
Williams, Gordon. 1958. "Some Aspects of Roman Marriage Ceremonies and Ideals." *Journal of Roman Studies* 48: 16–29.
Williams, Gordon. 1968. *Tradition and Originality in Roman Poetry.* Oxford: Oxford University Press.
Williams, Mark. 1988. "Catullus 50 and the Language of Friendship." *Latomus* 47, no. 1: 69–73.
Williams, William Carlos. 1985. *Selected Poems*, ed. Charles Tomlinson. New York: New Directions.
Wiltshire, Susan. 1977. "Catullus Venustus." *Classical World* 70, no. 5: 319–26.
Wiseman, T. P. 1969. *Catullan Questions.* Leicester: Leicester University Press.
Wiseman, T. P. 1974. *Cinna the Poet, and Other Roman Essays.* Leicester: Leicester University Press.
Wiseman, T. P. 1975. "Clodia: Some Imaginary Lives." *Arion* n.s. 2, no. 1: 96–115.
Wiseman, T. P. 1979. *Clio's Cosmetics: Three Studies in Greco-Roman Literature.* Leicester: Leicester University Press.
Wiseman, T. P. 1985. *Catullus and His World: A Reappraisal.* Oxford: Oxford University Press.
Wiseman, T. P. 1987. *Roman Studies Literary and Historical.* Liverpool: Francis Cairns.
Witke, Charles. 1968. *Enarratio Catulliana: Carmina L, XXX, LXV, LXVIII.* Leiden: Brill.
Witke, Charles. 1980. "Catullus 13: A Reexamination." *Classical Journal* 75: 325–31.
Wlosok, A. 1980. "Nil Nisi Ruborem—Ueber die Rolle der Scham in der Roemischen Rechtskultur." *Grazer Beitraege* 9: 155–72.
Wright, G. T. 1975. "Four Poems" and "On Translating Catullus." *Centennial Review*, 70, no. 3: 172–74.
Yardley, J. C. 1981. "Catullus 11: The End of a Friendship." *Symbolae Osloenses* 56: 63–69.
Yeats, W. B. 1956. *The Collected Poems of W. B. Yeats.* New York: Macmillan.
Zanker, Paul. 1988. *The Power of Images in the Age of Augustus.* Ann Arbor: University of Michigan Press.
Zarker, J. W. 1972. "Lesbia's Charms." *Classical Journal* 68: 107–115.
Zetzel, James. 1983. "Catullus, Ennius and the Poetics of Illusion." *Illinois Classical Studies* 8: 251–66.

# General Index

Achilles, 162, 163, 165, 166
Acme, 183
actors, Roman status of, 57
Adams, J.N., 65, 68
Adler, Eve, 22–23
Aegeus, 141, 152
Aemilius, 79–80, 82
Aeneas, 218
aesthetic, 1–2, 34, 35, 38, 43, 44, 55, 229; and lyric, 15–16
"After Catullus" (Turnbull), 233
aggression, language of, 69
Alexandria, 18, 186, 200, 205, 206, 207, 210
Alexandrianism. *See* Catullus, Alexandrianism of
Alfenus, 234
Allinson, A.C.E., 216–18
Allius, 186, 207, 208, 222
Alpers, Svetlana, 238
Ameana, 72, 103–4, 215
Amphitrite, 151
Andromeda, 144, 145, 146
Antony, 62
Aphrodite, 79
Appius, 130–31
Argei, ritual of, 204
Argo, 150–51, 217
Ariadne: as Bacchant, 154, 155; in Boscotrecase Panels, 144–45, 153–54, 155; as Diva, 156–58; as figure for betrayed Catullus, 147; as figure for poetic power and impotence, 155; as figure for reader, 155; as figure for Roman cultural belatedness, 170; as gazer, 149, 153, 154, 161, 162; lament of, 156–58; and myth, 155; as spectacle, 146, 147–48, 149; symbolic import of, 156, 158
aristocratic obligation, language of, 17, 115, 118, 119, 120, 128, 130–32, 134
Asinius Gallus, 44–45
Asinius Marrucinus, 94–97, 100, 101, 102
Asinius Pollio, 94, 220
Atalanta, 43, 137
Atticus, 26
Attis, 222
Auden, W.H., 15
Augustus, 62
Aurelius, 46, 47, 49, 50, 51, 53, 55, 170, 172, 181–82, 183, 214, 230; and *irrumatio*, 65–66
Ausonius, 76
author, 11–12, 30–31, 111; construction of Catullus as Roman, 19–21; position of, 13; and relation to work, 29–31; role of, 212

Bacchus, 157
Baehrens, Aemilius, 32, 33
Bagg, Robert, 228, 229
Battus, 55

## INDEX

Baxter, James, 222–25, 228; and misogyny, 224
Beardsley, Aubrey, 216–17, 226
belatedness, 142, 160, 167, 170
Bignone, Ettore, 126, 127
birth metaphor, 192, 194, 195
body, 81–83, 83, 85, 86; of Ariadne, 149
book, 39–42
Boscotrecase Panels, and spectatorship, 146, 147–48
Bramble, J.C., 143
breasts, in Song of Fates, 165
Britain, 175
Brixia, 205, 206
Bryson, Norman, 167
Buechner, Karl, 125

Caelius Rufus, 10, 21–22, 26, 75, 76, 130–31, 132, 234; as character in Baxter, 223; as character in Jaro, 217, 221–22
Caesar (Julius), 9, 62, 84–85, 115, 120, 181, 204; as character in Wilder, 218–21, 225
Callimachus, 47–49, 54, 55, 186, 189, 191, 193, 195–96, 197–98, 199, 202
Callipho, 56, 58
Callistratus, 71
Calvus, Licinius, 6, 45, 46, 62, 112
Campesani, Benvenuto, 240
Cato (Marcus Porcius), 62, 77, 78
Cato (Valerius), 6, 78
*Catullan Self-Revelation* (Adler), 22–23
Catullus: Alexandrianism of, 41, 44, 95–96, 142, 143, 185, 186, 189, 197, 199, 201; and bacchic mysticism, 125–26; brother of, 18, 185–86, 187–89, 194, 195, 201, 208, 209, 210–11, 215, 216, 217–18, 218, 225, 237; as canonical author, 11–12, 19–21, 26–27, 30–31, 44, 115; as character in Lindsay, 231–33; as character in Wilder, 218, 219–21; as character in Wright, 228; and Christianity, 24, 125–26, 231–32; cultural displacement of, 9–10, 18; and *domus*, 201–2, 203, 218; early reception of, 24–26, 44–45; echoed in Baxter, 223; editorial traditions of, 43–44; as emblem of self-divided Roman poet, 20; and ethic of slightness, 14–15; and fallen flower image, 179, 180, 227; father of, 221; and Golden Age, 17, 140, 141, 142, 143, 146, 148–51, 149–50, 152, 156, 160–61, 162, 166–67; and Greek literature, 199, 202; Havelock's biographical account of, 246–47n32; and "I hate and I love" motif, 20, 23; imitations of, 50–51, 227; and innumerability topos, 54; as *irrumator*, 71–72; manuscripts of, 24–25; and mastery of poetic discourse, 179; modern reception of, 41, 44, 106–7, 110, 118, 119–20, 122–23, 125–27, 142–44, 146–48; and myth, 144, 146, 153, 154, 155, 159; New Critical reception of, 106–7; obscenity in, 16; and order of poems, 24–25, 28–29, 33, 35, 43–44, 78, 79, 80, 280n1; parodies of, 105–6; and physical book, 39–42; provocations of, 13–14, 16, 34–35, 36–44; reception of, 13, 14–15, 23–25; relation to reader, 13, 17, 34–35, 37–44, 46, 120–21, 125, 126–27; Renaissance reception of, 73–75; resistance to translation, 229–30; and 'reverse theft,' 101–2, 103–4; as "Rilke of antiquity," 212; in Roman canon, 20–21; and Roman imperialism, 20; and scholarly tradition, 14–15; and Shakespeare, 228, 229; *The Sparrow*, 28–29; translations by, 195–96; translations of, 60, 61, 216, 227–28, 229–34; as Transpadane, 9–10, 18, 185, 186, 200–201, 202, 203–4, 205–6; and triangulated readership, 13; and urbanity, 16, 20; use of diminutives, 102; use of invective, 100–101; values of, 29; and Vergil, 197; as victim, 17–18, 23, 68, 69, 70, 72, 169–70, 184, 189; Victorian reception of, 32, 59–60, 224; and women, 13, 17–18; as wronged lover, 115–16
Celan, Paul, 188
Chrestillus, 50, 51
Christianity, 24, 125–26, 231–32
Cicero, 6, 10, 19, 20, 25–26, 45, 63, 64, 119, 125–29, 130–31, 132, 133, 134, 175–76; as first critic of Catul-

## INDEX

lus, 22; style of, 128–29; use of *urbanitas*, 91–92, 97
Cinna (Gaius), 9
Clodia, 21–22, 64, 130, 221; as character in Lindsay, 231; as character in Wilder, 218–21
Clodius, 21
closure, 3–4, 179; and obscenity, 75–78, 79–80
Commager, Steele, 119–20
commendation, 48, 49
confessionalism, and Catullan scholar, 212
Conon, 196
*convicium*, 62
Copley, Frank, 23, 106–8, 116, 117
Cornelius Nepos, 35, 39, 40, 41, 42, 43, 47, 51, 52
Cornificius, 213
Cotton, John, 213, 214–15
criticism, as performance of the text, 242n10
Croce, Benedetto, 122–23
Culler, Jonathan, 3
Cybele, 126, 222
Cycnus, 205

dedication poem, 34–35, 38–39
*delicatus/delicati*, 36, 37, 45–46, 51, 53, 111, 112, 113, 250n7
*deliciae*, 35–36, 37, 44, 52, 54, 268n52
de Man, Paul, 5, 212, 215, 229
*dicacitas*, 62
Dido, 218
diminutives, Catullan use of, 102
displacement, 185, 186, 188, 196, 200, 207, 210; cultural, 9–10, 18
*domus*, 201–2, 203, 218

Ecnomus, 74
editorial traditions, 43–44. *See also* Catullus, order of poems
effeminacy, 43, 46, 49, 51, 53; of book, 41
Egnatius, 82, 203–4, 222
ekphrasis, 140
elegy, 26, 114, 117, 118, 121, 135; Roman semiotic game of, 8–9; and sincerity, 7–8
Eliot, T.S., 119
elite, Roman, 8–9

epigrams, 47–49, 117–18, 119, 120, 123, 136, 137–38
epithalamia, 180–81
epyllion, 140, 167, 273n1
eroticism: and Roman imperialism, 177; versus obscenity, 59
ethics, dual standard of Roman, 8–9
Europa, 159
exclusion, and urbanity, 87, 90, 95–96, 100
*expressa*, 189, 191–92, 194

Fabullus, 98–99, 100, 113; as figure for reader, 267n35
fallen flower image, 179, 180, 227
Fates, Song of the, 162–65, 166, 167
Fénelon, 59
Festus, 193
Fidentinus, 97
film theory, feminist, 147–48
*flagitatio*, 62
Flavius, 52, 53–54, 55
Fordyce, C.J., 40, 59, 75, 130
*Fortuna*, 216, 217
Foucault, Michel, 12, 29–31, 70, 236
Frank, Tenney, 122
Freud, Sigmund, 174
Friedricksmeyer, Ernst, 12
Furius, 47, 49, 50, 51, 53, 55, 82–84, 170, 172, 181–82, 183, 214, 230

Galatea, 144, 145, 146
gaze, 140, 145, 146, 148, 149, 152, 153; overlay of, 161–62
Gellius, 67, 71, 72, 80–81, 81–82
gender, 169, 170, 174, 215
Ginsberg, Allen, 213
*glubit*, 75–76, 77, 261n56; in Jaro, 222; in Sisson, 232
Golden Age, 117, 140, 141, 142, 143, 146, 148–51, 149–50, 152, 156, 159, 160–61, 166–67, 275n15; Catullus' relation to, 17; soft versus hard, 275n15
Granarolo, Jean, 125, 126, 127
Greek: literature, 142; and obscenity, 11
*gremium*, 193, 196, 198, 199, 200
Griffin, Jasper, 147

"hail and farewell" paradox, 213, 214, 215, 237

Hallett, Judith, 28, 170
happy family theme, 84–85
Harpocrates, 67
Havelock, E.A., 20, 30
Hellenism, 186, 256n44
hierarchy, 82, 85
Hollis, Christopher, 14
home. See *domus*
homosexuality, 30, 31–32, 45–46, 49–50, 82, 85; Roman attitudes toward, 254n31. See also *irrumatio*
homosociality, 181–82, 183, 214–15, 216, 284n7
Horace, 10, 19, 20, 40, 109–10, 155, 159; and *urbanitas*, 109, 110
humor, and obscenity, 61

"I hate and I love" paradox, 135, 136, 138, 213, 216, 272n42
imperialism, Roman, 20, 42, 142; and women, 169, 170, 173, 174, 175–78, 180–81
impure mouth, 10–11, 63, 64, 73, 74, 80, 81
incest, 82, 83
innumerability topos, 54
invective, 85; Catullan use of, 100–101; obscenity in, 61, 62; Roman, 70, 71, 72–73; scholarly, 73–74, 75
*irrumatio*, 11, 64–72, 177, 259–60n34; and Aurelius, 65–66; derivation of, 65; and poetic agency, 63, 66–67; untranslatability of, 64–65
Isidore of Seville, 24
isolation, of performing poet, 114, 120–21, 131–32, 134, 139

Janan, Micaela, 13
Jaro, Benita Kay, 24, 221–22
Jenkyns, Richard, 143–44, 154–55, 163
Johnson, W.R., 28–29, 30
*Jokes and Their Relation to the Unconscious* (Freud), 174
Juvenal, 10, 20

Keats, John, 3–4, 154–55, 229; "The Fall of Hyperion," 3
Kerouac, Jack, 213
Klingner, Friedrich, 143

Konstan, David, 161
Kroll, Wilhelm, 30
Kyrnos, 47

Lahr, John, 51
Landor, Walter Savage, 60–61, 213
language: aesthetic, 35–38; of aggression, 69; of aristocratic obligation, 17, 115, 117, 118, 119, 120, 128, 130–32, 134; neoteric, 117; of pleasure, 69; poet's isolation from, 114. See also obscenity
Laodamia, 208, 209, 218
Leach, Eleanor, 144–45
Lenz, Friedrich, 76
Lesbia, 75–76, 78, 79, 90–91, 103–4, 134–37, 138, 169, 172, 173, 179; in c. 67, 207, 208, 209, 210; in c. 68, 202; Catullus' repudiation of, 221; as character in Jaro, 222; as character in Squire, 226, 227; as character in Turnbull, 233; critical traditions regarding, 22; identification of historical, 21–22; as Nemesis, 29; and obscenity, 61; relation to Catullan scholar, 12–13, 22, 76, 77, 127; relation to reader, 127, 137; and Roman imperialism, 180–82, 183; sincerity of, 114, 135, 136–37; and sparrow, 36–38, 43, 44
Lesbia poems, 17, 26, 26–29, 114, 118–27, 131–32, 133–39; critical reception of, 117; liminality in, 134; as 'novel,' 26–29
liminality, 134
Lindsay, Jack, 231, 233–34
literary culture; Roman, 6, 8–9
Lucretius, 9, 20
lying, and poetry, 173, 174–76, 177, 178, 179, 184
Lyne, R., 117, 119
lyric: aesthetics of, 15–16; Paul de Man on, 5; and position of poet, 5; and position of reader, 7; and process of provocation, 14; relational dynamics of, 100; and slightness, 14–15; unconscious of, 237; and victimized speaker, 169

Macaulay, Thomas, 213
MacLeod, Colin, 31–33

## INDEX

Mallius, 186, 202, 207
Mamurra, 72, 85, 103, 104
Marmorale, Enzo, 125
Martial, 19, 20, 50–51, 70–71, 75, 97; theater analogies in, 61–62
Marullus, 74, 75
McAfee, Thomas, 125, 213, 234–35, 236
Medea, 217, 218
Memmius (Gaius), 68, 69, 70, 182–83
Metelli family, 56
Metellus (Quintus), 21
Mill, John Stuart, 4
Minyard, John Douglas, 119
misogyny, 12–13, 18, 216, 217; in Baxter, 224; of Catullan scholar, 12–13; in Cotton, 215
mouth. *See* impure mouth
Muretus, 74
mysticism, Bacchic, 125–26
myth, 142, 144, 145, 146, 153, 154, 155, 159; and Verona, 205–6

Naevius, 56
napkin, 94–95, 96–97, 98, 100
*neglegentia*, 173, 184
*negotium*, 8, 9
neoterics, 6, 41, 117
New Criticism, 106
Nicomedes of Bithynia, 62
"novel" of Catullus, 28–29

obscenity, 16, 33; and closure, 75–78, 79–80; defined, 258n21; derivation of, 62–63; as figure for poetic discourse, 81; Greek, 11; and humor, 61; in invective, 61, 62; and Lesbia, 61; as perverse cleanliness, 84; and poet/reader relationship, 63–64, 79; reception of, 59–61; and relation to reader, 79; in Roman culture, 10–11, 61–62, 63, 64, 86; in Sisson, 232; in translation, 60; and urbanity, 10; versus eroticism, 59
Ocean, 181
Oceanus, 81
Odysseus, 145, 146, 187, 188–89, 199
Ortalus, 189, 191, 192, 195, 200
Orton, Joe, 51
*otium*, 8, 9
Ovid, 9, 10, 19, 20, 30, 128

painting: Campanian, 168; Pompeiian, 147; Roman, 144–46, 147, 167. *See also* Boscotrecase Panels
*parasiti*, 6
parodies, 105–6
Parthenius, 73, 74
*patronus*, 6
Peleus, 153
Penelope, 199
performance: and isolation of poet, 114, 128; oral versus written, 6; and urbanity, 93, 94–95
perfume, 97, 98–100
Perseus, 144, 145
Philodemus, 25
Piso (Lucius Calpurnius), 25, 68
Plautus, 56, 58
pleasure, 86; language of, 69; of viewer, 153–54, 160
Pliny the Younger, 25, 44–46; and obscene verse, 63
poet: position of, 178–79, 184; as *scurra*, 7
poetic mind, metaphors for, 192–93, 194
poetic production, birth metaphor for, 192, 194, 195
poetry: confessional, 5; and lying, 173, 174–76, 177, 178, 179, 184; overheard, 4–5; and societal self-definition, 100; as talk, 10
Poliziano, Angelo, 25, 73–75
polymetrics, 26, 28, 116–17, 121, 129
Polyphemus, 144, 145, 146
Polyxena, 162, 163, 165–66
Pompey, 62, 120, 132, 133
position: of Catullan scholar, 12, 14, 16, 19, 21, 22, 23, 64, 70, 73, 75, 79, 143; of poet, 17, 18, 21, 34, 37, 86, 104–5, 114, 120–22, 137, 138, 194, 195, 199; and lyric, 5; of reader, 4–5, 7, 16, 22–23, 80, 86, 111–13, 139, 167–68, 188, 212, 227, 233
positionality, 16, 55, 72, 86; aesthetic, 1–4; erotic model of poetic, 59
power: poetic, 179, 180, 184; relations between poet and reader, 34–35, 46–47, 49–51, 52; secondary, 17; and *urbanitas*, 16–17
power relations: Roman, 51; in Roman comedy, 56–58
Priapus, 61, 64, 66

private life, 25
Procne, 199
Propertius, 9
Protesilaus, 208, 209, 218
provocation, 16, 34, 237; between Catullus and Calvus, 36–38; between Catullus and Nepos, 38–44; between Catullus and Pliny, 44–46; between Catullus and reader, 34–35, 36, 37–44; and lyric, 14
Ptolemy II, 199, 200
Ptolemy III, 196, 198, 199
publication, anxiety of, 44, 46, 47–48
pumice, 40–41
puritanism, aesthetic, 143–44
Putnam, Michael, 107–8, 109
Pyrrha, 222, 223, 224–25

Quinn, Kenneth, 4, 6, 15, 30, 112, 151, 222
Quintia, 90, 91
Quintilian, 32, 94

reader: position in Squire, 227; in Turnbull, 233
reception: of obscenity, 59–61. *See also* Catullus, relation to reader
representation: of Golden Age, 149; ideology of, 167
Richlin, Amy, 13, 64
Rilke, Rainer Maria, 212, 215, 229
Roman: canon, 19; concern with impure mouth, 63; concern with obscenity, 10–11, 61–62, 63; cultural schizophrenia, 9; culture, 236–37; elite, 8–9; ethics, 8–9; Hellenism, 256n44; imperialism, 20, 42, 142, 164, 170, 173, 174, 175–78, 180–81; literary culture, 6; painting, 144–46, 147, 167; power relations, 51; relation to Greek culture, 197; socio-political milieu, 114; speech, 10, 17
Romanticism, 23
Rome, 186, 188, 189, 201, 202, 203, 232, 236
Ross, David, 118, 119
Rubino, Carl, 118
*rusticitas*, versus *urbanitas*, 9

Sappho, 22, 196
Schefold, Karl, 144

Schmidt, Ernst, 118
scholar, Catullan: and confessionalism, 212; and relation to betrayed lover, 115, 118, 122–23; and relation to Lesbia, 12–13, 22, 76, 77, 127
Schwabe, Ludwig, 21, 26
Selden, Daniel, 13
self-division, of poet, 20
Seneca, 20, 191
Serapis, cult of, 178
severance, 179–83, 184, 189, 200
sexual stimulation, role of, 55
Shakespeare, William, 228, 229
Silverman, Kaja, 147–48, 274n13
sincerity, 7–8, 189, 196, 197, 198–99, 210; of Roman elegy, 7–8
Sisson, C.H., 230–33
Skinner, Marilyn, 11–12, 13, 95, 96, 118, 278n4
slave/playwright analogy, 57–58
slightness, ethic of, 14–15, 16
Sophocles, 220
Sotades, 200
sparrow, 35, 36, 37, 38; as phallic symbol, 252–53n24
spectatorship, 147, 159, 160, 161
speech; nature of poetic, 18; Roman, 10, 17
Squire, J.C., 225–27, 229; imitation of flower image, 227
stepmother figure, 83
Suetonius, 62, 85
Swinburne, Charles Algernon, 213, 215–16, 227

Tacitus, 10
Tethys, 81
Thallus, 101–2, 103, 109
Theognis, 47, 48
Thetis, 153
Tibullus, 9
Tompkins, Jane, 7
translation, 194; by Catullus, 195–96, 197–98, 199, 202; displacement and, 196; as *expressa*, 191. *See also* Catullus, translations of; Catullus, translations by
triangulation, 13, 18, 191, 216; involving women, 170
triviality. See *delicatus/deliciae*
Troy, 186, 187, 188, 202, 209, 211, 218

Turnbull, Gael, 233
Tyrell, Robert, 122

*urbanitas*, 104, 113; Catullan agressive use of, 87, 88, 91–92, 93–96, 97–100, 102; Ciceronian use of, 91–92, 97; Horatian characterization of, 109, 110; instability of meaning, 90, 91; poet as arbiter of, 93–94, 95, 96; and power, 16–17; undefinability of, 88–89, 90, 91, 100; and Verona, 204; versus *rusticitas*, 9, 98, 91. *See also* urbanity
urbanity, 16, 20, 26; as aestheticized morality, 88, 89; and exclusion, 87, 90, 95–96, 100; and obscenity, 10; and performance, 93, 94–95; as poetic performative game, 11. See also *urbanitas*

Valerius, 217
Varus, 176
Vectios Philocomus, 74
*venustus*, 35–36, 175
Vergil, 19, 20–21, 24, 197, 218
Vermeer, Jan, 238–39
Verona, 186, 201, 202, 205, 207, 208, 211, 240; and myth, 206; and *urbanitas*, 204

Veyne, Paul, 7–8, 9, 62, 70, 86, 123; *Roman Erotic Elegy*, 7
viewer, castrated, 148
virtuosity, 151
vision, theory of, 161

Weinrich, Otto, 76
Whigham, Peter, 60, 61
Wilamowitz-Moellendorff, Ulrich, 105, 107
Wilder, Thornton, 218–21, 225
Williams, William Carlos, 2–3, 4, 10, 113, 239, 240; "This Is Just to Say," 2–3, 4, 10, 113, 239, 240
Wiseman, T.P., 32–33, 147, 203, 205–6
womb, poetic mind as, 192–93
women, 193, 216, 218; as alibi for creative genius, 225; in Allinson, 217; Catullus as victim of, 17–18; and imperialism, 169, 170, 173, 174, 175, 176–78, 180–81; as medium of intermale communication, 216; status of, 177–79
Wright, G.T., 227–28, 230

*xenia*, 168

Yeats, William Butler, 22, 25; "The Scholars," 22, 24

# Index of Catullan Poems Cited

C. 1: 34, 35, 37–38, 222
C. 2: 27, 31, 34, 35, 37, 38, 42–43, 53, 137
C. 3: 27, 35–36
C. 4: 104–110, 227, 263
C. 5: 27, 30, 31, 37, 53, 54, 55, 183, 228
C. 6: 52, 153–54, 155
C. 7: 27, 30, 31, 37, 53, 54–55
C. 8: 27, 121–23, 213, 214
C. 10: 17–18, 68, 169, 170–72, 173–175, 176–79, 180–82, 183–84, 214, 227, 259
C. 11: 17–18, 31, 32, 61, 169, 170, 172–73, 179–82, 183–84, 221, 223, 228, 248, 263, 285
C. 12: 93–98, 100, 102, 103, 263, 267, 277
C. 13: 98–100, 103
C. 14B: 47
C. 15: 31, 34, 38, 46–47, 48–49, 51–52, 55, 248, 254
C. 16: 31, 34, 38, 46, 47, 48–50, 51–52, 53, 55, 63, 64, 226, 241, 248, 249, 263, 279
C. 17: 204
C. 21: 31, 65–66
C. 23: 31, 83–85, 86, 248, 279
C. 24: 31, 279
C. 25: 100, 101–3, 104
C. 28: 68–70, 86
C. 31: 107
C. 32: 258
C. 35: 245, 250
C. 36: 265
C. 37: 66, 251
C. 38: 213
C. 39: 203, 262, 264, 265
C. 41: 72, 215, 271, 287
C. 42: 62, 100, 243, 251, 281
C. 43: 264, 265
C. 44: 242
C. 45: 183, 214, 262
C. 46: 107, 182–83, 279
C. 47: 242, 251, 263, 266
C. 48: 30, 251
C. 49: 129
C. 50: 31, 36–7, 45, 46, 110–12, 196, 250

C. 51: 228, 280, 281–82, 285
C. 54: 243
C. 55: 31, 268
C. 56: 77–79, 251, 258, 267, 268
C. 57: 86, 263, 264
C. 58: 31, 61, 75–79, 221–22, 232
C. 59: 263
C. 61: 28, 61, 276
C. 62: 180, 276, 279
C. 63: 222
C. 64: 140–44, 146–68, 170, 281
C. 65: 18, 185, 189–95, 197–98, 199, 200, 201, 203, 207, 208, 210, 248
C. 66: 18, 186, 189, 197, 198–99, 201, 203, 205, 206, 207, 208, 281
C. 67: 18, 202–3, 205–7, 208
C. 68: 18, 28, 126, 185, 186, 201–2, 203, 207, 248, 250
C. 70: 137, 139, 228
C. 72: 117, 135–36, 245
C. 74: 67, 259
C. 75: 133–35
C. 76: 117, 119, 121, 123–27, 128, 130–31, 132–33, 213
C. 77: 262
C. 78B: 262
C. 79: 244
C. 80: 71–72, 80–81
C. 83: 272
C. 84: 265
C. 85: 135, 136–37
C. 86: 90–91, 104
C. 87: 117, 129–30, 131–32
C. 89: 31
C. 92: 135, 137–38
C. 93: 266
C. 97: 79–80, 81, 257, 262
C. 98: 72–73, 75–76, 79
C. 99: 30, 262
C. 101: 13, 19, 185, 186, 187–89, 195, 200–201, 202, 213, 215–18, 237, 244
C. 102: 260
C. 109: 115–16, 117, 130, 135, 138–39
C. 110: 260
C. 111: 260

310